MW01251418

Islamic Capitalism and Finance

STUDIES IN ISLAMIC FINANCE, ACCOUNTING AND GOVERNANCE

Series Editor: Mervyn K. Lewis, *Professor of Banking and Finance, South Australia and Fellow, Academy of the Social Sciences, Australia*

There is a considerable and growing interest both in Muslim countries and in the West surrounding Islamic finance and the Islamic position on accounting and governance. This important new series is designed to enhance understanding of these disciplines and shape the development of thinking about the theory and practice of Islamic finance, accounting and governance.

Edited by one of the leading writers in the field, the series aims to bring together both Muslim and non-Muslim authors and to present a distinctive East–West perspective on these topics. Rigorous and authoritative, it will provide a focal point for new studies that seek to analyse, interpret and resolve issues in finance, accounting and governance with reference to the methodology of Islam.

Titles in the series include:

Islamic Banking and Finance in the European Union
A Challenge
Edited by M. Fahim Khan and Mario Porzio

Islamic Capitalism and Finance
Origins, Evolution and the Future
Murat Çizakça

Islamic Capitalism and Finance

Origins, Evolution and the Future

Murat Çizakça

INCEIF, Kuala Lumpur, Malaysia

STUDIES IN ISLAMIC FINANCE, ACCOUNTING AND GOVERNANCE

Edward Elgar

Cheltenham, UK • Northampton, MA, USA

Published by
Edward Elgar Publishing Limited
The Lypiatts
15 Lansdown Road
Cheltenham
Glos GL50 2JA
UK

Edward Elgar Publishing, Inc.
William Pratt House
9 Dewey Court
Northampton
Massachusetts 01060
USA

A catalogue record for this book
is available from the British Library

Library of Congress Control Number: 2011925757

ISBN 978 0 85793 147 4 (cased)

Printed and bound by MPG Books Group, UK

To my uncle Saadet Kavukçu, sisters Prof. Dr. Çiğdem Kâğıtçıbaşı,
Leyla Çizakça Özalan and to the family Howe,
who contributed so much to my life.

Contents

Figures

Tables

Foreword

The day I met the late Dr Ahmad Al-Naggar, 'the father of Islamic banking' in the spring of 1982, turned out to be a turning point in my life. I was at that time a young PhD trained as a comparative economic historian. Dr Al-Naggar introduced me to Islamic finance. Combining the two disciplines has been an inseparable part of my academic life ever since.

As a comparative economic historian, I have two strong objections to the way Islamic economics and finance are currently studied. First, I object vehemently to the argument that Islamic finance is just 40 years old. Definitely not, it is actually fifteen centuries old! Second, I object, equally vehemently, to the conventionalization of Islamic economics and finance. I am convinced that much of this conventionalization occurs because financial engineers are simply not aware about the achievements of their forefathers. Ignorance about these achievements leads to inferiority complexes and to a highly dynamic process of institutional borrowing. This process is so dynamic that much of modern Islamic finance boils down to the endless struggle between the financial engineers trying to imitate Western instruments and the *Shari'ah* authorities who are trying to control them. A major purpose of this book is to link Islamic economic/financial history not only to the present but even to the future and thus reduce institutional borrowing only to the most essential, so as to preserve the authenticity of Islamic economics and finance.

I agree with Professor Abbas Mirakhor that the principles, laws and theoretical foundations of Islamic economics are already enshrined in the classical sources of Islam. Therefore, current research on Islamic economics should focus not so much on the theory but on application. This book will therefore focus on, first, the principles and then their implementation through the institutions. An objective analysis of the evolution of Islamic economic/financial institutions and the consequences of this evolution constitute an essential part of this book. A focus on the consequences of the evolution brings us inevitably to reform proposals and hence to the future. That is why the past, the present and the future are organically intertwined in this book. Readers may find sudden and massive shifts across centuries a little disturbing, so I offer my apologies in advance and ask them to bear with me.

I could have called this book *Islamic Economics and Finance: Historical Approach*. In fact, some of my colleagues even urged me to do so. I have called it as it is for two reasons: first, as mentioned above, this is not a book on theory but on application. Calling it *Islamic Economics* would have given the wrong impression. Second, and more importantly, my life-long research has convinced me that the grand economic design laid down in the classical sources of Islam was capitalistic. Yes, a capitalist system that preceded that of the West by several centuries. It was this capitalism and its institutions which translated the economic/financial principles enshrined in the classical sources into daily life.

Whether contemporary Muslims will be able to modernize their historical institutions and mobilize them for their economic development remains to be seen. It is hoped that this book will contribute to their efforts by proposing how this can be done.

'There are still only two kinds of capitalism. There is authoritarian capitalism, as in China and Singapore, and there is democratic capitalism, as in the U.S. and Europe. If there is anyone out there who has a better idea, I am sure the world would love to hear about it.'

Robert Reich, former US Secretary of Labor and a professor of economics at the University of California, Berkeley, on calls for the reform and evolution of capitalism. *Newsweek*, 13 October 2008, p. 28.

Introduction

Can Islamic capitalism, which has served Muslims so well for centuries in different periods in history, provide a viable alternative economic system to humanity? In this age of recession, the worst since 1929, this is surely a provocative question. But if this alternative is to emerge and serve mankind as a gift of the Islamic world, it must, first of all, be well understood. To start with, was there, indeed, an Islamic capitalism? Are we justified to call this system that emerged a thousand years before Adam Smith, capitalistic? What are the principles upon which this system has been built? What were the institutions which developed from these principles? How have they functioned and evolved, and most important of all, can they be modernized to address today's needs? This book aims to address these problems.

It would be appropriate to provide now a brief explanation of the term Islamic capitalism. Indeed, capitalism, for many not exactly a respectable term, is strongly associated with the West. It may therefore seem strange that the economic system practised by the Islamic world from the seventh century to roughly the middle of the thirteenth century, also known as the classical age of Islam, should be referred to with this term. But, subject to certain caveats, the characteristics of this economic system to which I will refer shortly can be best described with the term capitalism. What these caveats are will become clear below. Meanwhile let us note that the two capitalisms share important characteristics. Indeed, the three most important rules crucial to economic development identified by the Western new institutional economics – property rights protection, enforcement of contracts and good governance – constitute the essential principles of Islamic capitalism as well.

Islamic capitalism of the classical age was an economic system derived basically from the Qur'an and Prophetic traditions. Sincere Muslims, who have great respect for these sources, may therefore, with some justification, find the term irksome. But there is strong evidence that Islam had developed its own capitalism. Consider for instance that the bulk of the Islamic jurisprudence was written down by men most of whom were merchants. More importantly, even Prophet Muhammad, himself, was a merchant, who firmly believed in free markets and refused to interfere in prices. Moreover, of the four righteous Caliphs, Abu Bakr was a cloth merchant and Uthman was an importer of cereals.[1]

Great Islamic philosophers also had firm opinions about markets. This is not surprising, because most of them had been appointed as *muhtesibs*, officials in charge of markets, and earned their living as such. Consequently, being in charge of the smooth functioning of markets, they had a profound understanding of the way markets actually functioned. Continuous and close observation of markets instilled in their minds respect for private property. For instance, Al-Shatibi and Al-Ghazali consider the protection of property, *hifz al-mal*, as one of the five purposes of Islamic jurisprudence, *Maqasid al-Shari'ah*.[2] The great fourteenth-century historian and philosopher Ibn Khaldun had highly sophisticated ideas about economics and, reflecting the Prophet, favoured minimum state interference in the economy.[3]

The immense importance of trade for Muslims is also demonstrated by the transfer of mercantile concepts to the religious sphere: the good and bad deeds of each person are *registered* in a *personal account book*. The Muslim will be judged according to these deeds recorded and will be rewarded with paradise if his good deeds exceed his sins. Having faith is like a *profitable transaction*; participating in the struggle of the Prophet is like *giving a loan* to God; each Muslim has a *covenant* (*contract*) with God.[4] It is believed that *Allah* buys Muslims' lives and properties and sells them, in return, the paradise.[5] This means that if a Muslim spends his/her life and property in the cause of *Allah,* he/she would be rewarded with entry to the paradise. But to be able to spend one's property in this way, property needs to be earned first. Therefore, it is believed that an honest merchant struggling to earn and enlarge his assets legitimately will be exalted and shall join the ranks of the martyrs.[6]

Therefore, there is nothing surprising about the fact that Islam, a religion born in the Arabian Desert, where trade constituted the most important, perhaps even the sole economic activity, favours merchants, property rights, free trade and market economy.[7] The Prophet himself has informed us that trade constituted nine-tenths of the livelihood of early Muslims.[8]

Because an economic system which favours merchants, and respects property rights and free trade, applies the principles of market economy and market wage rate and treats interference in the markets as transgression and sinful would be considered capitalist,[9] I have no qualms about calling this Islamic economic system as such, even though this term is so closely associated with Western experience.[10] Moreover, another condition of capitalism, the ownership of the factors of production by private persons, can also be observed in the Arabian Peninsula during the age of the Prophet. Not only is the market wage rate mentioned in the Qur'an, there is also definitive evidence about its widespread application across centuries.[11] Still another condition of capitalism is the existence of buyers who purchase goods not only for their own immediate consumption but also for further sale to third persons.[12] The fact that classical Islamic jurists had felt the need to approve certain popular partnerships such as *wujuh* (*sharikat al*-mafalis), which specifically focused on the resale of merchandise to third parties, indicates that this condition also found widespread application. Furthermore, the West should not have a monopoly over this term, particularly because many important principles, institutions, even laws, of the medieval Western European economy, which formed the nucleus of the modern Western capitalism later, have been borrowed from the Islamic world.[13]

Thus, the fact that the medieval Islamic economy was not industrialized, does not disqualify it from being capitalistic.[14] That capitalism is not necessarily associated exclusively with industrialization, has been confirmed long ago by Fernand Braudel.[15] Indeed, some eminent historians from Mommsen to Pirenne have considered many ancient civilizations such as Babylonia, ancient Greece, Rome and China as capitalist. This has led to a fierce and ideological Marxist counterattack. Karl Polanyi, for instance, ridiculed historians for arguing that capitalist merchants existed in ancient Mesopotamia. This is despite the fact that thousands of cuneiform tablets have survived, proving the existence of commercial correspondence between Assyrian and Anatolian capitalists. Van Leur and Steensgaard, fearing the Marxist witch hunt, have put all the powerful capitalist merchants of the oriental spice trade under the category of 'pedlars'.[16] In short, orthodox Marxism refuses to accept capitalism before the industrial revolution and in doing so it contradicts Marx himself, who did recognize its existence in medieval Italian city states.[17] It goes without saying that I do not feel bound in this book by the confines of this orthodoxy.

The capitalism that I am referring to here is pre-industrial, commercial capitalism. It naturally differs from the industrial capitalism referred to by Adam Smith and Karl Marx.[18] Why this Islamic commercial capitalism differs from the industrial capitalism and why the latter did not emerge in the Islamic world will be discussed below.

There are essentially two traditional approaches to characterizing a society capitalistic: statistical or institutional. The former assumes that more than 50 per cent of the total output was produced by capitalistic methods, while the latter focuses on the government and customs of the country, its written and unwritten laws and whether capitalistic forms of production and exchange were preferred over other forms.[19] I have already mentioned above that the capitalistic commercial sector of the classical Islamic economy probably constituted some 90 per cent of the total economy. Since it is very difficult to confirm this quantitatively for an economy that emerged fifteen centuries ago, I will prefer the second method and focus in this book not so much on the theory and statistics of capitalism, but rather, on its institutions and their evolution.

In addition to these two traditional approaches, there has emerged in the 1970s a third, 'new', approach to determine whether a society was capitalistic. This is the entrepreneurial history. As the name suggests, this approach focuses on explaining economic change by focusing on business management. All the traditional three factors of production – land, labour and capital – are given equal weight while the fourth element – entrepreneurship – is given prime importance. Even profit maximization, the most traditional guide of economists, becomes modified by the personal preferences of the entrepreneur in this scheme.[20] This third approach will also be adopted in this book. This is not only because of the wealth of information we have on Islamic entrepreneurship but also because of the modified character of profit maximization practised by the *homo-Islamicus*.

Finally, Immanuel Wallerstein pursues a different approach and first identifies the conditions necessary for the emergence of a capitalist system and then explains how and why these conditions could not develop before the late fifteenth century in Europe.[21] Nearly all of these conditions, which Wallerstein approaches negatively, actually, existed in classical Islam. First, he makes the point that in history, societies had many considerations and these usually intruded upon the process of capital accumulation. Then he says:

> Whenever, over time, it was the accumulation of capital that regularly took priority over alternative objectives... we are observing a capitalist system in operation.

As we will see below, classical Islam considers capital accumulation as the *conditio sine qua non* for the performance of the pilgrimage as well as the payment of *zakat*, two of the five pillars of Islam. Thus, capital accumulation is given a sacred status, which enables a Muslim to perform his prayers.

Another condition Wallerstein identifies is the ability to make profit – endless profit. This condition was also fulfilled. In classical Islam it was not any public authority but competition which controlled profits. Classical Islam does not impose any maximum limit upon the profits a Muslim can generate. The only condition that is imposed is that profits should be earned through legitimate, *halal*, means. A Muslim merchant would certainly wish to make endless profits because this would not only enable him to finance his and close relatives' pilgrimage expenses and *zakat* payments, but it would also enable him, by establishing a waqf, to finance the needs of other Muslims. As we will see below, establishment of a waqf would save a Muslim's soul in the Hereafter.

Wallerstein then refers to the non-availability of one or more elements of the process – the accumulated stock in money form, the labour power, the network of distributors, the consumers, etc. – to explain why capitalism rarely emerged in history. Of these, only the availability of money appears to have been a serious impediment, but as will be explained below, this problem was solved within a very short time after the revelation. The solution was so definitive and money became so widely available that even Europe was re-monetized thanks to Islamic coins.[22]

In view of all the arguments presented above, we are justified to claim that there is an economic system called Islamic capitalism, in which objectives of capital accumulation and religion are intimately fused and inseparable. Remarkably, this Islamic capitalism was born more than a thousand years before Adam Smith.

Finance and financial entrepreneurship may be the most important components of any capitalist system. Islamic finance, however, has a rather remarkable feature: a segmented time frame. While, on the one hand, it is based upon the classical sources of Islam dating from the seventh century, it is generally believed that this is a new field of finance and that all its major institutions have been invented during the last 40 years or so. This way of thinking is reflected in the organizational structure of every Islamic bank. Indeed, each Islamic bank has a *Shari'ah* board, which supervises the directors of the bank. Thus seventh-century Islamic jurisprudence and modern finance try to coexist.

Focusing exclusively on classical Islamic jurisprudence, *fiqh*, the bulk of the literature on Islamic finance implicitly assumes that from the end of the eighth century, when the most important works of Islamic jurisprudence were completed, until the 1960s, when Ahmed al-Naggar started his Mit Ghamr experiment,[23] that is, for more than a millennium, nothing of any significance happened in Islamic finance. Thus the entire field of *applied fiqh* is simply ignored and consequently there is near total ignorance about how the *fiqh* had been actually applied across centuries. The by-product of this ignorance is that, with a few exceptions,[24] the evolution of Islamic financial institutions remains largely unknown.

A basic point of this book is that Islamic finance is actually fifteen centuries old. Therefore, like its Western counterpart, it is actually the end product of a long-lasting evolution. The continuity of Islamic finance is even more remarkable than that of Western finance. This is because its basic principles, particularly the stringent interest prohibition enshrined in the Qur'an, have remained unchanged ever since the seventh century. This cannot be said for Western finance, which not only went through a very gradual dilution of the interest prohibition, but also the cataclysmic 'Enlightenment' of the eighteenth century. With its basic principles remaining intact, Islamic finance exhibits a much greater degree of continuity than Western finance. One of the main purposes of this book is to demonstrate this continuity as well as the evolution of Islamic financial institutions.

Indeed, the origins of Islamic finance can be traced back to the very birth of Islam, and even earlier, to the pre-Islamic era. This is attested by the fact that Prophet Muhammad had been involved in *mudaraba* ventures, a pre-Islamic partnership form, before the revelation.[25] Thus, there is no doubt that the wisdom of pre-Islamic civilizations was incorporated into Islam. This was done through a process of Islamization, that is to say, by a process of selection and elimination whereby pre-Islamic institutions were closely examined and those that did not conflict with the basic teachings of Islam were accepted.

Many pre-Islamic institutions were incorporated into the Islamic jurisprudence this way.[26] It is generally agreed that this process was completed by the end of the eighth century.

At this point, the term Islamic finance must be explained. By this term, a whole spectrum of financial activities is meant. But banking in the Western sense is not. This is because, whereas Western banking is based upon deposit and its commercial exploitation, i.e., relending it with a premium, Islamic law recognizes deposit in the form of *wadia* only. That is to say, safe-keeping plain and simple without any further benefit either to the depositor or the depositary. These radically different financial concepts had far-reaching consequences, which will be explained later. But one consequence must be mentioned here. In the Islamic world, although banking activities and a host of financial transactions existed, they were practised by merchants, who needed to finance their commercial transactions. But specialized institutions, as we know them today, focusing entirely on financial transactions cannot be observed in medieval Islam.[27]

What then were these financial transactions and how were they carried out in the absence of banks? They can be categorized into two main groups: financing the entrepreneur and transferring capital across time and space. The former was done primarily by utilizing various forms of business partnerships, such as the *mudaraba*, *mufawada*, *inan*, *wujuh* etc., while the latter was done by instruments called *hawala* or *suftaja*. Sales based upon deferred payments were also very important.[28] These institutions and instruments will be explained later. But it should suffice here to note that in the period from the seventh to the thirteenth centuries, they were the most advanced financial institutions. Indeed at least one of them, actually the most important one, the *mudaraba*, was borrowed, in all probability, by Europeans from Muslims.[29] Actually, there is a substantial body of evidence that other important Islamic institutions such as waqfs were also borrowed by the Europeans.[30]

At this point one may wonder why Europe, in the medieval era, should have borrowed some of its most important institutions from the Islamic world. Since detailed studies of this phenomenon have been made elsewhere,[31] it will be briefly stated here that Europe went through a dramatic period of discontinuity after the collapse of the Western Roman Empire. This discontinuity was exacerbated by the Catholic Church trying to establish its complete monopoly over the pre-Christian heritage. Muslims, by contrast, openly embraced the combined wisdom of ancient Greece, Rome, Iran and India and expanded it considerably further.[32] Consequently, the Islamic world enjoyed a higher level of civilization in the medieval era.

It has been argued that between the eighth and the eleventh centuries Europe came to be increasingly dominated by the Church. The Church imposed a very strict prohibition of interest and discouraged trade and capitalist accumulation.

In this period Western Europe was deprived of its bankers, great merchants and contractors. Europe increasingly succumbed to barter, the only method of commerce according to the church that was free of any suspicion of usury.[33]

Meanwhile, the Church came to own one-third of all land in continental Europe. It was this huge wealth that provided seed finance for the crusaders. Ironically, it was the crusaders, who, by establishing close contact with the Islamic Middle East, lifted up Europe from the dark ages described above.

How could the Islamic world have such a positive effect on Western Europe? What the crusaders found in the Islamic world was fabulous wealth, created and maintained by the classical Islamic capitalism. We will return to these principles in detail.

Thus, we have two capitalist systems: Islamic and, its follower, the Western European capitalism. The latter followed the former with a lag of some 200 to 450 years.[34] Despite this lag, these two capitalisms had much in common. Most significantly, they both applied a stringent prohibition of interest.

Once interest prohibition is taken as a starting point, financial institutions that developed from this maxim in the two capitalist systems had to be quite similar. Moreover, the West did not have to re-invent these institutions developed by Muslims centuries ago. Institutional borrowing rather than invention would generally characterize the follower and the follower increasingly becomes similar to the leader. Indeed, this was the case.[35]

Despite the initial institutional similarity, however, the two systems eventually began to follow different evolutionary paths. To start with, in Europe, the Church itself began to evolve into the very first corporation. This concept, originally developed by the Church, was then borrowed by independent cities, guilds, universities and finally merchants. When merchants began to apply the idea of corporation to business, they quickly combined it with the partnerships they had borrowed from the Islamic world. The resulting synthesis paved the way to the powerful incorporated joint-stock companies of the sixteenth century.[36]

The sixteenth century was also the period when a belated but powerful reaction against the Catholic Church and its corrupt and ruthless Inquisition emerged. The Inquisition represents the most horrifying example of what an alliance of a powerful state and a corrupt Church could do to a society. In a nutshell, it can be asserted that the Inquisition violated two basic human rights: the right to live and to own property. It is well known that whenever the King of Spain needed extra funds, the Inquisition descended upon the rich individuals with the false pretence that they were disguised Muslims or Jews and subjected them to torture beyond human imagination. Nearly always, the torture, which lasted many months, ended with the hapless victims being sent to the stake to be burnt alive. Needless to say, all the properties of the victims were confiscated.[37]

Obviously, this lethal combination of corrupt state and Church had to be stopped. The initial reaction came from the Church itself. Led by a fearless monk and a great leader, Martin Luther, Protestantism started. Helped by the Ottomans, who were quick to appreciate the enormous potential of the movement in splitting the power of their adversary, the Catholic Holy Roman Empire, Protestantism spread rapidly in Central and Northern Europe.[38]

One of the most important disagreements Luther had with the Catholic Church was the established belief and practice that one could save his soul by purchasing indulgences from the Church. This meant that only the rich could go to heaven. Luther vehemently opposed this and argued that heaven could only be reached through faith and hard and honest work. This concept is known as 'justification through faith and work'. Thus, an important by-product of Protestantism was a new attitude towards work, profit and business in general. Hard work, honesty and well-deserved profit were now regarded as pious deeds.[39]

But Protestantism, initiated by Martin Luther and expanded further by Calvin and others, was just the beginning. Two centuries later a group of French philosophers started a new movement, the 'Enlightenment', which also proved to be lasting and powerful. This time not only the Catholic Church, but religion itself was attacked.[40] Pushed to the extreme during the French Revolution, nearly all the values preached by the Church for more than a millennium were now discarded. Gone were not only the confiscated properties of the Church but also many of the moral controls with which businessmen had been conducting their businesses for centuries. Uncontrolled profit, exploitation of labour, in short, all the tenets of a new and ruthless form of capitalism, the modern Western capitalism, came out of Pandora's box.

If we return to the Islamic world, we observe a considerably different evolution. To start with, not burdened by a centralized universal Church and its corrupt Inquisition, the Islamic world experienced neither a universal Protestant movement nor Enlightenment. Islam neither went through cataclysmic transformations, as Protestantism and Enlightenment, nor experienced a dilution of its influence.[41]

What affected the evolution of Islamic capitalism was not a transformation of the religion itself, but rather the political economy of the various Islamic empires. What we observe in this context is a gradual divergence from the *sunnah* of the Prophet, which represents the origin of Islamic capitalism.

Concerning the system of land ownership, for instance, whereas the Prophet had distributed conquered land to the warriors and thus confirmed private ownership of land, beginning with Omar the Second Caliph, the Roman system of landownership was introduced in the newly conquered territories of the Sawad (Iraq and parts of Syria). Thus, the pure private ownership of land as practised and confirmed by the Prophet was replaced by this complex

Roman system.[42] Omar was able to push his scheme through by referring to the Qur'an,[43] and the result was that private ownership of land was subordinated to state ownership. It should be noted here that these two different land distribution systems applied by the Prophet and Omar the second caliph were both based upon the Qur'an, the former on 8: 41 and the latter, 59: 7. Omar was able to alter the Prophet's system by both referring to the Qur'an and by consultation.[44]

The next divergence from pure Islamic capitalism of the Prophet was introduced by the famous jurist Ibn Taymiyya during the late thirteenth to early fourteenth century. This was the concept of 'fair prices'. Ibn Taymiyyah asked what price would be the fairest price, and concluded that it is the price practised by the majority of the merchants in the market. Ibn Taymiyya even advised how in practice this price could be found. He suggested two procedures.[45]

Once again, these procedures represent a deviation from the *sunnah* of the Prophet, who refused to interfere with prices. This is because both of these alternatives actually involve, however 'fair', a process of price fixing by an authority. Moreover, the second procedure also introduces inadvertently the concept of 'fair profit'. 'Fair profit' suggests that any rate of profit that exceeds it is actually unfair, unjust – something to be avoided or ashamed of. Yet, a combination of 'fair prices' and 'fair profits' powerfully impedes entrepreneurship. With 'fair prices' prevalent in the market, the entrepreneur no longer tries to minimize his prices and with 'fair profits', he loses interest in cost minimization and revenue maximization.

Another deviation from pure classical Islamic capitalism concerns taxation. It is well known that when the Prophet established the Madinah bazaar he had declared that no taxes were going to be imposed on transactions conducted in that market.[46] Thus the *sunnah* of the Prophet suggests clearly that an Islamic state should abolish taxes in order to encourage trade or that the tax burden should be relatively light.[47] In this context, particularly the abolition of the internal customs by the Prophet can be mentioned.[48] These taxes used to be imposed in pre-Islamic Arabia on all imports as well as commercial transactions at the rate of one-tenth. Obviously, with the abolition the Prophet must have aimed at enhancing trade within the realm of Islam. Taxes on foreign trade, however, were not abolished. This was because of reciprocity – Muslim merchants were taxed when they went to trade to non-Muslim countries. So, when non-Muslim merchants from Europe visited the lands of Islam, they had to pay the same rates. Muslim as well as local non-Muslim merchants, *zimmis*, involved in external trade, appear to have been exempted from export taxation. These merchants, initially, were only liable to pay their *zakat* and *jizya* respectively.[49] During the reign of Omar the second Caliph, a more concrete system was established: Europeans were to pay customs duty at the rate at which they charge Muslims in Europe, i.e., full reciprocity, usually 10 per cent; local non-Muslims, *zimmis* were to pay 5 per cent and Muslims only 2.5 per cent, which was of course, the *zakat*.

It is well known that in the following centuries nearly all Islamic states violated these early traditions and began to impose heavier taxation on trade. With the Mamluk rule in Egypt, further deviations from classical Islamic capitalism took place. When the Mamluk Sultan Baybars introduced trade monopolies in 1432, the state monopolized the pepper and spice trade along the Red Sea. This was the end of the famous Karimi merchants, who had dominated this trade ever since the thirteenth century. The rebirth of the Egyptian mercantile class had to wait until the Ottoman conquest, which peripheralized Egypt. Becoming periphery of a huge empire meant that state control came to be diluted, which gave Egyptian merchants and craftsmen a breathing space to flourish.[50] The same, however, cannot be said for the merchants of the Ottoman heartlands. In those regions, the mercantile class was subjected to the 'Ottoman proto-quasi-socialism' and could not flourish. Consequently, Arab merchants from Syria, which was too near to the Ottoman heartlands for comfort, appear to have consistently emigrated to Egypt. From the sixteenth to the nineteenth centuries, there was a substantial Syrian merchant community in Egypt.[51]

Recent research by Gad Gilbar, who showed that major Muslim merchant families were observed primarily in the Eastern and the Southern parts of the Middle East, i.e., the periphery of the Ottoman empire, rather than in its Western and Northern parts, has provided powerful support to this argument.[52] Gilbar has observed such powerful merchants in Iran as well. This is not surprising in view of the fact that the Iranian state did not actively interfere in mercantile activities and pursued a decentralized economic policy. Unlike the Ottoman economy, the Iranian economy was left to the private sector; governments were happy to collect taxes and leave the bazaars alone. Even when a national central government was formed, the economy was left alone other than major public works undertaken by the government. Indeed, the full notion of a centrally designed and implemented national economic policy framework came into being in Iran only in the 1950s.[53]

Thus the Ottoman economic doctrine constitutes probably the most radical divergence from the classical Islamic capitalism. This doctrine has been called 'proto-quasi-Ottoman socialism'.[54] 'Proto' because it antedates Marxism by several centuries and 'quasi' because, it was not based upon the Marxian class conflict but on the preservation of social harmony. In any case, albeit possible theoretical differences, the Ottoman system functioned in reality by and large akin to the modern socialism as we know it.[55] This is attested by the fact that the Ottoman state firmly controlled all the basic factors of production and physical capital, possessed nearly all mines and metallurgical establishments, and exerted a firm control over factor prices and mercantile profits – in short, it effectively controlled and dominated the economy.[56] This is clearly a major divergence from the classical Islamic capitalism of the first two centuries of Islam.

As the political economy of the Islamic empires evolved from the classical Islamic capitalism towards greater state control and gradually culminated in the proto-quasi-Ottoman socialism, financial institutions also evolved to respond to the changing needs.

Notwithstanding its divergence from the classical doctrine, the Ottoman experience is still important because it is the most important source with rich archival evidence informing us how a major Islamic state functioned in reality.[57] Moreover, Ottomans succeeded in establishing a powerful state, which could protect a large part of the Islamic world for centuries. It was also able, by and large, to eliminate poverty.[58]

On the negative side, it insisted on embracing its time-tested doctrine and failed to respond to the rise of modern Western capitalism. Thus, it has the dubious honour of succumbing to Western capitalism first, even before Soviet socialism. The demise of the Ottoman Empire was followed by colonization of the bulk of the Islamic world. This was followed by the abolition of the Caliphate, replacement of the *Shari'ah* by the French or British civil or common laws and the dismantlement of waqfs by the modernists. In short, all the Islamic countries, even those who could maintain their independence, were exposed to powerful Western influence. Things began to change only after the Second World War, when the Islamic world regained its independence. Attempts to recover the lost heritage began in earnest soon after. Emergence of modern Islamic finance, as the heart of modern Islamic capitalism, should be viewed within this historical framework.

Exposed for far too long to the debilitating effects of proto-quasi-socialism, it is high time that the Islamic world rediscovers its original capitalism established by the Prophet himself. One of the purposes of this book is to do precisely that.

Thus, modern Islamic finance is built upon three sets of institutions: classical Islamic capitalism and the institutions it has created; Western capitalism (pre- and post-Enlightenment) and the institutions that emerged out of them; and finally the Ottoman proto-quasi-socialism and its institutions. We will focus primarily on the two Islamic systems and their institutions and refer to the Western institutions only selectively and by way of comparison.

Currently, modern Western (conventional) finance is having a huge impact on Islamic finance. So much so that conventionalization appears to have emerged as the greatest danger to modern Islamic finance. If it is conventionalized, Islamic finance will become a mere imitation of Western finance and will fail to contribute to the birth of modern Islamic capitalism as an alternative economic system. To the extent that an observation made by Prof. Zubair Hasan can be generalized, jurists sitting on the *Shari'ah* boards of Islamic banks share much of the blame. One such jurist who sits on the boards of two banks admitted that they inevitably avoid initiating new products. Instead, they prefer to ask bank managers the details of the conventional product for which they need an Islamic counterpart: for 'it is much easier', this jurist said, 'to put on it the Islamic face than to structure an entirely new one'.[59]

Danger of conventionalization, with even more serious implications, is not limited to finance alone but is relevant for Islamic economics as well. With the expulsion of moral Church-imposed controls, Western capitalism ended up relying on state-imposed external controls.[60] The expulsion of moral controls was followed by the entire Western economic thought being focused upon the imaginary and supposedly rational, profit-maximizing *homo-economicus*. Conventional economics then attempted to discover how this fictitious being would behave.

Recently, with Kahneman receiving the 2002 Nobel Prize in economics, economic theory began to borrow from psychology and behavioural economics and started to move the latter to the mainstream. Kahneman challenged the standard economic theory that everybody acts like the *homo-economicus* and is a rational, calculating profit maximizer. He showed that psychological motives determine people's behaviour and that these motives are important for economic phenomena. The main paradigm here is the discovery of the laws, which govern actual human economic behaviour. It is believed that failure to understand these laws has caused the present crisis.

With respect to the above, Islamic economics has a huge advantage: Islam not being burdened by a powerful, centralized and an incorporated Church and its oppressive institutions, particularly the Inquisition, did not need an Enlightenment. Thus, moral controls imposed by the original sources of Islam were never discarded. The world of *homo-Islamicus*, which comprise about one-fourth of humanity, is still governed by an inbuilt auto control system spelled out in the classical sources of Islam. There is therefore no need to discover the laws that govern this Islamic capitalism. These have been laid down about 1400 years ago and are well known.

More specifically, rules that govern market participants, producers, traders and consumers alike are determined outside the market. They are internalized by participants before entering the market. These laws are clearly stated in the Qur'an, *ahadith* and *sunnah*. Rules such as no waste, no overconsumption, no harm or injury, faithfulness to contracts as well as trustworthiness, no fraud, no cheating, no short-changing of weights and measures, no interfering with the flow of supplies, no hoarding of commodities or money are general rules of behaviour that are internalized by Muslim consumers, producers and traders. These rules permit free and unrestricted interplay of demand and supply.[61]

Thus, the field of behavioural economics, for Muslims, boils down to the study of the relationship between the ancient code of life provided by the

Shari'ah and the actual economic behaviour of Muslims. Conventionalization, to the extent that Islamic economists borrow laws and concepts from Western economics, has the implicit danger that the laws developed for the *homo-economicus* are being super-imposed on the *homo-Islamicus*.

The code of life as embodied in the Qur'an and the Prophetic traditions was actually translated into daily economic life through institutions. What economic and financial institutions emerged out of this code of life and how they evolved over the centuries is the main subject of this book. By focusing on institutions – past and present – this book tries to shed light on the economic behaviour of Muslims determined not only by the ancient code but also by modern institutions.

We will start our inquiry with the basic principles of classical Islamic economy or capitalism and the financial institutions that developed from these principles. Throughout the book, I will try, whenever possible, to explain each major economic or financial institution by first providing its historical origins, then its evolution and then, finally, its present. Since I consider history, present and future as inseparable parts of the same continuum, in Part V some thoughts on the future of Islamic capitalism and finance will also be provided.

NOTES

1. Goitein, 'Middle-Eastern Bourgeoise', p. 223.
2. For a major modern study of the *Maqasid* see Ibn Ashur, *Treatise on Maqasid al-Shari'ah*.
3. Khaldun, *The Mukaddimah*, vol. II, ch. 5.
4. Zaim, 'Ekonomik Hayatta', p. 4; Al-Attas, *Prolegomena to the Metaphysics of Islam*, p.144.
5. Erkal, *İslam'ın Erken Döneminde*, p. 77.
6. Qur'an 73: 20; Zaim, 'Ekonomik Hayatta', p. 105.
7. For evidence that there was no textile production, tailors nor even mills in Mecca at the time of the Prophet, see Kallek, *Devlet ve Piyasa*, pp. 85–6. Thus trade, indeed, appears to have been the sole economic activity.
8. Gülen, *Iktisadi Mülahazalar*, p. 319.
9. That there were many types of capitalism classified according to chronology and function is now generally recognized. The salient characteristics of all capitalist economies were the use of market for allocation and distribution of goods and factors of production. Hartwell and Engerman, 'Capitalism', in J. Mokyr, *Economic History*, p. 319. For an excellent account of a non-Western, Chinese capitalism, see Faure, *China and Capitalism*, p. 48. On the Islamic disapproval of market interference see Mirakhor and Iqbal, *An Introduction to Islamic Finance*, p. 48.
10. For a very detailed and rigorous discussion on whether the Islamic economic system can be called capitalistic, see Rodinson, *Islam and Capitalism*, 1974. Rodinson first approaches the problem from the Marxist perspective and declines to call the Islamic economic system capitalist but then admits that it possessed a highly sophisticated 'capitalist sector'. This sector was, naturally, the trade sector and with the near total absence of agriculture and industry in the Arabia of the Prophet's time, it must have constituted some 75 to 90 per cent of the economy. Thus, Rodinson's admission should actually be considered as a confirmation that the early Islamic economy was capitalistic. He also admits that 'the merchants of the Muslim Empire conformed perfectly well to Max Weber's criteria for capitalistic activity',

ibid., pp. 28–30. For substantial empirical evidence about medieval Islamic capitalism see Labib, 'Capitalism in Medieval Islam', vol. 29, no. 1.

11. On the Qur'anic injunctions about the market wage rate see Döndüren, *Ticaret ve İktisat İlmihali*, 1993, pp. 452–3. On the widespread application of the market wage rate in an Islamic (Ottoman) economy see Çizakça, *A Comparative Evolution,* pp. 89–90, 95.
12. Lane and Commentators, 'Meanings of Capitalism', p. 7.
13. Çizakça, 'Cross-cultural Borrowing'. There will be a further discussion of this borrowing process below.
14. Although the term 'medieval' normally refers to the period from the fifth to the fifteenth century in Europe, it can and has been borrowed for the Islamic world. In this case, 'medieval Islam' refers to the period from the seventh century, when Islam was revealed, to the mid-fifteenth century, when Constantinople was conquered and walls ceased to protect cities.
15. Braudel, *Ekonomi ve Kapitalizm, XV–XVII Yüzyıllar*, 3. cilt, pp. 199–200.
16 Van Leur, *Eenige Beschouwingen*; Steensgaard, 'The History of European Expansion' in Blusse and Gaastra (eds), *Companies and Trade.*
17. Braudel, *Ekonomi ve Kapitalizm*, vol. II, p. 207.
18. For a brief account of these differences, see Lane and Commentators, 'Meanings of Capitalism', pp. 8–9.
19. Ibid., p. 10.
20. Ibid., p. 12 (comment by Arthur Cole).
21. Wallerstein, *Historical Capitalism*, pp. 13–19.
22. McCormick, *Origins*, pp. 344–54. Consider the following statement by McCormick: 'I know of 54 finds of Arab coins issued between the late seventh and early tenth centuries and discovered in 42 places in the Carolingian empire and its neighbors', ibid., p. 344.
23. Establishment of the first Islamic bank. To avoid any possible misunderstanding, it might be appropriate to reiterate the three very important terms referred to in this page: *Shari'ah* is the revelation that the Prophet received, *fiqh* is the collection of Islamic juridical opinions regarding *Shari'ah's* application, applied *fiqh* is the actual application through institutions and institutional evolution of the jurists' rulings.
24. Çizakça, *Comparative Evolution, id.*, *Philanthropic Foundations* and, *id.*, 'Cross-cultural Borrowing'.
25. It has been argued that Hashim, the grandfather of the Prophet, had perfected the *mudaraba.* See Şencan, *Homo-Islamicus*, p. 4.
26. For example, for the incorporation of the Roman land system into the Islamic Caliphate, see Inalcık and Quataert, *An Economic and Social History*, pp. 103–8.
27. Udovitch, 'Bankers Without Banks', p. 271.
28. Udovitch, ibid., p. 265.
29. The Islamic origins of the medieval European partnership *commenda* has been hotly debated ever since Udovitch published his groundbreaking article; 'At the Origins of the Western Commenda', 1969. For a summary of this debate see Çizakça, *Comparative Evolution*, pp. 10–12.
30. Çizakça, *Philanthropic Foundations*, pp. 8–12.
31. For a theoretical explanation of this topic supported with substantial evidence, see Çizakça, 'Cross-cultural Borrowing'.
32. Borrowing the wisdom of other cultures was encouraged by Prophet Mohammad himself. Consider the following statement attributed to him: 'A word of Wisdom is the lost property of a believer. He can take it wherever he finds it, because he is more entitled to it', Al-Tirmidhi, *Kitab al-'ılm, hadith* 2687. On striking examples of how Muslims borrowed the scientific achievements of Greeks, Persians and Indians and expanded them further, see Sezgin, *Einführung in die Geschichte*, vol. I.
33. Heck, *Arab Roots of Capitalism*, ch.1.
34. The exact length of the gap depends on the beginning of Islamic and Western capitalisms. The latter can be assumed to have begun roughly with the first Crusade in 1095 AD. If we consider the year 622 AD, when the Prophet migrated from Mecca to Medinah, an event known as the *Hejrah*, as the beginning of Islamic capitalism, the gap would be about 450

years. If, on the other hand, we consider the year 900 as an approximate date, when Islamic jurisprudence with respect to commerce and finance was more or less completed, then the gap would be about 200 years. If we accept the thirteenth century as the beginning of Western capitalism, the gap increases even further.

35. Çizakça, *Comparative Evolution*, pp. 10–12; Çizakça, 'Cross-cultural Borrowing', passim; Çizakça, *Philanthropic Foundations*, pp. 8–13; Heck, *Arab Roots of Capitalism*, chs. 5 and 6. In the area of public finance, however, autonomous European city-states invented institutions, which differed substantially from those invented by the centralized Islamic empires. Thus, eventually different political systems, quite naturally, led to different institutions of public finance.
36. Çizakça, *Comparative Evolution*, ch. 2. A joint-stock company is a company having a certain amount of capital, divided into a number of transferable shares, managed for the common advantage of the shareholders by a body of directors chosen by and responsible to them.
37. Baigent and Leigh, *The Inquisition*, p. 69.
38. Çizakça, 'Islam und Christentum'; see also Inalcık, *Turkey and Europe in History*, pp. 107–112, and Blockmans, *Emperor Charles V 1500–1558*, p. 42.
39. Weber, *the 'Spirit' of Capitalism*.
40. This happened particularly in France and, under its influence, in continental Europe. English and American Enlightenments did not lead to such a hatred of religion. For the subtle but important differences between the various forms of Enlightenments, see Himmelfarb, *The Roads to Modernity*, pp. 152–3.
41. During the nineteenth and twentieth centuries, under the influence of the French Revolution and colonialism, a dilution of religion did take place in the Islamic world. After the Second World War, however, most newly independent Muslim countries began to restore their Islamic heritage. Today, Islamic values are making a strong comeback everywhere.
42. Actually, although the system of land ownership as introduced by Omar, indeed appears to have been nearly identical to the Roman system (for details of this similarity the reader is referred to Inalcik and Quataert, *Economic and Social History*, p. 106), it is possible to deduce from the Qur'an a system of land ownership based on a full right of possession for the individual *without* the state (representing the Creator or the collectivity) losing its initial right of possession. For this deduction, see Mirakhor and Hamid, *Islam and Development,* forthcoming. Thus, it is also possible that Omar may have reached the same system by deduction from the Qur'an. Some authors, usually those unaware of the Roman system, argue that Omar simply imposed the *kharaj* on the previous owners and allowed them to keep their lands. What he granted, of course, were the *usus* and *fructus* rights, with the *dominium eminens, raqaba,* remaining firmly with the state. Thus, while deduction from the Qur'an was certainly possible, simple continuation of the previous Roman practice must have been far easier. In any case, Omar's practice of learning the ancient customs of conquered territory before drawing up any system of administration for it has been acknowledged. Moreover, it is known that Parsis, Greeks and Copts employed in the land revenue departments of the conquered states were allowed to maintain their posts as before. It is only natural that, providing they were permitted to do so, they would simply continue the systems they knew. See on this, Shibli, *Al-Farooq*, pp. 233, 235, 238.
43. 59:7.
44. For details, see Erkal, *İslam'ın Erken Döneminde*, pp. 200–4.
45. Essid, *A Critique of Islamic Economic Thought*, pp. 159, 162.
46. Kallek, *Devlet ve Piyasa*, pp. 32–3.
47. Indeed, there is evidence that the *jizya* imposed by Muslims when they conquered an area was usually lower than the taxes that prevailed before the conquest. Erkal, *İslam'ın Erken Döneminde*, p. 86.
48. Erkal, *İslam'ın Erken Döneminde*, p. 46.
49. Erkal, *İslam'ın Erken Döneminde*, pp. 65, 167–8.
50. Hanna, *Making Big Money in 1600* (Cairo: The American University in Cairo Press, 1998), p. 73; Faroqhi, *Artisans of Empire*, p. 86.
51. Ibid. and Gilbar, 'Muslim Tujjar', Session 121.

52. Gilbar, 'Muslim Tujjar', p. 5.
53. I am grateful to Abbas Mirakhor for this point. Personal correspondence, 21 March 2009.
54. Çizakça, 'The Economy, 1453–1606', forthcoming, vol. II.
55. I have been criticized by Hans-Georg Majer for using a term invented by Karl Marx for the sixteenth-century Ottoman economy. But my depiction of the Ottoman economic system as 'proto-quasi-socialism' simply argues that just as there were capitalist or quasi-capitalist systems before Adam Smith, so was there an Ottoman proto-quasi-socialism before Marx. Actually, it was Ömer L. Barkan who, more than half a century ago, probably for the first time, applied the term socialism to describe the Ottoman system. The precise term he used was: 'a type of war socialism' (*Bir nevi harp sosyalizmi*). See Barkan, 'Bazı Büyük Şehirlerde Eşya', p. 327.
56. Genç, 'Osmanlı İmparatorluğu'nda Devlet ve Ekonomi', p. 67; Genç, 'Osmanlılar: Ticari ve İktisadi Yapı'.
57. None of the other great Islamic empires, not even the relatively recent Safevid and Mughal empires, have left any archives comparable in quantity and quality to the Ottomans. The Prime Ministry Archives of Turkey alone is estimated to contain some 400 million documents. For an exceptionally important pre-Ottoman source primarily based upon Arabic papyrus documents on early Islamic Egypt, see Morimoto, *The Fiscal Administration*.
58. Latest research has yielded that in 1736 there were 322 beggars in Istanbul. Out of these, only 70 persons were considered by the authorities as genuinely poor and permitted to beg. This figure was less than 0.1 per cent of the population of Istanbul. By contrast, Paris, which had a smaller population than Istanbul, had more than a hundred times more beggars. See Genc, 'Osmanli Dunyasinda Dilencilik', and, Geremek, *Poverty, A History*, p. 119.
59. Hasan, 'Islamic Finance: What Does it Change'.
60. Lecture given by Mervyn Lewis on 'An Islamic Economic Perspective on the Global Financial Crisis', 16 April 2009 at the Securities Commission in Kuala Lumpur.
61. Mirakhor and Hamid, *Islam and Development*, forthcoming.

Acknowledgements

This book was commissioned by INCEIF, also known as the Global University for Islamic Finance in Kuala Lumpur, Malaysia. My foremost thanks, therefore, go to Dr Zeti Akhtar Aziz the Founder and Chancellor of INCEIF as well as the Governor of Bank Negara Malaysia. It was Prof. Dr Sudin Haron, the Founding Dean, who offered my first contract with INCEIF. Special thanks are due to the President and CEO of INCEIF, Dato'Agil Natt, as well as to Prof. Dr Malik Muhammad Mahmud Al-Awan and Prof. Datuk Dr Syed Othman Al-Habshi, the successive deans.

Professors Obiyathulla Ismath Bacha, Zubair Hasan, Saiful Azhar Rosly and Mahmood Sanussi as well as Dr Asyraf Wajdi Dusuki, Dr Mohammad Akram Laldin and Shabnam Mokhtar of INCEIF discussed with me various parts of my work. I am grateful to them for their valuable comments and insights. Professors Bacha and Hasan each contributed to the chapter on the gold dinar substantially. The chapter itself was inspired by a challenging discussion I had with the Royal Professor Ungku Aziz, the Governor Dr Zeti Akhtar Aziz and Dr Tawfiq Ayman.

Securities Commission, Project Director of the ICM-CMDF Development Project Wan Abdul Rahim Kamil, a former student of mine at the International Institute of Islamic Banking and Economics at the Turkish Republic of Northern Cyprus, and now a colleague, invited me to the Malaysian Securities Commission to discuss with the staff the section on venture capital.

Prof. Dr Abbas Mirakhor contributed to this manuscript not only by allowing me to read his forthcoming *opus magnum*, from which I benefited enormously, but also by reading it. I benefited greatly from his comments. Professor Dr Muhammad Hashim Kamali invited me to his International Institute of Advanced Islamic Studies in Kuala Lumpur and gave me the opportunity to discuss openly the chapter on *Maqasid al-Shari'ah*. The original idea of this chapter had emerged during a discussion with Alparslan Acikgenc of Fatih University, Istanbul. The concept of Al-Ghazali optimum was reached independently yet jointly with Sabri Orman of the University of Commerce, Istanbul. The insight regarding the *hifz al-nasl* actually constituting the essence of the twentieth-century concept of intergenerational Pareto Optimum was provided by Emin Koksal of Bahcesehir University, Istanbul.

Prof. Dr David Faure of the Chinese University of Hong Kong invited me to discuss Islamic waqfs. It was in Hong Kong that we were able to compare, probably for the first time, Islamic waqfs with the Chinese Tang.

INCEIF librarians Siti Salbiah Raduan and Zain Azreen Zainoren contributed greatly to this book by regularly sending me the latest information on the current Islamic finance practices. Muhammad Muhaizam bin Musa, my research assistant, collected original data from the Corporate Communications Department of *Tabung Haji*. Table 12.1 could not have been formed without his help. I am grateful also to the officials of this department for their valuable cooperation. Another student of mine, Buerhan Saiti, provided valuable and much appreciated help in preparing the manusript for publication. My personal assistant Abdul Rais Abdul Rashid also helped along the same lines and many others.

My former student at the International Institute of Islamic banking and Economics in Northern Cyprus and current friend, Cemal Rodoplu, has kept in touch with my work ever since 1982 and has continued sending me information about the current situation of Islamic finance in Turkey. I am indebted to him for much of the information about the latest Revenue Participation Documents. I would also like to thank professors Süleyman Kaya and Mesud Küçükkalay on their views regarding the *icareteyn* waqfs.

I benefited greatly from my conferences and lectures delivered to the graduate students of INCEIF. They were the very first student body to be exposed to my ideas and their comments were therefore most valuable. I would like to thank particularly Servet Bayındır and Nidal Al-Sayyed; with both, the learning experience was mutual.

Finally, I am most grateful to my wife not only for sharing my life in Kuala Lumpur but also for her constant encouragement. She has read the entire manuscript and thanks to her penetrating comments I rewrote and corrected many sections. Without her comments and the ensuing improvements, readers would have found this book far less readable.

While I acknowledge with gratitude my debt to all these family members and colleagues, I must emphasize that I, alone, am responsible for any mistakes in this book.

Notes on transliteration and pronunciation

All foreign words, excluding foreign names, are italicized except the word waqf and its plural awqaf. These words appear so frequently throughout the text that it has been decided not to italicize them. Throughout the book, I have used the generally accepted forms of Arabic words in Latin alphabet. For Arabic words in Ottoman context, however, I have used the generally accepted Ottoman/Turkish spelling and punctuation. For words that have become part of English in their Arabic versions, then their Arabic transliteration has been preferred. Thus, waqf (and not *vakıf*) has been used. Turkish words, which have become anglicized, have been kept in the latter form. Thus pasha (and not *Paşa*) has been used. For those who are unfamiliar with the pronunciation of modern Turkish spelling, the following rudimentary rules (according to Geffery Lewis's grammar) may be of some help: *c* is pronounced *j* as in *jam*; *ç* is pronounced *ch* as in *church; g* is pronounced as in the word *goat; ğ* lengthens the vowel preceding it; *y* sounds like the *u* in *radium*; *ö* and *ü* as in German *könig* and *führer* respectively; and *ş* is pronounced as *sh* in *shall.*

Explanation of Islamic terms of reverence

As it is well known, every time the name of Prophet Muhammad is mentioned, Muslims express their respect by saying 'salla Allahu 'alayhi wa sallam'. This is the universal rule of respect in the Islamic world. The problem, however, is that when put in writing this reverential term is far too distracting for readers. If the Prophet's name is mentioned frequently, as is often the case in this book, the reader finds it nearly impossible to concentrate on the topic. Originally I tried to abbreviate and used (SAS) after each time I referred to the Prophet. But then Western colleagues, who kindly read this book in manuscript form, complained bitterly for being distracted. This, surely, could not have been the intention of the Prophet. If he had to choose between the formal expression of respect and a higher level of understanding of his teachings, there is no doubt that he would have chosen the latter. Muslim readers of this book are therefore requested to recite the term of reverence silently in their hearts and thus show tolerance and understanding for non-Muslim readers. It goes without saying that I share the respect of all of my readers for all religious figures.

Part I

Value systems behind institutions

1. Two approaches to Islamic economics and finance

Two distinctly different approaches rival each other in modern Islamic finance. One of them, the *Shari'ah* compliant approach, dominates the field with important consequences. In this chapter we will focus on this problem.

To the extent that modern Islamic finance is not built directly from the *Shari'ah* (*Shari'ah* based approach) but rather from the Islamically modified conventional banking (*Shari'ah* compliant approach), the result is high costs, low profits and most importantly, a dilution of respectability. If Islamic finance is to emerge as the heart of a viable alternative capitalist system, it must progress from being *Shari'ah* compliant to being *Shari'ah* based. While the former briefly means borrowed from the West after being made compliant to the *Shari'ah,* the latter simply means not borrowed from the West but evolved from the original sources of Islam.[1] *Shari'ah* based also means, not only a system built up from the roots, based upon the true teachings of Islamic law, but also a profound understanding of how that law was practised over the centuries leading to specific financial institutions in history – thus comprising law as well as its centuries-long application and evolution.

It will be argued here that Islamic financial engineers can develop truly *Shari'ah* based instruments only if they are well informed about the existence of such institutions in the past. Failure to be equipped with such knowledge would lead to an embarrassing waste of creative talent with financial engineers reinventing institutions that have actually existed for centuries.

Thus the other essential goal of this book is to inform financial engineers about historical Islamic financial institutions as well as their evolution so that they can focus their creative talent into modernizing these historical instruments or designing completely new ones, really new ones! After all, as Abraham Lincoln once said, 'I know of nothing so pleasant to the mind, as the discovery of anything which is at once *new* and *valuable*.'[2] It would therefore be a great disappointment if these financial engineers one day found out that what they have 'discovered' has actually been known for centuries and their 'discovery' is therefore less 'pleasant to the mind'.

But the reader is also warned here against direct borrowing from historical instruments. Such borrowing could be as misleading as borrowing from the

West. Historical instruments should be a source of *inspiration* for creating new instruments rather than models to be emulated to the letter.

Furthermore, the *Shari'ah* compliant approach suffers from a dilemma. While on the one hand, it tries to be similar to conventional finance, on the other hand, it tries to exhibit an Islamic character by emphasizing Arabic contract names and obtaining, often at huge expense, certification by *Shari'ah* experts.[3] The dilemma pertains to the inherent contradiction: Imitation of the Western instruments is done in order to minimize costs and gain efficiency but maintaining an Islamic character increases the costs. Imposing an Islamic character on conventional instruments increases costs because, inevitably, some additional transactions are added to the existing *modus operandi* and every additional transaction means an additional office and is subject to taxes.[4] Moreover, additional transactions reduce efficiency.

There is an inherent danger in all this. If the classical Islamic contracts are relaxed, the substantive content of the classical contract forms may be lost forever. Furthermore, Islamic finance will continue being an imitation of conventional finance, always one step behind it, with the result that the clients of the industry will lose hope that it will ever provide a hope of a bona fide alternative to conventional finance.[5]

The hope for Islamic finance lies in a third alternative, namely, to try to understand and apply the substantive spirit of Islamic law. This can be accomplished by understanding the economic functions served by classical legal provisions and principles which prompted jurists to impose those rules. This understanding necessitates a thorough study of applied *Shari'ah* – that is, the way the substantive spirit of Islamic law has been applied throughout history. Thus a grand synthesis of legal/economic thought combined with historical application leading to a study of institutional evolution emerges as *conditio sine qua non* for the *Shari'ah* based approach.

The *Shari'ah* compliant approach is relatively easy and therefore dominates. It involves looking at the West for viable economic or financial institutions and instruments. After the identification, it reverse engineers and dismantles them into their essential components. This is followed by an introduction of additional transactions trying to make each component comply with the *Shari'ah*. It then claims to have invented a new instrument that is *Shari'ah* compliant. The basic advantage of this method is the instant recognition and understanding by the conventional sector.

But, there are four basic weaknesses of this *Shari'ah* compliant approach. First, because its initial starting point is a Western institution or instrument, it is basically imitative. Consequently, it does not contribute anything new to humanity's treasure box of accumulated wisdom and does not command respect. After all, it is a universal rule that imitators do not deserve respect but original contributors do. Second, although it is claimed that this approach allows Muslims to perform in an economic environment dominated by Western modes, it has been shown that it does so at the expense of increased costs and reduced profits.[6] Indeed, reverse engineering of financial products and the additional transactions it inevitably introduces constitute an expensive and time-consuming process. Seen from the perspective of public finance, every additional transaction constitutes a newly taxable resource leading to a substantially increased tax burden. Moreover, fees are also expensive. Actually, not only the very expensive fees of financial engineers, but also the equally expensive fees of the very limited numbers of *Shari'ah* experts, need to be paid. Moreover, for each newly invented instrument and transaction, *fatwas* need to be obtained, another very time-consuming and expensive affair. Third, all of these bear with them substantial *Shari'ah* risks, in the sense that the public may become disenchanted by these instruments so similar and even benchmarked to the interest rates prevalent in the West.[7] Fourth, highest profits are usually obtained when a new financial instrument is introduced for the first time. Since reverse engineering focuses on Western instruments introduced long ago, it tries to convert models whose profits have already diminished.[8] Fifth, Mirakhor and Iqbal have written almost prophetically one year before the current crisis that 'there are now USD32 trillion of sovereign and corporate debts alone'. The Western system has become an inverted pyramid of huge debt piled upon a narrow production base. 'This growth in debt has nearly severed the relationship between finance and production... For each dollar of production there are thousands of dollars of debt claims.' An Islamic financial system can address this problem by its fundamental operating principle of a close link between finance and production and because of its requirement of risk sharing. But to the extent that Islamic finance emulates the West, it loses its ability to do so.

Islamic finance has to develop its own genuinely Islamic financial instruments. So far, Muslims have been free-riding on financial theories and instruments developed by the West. Unless Islamic finance develops its own genuinely Islamic financial instruments, it cannot achieve the dynamism of a system that provides the security, liquidity and diversity needed for a globally accepted financial system, which would be a genuine alternative to the present debt–interest-based international system.[9]

It is for these disadvantages that the other, *Shari'ah* based, approach is needed. This is, however, more difficult to achieve. The essence of this approach is the realization that there is a substantial difference between the Western *homo-economicus*, the rational man, who has discarded all religious and ethical teachings and acts purely to maximize his profit, and the *homo-Islamicus,* the Muslim person, who also tries to maximize his profits but does so subject to the laws and ethics of Islam. Since it is assumed that the *homo-economicus* has discarded all ethics and the laws derived from them, a new set of laws are needed for him and the identification and designing of these laws is what conventional economics has been doing ever since Adam Smith. After all, Smith was trying to understand how the human society was able to remain orderly and predictable despite the prevalence of *homo-economicus* not governed by the fear of a deity.[10] These laws are needed to understand and predict how the *homo-economicus* will respond to certain economic phenomena. Without such laws, the conventional system, which assumes rationality, simply cannot function.

By contrast, Abbas Mirakhor has argued that the *homo-Islamicus* has his laws already given. Muslims act within the laws and constraints given to them by the *Shari'ah* and therefore do not need a new set of laws.[11] The *homo-Islamicus* considers these laws as given in perpetuity and tries to maximize his profits subject to them. If this is so, then the *Shari'ah* compliant approach, to the extent that it borrows economic laws and financial institutions from the West, ends up subjugating the *homo-Islamicus* to the laws designed for the *homo-economicus*.

This is not to say that ideas, laws and institutions should not be borrowed from other civilizations. On the contrary, Muslims have been encouraged by the Prophet himself to borrow the wisdom of other civilizations. But institutional borrowing is not a simple matter. There is no guarantee that the borrowed institutions will survive or flourish in the borrowing civilization. Recent research has shown that of a set of institutions borrowed, only those in harmony with the traditions of the borrowing civilization have the best chance of survival. This is because, after all, each borrowed institution must function within the institutional matrix of the borrowing society.[12] The gist of my argument is that institutions developed through the *Shari'ah* based method are in much better harmony with the traditions and values of Islam and therefore have a much greater chance to flourish in the Islamic world. Institutions introduced by the *Shari'ah* compliant method, however, are implants and their performance in the Islamic world is at best uncertain.

If indeed, as Mirakhor argues, Islamic economics should not be an endeavour to discover new laws, then the *Shari'ah* based approach boils down to the search of the basic framework of economic behaviour that has been laid down by the Qur'an.

This is the first task of the *Shari'ah* based Islamic economics and must be followed by the search of how the Prophet of Islam has applied these principles in economic reality and which institutions he has established for this purpose.[13]

Applications of the Qur'anic principles to the real world, however, have not stopped with the death of the Prophet. The Prophet was the first ever human being to have translated the principles laid down in the Holy Qur'an to the real world. But this endeavour, once started, continued throughout the history of Islam.

The second task of *Shari'ah* based Islamic economics is therefore to refer to Islamic legal/economic/financial and institutional history (ILEFIH) and find out how the laws and institutions established by the Prophet of Islam in order to apply the Qur'anic principles into reality have evolved over the next 14 centuries. This is nothing less than the birth of a new field of intellectual inquiry which can be called *applied Shari'ah,* because this particular and complex perspective of history actually explains how the *Shari'ah* was applied by Muslims over the centuries. The next question ILEFIH or applied *Shari'ah* deals with refers to the consequences. Indeed, what were the consequences of this particular Islamic legal and institutional evolution and how do they fare when compared to the evolution of similar laws and institutions in other civilizations? Finally, ILEFIH also refers to the question whether in view of this assessment there is a need to reform these institutions. In short, various forms of Islamic history, ILEFIH or applied *Shari'ah*, assume a profound importance for the *Shari'ah* based approach to Islamic economics and finance. It can even be argued that research in Islamic historiography becomes the *conditio sine qua non* for this progress towards the *Shari'ah* based approach.

Fortunately, thanks to the surviving Ottoman archives, progress in various forms of Islamic historiography is well on its way. There are well over 400 million documents in these archives excluding the more than eleven thousand volumes of *Shari'ah* Court Registers of the city of Istanbul alone. The Islamic Court Registers are of particular relevance here because they give direct evidence about how the *Shari'ah* was actually applied in history.

Can these historical institutions be considered as the basic underlying structures for modern ones? Consider the following obvious but often overlooked fact: interest prohibition and all the other principles of Islamic finance have been around and enforced for the last 14 centuries. Therefore the current problems that the financial engineers are facing are not at all new – they are 1400 years old! Muslims have lived with these rules for all those 14 centuries and have invented institutions to address their needs, which obey the rules of the *Shari'ah*. The institutions they have developed have also been confirmed by the jurists in past centuries. Thus these *Shari'ah* based institutions, accompanied by their *fatwas*, constitute the basic building structures from which, according to the spanning theory,[14] an infinite number of modern derivatives can be designed. If financial engineers do not progress towards the *Shari'ah* based method and learn thoroughly from these past institutions and their *modus operandi* and insist on the *Shari'ah* compliant method, there is a serious danger that they will end up 'inventing' what has been already invented centuries ago. This is a huge waste of creative talent of financial engineers, which is a very scarce resource and the Islamic world cannot afford to waste it.

The third task of *Shari'ah* based Islamic economics is to determine how Muslim thinkers have responded to the ever-changing economic phenomena throughout history. This is the history of Islamic economic thought. Only a thorough understanding of the evolution of Islamic economic thought and its comparison with the history of economic thought of other civilizations can inform us about where we stand today.

Only after these tasks are accomplished, can Islamic finance progress from reverse engineering of Western forms towards a new era of forward engineering based upon authentic sources. This involves designing new instruments *inspired* from the established menu of historical Islamic financial instruments. The word inspired is deliberately emphasized here. Because picking up institutions from history, and then applying them directly to modern times, can be dangerous. Being thoroughly informed about and *inspired* by historical instruments in order to design modern instruments is a more difficult and long-term project but with far greater potential for the Islamic world as well as humanity than reverse engineering.

Finally, a few words for the Islamic financial engineers: economic history of both the medieval West and the Islamic world demonstrates that usury prohibition did not act as an impediment to economic growth in the long run. This is because both European and Muslim merchants, the financial engineers of the medieval era, used their creativity to design financial instruments which obeyed the prohibition. It was these instruments which triggered massive and sustained economic growth. Modern financial engineers should therefore regard the prohibition as a challenge to their creativity. It would be appropriate here to quote John Munro, an eminent medieval European historian:

> Thus the responses to the prohibition of usury promoted rather than retarded European economic progress.[15]

NOTES

1. Laldin, '*Shari'ah* Compliant vs *Shari'ah* Based Product', pp. 2–3. These otherwise neat definitions can be problematic because, in reality, it is difficult to establish a clear cut separation between the two approaches. This is because an originally *Shari'ah* based instrument can eventually be misused as a tool to borrow conventional methods. In what follows, many examples of this will be presented.
2. Italics are Lincoln's.
3. There are only a handful of international *Shari'ah* experts capable of understanding Islamic law as well as the demands of modern banking. This has led to an oligarchy of *Shari'ah* scholars. An analysis covering Bahrain, Dubai, Kuwait, Qatar, Saudi Arabia and Abu Dhabi found that the top ten scholars share 253 positions in these countries with 25 *Shari'ah* board memberships per scholar. See *The Malaysian Reserve*, 14 September 2009.
4. This is not always true. A government determined to enhance Islamic finance can show some sensitivity towards the Islamic financial sector. This is the case in Malaysia, where issuance costs of Islamic securities are tax exempt if the transaction has been approved by the Bank Negara Malaysia or the Securities Commission. All profits pertaining to *sukuk al-ijarah* are also tax exempt since this instrument has been approved by the authorities. See Ram Ratings, 'Malaysian *Sukuk* Taxation', p. 18.

5. El-Gamal, *Islamic Finance*, p. 24.
6. El-Gamal, *Islamic Finance*, p. 1.
7. For the detailed study of the *Shari'ah* risk in Malaysia, see Rosly, *Critical Issues*. Also see his latest joint article under review with Lahsasna and Naim, 'Shari'ah Risk and *Clawback* Effect'.
8. Ibid.
9. Mirakhor and Iqbal, *Introduction to Islamic Finance*, p. 21.
10. Evensky, *Adam Smith's Moral Philosophy,* passim.
11. Consider the following letter written by Professor Mirakhor to this author on 20 March 2009: 'There is this fundamental fascination of some Islamic economists with Western economic, particularly the neoclassical thought. They do not seem to realize that whereas in Western economic tradition theory is in search of explaining, predicting, and controlling economic behavioral phenomenon to discover economic laws and regularities, Islamic economics has to take laws of behavior as given by the Law Giver in the Quran. The job of Islamic economics becomes discovering ways and means of efficient implementation of these rules and laws of behavior which Douglass North refers to as institutions. In the short run, however, the main job of Muslim economists is to discover these rules from the Quran and their corresponding application by the Sunnah. Concurrently, Islamic economics has to explore the economic history of Muslim societies for application or non-application of these theoretical rules (the Quran) and their Archtypal operationalization (the Sunnah) in these countries and consequences thereof.'
12. Çizakça, 'Cross-cultural Borrowing', 2006. Also see Pistor, Berkowitz and Richard, *Economic Development,* 2003 and Pistor, *Standardization of Law*.
13. Mirakhor and Hamid, *Islam and Development,* forthcoming. I am grateful to Professor Mirakhor for allowing me to refer to his yet unpublished manuscript.
14. A subset of game theory. The reader is warned here that not every historical institution was perfectly legal. This is another reason why such institutions should not be modernized verbatim without a thorough analysis.
15. Munro, 'The Medieval Origins', p. 561.

2. Basic principles of Islamic capitalism

In this chapter we will observe the basic principles upon which Islamic capitalism is based. It is from these principles that Islamic economic institutions have been designed.

BASIC AXIOMS OF ISLAMIC CAPITALISM

In this book, Islamic economics will be understood as capitalism practised by Muslims, which is based upon the following axioms:

1. The unity and oneness of the creator (*Tawhid*). This means that all creation has only one omnipotent creator – *Allah*.
2. Muhammad is the last and the final messenger of *Allah*.
3. *Allah* will call forth all mankind for a final, definite and complete account, followed by a judgement. At that point each person will see the results of his/her actions and will have to live forever with the consequences in the form of either rewards or punishments in the hereafter. This axiom introduces the concept of 'life hereafter' and extends the time horizon of a believer beyond the short span of life on this earth.
4. A Muslim is constantly aware of the presence of *Allah*, who is believed to be 'closer to him than his jugular vein'. This awareness extends to his day-to-day relationship with others. He knows his actions will be judged in the Day of Judgement and it is through this fear that he can distinguish between what is right and what is wrong.[1]
5. A primordial contract between *Allah* and the mankind is believed to exist, according to which man agreed to serve and worship no one but *Allah*.[2]
6. Vis-à-vis *Allah* the entire humanity is created equal. This equality is based upon the fact that we are all created by Him. With respect to our position to Him, we only differ from each other in goodness, virtue and service to *Allah*.[3] But with respect to the next fellow human being, we are not created equal. He has raised some of us above others so that we shall be tried by means of what He has bestowed upon us.[4]
7. Islamic community was created as a 'community of the middle', 'justly balanced'. The community is called upon by the Qur'an to be a nation in the middle.[5]

8. The central function of this community is to 'command the good and forbid the evil'.[6]

The importance of these axioms from the perspective of Islamic capitalism lies in the fact that they affect rule-compliance and strength of institutions. The stronger the ideology, the lower the cost of enforcement of contracts and hence the transaction costs. Moreover, strong ideology also minimizes information asymmetry problems and moral hazard.[7] All of these concepts are expressed in the verse that,

> We are nearer to him (mankind) than his jugular vein.[8]

Thus, a Muslim believes that all of his actions are recorded for a final assessment in the Day of Judgement. Moreover, unlike Jesus Christ (and by extension the Catholic Church), who is believed to have the power to forgive Christians' sins, Muslims are told that:

> Who receiveth guidance receiveth for his own benefit, who goeth astray doth so to his own loss. No bearer of burdens can bear the burden of another...[9]

Thus, if a Muslim commits sins, he alone is responsible for them. He cannot hope that Prophet Muhammad will have him forgiven. A Muslim, furthermore, believes that if he does injustice to someone else, there is always reciprocity in that through injustice to others, ultimately, he does injustice to himself and receives its results both here and in the hereafter.

These beliefs lead to powerful auto-control, contract fulfilment and a reduction of transaction costs. It has been argued that Islam first equips a Muslim with ethical principles and then leaves him free to compete.[10]

INTEREST PROHIBITION

As it is well known, interest prohibition is one of the most important tenets of Islamic capitalism. But this prohibition is merely a reflection of a more subtle principle. This is the idea of sharing. Islam demands that profits, risks and losses must be shared fairly between the transacting parties. This fair sharing constitutes the essence of justice, *adl*, which must dominate the economic system.[11]

Interest transactions are prohibited because it is recognized that these so-called *riba* transactions impose all the business risks upon the borrower. Consequently, such transactions are considered unjust and are prohibited.[12] Another reason for the prohibition is that interest income is not earned through work. This violates the fifth rule of property rights to be explained below.

With interest prohibited, the nature of deposits differs substantially between the two capitalisms. Whereas classical Islam considers deposits made in a banking institution as *wadia*, i.e., purely for safe-keeping, Western capitalism permits the banker to utilize it and, in return, obliges him to reward the depositor with the rate of interest. It is only natural that, theoretically speaking, out of these very different concepts, two very different systems of banking should emerge.

The question as to under what conditions a transaction would be condemned as usury, will be answered in Chapter 6.

PRICES AND PROFITS

Classical Islamic capitalism's approach to the concept of profits also differs substantially from Western capitalism. The starting point of both is the same: profits are desirable. But the Islamic system allows profits subject to the concept of *halal* or *haram*, i.e., permitted or prohibited. Generating profits by hurting others, or by violating the basic principles of Islam, is considered as transgression. Consequently, a Muslim businessman is obliged to control himself and to see to it that his profits are earned through *halal* transactions.

Classical Islamic capitalism, based upon self-control, does not impose a maximum limit on profits or prices. This argument is supported by a *hadith* attributed to Prophet Muhammad. Accordingly, when during an inflationary period he was asked to fix the prices, he replied: 'prices are fixed by *Allah*', and refused to interfere in the price mechanism. He explained his refusal by saying that to do so would lead to injustice.[13] There are also many judicial treatises which have condemned fixing prices, the *narh*. Price fixing is condemned as *mazlama,* arbitrariness, injustice and usurpation of the property of others.[14]

In the following centuries, however, as Muslims experienced shortages, market distortions and *de facto* monopolies, jurists began to consider price fixing by state. While Abu Yusuf rejected it, other Hanefite jurists sanctioned it. The Hanbelis rejected it on the grounds that it would merely serve to increase the prices. Imam Malik not only sanctioned it, he also determined the *narh* price for butchers. Although Imam Shafi'i rejected it, some of his followers sanctioned it at inflationary times.

The most sophisticated analysis of the question was attempted by Ibn Taymiyya and his student Ibn Qayyim. They asked, if *Allah* fixes prices, shouldn't hoarders be punished or their goods be confiscated by the state? Moreover, they argued, the Prophet had not declared that price fixing by the state in response to the need of the society was expressly prohibited, *haram*. He had merely stated that prices are fixed by *Allah*. Ibn Taymiyya considered two types of *narh*: if the ruler prohibited profits and forced the merchants to sell at a price they did not think was fair, this would be an act of oppression and should not be sanctioned. If, however, the *narh* prevented illegal profits and forced merchants to sell at the prevalent market price, this type of *narh* should be sanctioned. Ibn Taymiyya argued that it was the first type which the Prophet had refused to apply. Based upon such legal reasoning, price fixing by the state was eventually sanctioned, thus preparing the ground for the widespread *narh* applications by the Ottomans.[15]

There are also *ahadith* reporting that the Prophet approved of profits exceeding even 100 per cent providing they were made through permissible, *halal*, means. It has also been reported that some individuals were blessed by the Prophet and consequently made huge profits in the market.[16] From the recorded debates among the classical jurists it is possible to deduce the following: first, there is no consensus on a specific maximum profit rate. Profits up to 100 per cent had not even triggered discussion among the jurists. Imam Malik has clearly permitted profit rates exceeding 100 per cent.[17] Second, debate focused only on the question of whether repeated *murabaha* transactions, each with 100 per cent or more profit rates, would be permitted. Abu Hanife ruled that if a person manages to sell a commodity with 100 per cent or more profit, he should not be permitted to repeat the transaction unless he clearly informs the second buyer about the profit he has made. Imams Shafi'i, Abu Yusuf and Muhammad al-Shaybani, however, considered each transaction as separate and permitted the resale without any condition attached.[18] Consequently, we conclude that Islam does not impose a maximum profit rate and freely functioning market mechanism is the accepted norm by classical Islamic capitalism.

But if there is market distortion and hoarding occurs, then the *muhtasib* would be authorized to interfere and even confiscate the hoarded commodities. Once confiscated, these goods would be sold at fair prices. The capital of the hoarders would then be returned but the profits generated by the *muhtasib* would be distributed as alms.[19]

Although normally prices were to be determined by the market forces, under extraordinary conditions price fixing, *narh*, could be imposed. If so, the procedure was as follows. First, the *muhtasib* would summon the traders, ask them what the fair price is and then impose it. Alternatively, he would calculate the cost of the raw material plus labour and then add a fair profit.[20] Since, either way, the *sunnah* of the Prophet would be violated, such price fixing was supposed to have been considered only under extraordinary circumstances.[21]

INCOME INEQUALITIES

Islamic capitalism considers income inequalities as inevitable and a trial upon the rich.[22] Islamic law commands complete equality only under life-threatening emergencies, such as famines. But such situations are rare and 'non-repetitive'.[23] A major outcome of policies designed to curb inequalities through taxation in all economies is the problem of disincentives. The problem of disincentives caused by taxation is not relevant for Islamic capitalism. This is because Muslims are expected to notice income inequalities and act upon them *voluntarily* by paying *zakat*, *sadaqa* and establishing waqfs, to be explained below.

PROPERTY RIGHTS

The first rule/principle of property rights is that all creations, including human beings, are the property of the Creator, *Allah*. Therefore, true ownership, that is, permanent, constant and invariant ownership of all property, belongs to the Creator. But the Creator has transferred to mankind the right of possession, usufruct. Thus, true ownership and the right of possession are clearly demarcated. Property rights over natural resources are placed in trust of either the state or the society in the form of commons.

The distinction between the rights of ownership and possession is of particular relevance for land. True ownership of land belongs to the Creator or to the state, which represents Him. This land can be possessed by an individual so long as he cultivates and takes good care of it. If the land is not used for three consecutive years, the person would lose his right of possession. In an Islamic society the right of possession of land is granted to Muslims and non-Muslims alike.

The second rule is based on the observation that the Creator has created all the natural-physical resources for the benefit of all mankind. Therefore, the human collectivity has rights over these resources. The condition for possession (to take good care of the land) is imposed as a result of the recognition of this right of the human collectivity.

The third rule establishes a full right of possession *without* either the Creator or the collectivity losing its initial right of possession to these resources.[24]

The fourth rule recognizes only two ways for individuals to gain legitimate property rights:

(a) through their own creative labour; and
(b) through transfers (via exchange, contracts or inheritance) from others who have gained property rights to an asset through their own labour.

There are a number of *ahadith* emphasizing the legitimacy of earning property rights through labour. While property ownership is thus respected, waste and extravagance are discouraged.

The fifth rule is a corollary of the fourth and forbids gaining instantaneous property rights without having to perform the work. The exception is the lawful transfers mentioned in 4b above. Rights gained to assets through gambling, theft, *riba* and bribery are prohibited. Usurpation of the property rights of others by force is also prohibited. These rules are also clearly stated in the Qur'an.[25]

The sixth rule is the rule of 'immutability of property rights'. Although all humans have equal right and opportunity to have access to resources, when individuals apply their creative labour to resources, they gain a right of priority in the use and exchange of the resulting product without nullifying the original property rights of the Creator. This provides the justification for the next rule.

The seventh rule emphasizes the duty of sharing the product or the income derived from it or the wealth obtained from its sale. Such income or wealth is cleansed from the rights others have in them through the payment of *zakat*. This word comes from a root word meaning cleaning, purification and growth. It is believed that wealth cleaned and purified through *zakat* would grow.

The eighth rule imposes limitations on the right of disposing of property. While this right is absolute in the West, in Islam individuals have the obligation not to waste, squander or destroy, or use property for opulence or unlawful purposes, such as bribery. But once these obligations and the rules stated above are obeyed, property rights on the remaining part of income, wealth and assets are held sacred. Such legitimate property rights are fully protected by the Prophet, who said, 'humans have sovereignty over their wealth'. This has led to the exercise of *dominium eminens* for development of public utilities and services only after adequate compensation is paid to the owner.[26]

The sacredness and legitimacy of property rights are confirmed by a well-known verse of the Qur'an, which confirms it beyond any doubt whatsoever:

> It is We who portion out between them their livelihood in the life of this world: and We raise some of them above others in ranks, so that some may command work from others. But the mercy of thy Lord is better than the (wealth) which they amass. (43: 32)

This verse confirms the inevitable inequalities in the economy and the need for those who have talent, ambition, knowledge and opportunity to employ others. Yet, the verse also confirms their need to obtain the mercy of the Creator while doing so. Thus, this verse, which legitimizes wealth and yet at the same time urges the employers to obtain the mercy of God, may well be considered the very heart of Islamic capitalism.

Finally, it has been argued that property rights are actually on a stronger footing in the world of Islam than in the West. Indeed, in the secular West private property is protected by law. In the Islamic world, however, once the wealth is 'cleansed', the remainder is held inviolable and to the protection of the law is added the great weight of religion. Thus infringing someone's property right does not only violate the law, it is also considered to be a great sin.[27] To all this might be added the severity of the so-called *hudud* punishments. Indeed, while in the West theft is punished by a relatively mild prison sentence, in those Islamic countries where *hudud* are applied, amputation of the hand that stole, is the punishment.

FREE TRADE, EXCHANGE AND MARKETS

Free trade constitutes an inseparable characteristic of Islamic capitalism. Pilgrimage, one of the five pillars of Islam, can be considered as the foundation upon which free trade is built.

The Prophet encouraged trade among Muslims as well as non-Muslims by considering the latter as guests of Muslims and guaranteeing their merchandise, wealth and income against all losses. After the migration to Medina, the Medina market was organized based upon two principles: competition and minimum government interference. To achieve this, the Prophet declared that merchants were not allowed to reserve for themselves specific places in the market and that market transactions would not be taxed.[28] After the conquest of Mecca and the rest of Arabia, the rules governing trade and market were institutionalized. The general policy was to impose no restrictions on international trade. Imposition of no taxes was also part and parcel of this policy. Resources, goods and services were to move freely from market to market and there were to be no barriers to entry and exit. Markets were organized according to the commodities sold and sellers of the same goods were to sell in the same location. This not only ensured price competition among the vendors, it also facilitated the control mechanism. The very first *muhtasib* in Islamic history was appointed by the Prophet.[29] In the following centuries some of the greatest jurists and scholars emerged out of this profession. This is not surprising in view of the fact that these *muhtasibs* were very well informed about the day-to-day functioning of markets. During the second and the third centuries the official market controls were supplemented by the vendors' and producers' own guilds. This was a form of auto-control.

As already mentioned, the idea of contract constitutes the very essence of Islam. Indeed, the whole fabric of Islamic law has been envisaged as a contract. More than a billion Muslims refer to this primordial contract between their souls and *Allah* in their daily prayers. Indeed, the Qur'an urges believers to fulfil the primordial covenant of *Allah* and then generalizes this command to all contracts:

> O you who dynamically believe! Fulfil all contracts![30]

Contract enforcement therefore is also given great importance. Every contract has to specify clearly the property and other rights of all participants. Contract enforcement is guaranteed by the state and its legal institutions.

In general, it can be argued that the moral-ethical foundation of market behaviour prescribed by the Qur'an and implemented by the Prophet ensured the minimization of risk and uncertainty for market participants and increased efficiency in exchange. Moreover, the duty of remaining faithful to the terms of a contract as specified in the Qur'an[31] and the knowledge of its enforcement increased certainty and reduced transactions costs of entering into contracts.

The enforcement of the above-mentioned rules were to be provided by the market supervisors known as *muhtesib*. Their primary responsibility was to ensure rule-compliance. It has been reported that the Prophet himself, every now and then controlled the markets to exhort rule-compliance. He also strongly urged the duty of *commanding the good and forbidding evil* by market participants to induce self-regulation and rule-compliance.[32]

THE PILGRIMAGE

It was thanks to the pilgrimage that Muslims were able to link the Mediterranean and the Indian Ocean world-economies a thousand years before Western capitalism was able to do so. Moreover, they have successfully maintained this linkage for a millennium.[33]

The pilgrimage literally brings together millions of Muslims from the four corners of the world in Mecca. Although most Muslims consider the pilgrimage as a purely religious act, in reality it is nearly impossible to draw a line between religion and business. First of all, Muslims are specifically permitted to trade during the pilgrimage.[34] Second, this duty is incumbent upon those Muslims who can afford it, which means primarily merchants. Thus the bulk of the mercantile class of the Islamic world is ordered to go to Mecca (and trade there) at least once in a lifetime. Third, unlike the Christian pilgrimage for which there are several centres, in Islam there is absolutely one centre, Mecca, forcing in fact all the pilgrims to convene there. Fourth, throughout history the number of pilgrims was huge. The scattered evidence that we have indicates that these numbers fluctuated between 70 000 and two million throughout the history of Islam. It is doubtful if the much publicized medieval European fairs of Champagne could ever muster such numbers. Moreover, the Champagne fairs were relatively local affairs bringing together mostly Italian and Flemish merchants. By contrast, Muslims from all continents convene in Mecca. Fifth, when pilgrims approach Mecca, they are ordered to stay and set up camp at the nearby plains where it is the responsibility of the ruler that free trade and security prevail. Any ruler who fails to fulfil these conditions would lose his legitimacy.[35] In short, beginning from the seventh century, the pilgrimage considerably facilitated the establishment of a worldwide trade network. The West simply incorporated itself into this system.[36]

HONEST WORK AS A FORM OF WORSHIP

The importance of honest work has been confirmed by the Qur'an.[37] Indeed, the Prophet is reported to have said that 'legitimate work for oneself and family is nine-tenths of worship'.[38] Imam al-Ghazali explained the sacred status given to work by linking it to the pilgrimage. His reasoning was straightforward: pilgrimage is one of the five pillars of Islam, a duty that every well-to-do Muslim must perform at least once in a lifetime. To fulfil this duty, capital accumulation is needed. Therefore, honest work aiming at capital accumulation, which makes pilgrimage possible, is actually a form of worship.[39] In short, Islamic capitalism allows, even encourages, accumulation of capital subject to ethical and *voluntary* self-controls and redistribution of wealth.

REDISTRIBUTION OF WEALTH

Muslims are not ordained to redistribute their wealth excessively. A moderate and voluntary redistribution of the accumulated capital is clearly the message of the Qur'an.[40] The Prophet applied this principle by prohibiting the imposition of taxes on individual merchants as well as on transactions which were customarily imposed in all other markets in the Arabian Peninsula.[41]

The requirement of moderate and voluntary redistribution is strengthened by the belief that a Muslim will be asked five questions in the day of judgement. Two of these are the following:

1. 'How did you earn your wealth?'
2. 'How did you spend your wealth?'[42]

If wealth has been earned through permissible, *halal*, methods, and the rich person has utilized his wealth wisely, for the good of his family and the society, then his soul would be saved. This is in sharp contrast with the Bible, which is much harsher for the wealthy Christians. Consider the following:

> But woe on to you who are rich, for you have received your consolation.[43]

> It is far easier for a camel to pass through the eye of a needle than for a rich man to enter the Kingdom of Heaven.[44]

> If any will come after me, let him deny himself and take up the cross and follow me.[45]

In short, in contrast to Christianity, which urges Christians to give up their worldly goods and strongly discourages them from accumulating wealth, Islam considers *halal* accumulation of capital as a form of worship and puts no upper limit on profitability or wealth.[46] Excessive profit generated by sales when demand is rising is permitted. Ibn Taymiyya considers this as the bounty of *Allah*, *rizq*.[47] These values can be seen clearly in the following verse of the Qur'an:

> Alluring to man is the enjoyment of worldly desires through women, children, heaped-up treasures of gold and silver, thoroughbred horses, cattle and lands. All this may be enjoyed in the life of this world – but the most beautiful of all objectives is with God.[48]

Consequently, whereas we can certainly talk about an Islamic capitalism, which does not forbid legitimate acquisition of wealth,[49] it is very difficult to talk about a Christian capitalism, at least not until the Reformation and the rise of Protestantism. The impact of the Church on the rise of medieval European capitalism in Flanders and Northern Italy is ambiguous.[50] Indeed, the disastrous effect of the rise of the Church's power on the Carolingian economy has been thoroughly documented.[51]

Taxation is another area that confirms the above arguments and it is imposed because the Qur'an recognizes the rights of the poor in each person's income. While taxes are thus legitimized, there are actually only a few taxes specifically stated in the Qur'an. The *jizya*[52] was imposed on non-Muslims living in an Islamic state and was paid in return for the protection of their lives and property. Since these non-Muslims were not obliged to participate in *jihad*, this tax is also considered as a commutation of obligatory military service. The *jizya* was imposed for the first time by the Prophet upon the peoples of Bahreyn and Yemen at the rate of one gold dinar per year.[53] It is generally accepted that one dinar weighed approximately 4.25 grams.[54]

The *Kharaj* is mentioned in the Qur'an several times under different contexts.[55] It was, basically, an agricultural tax and was imposed either according to the productivity of land, *kharaj al-mukasamah*, or a fixed amount on the size as well as the location of the land, *kharaj al-muvazzafa*.[56]

Finally, the *zakat*, one of the five pillars of Islam, was imposed, generally, at 2.5 per cent on those who possessed at least 200 dirhems of silver. With one dirhem equal to 2.975 grams, this makes a *nisab* of 595 grams of silver. In terms of gold, the *nisab* was 20 dinar, or 85 grams of gold, and the *zakat* rate, again, 2.5 per cent.[57]

These *nisab* calculations and *zakat* rates found widespread application in commerce. *Zakat's* application in agriculture was the *Ushr,* and was imposed at the rate of 10 per cent if the land in question was irrigated naturally and at 5 per cent if irrigated by labour. Although these rates should be taken with a grain of salt, as there were wide variations and many exceptions in application, it is generally agreed that taxation did not impose an overwhelming burden during the early centuries of Islam. The fact that *zakat* rate was determined merely at 2.5 per cent in commerce but a hefty 10 per cent in agriculture may indicate that commerce was the preferred, even the sole occupation among the Arabs and that agriculture was viewed as a mere additional activity.

As for mining, the Qur'an does not state a specific rate and merely ordains Muslims to 'give... of the fruits of earth, which We have produced for you'.[58] The classical jurists have not been able to reach a consensus, while the Hanefites have imposed a *zakat* rate of 20 per cent, the remaining three schools have imposed the standard rate of 2.5 per cent. Some Malikite jurists have approached the Hanefites and imposed the standard 2.5 per cent on mines that demand a lot of labour and 20 per cent on those that yield with little work.[59] The reason why the Hanefites have imposed a higher rate on mining is because they have considered mining as similar to finding a buried treasury, *rikaz*. Since the Prophet has imposed *hums*, one-fifth tax, on buried treasury, this rate has been applied by *qiyas*.

Thus, the basic sources of tax revenue for the early Islamic state were *kharaj* and *jizya,* one-fifth of the booty, *hums al-ganaim* and *zakat*. Having provided this basic information about Islamic taxation, it should be acknowledged that taxation is not given the primary role in income redistribution. Al-Jarhi and Zarqa have argued that four institutions in *decreasing importance* alleviate poverty in Islam:

1. intra-family maintenance, including the family waqf or other types of waqfs;
2. *zakat*;
3. public treasury, *bayt al-mal*;
4. ad hoc taxation.

In general, lower level institutions are activated only if the more important ones fail to alleviate poverty. The low level ascribed to taxation is in conformity with the *sunnah* of the Prophet explained above. It has been argued that the reason why voluntary transfers, such as *qard hassan, sadaqa* and particularly waqf, are favoured over obligatory transfers such as taxation is to avoid disincentive problems on work effort.[60] Any remaining wealth that is accumulated is broken up at the end of the person's life and distributed through the law of inheritance among a large number of beneficiaries according to rules specified in the Qur'an.

It has been argued that in comparison to Western economic thought which, from Rawls to Sen and Nozik, requires comprehensive government intervention on a continuous basis, in an Islamic society the state's role is one of administrator, supervisor and protector of the society.[61] In such a society, it is the members of the society themselves, governed by their personal beliefs, who ensure that social justice prevails. It is argued further that in such a society poverty would be eradicated. If it is not, the mere existence of the phenomenon constitutes prima facie evidence of non-compliance with the rules of Islam.[62]

Having stated these, what we may call, liberal economic principles, we must also point out to other verses which ordain Muslims to redistribute their wealth.[63] Thus accumulating wealth through *halal* actions is perfectly legal and no upper limit is imposed on such wealth.[64] But massive wealth circulating forever among a few is considered a great sin. In short, while Islamic capitalism has all the necessary conditions for private accumulation of wealth, it also orders Muslims to redistribute this wealth, preferably through voluntary means. If such redistribution does not materialize, the Apostle, or representing him the state, can interfere and redistribute. Thus in addition to all the traits of capitalism explained above, in these verses one can also find the essential characteristics of a proto-quasi-socialist perspective.[65] It is based upon this perspective that the proto-quasi-Ottoman socialism emerged in the following centuries.

If a Muslim is properly imbued with these values, it has been envisaged that they would lead him to behave as follows:[66] if the person is a worker: he would be satisfied and pleased with his hard work as this work would be recorded and help him to be rewarded in the Hereafter.[67] Moreover, he would try his best to produce good quality work as he has been informed about the Prophet's statement that each Muslim will be responsible for his deeds. The Prophet is also reported to have said that a person who works for the livelihood of his family is close to God. Moreover, if a person goes to bed tired with a hard day's honest work, he will be forgiven in the Day of Judgement.[68] A Muslim worker would also be thankful to God for the wage he has received. He would not be full of jealousy for the wages of the others, nor would he have hatred for his boss. This is because he would be informed about the verse:

> If ye are grateful, I will add more favours unto you, but if ye show ingratitude, truly my punishment is terrible indeed.[69]

If the person is an employer: He/she would expect that his property rights would be fully respected by the Islamic state, which considers the protection of property, *hifz al-mal*, as one of its primary duties.[70] He can also be sure that his wealth would be freely transferred to the next generation. Moreover, he would make his decisions on the premise that state interference in free markets would be at the lowest possible level. In general, he knows that an honest merchant will be exalted and join the ranks of the prophets and martyrs.[71] He is ranked with the prophets because he, like the prophets, follows the path of justice; like martyrs because they both fight with heavy odds in the path of honesty and virtue.[72] He also knows that he has earned his wealth not only with his hard work but also thanks to *Allah*'s blessing.[73]

When he is using up his wealth he would not keep his assets idle, he would pay his *zakat* and would be neither extravagant nor miserly. He would pay his workers their fair wage promptly. His earnings would be in the form of wages, profits and rents. He knows that he cannot earn interest. His earnings would have been accumulated based upon hard work and risk taking. He would not be involved in gambling nor would he ever use his wealth to harm the society, fearing the verse 69: 30.

If the person is a consumer: He would not consume alcohol, gamble or be involved in prostitution. All his consumption spending would be on legitimate goods and services. He would avoid conspicuous consumption, for he would know that God does not forgive extravagance.[74] If he has to borrow, he would do so with full intention of paying back on time.

If the person is a saver: and if his wealth is such that he cannot spend it all within a year, he would become liable to pay the *zakat*. This would diminish his real income if he keeps it idle. He knows he cannot buy fixed income yielding financial instruments such as bonds. So, the only option open to him would be to invest it in business. If he is young, he would establish his own business; if not, he would invest it with a younger entrepreneur in a partnership. The most rational thing to do for such a person would be to invest his wealth.

Continuous investment would increase his wealth even further. Since he cannot spend this wealth on conspicuous consumption or gamble it away, he has to consume it somehow. But, after a certain limit, consumption would have diminishing marginal utility. This would lead him to be involved in charity or philanthropy. Thus, charity/philanthropy emerges as a rational choice for a wealthy Muslim. How he can channel his wealth to these causes will be discussed in the following chapters.

Having presented the basic values of Islamic economics, we will now return to history and observe which institutions have emerged out of these values throughout history. Studying these institutions is of crucial importance because only such a study can inform us as to how the values were translated into practice.

NOTES

1. The Qur'an: 50: 16; also see Mirakhor and Iqbal, *Introduction to Islamic Finance*, p. 4.
2. The Qur'an, 7: 172; Al-Attas, *Prolegomena*, p. 144.
3. Qur'an: 9: 20.
4. Qur'an: 6: 165.
5. Qur'an: 2: 143; 21: 92 and 2: 143
6. Qur'an: 3: 104, 3: 110.
7. Mirakhor and Iqbal, *Introduction to Islamic Finance*, p. 6.
8. Qur'an, 50: 16.
9. Qur'an, 17: 15.
10. Zaim, 'Ekonomik Hayatta', p. 103.
11. Muslims are ordained to share their wealth with the verse: 'and bestow upon them of the wealth of *Allah,* which He has bestowed upon you' 24: 33.
12. Saeed, *Islamic Banking and Interest*.
13. Akram Khan, *Economic Teachings*, p. 126.
14. Essid, *Islamic Economic Thought,* p. 151.
15. Kallek, *Devlet ve Piyasa*, pp. 90–3.
16. Canan, *Kütüb-i Sitte*, pp. 176–7.
17. Karaman, 'Islam Hukukunda Alış', in Karaman ve Şafak, *Islam Hukuna,* p. 119.
18. Assume a person buys a commodity for 100 and sells it for 200. Assume further that he buys back the commodity for 100. Abu Hanife did not permit reselling it for 200 again. Şafak, 'İslam Hukuku'nda Alış', in Karaman ve Şafak, *Islam Hukuna,* p. 79. Also see Döndüren, *Islam Hukuku'na*.
19. According to Ibn Taymiyya, fair prices were those prevalent among the majority of the merchants. Essid, *Islamic Economic Thought,* pp. 156, 159.
20. Imposing 'fair' profit levels on the market was a common Ottoman policy. But things eventually went out of way, when Ottomans began to impose these profit levels in order to pursue their unique economic policy. For further details see the 'Ottoman proto-quasi-socialism' discussed below.
21. The widespread application of price fixing in Ottoman markets is controversial. While in my opinion this indicates a serious diversion from classical Islam, Pamuk has warned that the Ottoman state applied a maximum price policy, *narh*, only during extraordinary times. See his *500 Years of Prices*, appendix 3.3, pp. 164–69. While this may be true, Pamuk's own data reveal that *narh* orders have been issued for 163 years out of a total of 319 years between 1520 and 1839. Moreover, this does not take into consideration multiple *narh* orders issued in a single year. Thus at least half of the period in question has witnessed *narh* imposition.
22. Qur'an, 6: 165.
23. Al-Jarhi and Zarqa, 'Redistributive Justice', p. 41.
24. *Dominium eminens* refers to the ownership of the state. See Mirakhor and Hamid, *Islam and Development,* ch. 5, forthcoming.
25. 2: 188 and 4: 29.
26. Mirakhor and Hamid, *Islam and Development,* ch. 5, forthcoming.
27. Ibid.
28. Şencan, *Homo-Islamicus,* p. 6.
29. Mirakhor and Hamid, *Islam and Development*, ch. 5, forthcoming.
30. 5: 1 and 9: 4.
31. 5: 1.
32. Mirakhor and Hamid, *Islam and Development,* ch. 5, forthcoming.
33. Wink, *Al-Hind,* pp. 34–6. Islamic domination of the Indian Ocean trade started in the seventh century and was challenged effectively only after the English and the Dutch entry into the region during the seventeenth century.
34. How this permission was granted is explained in a *hadith* narrated by Abdullah Ibn Abbas: 'The people used to trade in the beginning at Mina, Arafat and during the season of *Hajj*. But later on they became afraid of trading while they were putting on *ihram*. So *Allah* sent down

His verse: "It is no sin for you that you seek the bounty of your Lord during the seasons of *Hajj*". Dawud, *Kitab al-Manasik wa'l-Hajj, hadith* 1730.

35. Faroqhi, *Herrscher über Mekka*.
36. Wink, *Al-Hind*.
37. 53: 39–41.
38. Mirakhor and Hamid, *Islam and Development,* ch. 5, forthcoming.
39. Orman, *Gazali'nin Iktisat Felsefesi*, p. 79.
40. Qur'an, 47: 36–37.
41. Mirakhor and Hamid, *Islam and Development,* ch. 5, forthcoming.
42. He will also be asked how he spent his lifetime, how he spent his youth and what he did with his knowledge. See for this *hadith*; Sunan al-Tirmidhi, *hadith* no. 2417.
43. Luke, 6: 24.
44. Matthew, 19: 24.
45. Matthew, 26: 24.
46. Accumulation of wealth certainly took place in the West. This was made possible by the Church indoctrinating the wealthy that they can redeem their sins by making donations to, and better still, by purchasing indulgences from the Church. In this way, accumulation of wealth was made possible. Private and Church wealth expanded in tandem.
47. For further details see Rosly, *Critical Issues*, p. 559.
48. Qur'an: 3: 14.
49. Ibn Ashur, *Maqasid*, pp. 269, 271.
50. Although not intentional, the Church did have some important contributions to the emergence of Western capitalism. The emergence of the Church as the very first corporation is referred to here. Transfer of Church taxes from all over Europe to Rome also contributed to the development of cash transfer techniques and institutions.
51. Heck, *Arab Roots of Capitalism*, pp. 19–21.
52. Qur'an, 9: 29
53. İnalcık, 'Cizye', *İslam Ansiklopedisi*.
54. Erkal, *İslam'ın Erken Döneminde*, p. 132.
55. Qur'an, 23: 72; 18: 94; 2: 267.
56. Erkal, *İslam'ın Erken Döneminde*, pp. 195, 227.
57. Erkal, *İslam'ın Erken Döneminde*, pp. 132–5. Since the pure precious metal content of coins at this period is not known with certainty, these calculations need to be considered with caution.
58. 2: 267.
59. Erkal, *İslam'ın Erken Döneminde,* p. 162.
60. Al-Jarhi and Zarqa, 'Redistributive Justice', pp. 44, 46.
61. Adam Smith constitutes a very important exception. In his *Theory of Moral Sentiment* he realizes the importance of the compliance with the rules prescribed by the Creator and approaches to Islamic economics. For details, see Abbas Mirakhor and Idris Samawi Hamid, *Islam and Development, the Institutional Framework*, forthcoming.
62. Mirakhor and Hamid, *Islam and Development,* forthcoming. Recent research has shown that in comparison to Paris, Ottoman Istanbul had a much lower rate of poverty. See Genc, 'Dilencilik', and, Geremek, *Poverty, A History*, p. 119.
63. 'Thus have we made of you a community justly balanced…', the Qur'an, 2: 143 and 'What God has bestowed on His Apostle (and taken away) from the people of the townships, belongs to God – to His Apostle… in order that it may not merely make a circuit between the wealthy among you. So take what the Apostle assigns to you, deny yourselves that which he withholds from you. And fear God, for God is strict in punishment', the Qur'an, 59: 7.
64. Canan, *Kütüb-i Sitte,* pp. 176–7 and p. 261.
65. While 'proto' refers to the fact that this Islamic perspective antedated Marx by more than a millennium, 'quasi' refers to the lack of class conflict – an essential trait of Marxist socialism. Islamic quasi-socialism did not aim at a revolutionary class conflict, but at creating a 'justly balanced' society as stated in the Qur'an (2: 143 and 59: 7).
66. Zaim, 'Ekonomik Hayatta', pp. 101–8.
67. The Qur'an, 53: 39–41. Zaim, 'Ekonomik Hayatta', p. 103.

68. Zaim, 'Ekonomik Hayatta', p. 103.
69. 14: 7.
70. This will be treated in much greater detail in the chapter on *Maqasid Al-Shari'ah*.
71. Zaim, 'Ekonomik Hayatta', p. 105.
72. Mirakhor and Iqbal, *Introduction to Islamic Finance*, p. 47.
73. 13: 26.
74. 7: 31.

Part II

Historical institutions of private enterprise: capital accumulation

3. Financing the entrepreneur: the medieval Islamic business partnerships

Verse 2: 275 of the Qur'an, which prohibited *riba* in the most stringent terms but encouraged trade and exchange, has laid the foundations of many institutions. Indeed, exchange and trade require freedom of parties to contract. This, in turn, implies freedom to produce, which calls for clear and well-protected property rights. Moreover, to freely and conveniently exchange their commodities the parties need a market. But the market itself needs to be controlled according to certain rules and measures facilitating exchange. The level of mutual trust prevalent in the market would lower transactions costs. The level of trust would be enhanced if institutions were to emerge which enforce rule-compliance.[1]

Probably the most important institutions that emerged in response to the basic principles of Islamic capitalism mentioned above were the various business partnerships. This is because, in a culture which prohibits the rate of interest in the most stringent manner, combining the factors of production emerges as a major problem.[2] Indeed, if capital, labour and entrepreneurship are factors owned by different individuals, how can transactions between these persons materialize? If the owner of capital is not rewarded for the risks he takes by the rate of interest paid over and above the capital he has loaned, why, indeed, should he make his capital available for the entrepreneur?

In Islam, it is the institution of business partnerships which solves this problem. Put simply, the owners of these diverse factors of production form partnerships and it is in this way that they transact. Thus, business partnerships constitute one of the institutions, probably the most important one, by which the rate of interest is substituted in the Islamic economy. The great achievement of these partnerships was to transfer capital from the principal to the entrepreneur without recourse to the prohibited rate of interest. We can therefore safely claim that without business partnerships, Islamic capitalism simply could not have been born.

There is no doubt that the *mudaraba* or its synonym, the *qirad*, constitutes the most important type of business partnerships resorted to by Muslims in history. The honourable position of *mudaraba* in Islamic finance is due to the fact that it was practised by the Prophet himself. Consequently, its legitimacy is beyond any doubt whatsoever. Indeed, the other partnership forms practised may be considered as derivatives of the *mudaraba*.[3] Actually, it should come as no surprise that other partnership forms have emerged from the basic *mudaraba*. This is in conformity with spanning theory, itself a component of game theory. The basic point of spanning theory is that it is mathematically possible to develop an infinite number of derivatives from each basic structure. Each of the classical business partnerships to be considered in this chapter can be considered as a basic structure for modern Islamic finance.[4] This is because each of these financial instruments have been scrutinized to the smallest detail and confirmed by medieval Muslim jurists. The relevance of all this for the modern financial engineer is that it is theoretically possible to design an infinite number of modern Islamic financial instruments from each one of these classical basic structures.

THE *MUDARABA*

The classical *mudaraba* was an arrangement in which a principal, *rab al-mal*, entrusted his capital to an agent, *mudarìb*, who was to trade with it and then return to the investor the original capital plus a previously agreed-upon share of the profits. As a reward for his entrepreneurship the agent received the remaining share of the profits.[5] Any loss resulting from unexpected dangers of travel or from an unsuccessful business venture was shouldered exclusively by the investor. The agent was in no way liable for a loss of this nature, losing only his expended time and effort. The *mudaraba* was a true capital-labour partnership in the sense that the entire capital of the partnership was provided by the principal. The agent's input was in the form of entrepreneurship and effort only.

In general, profit and loss are shared according to the rule: profit follows mutual agreement and loss follows the capital invested. This is the Hanefite view, which allows profits to be distributed differently from losses. According to Ibn Rushd, however, both Malik and Shafi'i prohibited the division of profits to diverge from the division of losses. On the other hand, they both agreed with the Hanefite view that losses should follow the partners' shares in the capital.[6] Consequently, the Maliki and the Shafi'i schools differ from the Hanefis and insist that profits as well as losses should be divided in proportion to the capital invested.

Since in *mudaraba* the entire capital was provided by the principal, it follows that in case of loss, the entire pecuniary loss belongs to him. The maximum loss of the principal, however, is limited to his invested capital. In this sense, *mudaraba* was a limited liability partnership in that the principal's loss cannot exceed his investment. The complete freedom granted to the agent from any liability for the capital in the event of loss and the disjunction between the owners of the capital and third parties constitute the novel and distinctive characteristics of the *mudaraba*.[7]

In the *mudaraba* agreement the partners enjoy absolute freedom in the determination of the division of profit. There is only one requirement which is the *conditio sine qua non* of a *mudaraba* contract: that the division of profits between the parties must not be in absolute amounts but in proportions.

To sum up, the simple *mudaraba* had the following characteristics:

1. There are two partners, a principal (*Rab al-mal*) and an agent (*Mudarìb*).
2. Entire capital is provided by the principal.
3. Agent contributes only his time, effort and knowledge. He does not contribute to the partnership with capital.
4. Agent takes the capital and tries to generate profit with it.
5. Venture is concluded when the agent returns the original capital to the principal.
6. Profit, if any, is shared either according to mutual agreement or capital invested. This mutual agreement is in the form of percentages and it is clearly stated in the contract at the beginning of the venture.
7. If there is loss, entire pecuniary loss accrues to the principal. Agent goes unpaid for his effort but does not suffer any pecuniary loss.
8. In general, profit and loss sharing is done according to the Hanafite rule: *profit follows mutual agreement, loss follows capital*. Since, in *mudaraba*, the entire capital has been provided by the principal, entire pecuniary loss accrues to him. Principal may lose his entire investment in the venture. But notwithstanding this, the principal's liability is limited in the sense that he is not responsible for the agent in transactions with third parties. Indeed, third parties may not even be aware of the investor's existence. The responsibility for all contact with third parties resides with the agent.[8]

THE SIMPLE *INAN* PARTNERSHIP

It is in the area of profit shares that the other classical Islamic partnership form, *inan*, was conceived. In a simple *inan* partnership, the agent seeks a greater profit share than is possible in *mudaraba* for which he agrees to shoulder greater risk. He does this by contributing to the capital of the partnership and it is this capital input, in addition to his entrepreneurial input, which qualifies him for a greater share of the profit. *Inan* partners usually contribute unequal amounts to the partnership capital, with the passive partner contributing the larger and the active partner the smaller part. But once committed, this combined capital becomes the joint capital of the partnership. Ibn Rushd describes this combined capital as 'in a single box', *fi sanduq wahid*.[9] While establishing an *inan* partnership, as in *mudaraba*, it is important that the profit shares are stated in the contract in proportions and not in exact amounts of cash. The partnership can be established with a fixed or flexible term. If the former, the partnership ends at the end of the term. If the latter and the partnership has only two partners, it can continue until one of the partners dies or goes insane.[10] The impression one gets from Nuwayri is that the latter alternative, that is a flexible term, is preferred. Nuwayri describes the duration of partnership as 'situation after situation, act after act'. Research in the Ottoman archives has confirmed long-lasting partnerships.[11]

Both partners participate in profit as well as loss in proportion to their capital contribution. But, according to the Hanefite school, the partners who are actively involved in the management, while still sharing the loss in proportion to their capital contribution, share the profit according to the mutual agreement reached when the contract was signed. The Maliki and Shafi'i schools insist on sharing both profits and losses in proportion to the capital contribution.[12] Partners do not have to contribute to the capital at equal amounts. These dynamics of a simple *inan* partnership are depicted in Figure 3.1.

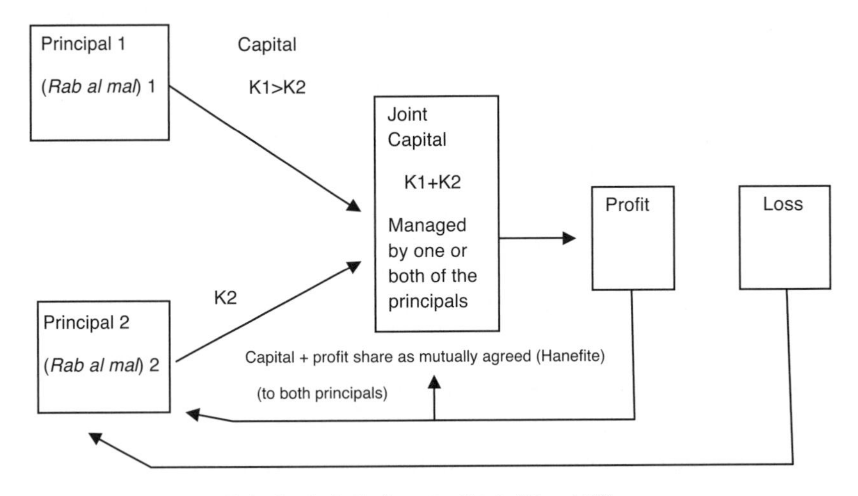

Figure 3.1 The simple inan *partnership*

THE *MUFAWADA*

In still another classical partnership form, the *mufawada*, partners contribute capital in exactly equal amounts to the venture and share profits, as well as losses, in exactly equal proportions. Certain scholars have argued that *inan* and *mufawada* mean the same thing. But this view has not been generally accepted. This is because, whereas in *inan* each partner's contribution is specified, in *mufawada* the communality comprehends all things.[13] Thus, *mufawada* is understood as an unlimited liability partnership. By contrast, in an *inan* partnership managed by both partners, third parties are compensated for their claims only from the partner with whom they had transacted. He alone is responsible for the entire sum involved. But if both parties have jointly undertaken an obligation, third parties can demand restitution from each of them in proportion to the share of liability assigned to them in the contract.[14]

The termination of a *mufawada* occurs, both according to the Hanefis and the Malikis, by the mutual consent of the partners, by the accomplishment of its aim, by the expiration of the term stipulated in the contract or upon the death of one of the partners.[15]

THE *WUJUH* (*SHARIKAT AL-MAFALIS*)

This is also known as the partnership of the penniless. This occurs when two merchants, who have lost their capital but maintain good reputations, come together to re-enter the world of commerce. Their capital consists of their good reputations (*al-wujuh*). The partnership is officially established when the partners declare that they have bought their merchandise on credit and shall sell it to a third party for immediate cash with profit to be shared among themselves.[16] After repeating the process a few times, they pay their debt to the original seller who had sold them the merchandise with credit. This partnership has been rejected by the Shafi'i and the Maliki schools but accepted by the Hanefites, Hanbelites and the Shi'ites.[17] Kasani, a well-known Hanefite scholar, considers this credit partnership as a method for creating or augmenting capital. A *wujuh* partnership can be established in *mufawada* form with strictly equal profit and loss sharing or in *inan* form with unequal shares.

As far as profit distribution is concerned, the *wujuh* is unique in the sense that it is the only Hanefite partnership in which profit is not distributed according to mutual agreement but strictly according to the respective shares in investment.[18] As we will see below, this partnership has assumed enormous importance in modern Islamic finance.

The reader is cautioned that the Shafi'ite jurists allow only the *inan* and the *mudaraba*. The Hanbelites allow all types but reject the *mufawadah*. The

Table 3.1 Basic contracts and their characteristics

Name of contract	Capital contribution	Profit sharing	Loss sharing	Termination	Liability towards third parties	Liability within the partnership
Mudaraba (simple)	One partner provides the entire capital.	According to mutual agreement (Hanefite) or capital (others).	According to capital. Entire pecuniary loss goes to the investor. Agent loses his effort.	Immediate termination in case of death, insanity, mutual agreement, unilateral abrogation, apostesy from Islam.	Investor's liability limited to the amount invested. Agent not liable.	
Inan	Both partners contribute unequal amounts of capital.	According to mutual agreement (Hanafite) or capital (others).[1]	According to capital contribution.	As in *mudaraba* if two partners. If more than two, partnership can continue.	Limited or unlimited, several but not joint.[2]	Joint
Mufawada	Both partners provide equal amounts of capital.	Equal for both partners.	Equal for both partners.	As in *mudaraba*. Termination also occurs if equality in capital lapses.	Unlimited, several and joint.	Joint

Notes

1. Actually, Hanafites also accept profit distribution in an *inan* partnership according to capital. But since they also permit unequal sharing in profits with equal capital shares, and this is possible only with mutual agreement, they *ipso facto* accept division according to mutual agreement as well. Al-Zuhayli, *Financial Transactions,* vol. I, pp. 465–6.
2. A liability is said to be joint and several when the creditor may sue one or more of the parties to such liability separately, or all of them together at his option. Liability of partners is one of the most difficult areas in Islamic finance and sources may contradict each other. Whereas Udovitch considers that in all partnerships liability is unlimited (*Partnership and Profit,* p. 100), Al-Zuhayli calls *sharikat al-inan* a limited partnership with each party only responsible for dealings that he himself performed (*Financial Transactions*, vol. 1, pp. 451–2).

Malikites permit all but reject the *wujuh* and the *mufawadah*. Finally, the Hanafites exhibit the most tolerant approach and permit all the partnerships mentioned above.[19]

Meanwhile, let us now summarize the basic characteristics of all the major contract forms (Table 3.1).

NOTES

1. Mirakhor and Hamid, *Islam and Development*, forthcoming.
2. For a comparison of the relative stringency of the interest prohibition in the three monotheist religions, see Al-Qusi, *Riba*, ch. 3.
3. The relative importance of *mudaraba,* at least for the Ottoman era, has also been quantitatively determined. See Gerber, 'The Muslim Law of Partnerships', vol. 53.
4. Fourteen such basic structures have been identified by Iqbal and Mirakhor. See *Introduction to Islamic Finance*, p. 79.
5. Udovitch, *Partnership and Profit*, p. 170.
6. Ackerman-Lieberman, *A Partnership Culture*, p. 87.
7. Udovitch, *Partnership and Profit*, p. 171.
8. Ibid., pp. 171, 239, 242.
9. Ackerman-Lieberman, *A Partnership Culture*, p. 82, fn. 19.
10. If there are more than two partners, the situation changes significantly as will be made clear below.
11. Ibid., p. 90; Çizakça, *A Comparative Evolution,* ch. 4.
12. Gözübenli, 'Inan'.
13. Udovitch, *Partnership and Profit*, pp. 121–2.
14. Udovitch, *Partnership and Profit*, p. 135.
15. Ibid., p. 169.
16. Şekerci, *Şirketler Hukuku*, p. 238.
17. For a critique of the Shafi'i position by the Hanafis, see Udovitch, *Partnership and Profit*, pp. 81–2. See also Şekerci, *Şirketler Hukuku*, p. 238.
18. Ibid., p. 83.
19. Al-Zuhayli, *Financial Transactions*, vol. I, pp. 449–50.

4. Evolution of medieval Islamic business partnerships in the Islamic world and the West

THE MULTIPLE *MUDARABA*

Since Islamic law of partnerships allows the agent to pool the capital of several principals, total capital entrusted with a single agent can be considerably enhanced.[1] This brings us to the 'multiple *mudaraba*'. The term 'multiple' here refers to the multitude of principals, who pool their capital and entrust the thus pooled capital to a single *mudarìb,* agent.

The advantage of this arrangement is that economies of scale are achieved. That is to say, the agent with the now much greater capital at his disposal can bargain more effectively with the suppliers. The arrangement also minimizes transaction costs per unit of commodity purchased.

The agent signs a separate *mudaraba* contract with each of the principals and with the thus combined capital larger profits are generated. Since the entire capital is provided, now, by a group of principals, the loss also accrues to them in accordance with the principle: *profit follows mutual agreement and loss follows capital*. This means losses are distributed among all the principals in proportion to the capital they have provided. The agent, as usual, does not suffer any pecuniary loss; his loss would be in the form of unpaid effort. Profits are distributed between the group of financiers and the *mudarìb*/agent, either according to their mutual agreement stated in the contract or according to their relative capital contribution.

The great achievement of the multiple *mudaraba* (and *inan*) is that it has made it possible for various merchants to pool capital to finance an agent. Conversely, a principal is also permitted to finance a multitude of agents, thus diversifying his risks. When a multitude of individuals come together to arrange their cooperation subject to reasonable rules acceptable to all, this is not an achievement to be taken lightly. Moreover, *mudaraba* (and *inan*) is considered as a nexus of contracts. Indeed, it is an investment contract, specifying what each partner would invest, an employment contract, laying down the rules how the agent should invest his time and effort, an agency contract, granting to the agent varying degrees of business freedom, finally a liability contract, determining the respective liabilities of each partner towards the third parties.[2] In short, we are talking about a highly sophisticated contract form, which spread from the Middle East to Europe, in the West, and all the way to China, in the East.[3]

THE EXPANDED *INAN*

If the partners empower each other with their full trust and allow each other to 'do with the capital as you see fit',[4] they obtain three additional freedoms. First, it is permitted for an active *inan* partner to enter into a separate partnership with a third person. If the new partnership is unrelated to the basic activity of the original *inan,* then there is no need to obtain the approval of the original *inan* partners. If, however, the activities are related, such permission is needed.[5] Second, the active partner can mingle the capital of the partnership with his own capital so as to have greater bargaining power vis-à-vis third parties; and third, he can use the partnership's capital to establish another *inan* partnership with a third party.[6] These freedoms had important implications for the future evolution of the *inan* partnership.

The management of an *inan* partnership can be undertaken either by the partners themselves or be entrusted to professional third parties. These professionals can be paid a salary by the partnership.[7] Thus the modern notion of hiring professionals to manage the company is permitted by Islamic law. The law, however, is more ambiguous when it comes to rewarding the active/managing partner with extra shares. The Hanefite and the Hanbelite schools grant this permission, while the Malikite and the Shafi'ite schools do not.[8]

If the *inan* partnership has two partners, the death of one of these partners causes the liquidation of the partnership. If, however, there are three or more partners, the partnership continues and only the share of the deceased partner is liquidated and paid to his inheritors.[9]

Moreover, a partner in good health can give his share as a gift to any one of his children, even to a minor. Transfer of shares even to third parties is permitted. Such gift transfers can take place without necessarily obtaining the approval of the other partners. If, however, exiting the partnership is made subject to the approval of the other partners and this is stated clearly in the contract, then such approval must be obtained.[10] Gift transfers are important in that they ensure the longevity of the *inan* partnership, which does not end as soon as one of the partners dies. This is because a partner who feels death approaching can easily transfer his shares to a person he prefers to ensure the continuity of the partnership.

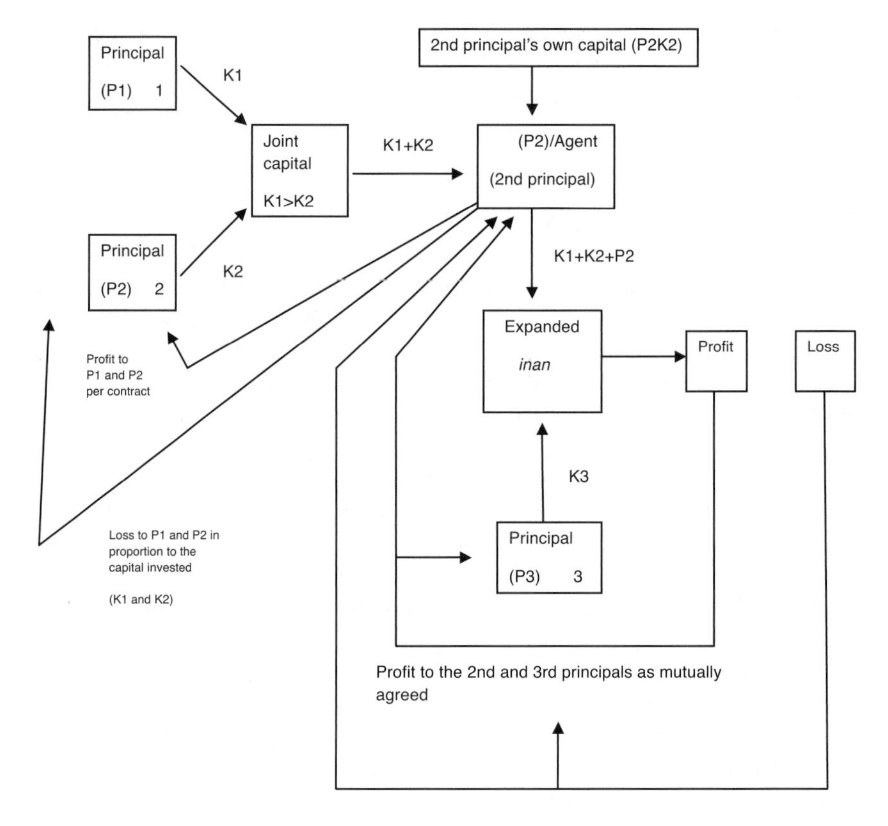

Figure 4.1 The expanded inan

These dynamics of an expanded *inan* partnership are depicted in Figure 4.1, where we observe, first, two principals: P1 and P2. These principals establish among themselves an *inan* partnership with P1, the passive partner, granting to P2, the active partner, an unlimited mandate. Both partners contribute capital and P1's capital K1 is greater than P2's capital, K2. The total capital K1+K2 is then entrusted to the second principal, P2, who also acts as the agent. The second principal, P2, then adds his own personal capital, P2K2, to the partnership. The total capital is thus expanded to K1+K2+P2K2. With this expanded capital, P2 then enters into a separate *inan* partnership with a third principal, P3, who contributes with his own capital of K3.

We then assume that the partners P2 and P3, both of whom belong to the Hanefite School, start trading and generate a profit. This profit would be shared between P2 and P3 as mutually agreed. If they belong to the Maliki or Shafi'i schools, however, it would be distributed in proportion to the capital invested. After P3's profit share is deducted, the profit share of the second principal's own investment, the P2K2 would be deducted. The remaining profit would then be distributed between P1 and P2 as the profit shares of the original partnership.

Exactly the same procedure would apply in case of loss, which would be shared also in sequence and in proportion to the capital invested by each partner. Naturally, it is also perfectly possible to have not two but three original partners, in which case there would be the additional advantage of longevity. This is because, in the case of three or more partners, an *inan* partnership is not automatically dissolved in the case of death of one of the partners.[11]

The question as to whether classical Islamic partnerships possessed judicial personality is a difficult one. A concept called *dhimma*, which is very similar to judicial personality, has been developed.[12] It has been argued that this concept, absolutely necessary for big partnerships with a multitude of partners, was not really needed in past Islamic societies.[13]

Modern Islamic companies, however, need judicial personality. Consequently, an Islamic perspective of judicial personality is now needed. To start with, it is possible to find certain clues in the writings of medieval jurists. For instance, mosques, *waqf*s and *bayt al-mal* are considered to possess judicial personality.[14]

Judicial personality of Islamic companies, however, is more complicated. It has been argued that if an *inan* partnership is established with surety, *kafala*, it is considered to have judicial personality. This is because all real person transactions can also be fulfilled by the partnership. If, however, it is established with *waqala*, representation, it is not considered to have judicial personality.[15] Most modern companies in the Islamic world, however, avoid such complications by simply incorporating themselves at the time of establishment. This means that they borrow a Western concept, the corporation, which embodies judicial personality.

THE *MURABAHA*

Although not a partnership, but a sale contract, the *murabaha* must be considered here. This is because this particular sale contract has turned out to be of great importance in the future evolution of Islamic finance during the twentieth and the twenty-first centuries.

Murabaha is defined by Saleh as 'the sale of a commodity for the price at which the vendor has purchased it, with the addition of a stated profit known to both the vendor and the purchaser'. Thus, it is a cost-plus-profit contract.

The cost includes all expenses made directly on the commodity indispensable to its sale. A value-added approach is envisaged here. This means that any expense that does not increase the value of the commodity in question cannot be included in cost.

Still another definition has been provided by Quduri: '*Murabaha* is the sale of an object for the price at which it was originally bought by the seller with the addition of some profit. It is important that the vendor informs the new buyer of the original cost of the object.'[16] The purpose here is to protect the innocent consumer.

According to Abu hanifa, if the buyer learns that the seller has lied about the contract, he has the right to cancel the contract.

If a movable object is the subject of a *murabaha* contract, it is not permissible, according to Quduri, for the buyer to resell it prior to its complete receipt. This is based upon the *sunnah* of the Prophet, who discouraged the sale of a movable thing prior to its receipt by the seller. It is understood that this rule was due to the consideration of risk (*gharar*) in the transaction. The sale of immovable goods in the same manner, on the other hand, is permitted by both Abu Hanifa and Abu Yusuf based on the consideration that such goods would be unlikely to perish at such short notice.[17]

Bargaining is not permitted in a *murabaha* contract since the whole point is resale at a known price. But it is essential that these transactions are mutually accepted by both parties.

A seller may sell his commodity for immediate payment, *thaman hall*, or for a deferred payment. If the latter, the price then becomes a future payment price, *thaman muájjal*. In this case, however, the exact date of the payment needs to be determined.[18]

In Chapter 9, how *murabaha* and its derivatives have become the core of modern Islamic finance will be explained in detail.

NOTES

1. For many examples of such cases from the Ottoman archives, see Çizakça, *Comparative Evolution*, ch. 3.
2. Harris, 'The Institutional Dynamics of Early Modern Eurasian Trade', http://www.usc.edu/schools/college/crcc/private/ierc/conference_registration/papers/Harris_final.pdf.
3. Çizakça, *A Comparative Evolution,* ch. 2 and Harris, ibid.
4. In other words, express the statement in Arabic: '*i'mal fihi bi raika*'.
5. Büyükçelebi, *İnan Şirketi*, p. 64.
6. Ibid., p. 64.
7. Ibid., pp. 67, 68–9.
8. Ibid., p. 69.
9. Gözübenli, 'Inan', p. 261; Çizakça and Kenanoğlu, 'Ottoman Merchants', pp.195–215.
10. Büyükçelebi, *İnan Şirketi*, p. 71.
11. Ibid., pp. 77–8.

12. Zahraa, 'Legal Personality', pp. 202–6.
13. Çizakça, 'Was Shari'ah Indeed the Culprit?', pp. 21-40.
14. Trustee of a waqf can borrow in the name of the waqf and can sue it. Thus the waqf itself could lend and borrow.
15. Büyükçelebi, *Inan Şirketi*, p. 76.
16. Baloğlu, *Law of sales,* p. 78.
17. Ibid., p. 83.
18. Ibid., p. 86.

5. Commerce and commercial institutions

We will study in this chapter what the classical sources of Islam, the Qur'an and the prophetic traditions, *ahadith*, have to say about commerce and what institutions have emerged as a result of these teachings in Islamic history. The gist of Islam's approach to trade has been summarized in the verse 2: 275 of the Qur'an:

> Allah has allowed trading and forbidden usury.

The verse 67: 15 is also revealing:

> He it is Who has made the earth easy to live upon. Go about then, in all its regions and partake the sustenance which He provides: but always bear in mind that to Him you shall be resurrected.

The verse 73: 20 mentions trade together with fighting in God's cause, thus bestowing merchants with great honour.

> and others who travelling through the land seeking God's bounty, yet others fighting in God's cause...

Still another verse (2: 282) is remarkable in that it directly teaches Muslims how to write a contract.

There are also many *ahadith*, statements of the Prophet, encouraging Muslims to do honest trade and earn their livelihood through *halal*, permitted means. Three examples should suffice:

> A person, who undertakes a journey to earn his livelihood and then returns with it towards his dependents, will be under the shade of Allah's throne.

> A person, who suffers pain to feed his dependents is like a person, who fights in the cause of Allah, the Mighty and Glorious.[1]

> A merchant honest in purchase and sale will be among the virtuous in paradise.[2]

Thus blessed, encouraged, even taught how to conduct trade by their religion, Muslim merchants did indeed 'travel through the land seeking God's bounty', that is, doing trade from the Atlantic to the Pacific. From the seventh century to the seventeenth, that is, for a millennium, they dominated the commerce of the vast territories from Morocco to the Malay world. At this point, Caliph Umar Ibn 'Abd al-Aziz (717–20 AD) and his reform must be referred to. It was this particular Caliph who famously declared the Islamic policy of unhindered trade by sea and land. He is reported to have said that:

> Both sea and land belong to God and He has subdued them to His servants to seek His bounty...in both of them. How then should we intervene between His servants and their means of livelihood.[3]

Let us now focus, once again, on the institutions which emerged to facilitate this intercontinental trade. We might start doing this by looking at money, without which long-distance trade would simply have been impossible. Indeed, in the absence of money, barter is the only other known method of commerce. Yet, barter necessitates a double coincidence of wants. That is to say, what merchant A wants to exchange should be needed by merchant B, and what B wants to exchange should be needed by A. Moreover, it is also necessary that both of these individuals should personally come together in a market. By contrast, in monetized trade A can sell his merchandise to third persons and with the money he receives he can travel to another market and there purchase B's goods in exactly the amount he wishes. Furthermore, since it is possible to send money over long distances, he does not even have to travel himself and can have the transaction completed by correspondence. The commercial advantage of trading with money over barter is thus obvious. Finally, since it is nearly impossible to measure the exact value of the goods exchanged in barter, any such transaction may involve an element of unjustified enrichment. It is probably based upon such concerns that Prophet Muhammad discouraged barter while encouraging monetized trade.

This policy is revealed in two *ahadith*, one clear and the other subtle. First the former, narrated in Malik's *Muwatta*:

> Someone brought some excellent dates to the Messenger of God as a gift. The Prophet asked 'are all dates of Khaybar like this?' The man said, 'No, Messenger of God! We take a *sa'* of this kind for two *sa's* or two *sa*'s for three'. Upon this, the Messenger of God said: 'Do not do that. Sell the assorted ones for dirhams and then buy the good ones with the dirhams.'

In this *hadith*, the Prophet clearly disapproves of barter and orders Muslims to resort to trade instead.[4] In the next *hadith*, narrated by al-Bukhari and Muslim on the authority of Ubadah ibn al Samit, the Prophet takes a dramatic step further and declares barter a form of *riba*, i.e., interest, and condemns it.[5]

> Gold for gold, equivalent for equivalent; silver for silver, equivalent for equivalent; dates for dates, equivalent for equivalent; salt for salt, equivalent for equivalent; barley for barley, equivalent for equivalent and whoever exceeds or asks for excess, he practiced *al-riba*. Sell gold for silver as you wish if it is hand to hand (prompt delivery), and sell barley for dates as you wish if it is hand to hand.[6]

The wisdom behind this *hadith* is not easy to understand. Actually, even today, more than 1400 years after it had been actually stated, some important scholars admit they do not really understand it.[7] The reason they do not understand it is because they consider the *hadith* from a legal perspective and ignore the historical circumstances in which it had been stated. With this *hadith,* the Prophet clearly makes barter almost impossible and encourages monetized trade. This is because, if the merchants wish to barter like objects, say, dates for dates, they are ordered to do so exactly equivalent for equivalent with total disregard to quality differences, actually a near impossibility. Indeed, they are told that when doing this particular case of bartering if one of them does not obey the rule 'equivalent for equivalent' and asks for his higher quality dates a higher amount of the lower quality dates from the other party, he would be committing *riba*. In short, merchants who wish to barter like-objects are not allowed to take quality differences into consideration and are restricted severely to barter only exactly 'equivalent for equivalent'. While with this particular *hadith*, the Prophet does not prohibit the barter of like-objects outright but makes it entirely unpractical and almost meaningless, with the previous one, he teaches the merchants how to trade like-objects by utilizing a medium of exchange, that is, dirhams or coins.

Bartering objects of the same genre, say, silver for gold, is less strict: it is permitted subject to prompt delivery. It has been argued that the wisdom behind this insistence on prompt delivery is the possible change in the relative values of the goods in question if deferred payment is allowed. Since this would lead to an unjustified enrichment for one of the parties, prompt delivery condition is imposed.[8] While this is certainly possible, I would argue that the real wisdom must be sought in the entirety of the *hadith*. What the Prophet has done here is to apply a hierarchy of restrictions with the purpose of gradually but surely leading the merchants from barter to monetized trade. Indeed, while the barter of like-objects (gold for gold) is most severely restricted, the barter of objects of the same genre (silver for gold, or, barley for wheat) is permitted subject to prompt delivery and finally the exchange (sale) of precious metals with commodities, say, gold for wheat, is not even mentioned in the *hadith*, implying that it is entirely unrestricted.

To sum up, by progressively relaxing the restrictions, the Prophet has catapulted Islamic community from the age of barter to the age of monetized exchange.[9] The significance of this seventh-century development would be appreciated better if we consider the fact that barter remained the general rule for trade over enormous areas of the world until as late as the eighteenth century. Barter dominated Russia until Peter the Great and was widespread in the USA during the 1790s. Eighteenth-century Naples practised barter routinely and even included it as an important instrument of business transactions in textbooks.[10]

This progress from barter to monetized trade must have been the *conditio sine qua non* for the establishment of an intercontinental trade system from the Atlantic to the Pacific, which Muslims, soon after the birth of Islam, came to dominate. If the gradual elimination of barter and its replacement by monetized trade was the *conditio sine qua non* for the establishment of an intercontinental trade network, the *conditio sine qua non* for the monetization of trade must have been the very existence of money. Indeed, the transition from barter to monetized trade could not possibly have materialized without a massive increase in the supply of money. In a bimetallic system, which dominated the world trade in this era, an increase in the supply of money was only possible with a corresponding increase in the supply of silver and gold. Under normal circumstances, a drastic increase in the supply of these precious metals is not possible. But during the seventh to eighth centuries circumstances were by no means normal. For this was the period when Islam expanded at the expense of the two great empires of the period: the Byzantine and the Sasanid. What dramatically changed the world economic history with the conquest of the Byzantine and Sasanid territories was the capture of massive amounts of hoarded gold and silver in the Byzantine and Sasanid churches and temples.[11] The gold and silver treasures hoarded by these institutions were melted down and then minted. Aggregate money supply increased in this way and a new economic system based upon monetized trade and dominated by the Muslims could thus become a reality.[12]

A closer look at the radical increase in the money supply reveals that this has been achieved in two steps. First, the coins of the conquered Byzantine and Sasanid territories continued to be the legal tender in the Islamic empire. Since Byzantine coins were gold and Sasanid ones silver based, this meant a *de facto* bimetallic system. The tolerance towards these coins meant that the now much enlarged economy of the Islamic community experienced minimum disruption. Second, when it was decided to mint new Islamic coinage, the precious metal content of these coins was kept deliberately lower than the earlier coins. Apparently, it was understood that the bad money would drive away the good money and in this way Islamic coins came to replace the earlier Byzantine and Sasanid coins. That bad money replaces the good money and the latter ends up being hoarded and taken out of circulation is, of course, known as Gresham's law and Muslims apparently had understood the principle behind it almost a millennium before Gresham.[13]

To sum up, Muslim coinage replaced the earlier imperial coins and spread rapidly and dominated the economies of Europe as well as India.[14] Van Der Wee, an eminent Belgian economic historian, also confirms that remonetization of Europe after the *Völkerwanderung* and the rebirth of the European banking system owe much to the flow of Muslim coinage to Europe.[15]

Discovery of Islamic coins everywhere in Europe, from Italy to Scandinavia, can only be explained by a sustained balance of payments deficit for the Islamic world. Europe exported to the Islamic world basically furs, lumber and slaves kidnapped by the Vikings from Northern and Eastern Europe. Thus Europe was exporting to the Muslims raw materials, even human beings, and the Muslims were paying for these goods in cash.[16] International trade, however, would not have been possible without a sophisticated maritime law. A well-known French historian, Daniel Panzac, has shown that this institution was also provided by Muslims. This originally Islamic law of maritime trade was transferred to Europe through various compilations.

The three most important compilations were made during the eleventh and twelfth centuries. These were the Maritime Laws of Rhodes, Oleron and the Consolato del Mare. It is now definitively established that the first one, previously considered to be a derivative of the Roman–Byzantine digests, was in fact based on Al-Mudawwana al-Kubra by Sahnun Ibn Sa'id al Tanukhi (d. 854). It was commented upon by Ibn Rushd (Averroes d. 1117) and drafted in Sicily or South Italy, both Muslim territories during the ninth to eleventh centuries. The second was authored by the Court of the Crusader Kingdom of Jerusalem in order to harmonize trade relations between the occidental and oriental Christians as well as Muslims. This compilation was brought to Europe partly by Eleanor of Aquitaine and partly by her son Richard the Lionheart. The contents of the Oleron compilation are identical to the Muslim laws of the ninth to tenth centuries. Finally, the Consolato del Mare was written in Spain. The document originates in the Muslim Middle Eastern texts of the eighth to ninth centuries and was later brought to Andalusia. It was translated during the reign of King Alphonse in thirteenth-century Castille as part of the great works of translation from Arabic.[17]

International trade soon necessitated a whole spectrum of new financial instruments. Indeed, invention of other business instruments facilitating monetary transactions did not have to wait very long. Bills of exchange, letters of credit (suftaja), promissory notes, ordinary cheque, and double-entry book keeping were all known to the Muslims. Historians are in general agreement that medieval Europe simply borrowed these instruments from the Muslims and could not improve upon them.[18] Without these financial instruments long distance trade would simply have been impossible.

THE *SUFTAJA* (BILL OF EXCHANGE OR LETTER OF CREDIT)

Of these, bill of exchange deserves our special attention. Because a bill of exchange allows a merchant to pay large amounts to a colleague who is in a far away city without ever carrying any cash. This was obviously an absolutely indispensable instrument for risk minimization. We have some information about how these instruments were actually used by medieval Muslim merchants. Consider the following case: 'Nasir-i Khusrau received from an acquaintance in Asuan a blank letter of credit addressed to his agent, *wakil*, in Aidhab of the following content: "Give Nasr all that he may demand, obtain a receipt from him and debit the sum to me."'

The case involves four individuals:

1. An unknown person, the 'deliverer', had written a letter of credit, most probably a *suftaja*, and handed it to 'the taker'.
2. 'The taker' of this letter of credit was the agent of Nasr's friend in Aidhab.
3. The agent passed the letter to his boss in Asuan. The latter was ordered to pay by the document. He is known as the 'payer'.
4. Finally Nasir himself was the 'payee'.

Thus, the deliverer who was in Aidhab managed to pay his debt to Nasr, who was in a different city in Asuan, without ever carrying any cash across long and dangerous distances.[19] This document is probably from the year 1047. Subhi Labib, referring to Mez, gives neither any explanation about the person of Nasir-i Khusrau nor the year in which this document was written. But we are informed by Suraiya Faroqhi that a Nasir-i Khusrau, the famous poet from the city of Balkh, went to the pilgrimage in the year 1047.[20] Assuming that both authors refer to the same Nasir-i Khusrau, we therefore conclude that the document was probably written in the middle of the eleventh century.

Although there is definitive evidence that *suftaja*s had been used since the very beginnings of Islam, in later periods jurists began to suspect them. Suspicion arose, referring to the example above, because of the very nature of what the 'deliverer' had delivered to the 'taker'. Had this transaction been an *amanah*, that is, depositing something with someone for safe keeping, then the liability of the 'taker' would have been nil. But the delivery is considered as a *karz*, a loan. The liability in a loan transaction, however, belongs solely to the borrower. Consequently, the jurists thought, the risks of transferring the loaned capital to the 'payee' becomes a burden upon the 'taker' and the 'payee' gains an unjustified advantage. Thus because the risks of the money transfer are imposed upon only one of the parties (and his partner), and this creates an unjustified advantage for the 'payee', Üsküplü Mehmed Efendi, an Ottoman jurist, objected to this instrument on the grounds that it violates the rule that a loan transaction should not yield an additional advantage to any one of the parties involved. The same logic can also be found in a treatise of Ebi'l Meali al-Guvayni.[21]

According to Halil Sahillioğlu, this objection was a typical example of narrow-minded legalistic thought. Indeed, says Sahillioğlu, such jurists failed to see the primary advantage of the *suftaja*. By transferring money across vast distances with minimum risk, this instrument made intercontinental trade possible. Moreover, all the parties involved gained, not just one.

Classical jurists with greater vision, such as Imam Sarakhsi, understood the importance of this instrument and were therefore more flexible. Sarakhsi probably saved the instrument by arguing that providing an obligation is not clearly stated in the contract, this instrument does not generate unjustified advantage for one of the parties and a burden for the other. The position of the party, which appears to be assuming the burden of transfer, could be considered as a generosity of a merchant towards his colleague. Providing this is not expressed as a legal obligation, there is no harm in it.[22] Finally, the loan, *karz*, characteristic of *suftaja* mentioned above, was understood as *karz hasene*, that is, loan without interest. By contrast, it is well known that the European bill of exchanges disguised interest in the different currencies utilized. This was done by disguising the rate of interest in the exchange rate.

To sum up, intercontinental trade and the successful Muslim linkage of the Indian Ocean and the Mediterranean world-economies[23] from the seventh to the seventeenth centuries simply could not have been achieved first, without money replacing barter and then an effective instrument of its transfer. *Suftaja*, though later on doubted by some jurists, nevertheless provided Muslim merchants with a means to transfer their money safely across vast distances.

IMTIYAZAT (COMMERCIAL PRIVILEGES, CAPITULATIONS)

Throughout the period from the seventh to the seventeenth century the route linking the Indian Ocean world-economy to the Mediterranean world-economy had two segments. The eastern segment from the Far East to Suez or to Basra, that is the Indian Ocean, was entirely controlled by Muslims and was considered a free trade zone. No major naval conflict was observed in its waters and the region was known as *Mare liberum*.[24] The western segment, linking the ports of the eastern Mediterranean to Europe, on the other hand, was contested by the hostile navies of Islam and Christendom as well as widespread piracy.

Thus trade had to be conducted in the western segment despite the prevalent hostility. Under such conditions of hostility trade can be feasible only if a certain minimum degree of security and mutual understanding for the traders prevail. These were provided by Muslim rulers to the European merchants by an institution known as the *imtiyazat*, or capitulations.

By capitulations, a set of terms or articles constituting an agreement between governments is meant. The second meaning of the word stated in most dictionaries, 'the act of surrendering or yielding', is totally irrelevant here because for much of its history capitulations have actually been granted by a powerful state to friendly powers to reward them in return for their loyalty. Indeed, the word capitulation is derived from the Latin word *caput* or *capitulum* as indicating the form in which these acts were set down in chapters. Capitulations were a special kind of treaties, unilateral contracts granted by a state and conferring the privilege of extraterritorial jurisdiction within its boundaries on the subjects of another state.

Thus, in the ninth century, the Caliph Harun al-Rashid granted guarantees and commercial facilities to the subjects of the emperor Charlemagne, who could visit the East with the authorization of their emperor. After the break-up of the Frank Empire, similar concessions were made to some of the practically independent Italian city states that grew up on its ruins. Thus, in 1098, the prince of Antioch granted a charter of this nature to the city of Genoa; the king of Jerusalem extended the same privilege to Venice in 1123 and to Marseilles in 1136. Salah ud-Din (Saladin), the great Ayyubid sultan and the conqueror of Jerusalem from the crusaders, granted a charter to the town of Pisa in 1173. The Byzantine emperors followed this example, and Genoa, Pisa and Venice were all granted capitulations.[25] Finally the Ottoman Empire also followed the tradition and granted numerous capitulations to friendly European powers, primarily to the French, English and the Dutch to obtain their support or at least neutrality in the fierce contest it had with the Habsburgs. These powers were also involved in a struggle for life or death against the Habsburgs, and the Ottomans utilized the capitulations to deepen the cleavage among the Europeans.

As long as the granting power enjoyed superiority vis-à-vis the grantees, capitulations were harmless treaties used to enhance trade. But when the relative power shifted and the granting power became weak and the grantees powerful, then they began to have an adverse effect and undermined the freedom of the granting power to exercise an independent economic policy.

Wansbrough has suggested that all of the capitulations had the following provisions with respect to the status of the European merchants in the Islamic world:

1. General security of person and property including:
   (a) testamentary rights, freedom of worship, burial and dress;
   (b) repairs to ships, emergency rations, aid against attack by corsairs;
   (c) permission to address complaints to the head of the Muslim community.
2. Exterritoriality, including:
   (a) consular jurisdiction;
   (b) consul's salary and exemptions.
3. Abolition of collective responsibility and its replacement by individual responsibility.[26]

The most important item provided above was obviously the general security of life and property of the European merchant. This was known as *aman*, which enabled a European merchant to travel in the world of Islam without being enslaved or having his goods looted. The precondition for granting to a non-Muslim European merchant *aman* was that his nation should apply for it with a promise of peace and friendship. It is in return for this promise that the Muslim ruler binds himself to guarantee *aman*. The *aman* was confirmed by an *ahd* or *ahdname*, a covenant, known in the West as a capitulation. If the European nation in question starts hostilities, the Sultan would revoke the capitulation and the merchants of that nation would no longer enjoy the protection provided by it. Every new Sultan at the accession to the throne had the right to revoke the *ahdname* granted by his predecessor. Thus, in return for the privilege of conducting trade within the world of Islam, the European nation was committed to maintain peace.[27]

The importance of the capitulations from the perspective of this book is that they have facilitated trade across the Mediterranean between hostile nations, thus completing the great intercontinental trade from the Malay world to Europe. Beginning with the sixteenth century, they were also important in that they facilitated the flow of precious metals first to the Ottoman Empire and then to the rest of the Islamic world. This is because European trade suffered a balance of trade deficit vis-à-vis the Ottoman empire and European merchants had to finance their imports with cash. Spanish silver dug out from the mines of Potosi in South America reached the Islamic world and then to India and the Far East, in no small part thanks to the capitulations.

NOTES

1. Akram Khan, *Economic Teachings of Prophet Muhammad*, p. 36.
2. Davudoglu, *Mevkufat Mülteka Tercümesi*, p. 338.
3. Abidin, 'The Fiscal Policy', *Islamic Culture*, 8: 120–24.
4. Ibn Ashur, *Maqasid*, pp. 288–9.

5. Malik, Book 31 (Business Transactions), *hadith* 31.12.21; see also Muslim, Book 10 (Book of Transactions), *hadith* 3861.
6. Al-Qusi, *Riba Islamic Law and Interest*, p. 144.
7. Consider the following interview conducted with Sheikh Esam M. Ishaq, a Board member of the *Discover Islam Centre* in Bahrain and *Shari'ah* advisor to several Islamic financial institutions. 'If I am going to exchange with you one bushell of a certain quality of rice with a bushell of lesser quality of rice, and if this is consensual and based on spot, people ask "Why is this forbidden?". I can try to extrapolate a reason but this will be purely deductive. Outwardly, I can't give you a single reason or explanation but I know that it is there explicitly in the theological text.' Parker, '*Shari'ah* Advisories', pp. 160–61.
8. Al-Qusi, *Riba, Islamic Law and Interest*, p. 149.
9. That the Prophet has condemned unequal barter exchange, encouraging instead monetized trade, has been acknowledged by Iqbal and Lewis as well. See *Islamic Perspective on Governance*, p. 83.
10. Braudel, *Civilization and Capitalism*, vol. I, p. 445.
11. Actually, substantial amounts of treasury had became available very early on. When Hayber was captured only seven years after the *Hejrah*, massive booty became available. When Bahreyn began to send regular revenue the next year, some 80,000 dirhems became available per annum. Kallek, *Devlet ve Piyasa*, pp. 82–3.
12. Wink, *Al-Hind*, p. 34.
13. Orman, *Iktisat*, p. 28.
14. On Islamic coins dominating European economies during the ninth century, see McCormick, *Origins of the European Economy*, pp. 332, 334–5, 340, 344. On their spread to India, see Wink, *Al-Hind*, pp. 30–34.
15. Van Der Wee, *A History of European Banking*, p. 74.
16. Van Der Wee, ibid., pp. 74–5.
17. Panzac, 'Le Contrat d'Affrément maritime en Mediterranée', pp. 351–8.
18. Braudel, *Civilization and Capitalism I*, p. 472; Sayous, *Le Commerce des Europeens*, pp. 132–3; Wink, *Al-Hind*, p. 12.
19. Labib, 'Capitalism in Medieval Islam', p. 89.
20. Faroqhi, *Herrscher Über Mekka*, p. 16.
21. Sahillioğlu, 'Bursa Kadı Sicillerinde İç, pp. 131–2.
22. Ibid., p. 133.
23. 'World-economy', with a hyphen, is a concept introduced by Fernand Braudel and Immanuel Wallerstein to denote large, more-or-less self-sufficient zones of the world. Each one of these zones has a centre and a periphery of its own. World economy, without a hyphen, denotes simply the economy of the world as a whole.
24. Utku, *Kızıldeniz'de*, p. 241.
25. http://www.answers.com/topic/capitulation-treaty.
26. Wansbrough, 'Imtiyazat'.
27. For details of the Ottoman capitulations and how they evolved from what has been described above into instruments of oppression on the weakened Ottoman empire during the eighteenth century, see Inalcik, 'Imtiyazat', ibid.

Part III

Historical institutions of capital redistribution and public finance

6. Obligatory redistribution of wealth: taxation and institutions of tax collection, the origins of modern *sukuk*

We will be discussing here the emergence of a fundamental component of public finance, the state (or government) borrowing from the public.[1] In the Islamic world, this problem appears to be particularly difficult in view of the interest prohibition. Indeed, how can the government of an Islamic country borrow much-needed funds from the public in an environment where the interest-bearing loan transactions are prohibited by the *Shari'ah*? But first, let us look at the taxes themselves, since states resort to borrowing only when taxes they collect do not suffice to cover their expenses.

ZAKAT

As it is well known, payment of *zakat* is considered to be as one of the five pillars of Islam. Some scholars consider it the third pillar, after the *kalimah* and the *salat/namaz*. The word *zakat* is mentioned 30 times in the Qur'an.[2] A careful study of the Qur'an reveals that during the Mecca period the concept was introduced and then during the Madinah era its details such as the taxable properties, the rate of taxation, its collection and disbursement became clear. It is generally accepted that every free and sane Muslim adult, providing he/she fulfils the conditions to be discussed below, is ordained to pay the *zakat*. Since *zakat* is a tax paid by Muslims, non-Muslims living in an Islamic state are not obliged to pay this tax.[3]

There are several conditions attached to the payment of *zakat*. First, the property or cash subject to *zakat* must be clearly in the possession of the person liable to pay. Second, the taxable wealth or property should be able to yield revenue. Third, a minimum amount of property, *nisab*, should be possessed. Until a person accumulates this minimum amount, he/she would not be responsible to pay the *zakat*. Fourth, *zakat* is due only after the primary needs have been satisfied. Fifth, before its due *zakat* is paid, an asset must be legally possessed for a full year.

If the asset in question is livestock, cash or tradable, the *zakat* is paid generally at the rate of one-fortieth. If it is land, only the produce of the land is subject to *zakat*. If the land in question can be irrigated naturally, the *zakat* is charged at the rate of one-tenth. If it has to be irrigated artificially, a very labour-intensive process given the technology of the time, then the rate is one-twentieth.[4] Remarkably, this ratio, the one-tenth, has also been widespread in Christian Europe, where it was known as *tithe*.

If the taxable asset is gold, the *nisab* has been calculated as 85 grams. If silver, it is 595 grams.[5] That is to say, a person fulfilling the five conditions mentioned above and possessing more than 85 grams of gold or 595 grams of silver is obliged to pay *zakat*. This obligation, however, is considered a personal one. In view of the fact that the exact amount of gold or silver a person actually possesses can be known only by him/her, it is preferred that the Muslim pays his/her *zakat* voluntarily as a form of prayer. This particular approach became even more pronounced when Othman, the third Caliph, decided that the *zakat* of assets in the form of gold, silver and merchandise, the exact amounts of which can only be known by individual Muslims, should be paid by themselves as a form of prayer.[6]

The Qur'an mentions eight categories of *zakat* recipients. These are: the poor; the needy; the *zakat* collectors or administrators; those whose hearts have been (recently) reconciled to truth; those in bondage and in debt; in the cause of God and for the wayfarer.[7]

This verse makes it clear that *zakat*, particularly in agriculture, should be collected by the state. This view is confirmed by the *sunnah* of the Prophet and the righteous caliphs, who had sent collectors to distant provinces. There were four offices for the taxes, *jizya*, *kharaj*, *zakat* and *ganimah* (booty). The first three are the Qur'anic taxes imposed by the early Islamic empires, while the *ganimah* refers to the booty gained during warfare. We will now focus on how these taxes were actually collected and how the institutions of tax collection evolved over the centuries.

It must be mentioned here that the actual tax load imposed by Islamic empires was by no means limited to these Qur'anic taxes. Based upon the prevalent local customs, a whole set of extra Qur'anic taxes were imposed particularly by the Seljukids and Ilkhanids. Under the Ottomans, the extra Qur'anic taxes were imposed by the sultans and were known as *takalif-i örfiye*, customary taxes. These came into being originally when the Ottomans faced serious challenges from the West. These extra Qur'anic taxes were legitimized by the argument that the Ottoman Empire was in continuous warfare with 'infidels' and the Sultan had the right to impose these taxes in order to defend the world of Islam, *Dar al-Islam*.[8] While originally these taxes, imposed temporarily and under extraordinary conditions, enjoyed certain legitimacy, in the long run they were not abolished and therefore began to have dubious legitimacy. The number of such taxes reached 97 in the late Ottoman state.[9]

INSTITUTIONS OF TAX COLLECTION: FROM *IQTA'* TO *TIMAR* AND *ILTIZAM*

In an age when direct tax collection by state officials was difficult or not possible, *iqta'* provided an indirect system of tax collection. In this system, the sultan granted the right to collect the taxes of a certain tax source, *muqata'a*, to a certain individual. This could be either in the form of a reward for a service or against a loan to the state or in order to reconcile an important person to the cause of Islam. The Prophet is known to have granted *iqta's* for this purpose. Actually the system was not an Islamic invention and has been observed in the Roman and the Sasanid empires as well.

An *iqta'* could take several forms. It could be given as private property pure and simple. It has been argued that the Prophet granted *iqta's* with the purpose of facilitating the expansion of Islam and to transform unused lands into arable and cultivable land. The Prophet was well aware of the difficulty of the latter and did not hesitate to grant private property *iqta's* in order to encourage the expansion of cultivated lands.

When the second Caliph Omar conquered the so-called *sawad* lands of Iraq and Syria, he applied a mixed system. Following the *sunnah* of the Prophet, those parts of the *sawad* conquered by force were distributed among the commanders as private property. One fifth of these lands, *khoms*, were taken as the share of the state. But once the supremacy of the Muslims was established, many tribes in the region voluntarily offered their submission, *bi'at*, to the Caliph. Thus, these parts of the *sawad* were incorporated into the Muslim empire without fighting. The Caliph refused to distribute these lands as private property. Instead, he allowed the previous users of these lands to keep their lands subject to the payment of *kharaj*.[10] Thus, the land regime of the previous Roman/Byzantine empires were maintained and incorporated into the Islamic empire.

When their expectations of private *iqta's* were ignored and the commanders demanded an explanation, the Caliph referred to the Qur'an.[11] Thus the Caliph prevailed and private ownership of land remained limited by and large to the Arabian Peninsula. The bulk of the rest of the Islamic world from North-West Africa and Spain to India was subjected to a different land system strongly influenced by the Roman Empire. In the Roman system the ownership of a given unit of land, the so-called *jugum*, usually measured by the amount of land a pair of oxen can till in a day, had three elements: *dominium eminens* (introduced to the Islamic world as *raqaba*) was the ownership claimed by the state. The state could legitimately claim this right on the basis of conquest. The second element was the *usus* (or *tasarruf*). This was the right to actually possess the land in question and was granted by the ruler usually to a military commander but also possibly to the members of the religious establishment.

What was granted here was the right to collect the tax revenue yielded by the land in the name of the state for a certain service, usually of the military kind. Finally the *fructus,* anglicized as the usufruct (or *istiglal*), was the right of the peasant, who actually tilled the land to benefit from the yield. Archives are full of documents informing us about land transactions. But the sale of land by a peasant should be understood as the sale of the usufruct right but not an actual transfer of ownership, which the state never relinquished.[12]

With the introduction of the mercenary Turkic troops by the Abbasid caliphs during the second half of the ninth century, military expenditure increased greatly. The problem was solved by granting military *iqta's* to these troops.[13] A commander granted an *iqta'* could collect the tax revenue paid by the peasants in his *iqta'* in return for maintaining a certain number of soldiers and joining with them to the Caliph's or the Sultan's campaigns. These military *iqta's* were granted in lieu of salary. Thus the system also solved another problem for the state – the shortage of cash.[14]

Under the Seljukids and the Buwayhids the system expanded further. The system was known as *jagird* in the Turkic empires of India, where the military type was prevalent.[15]

In Egypt the *iqta'* changes character and becomes a system of tax collection. Since the primary purpose of these *iqta's* was tax collection, they were known as *iqta' al-qabala*, meaning a land grant for the payment of a fixed amount of tax. The system, known also to the Abbasids, extended to the whole of Egypt and evolved into a system of auctioning.

Based upon Makrizi, Morimoto informs us that during the auctions all the interested parties assembled in front of a mosque. A man declared the names of the villages for which the tax amounts were agreed in contracts while the scribes noted down the villages for which the auction had been completed and the names of the individuals, tax farmers, who had made successful bids. Often the amounts of tax pledged were too high for a single entrepreneur and partnerships had to be formed. Thus the decision as to who would collect the taxes from each *iqta' al-qabala* was taken as a result of a competitive auction. The term of the contract was usually limited to four years.[16] The tax farmers, who bid in the auctions, were risk-taking entrepreneurs, who pledged to pay to the state a fixed amount in cash and expected to recuperate their investment by collecting the taxes from the tax source. If the total amount of taxes they collected exceeded what they paid to the state they made a profit, otherwise they suffered a loss. By the tenth century about half of the revenue of Egypt was collected by the *qabala*. Under the Ayyubids the system was extended to all the sectors of the economy and urban taxes also began to be collected in this way.

Thus land ownership in Islamic states was characterized by two institutions, the *iqta* and the *qabala*. The former had two basic versions, the private property *iqta's* as granted by the Prophet and military *iqta's* as envisaged by

Caliph Omar and the Abbasids under the Byzantine and Sasanid influence. Of these two versions, the former remained by and large limited to the Arabian Peninsula and the latter came to dominate throughout the Islamic world. The military *iqta's* were perfected by the Ottomans and came to be known as the *Tımar. Tımars*, though gradually losing their importance over the centuries, nevertheless survived in the Ottoman Empire until the nineteenth century. By contrast, private ownership of land, as originally envisaged and practised by the Prophet, has now become the norm practically all over the world!

The *qabala*, which was basically a system of tax farming, formed the basis of the Ottoman *iltizam* in the following centuries and under the Ottomans about 80 per cent of the revenues of Egypt were collected through this system.[17] In similar fashion to his predecessors in medieval Egypt and India, the Ottoman *mültezim* was also basically a risk-taking entrepreneur. The bidding for a tax source occurred in competitive auctions organized by the state and the highest bidder obtained the right to collect taxes from the tax source. If the *mültezim* succeeded in collecting more revenue than his total cost (which was equal to the auction price paid plus operational expenses) he enjoyed a profit, otherwise he suffered a loss. The risks were also similar: a *mültezim* not able to pay the state the promised amount risked confiscation and imprisonment.[18] On the upside, tax farming was highly profitable and the Ottoman state, in order to attract the available investable funds to the sector, allowed *mültezim*s to generate the highest profits in the economy.[19] Like *tımar, iltizam* was also long-lasting – although its importance gradually declined, it nevertheless survived as a system of tax collection until the end of the Ottoman Empire.

Thus, Ottoman public finance during the classical age of the Empire, that is during the fifteenth to seventeenth centuries, was dominated by two institutions, *timar* and *iltizam*. Both of these institutions were supplanted by newer institutional inventions in response to the changing needs and circumstances during the period 1695–1774 but they never disappeared until the end of the Empire. Of these two, *iltizam* is definitely the more interesting one for the history of finance, the main topic of this book. So, it is appropriate that we have a closer look at its actual functioning.

PARTNERSHIPS IN THE *ILTIZAM* SYSTEM

Before we examine the details of the *iltizam* system, we should note that both the *iltizam* and the *malikâne*, which followed it, contained the element of *gharar*, ambiguity. How these systems could be introduced and functioned for centuries, notwithstanding the forbidden *gharar* element and the exact nature of the prevalent *gharar* in *iltizam* and *malikâne* contracts, has been explained elsewhere.[20]

In his classical work on the history of the Egyptian public finance during the Ottoman period, Shaw informs us that when a *mültezim* obtained a tax source in an auction he was given a receipt, which had at the bottom the name of the tax farm, *muqata'a*, and the number of its shares which he had a right to control. These shares were known as *qirat*s and they may well have a linguistic as well as substantive links to the *mudaraba* partnership.[21] The tax farmer then had to find a guarantor, *kefil*, who wrote down his name on the receipt undertaking to compensate the treasury should the former fail to meet his obligation. The tax farmer then took the receipt to the appropriate scribe of the treasury, who wrote at the top a complete description of the tax farm, all those having a share in its auction price and the total amount of tax revenue owed to the treasury. This paper was then initialled by the *defterdar* and the governor and on it was inscribed an official order both authorizing the tax farmer to collect the taxes from the *muqata'a* and ordering the cultivators to obey his directions and perform their duties properly. Once the governor added his seal on the document, it became a legal deed, proof of the rights and obligations of the tax farmer.

Each tax farm was divided into 24 parts, *qirats*. A share could be held by a single *mültezim* in full, or by several in partnership. Each share, or part share, was measured in *qirat*s. At this point the relationship between the tax farmer and his guarantor, the *kefil*, needs to be examined in greater detail.

The need for these *kefil*s arose from the fact that tax farmers could not pay their pledge in advance. The state authorities had to accept that the tax farmer paid a certain amount in cash and the rest in instalments. The surety, *kefalet*, system was introduced in order to ensure some degree of reliability to the payment of these instalments. The liability of these *kefil*s to the state was limited to the amount they had guaranteed.

It has been argued that a disguised motive must have induced these guarantors to stand surety in such a risky enterprise as *iltizam* and that these individuals must have been actually passive partners, who were also providing finance to the tax farmers.[22] Indeed, it makes perfect sense to argue that in return for the risks shouldered, the guarantor must have been promised a proportional share of the profits to be earned by the tax farmer. It is also possible that the auction price paid to the state by the tax farmer was actually the capital of the partnership between the tax farmer and his *kefil*. We may therefore consider this guarantor as a *kefil/rab al-mal,* that is, both as a person who agrees to stand as surety (*kefil*) and the passive partner in a *mudaraba* or *musharaka* partnership (*rab al-mal*), who provides the capital. If *kefil*s were indeed principals or passive partners in a *mudaraba* partnership, this explains why their liabilities towards the third parties (state) was only up to the limit of the amount they had agreed to stand as surety, that is, the original investment capital of the partnership, and did not exceed it. This may well be because in a *mudaraba* partnership the responsibility for all contact with the third parties resides with the agent and the investor is never a litigant with outside third parties as a result of the agent's actions.[23] Thus the amount that was above the limit guaranteed by the *kefil/rab al-mal* was the responsibility of the tax farmer, whose liability to the state was unlimited.

As far as the state was concerned, the *kefil* was responsible up to the amount he guaranteed to the state and the tax farmer was responsible for any amount exceeding that. In case of failure, the state first tried to get the tax farmer to meet his obligations, that is, pay the instalments, and only in cases where he could not be located did it return to the *kefil*. The relationship between the two partners was not the state's concern, which explains why the documentation reflecting such partnerships are so difficult to find in state archives. But the fact that the state held the *kefil* responsible only for the amount he guaranteed and not for any amount exceeding that, indicates that the *mudaraba* element within the *kefalet* was recognized by the state.

As far as the structure of the *mudaraba* contract was concerned, it is clear that we are dealing with a multiple *mudaraba* involving a multitude of investors, *kefil/rab al-mal*s, and a tax farmer. Since sub-tax farming, that is to say, a tax farmer subcontracting his tax farm to several entrepreneurs, was a common feature of the tax-farming system, it is clear that we could also have a two-tier *mudaraba* involving a multitude of principals (*rab al-mal*s)/tax farmer (*mudarìb*) and another sub-tax farmer, who would, in fact, act as the agent of the original tax farmer. Alternatively, it was also possible to have tax-farming partnerships controlling a multitude of tax farms. Occasionally, mergers between such tax farms, which led to some of them losing their separate identity, were also observed. The state approved of such mergers as they were thought to provide more reliable revenue and avoid fluctuations.

After the disastrous second siege of Vienna in 1683, the Ottoman economy was hit by two calamities. While on the one hand, the long and costly campaigns had radically increased the government expenditure, on the other, the loss of extensive territories had reduced the revenues from these territories. These developments led to huge budget deficits never seen before.[24] As deficits began to increase, the first reaction of the state was to demand from the *mültezim*s an increasing portion of the auction prices in advance. When this proved insufficient, the tenure of the tax farmers was reduced from two to three years to one year only.

Tax farmers reacted to this increased insecurity by imposing heavier demands on tax payers. Tax payers reacted to this by, whenever possible, exiting from production altogether. Thus, in short, to the two calamities of increased military costs and declining revenues from the lost territories a third one was added: declining production in response to radically increased tax burden. This vicious circle from excessive taxation to declining production capacity was the most difficult paradox that the Ottoman state faced at the end of the seventeenth century.[25]

To sum up, the classical Ottoman tax-farming institution, *iltizam*, had a number of shortcomings. First, the tenure of the tax farmer, which was supposed to be for a period of two or three years, was in fact unreliable. Indeed, the state had the right to transfer the tax farm to another tax farmer, who offered to pay a higher amount, at any time. This had undesirable consequences, because the tax farmer, worried that he could lose his tax farm at any time, wanted to maximize his revenue collection as soon as possible. This led to an overexploitation of the tax source. Second, the system was loaded with risks for both the tax farmer and the state. When the state became risk-averse, it demanded from the tax farmer a fixed but guaranteed payment and in return permitted him to maximize his profits.[26] While this policy guaranteed the state a reliable revenue, it also led to, again, excessive exploitation of the tax source. Finally, *iltizam* was slow to generate revenue. By the early 1690s, the Ottoman state was involved in a fierce struggle for its very survival and needed urgent cash. The solution was found in a major institutional reform, the introduction of the *malikâne*.

MALIKÂNE

The paradox, excessive taxation leading to a decline in the production capacity, was solved by this new system. The crucial difference between the *iltizam* and the new *malikâne* was the length and reliability of the tenure of the tax farmer. With the new system, tax sources, *muqata'as*, were now auctioned off not for a few years but for the entire lifespan of the tax farmer. Thus, a tax farmer, now called *malikâneci*, who obtained the right to collect taxes from a tax source in a public auction, was now permitted to do so for as long as he lived. Moreover, he was granted complete freedom to manage his *muqata'a* and state interference in the management of the tax source was ruled out. It was understood by all parties that when the tax farmer died, the tax source would be taken over by the state and be auctioned off again. Although the *malikâneci* was permitted to sell his rights to third parties, he was not permitted to bequeath them to his offspring. Thus his property right over the *malikâne* remained limited to his lifespan and did not extend to the next generation. The negotiability of the *malikâne* shares came to be impeded by a 10 per cent tax after 1735.[27]

The *malikânecis* made two different types of payments to the state: the *muaccele*, a lump sum and usually a very large amount, was determined in public auctions, and the annuities, which were paid regularly every year. These annuities could be paid annually in three instalments. The state also guaranteed that it would not increase these annuities without obtaining the consent of the *malikânecis*. If during their tenure, the *malikânecis* made investments in the tax source they controlled and production and profits increased, these were to accrue to the *malikânecis* themselves. This was a win–win–win situation. Besides the *malikânecis*, peasants would also benefit from any increase in production. This is because share cropping was the most widespread method of cultivation, allowing all the parties to benefit from any increase in production according to a fixed proportion. Finally, the state would also benefit. This is because the investments made by the *malikânecis*, and the resulting production increases of the tax source, would enable the state to resell the tax farm, when the *malikâneci* died, at a higher price. Because of all these obvious benefits, the *malikâne* system was rapidly embraced by all the parties involved. It also rapidly expanded throughout the Ottoman heartlands and remained in force for a considerably long time.

It has been argued that the *malikâne* system should be considered as a form of domestic borrowing for the state.[28] This domestic borrowing had the additional advantage that it was *Shari'ah* based in the sense that the *malikâne* investments embodied considerable risks. First of all, there were three different investments: the auction price paid in cash, the *muaccele*, the annuities paid in instalments, and investments made voluntarily by the *malikânecis* in order to enhance profitability. All of these investments involved risks, basically because the *malikânecis* could never be sure that they would live long enough to recuperate their investments.

As larger and larger tax sources were auctioned off by the state, it became necessary to sell them in shares. Thus *malikâne*s gradually assumed a quasi joint-stock character, 'quasi' in the sense that the state did not grant an absolute freedom in the number of share owners but limited their numbers to about 20 participants. Moreover, although it was originally possible for any individual, regardless of his social class, to purchase these shares, gradually restrictions were introduced and women and civilian *reaya* were not permitted to do so.[29]

The *malikânecis* usually lived in major urban centres and entrusted the management of their tax farms to local managers. This led to a system of sub-tax farming, when *malikânecis* resorted to the former *iltizam* system for choosing their managers. They auctioned off their tax farms and the entrepreneur, *mültezim*, who pledged to pay the highest amount, became the new manager for the *malikânecis*. Thus, the former *iltizam* did not disappear and simply continued at a lower and private level within the *malikâne* system. Notwithstanding this, it is possible that the excesses observed in the earlier *iltizam* system were reduced thanks to the controls exercised by the *malikânecis*, who were interested in the long-term productivity of their tax farms. That, indeed, the long term productivity of tax farms had increased is confirmed by the fact that annuities of all *malikâne*s were increased by 50 per cent during the Russo-Ottoman war of 1714–17. Without prior productivity increases, such a substantial increase in tax burden could not have been sustained. This radical state interference notwithstanding, the system continued to expand albeit with a fall in the auction prices – a normal reaction on the part of *malikânecis*, who felt that they were facing higher risks and taxes. Confidence was restored only after the 1730s, when it became clear that another arbitrary state interference was unlikely. It has been estimated that whereas the *malikânecis* were prepared to invest only at a rate of expected profit of 30–35 per cent in the 1730s, these rates declined to 25 per cent in the 1760s and to 15 per cent at the end of the century, reflecting increased confidence.[30]

After 1762, apparently some major waqfs also began to resort to the *malikâne* system to farm out their extensive properties.[31] But we have as yet insufficient information of this particular form of *malikâne*. All in all, the expansion of the system continued unabated until 1775, when a new system, the *esham*, was introduced. But this did not mean that the *malikâne* was abolished: it continued until 1840, after which no new *malikâne*s were offered for sale.

A remarkable feature of the *malikâne* system was that in addition to its great success in enhancing state revenues and solving the acute problem of budget deficits,[32] it enhanced the entrepreneurial element in the otherwise proto-quasi-socialist Ottoman economy. Indeed, the entrepreneurial element already embodied in the *iltizam* system was significantly enhanced when under the *malikâne* the tenure of the tax farmer was extended to cover his entire lifespan. As we have seen above, this important improvement in property rights led to substantial increases in the productivity of the tax sources and consequently in tax yields. In view of the strong linkages envisaged between property rights and production, this comes as no surprise.[33] This enhancement of the entrepreneurial element, however, occurred at the expense of a massive crowding-out effect. Indeed, investable funds were attracted to the *iltizam* and the *malikâne* sectors by permitting tax farmers to earn significantly higher than normal profits prevalent elsewhere in the economy. This argument was confirmed by the observations that some merchants shifted their activities from trade, what they knew best, to tax farming.[34]

Ottoman public finance as a field of entrepreneurial activity came to an abrupt end in 1774, when a new system, *esham,* was introduced. When tax farms were transformed from *malikâne* to *esham*, their management were taken over by the state and the entrepreneurial element was therefore terminated. Thus, the transformation to *esham* was similar (but not identical) to the wave of nationalizations observed in modern times; consequently it can be argued that the quasi-socialist character of the Ottoman economy must have been enhanced even further by the transition from *malikâne* to *esham*.

When the Ottoman authorities were describing the new system, *esham*, they used the term '*ber vech-i malikâne*', meaning 'like the *malikâne*'. Thus, we get the impression that the new system simply evolved from the *malikâne*. But if we take securitization as the essential characteristic of *esham,* then we must be aware that this characteristic has a very long history.

EARLIEST EXAMPLES OF SECURITIZATION

It has been shown that the idea of securitization can be traced back to the seventh century in the world of Islam. The first example refers to the circulation of IOU documents based upon agricultural produce during the time of Caliph Mervan bin al-Hakem (d. 684).

The second one is from the eighth century and refers to similar documents called *sukuk*. These earliest *sukuk* were based on crops to be harvested from certain lands. Apparently, merchants who had purchased these crops still in the field and obtained IOUs from the peasants, wanted to resell their IOUs to third parties. When they asked for his approval, Said bin al-Musayyab (d. 712) did not object to this transaction on the condition that the crops should first be harvested. What is important here is that there was no objection to the transformation of a physical asset, crops, into a document.[35] Equally important, the condition of actually possessing the asset and then transferring its ownership still constitutes one of the most important aspects of modern Islamic finance. While these examples are obviously very important, to understand the *modus operandi* of securitization, we need to go to medieval Europe. This medieval European example is relevant for Islamic finance, due to the stringent interest prohibition that prevailed in Europe at that time.

THE MEDIEVAL EUROPEAN PERMANENTLY FUNDED PUBLIC DEBT

In view of the current and continuous interest prohibition in the Islamic world, it is easily forgotten that medieval Europe had also faced the same restriction. It is well known for instance that the Third Lateran Council in 1179 had declared that the usurers would be excommunicated and would be refused burial in consecrated ground. These decrees were confirmed about a century later by Pope Gregory IX in 1234. The council of Vienne declared in 1311–12 that the usurers would be declared heretics. Dante Alighieri placed them in his *Divine Comedy* in the Seventh Circle of Hell.[36] In short, the medieval West applied an interest prohibition as severe as that of the Islamic world. Therefore, financial institutions developed by medieval Europeans should be of interest for modern-day Muslims. One of these institutions, the Medieval European permanently funded public debt (PFPD), is of particular interest and relevance. For it is possible that although never acknowledged by the Ottoman authorities, this institution may have constituted the origins of the Ottoman *esham* that emerged in 1775. It will be argued here that these medieval European and the later Ottoman institutions together, can give important insight for the redesigning and improvement of the current Islamic financial institution for domestic borrowing, the *sukuk*.[37]

The first remarkable feature of this institution, PFPD, is the time dimension. Although domestic borrowing can be observed in the Italian city states as early as the thirteenth century, a similar system was introduced into the Ottoman economy only at the end of the eighteenth century.[38] There is yet no definitive explanation for this delay, which had striking consequences.

Ever since the thirteenth century the European states could borrow from their public huge funds, at very low cost. This Western European system of domestic borrowing actually started way back during the thirteenth century in the cities of northern France, Flanders and Tuscany. An invention of the quasi-democratic cities, the PFPD was later on successfully adopted by the nation states. This institution had the following characteristics. First, the debt was 'permanent' in that it consisted of perpetual annuities[39] (rentes). The debt was redeemable at any time at the discretion of the issuing authority. Thus, the issuing authority, usually the state or the municipal authorities, could redeem them when it suited them. This is in sharp contrast to ordinary loans with stipulated fixed redemption dates. Second, the debt obligation was national, i.e., a personal obligation of the prince or the state. It was created by the state through representative parliamentary institutions. Third, the annual payments on such annuities and their redemptions were authorized by the parliament, which undertook to fund that debt by levying specific taxes, usually on consumption. Fourth, the sale of these annuities occurred without any coercion on the part of the state. Members of the public purchased these annuity-yielding instruments voluntarily. Fifth, the state was able to give the public the confidence that it would always honour its obligation of paying the annuities on time. Sixth, annuities were freely negotiable through financial intermediaries in secondary markets for purchase by any buyer both inside and outside the national boundaries.[40]

Actually, the origins of these annuities go back to the eighth century Carolingian monasteries. In order to secure bequests of lands from the laity, the monastery guaranteed the donor that, in return for surrendering all his property rights to the land, the donor would receive an annual usufruct income from the lands donated for the rest of his life and sometimes also for the lives of designated heirs as well. Thus, rather than being an invention by the autonomous cities, the system was actually invented by the Church itself. But the Church was not applying a double standard here, because there was indeed no loan: annual payments were made in return for transferring the ownership of a piece of land.[41]

During the thirteenth century the Church started a fierce anti-usury campaign and a debate on the legality of these annuities started. The Dominican Roland of Cremona argued that, because the uncertainty of the buyer's death made the return of the rente uncertain, the contract was not usurious. A powerful confirmation came in 1251, when Pope Innocent IV declared that annuities were legitimate contracts and not usurious, providing that annual payments were based on real assets. Although based upon this, rente contracts became popular and widely circulated, doubts about their legitimacy never completely disappeared and the debate resurfaced once again during the fifteenth century. In 1416 the council of Constance was asked whether these transactions were usurious. The council ruled that rentes were licit and that the issuer had the right to redeem them, provided that the amount equalled at least the nominal purchase value. This ruling was followed by three other fifteenth-century papal bulls, which declared that these contracts were licit under three conditions: that contracts be tied to real assets, that annuity payments not exceed 10 per cent of the capital sum (almost never observed) and that, most importantly, it was the issuing authority but not the purchaser, crédirentier, who had an unrestricted right of redemption. These bulls settled the debate until the seventeenth century, when another confirmation came from the Leuven theologian Lessius, who summarized the whole debate with the dictum: *ubi non est mutuum, ibi non est usura*, that is, 'where there is no loan, there is no usury'. Thus, the whole seventeenth-century argument boiled down to whether these rente transactions constituted loans or not. What made them different from loans was the fact that anyone who purchased a rente was denied the right to demand repayment of the principal, so long as the seller, that is, the state or the prince, honoured the obligation to make annuity payments for which he had pledged real assets. Had the buyers, the crédirentiers, given the right to demand back their principals, their rentes would have become merely devices to cloak a usurious loan.[42]

Soon autonomous cities and then princes and kings began to borrow using this system of 'permanently funded national debt'. Thanks to these systems, European governments began to borrow ever larger amounts at constantly declining rates.[43] While during the eleventh century, mortgage rates of 100 per cent had been observed in France, in 1152, Genoa borrowed at 40 per cent and reduced the rate to 8 per cent in 1259. In 1171 Venice began to borrow at 5 per cent and this low rate became the norm in 1262.[44] This was because, between 1262 and 1264, the Venetian Senate consolidated all of the state's outstanding debts into one fund called the Monte Vecchio, mountain of debt, and decreed that debt holders would receive annuity payments at 5 per cent, which the state was obliged to pay twice yearly from eight specified taxes. During the fourteenth and the fifteenth centuries most French, Flemish, Dutch and German cities adopted rentes as the primary vehicle for public finance. Actually, in both

France and Flanders, it was the princes who were actually having the municipal governments sell the rentes on their behalf. This was because quasi-democratic municipal governments, where the rente buyers were well represented, were considered to be more trustworthy than the princes. The first national monarchy to establish a PFPD was the Habsburg kingdom of Spain. The first issue of hereditary, perpetual and redeemable rentes, known as *juros de heredad*, took place in 1489, when the newly united Spanish crown under Ferdinand II and Isabella wanted to finance their war against the Muslims of Granada. Thus, it can be argued with hindsight that the financial secret of their success against the Muslims were these rentes, which had been developed in medieval times under severe interest rate prohibitions – as severe as any that could be observed in the world of Islam.

Negotiability, that is, the unrestricted ability to transfer the ownership of a financial document to third parties, constitutes a very important aspect of all such transactions. Already during the thirteenth century a rente buyer was permitted to sell his document to a third party. By 1320, at the latest, a secondary market for these annuities had developed.[45] But true negotiability in the modern sense did not emerge in France even during the sixteenth and seventeenth centuries.[46] This was because the transaction process was difficult and costly – both parties or their attorneys had to appear before a notary public. Because of these costs, so long as the annuity payments were made regularly and some redemptions of the principal were made, the claims traded between par and 75 per cent. But when, for instance, the French crown failed to make regular payments of the annuities in the 1570s, the few buyers demanded discounts of 50 per cent.[47]

In comparison to France, the Habsburg Empire had a much better system of rents. The system developed by the Habsburg Netherlands was so successful that Holland's government was able to redeem its *renten* without any difficulty. Much of this success was due to the opening of the Antwerp bourse in 1531. There, trade in *juros* and *renten* had become the principal activity of the South-German banking houses such as the Fuggers and others. A second bourse was established in 1608 in Amsterdam. Such secondary markets depended in turn upon the adoption of fully fledged negotiability between 1537 and 1543 in the Habsburg Netherlands – that is to say, protection of the property rights of third party creditors.

The PFPD was well known in Flanders[48] as well, where it took two distinct forms: the traditional perpetual hereditary rent, known as the *erfelijke rente*, and the newer form of life rent, the *lijfrente*. The latter was supposed to be extinguished on the death of the holder, but its duration was eventually extended to cover two or even three designated lives. They could be transferred at death to a spouse, child or close relative. The annuity payments on single-life rents were always higher than, and sometimes twice as high as, those on perpetual or hereditary rentes. In the late thirteenth-century Flemish towns, the annuity rate on perpetual rents, *erfelijke rente*, was 10 per cent, falling to 6.25 per cent in the fifteenth century. The rate on *lijfrente* in the late thirteenth century was 12.5 per cent falling to 10 or even 8 per cent.[49]

The rates were declining most probably due to the confidence the public felt towards the issuing authority that the annuities would be paid regularly. Thanks to this confidence, these low rates prevailed in the very long run. Indeed, in Catalonia as in the rest of Western Europe during the fourteenth and fifteenth centuries, rates on these annuities were as low as 5, 4 and even 3 per cent.[50] The Genoese public debt stood at 4 720 000 ducats in 1407, for which the government paid 220 000 ducats annually. The debt increased to 6 440 000 in 1509 with a debt service of only 180 000 ducats, i.e., an annuity rate of 2.8 per cent.[51] In 1624 the yield was reduced to 1.03 per cent, a world record that has been broken only at the end of the twentieth and in the early twenty-first century.[52] The Genoese public debt was considered so safe that although nominally it was less than the total GNP, the market valued it at more than double the national income. Charles V, the Holy Roman Emperor and the arch-rival of the Ottomans, was also able to borrow in addition to the huge American funds that were flowing into his treasury. The *juros*, as the Castilian annuities were called, represented perpetual indebtedness rather than indebtedness for life. They were sold at yields that started out at around 10 per cent and then declined after 1530 to 5 per cent.[53]

Between 1749 and 1752 the Chancellor of the Exchequer in England began to convert all annuity issues into the *Consolidated Stock of the Nation*, known as *consols*. These *consols* were fully transferable and negotiable. Although they were redeemable annuities, the public firmly believed that the state would not exercise its option to redeem them. Remarkably, this was the main reason why they were so popular among the public. This belief was confirmed, because they were not redeemed until 1888, when the Chancellor of the Exchequer, taking advantage of a sustained fall in interest rates, converted them from the original 3.5 per cent to 2.75 per cent *consols*. Unchanged to this day, they continue to be traded on the London Stock Exchange with a yield of 4.69 per cent (the coupon divided by the market price).[54]

Domestic borrowing through the PFPD has been a remarkably stable and effective form of public finance in Europe. It achieved an unprecedented and sustained reduction in the cost of government borrowing from 100 per cent in eleventh-century France to 3 per cent in eighteenth-century England. It has been shown that the PFPD has always been cheaper to maintain than interest-bearing loans and perpetual annuity payments cheaper than life annuities. With their greater marketability and lower transactions costs, PFPD instruments were definitively preferred by both the public and the governments to loans, bonds and debentures. Moreover, the perpetual rentes did not alienate government revenues so long as it had the right to redeem them at par. Redemptions occurred simply whenever it suited the governments to do so.[55] With the PFPD so successful, it has been concluded with hindsight that the medieval prohibition of usury has promoted rather than retarded long-term European economic growth.[56] Despite these successes, the PFPD has largely disappeared from European public finance as governments during the great wars of the twentieth century reverted to short-term loans and bonds, a transformation whose story still needs to be written.

In short, successful European governments were able to borrow up to twice as much as their GNP at very low rates. Moreover, when we compare the Genoese public debt with the total revenue of the Ottoman Central Treasury, we reach a striking conclusion: the Genoese public debt of 6 440 000 ducats in 1509 was about five times as much in terms of Venetian ducats as the revenue of the Ottoman Central Treasury for the same year.[57] Thus at the cost of merely 180 000 ducats, or 2.8 per cent, the Genoese government could borrow more than five times the amount of the annual revenue of the Ottoman Central Treasury for the year 1509.[58] This was the achievement of the European Financial Revolution and it is this sort of access to such huge funds that the Ottomans lacked. If we consider the fact that from Genoa to Lübeck and Hamburg[59] public borrowing was widespread all over Western Europe, resorted to not only by the city states but also by princes, kings and even emperors, it should become clear what a formidable yet disguised financial power the Ottomans were facing in the West.[60]

To complete this comparative perspective, it is necessary to reconsider the Ottoman methods of public finance. As we have seen, the dominant mode of Ottoman public finance during the sixteenth century; the period for which the comparison was being made, was the traditional tax farming, *iltizam*. This was not really domestic borrowing in the European sense, but rather, privatized tax collection. In this system the right to collect taxes from a tax source was delegated to entrepreneurs, *mültezims*, who offered to pay to the state in public auctions the highest amount.

It is very difficult to calculate what it cost the Ottoman state to collect taxes by this system. But in general we can say that the more competitive the auctions, the greater amounts the state could collect. Towards the end of the sixteenth century, however, a new tendency in the opposite direction was observed: tax farm yields began to freeze. The number of these 'frozen' tax farms began to increase during the seventeenth century so that by the middle of the seventeenth century roughly 31 per cent of the tax farms were frozen.[61]

A probable explanation might be the state's risk aversion. This is because competitive auctions generally reflect economic conjuncture. When the economy exhibits a tendency for growth, prospective tax farmers compete and promise to pay to the state ever higher amounts. But in times of depression, the reverse occurs and the state gets declining amounts. With firm annual commitments to the military corps, the state must have felt extremely uncomfortable with these fluctuations. Consequently, it may have reached an agreement with certain members of the military and, in return for fixed annual payments to the state, allowed them to collect the taxes from a tax source. Thus, after having paid to the state a fixed amount, these members of the military tax collectors were free to collect what they wanted, subject of course to the tax rates fixed by the law.[62] Since what percentage of the taxes collected actually reached the state treasury and what percentage was retained by the frozen tax farm *mültezims* is not known, we cannot calculate the exact cost of Ottoman tax collection in this period. But we can say that an increase in the number of frozen tax farms must have led to an increase in the cost of tax collection. This is exactly what was happening and the numbers of frozen tax farms were on the rise.[63]

Approximate calculation of the cost of taxation to the state in the form of 'revenue forgone' becomes possible after 1695, when the *malikâne* system was introduced. Genç has shown that out of 100 *gruş* collected from the public, only 24 *gruş* actually reached the treasury. Thus the cost of taxation to the state was approximately 75 per cent.[64] This is in sharp contrast with the West, where PFPD rates were as low as 3 per cent. Indeed, if we consider the cost of Ottoman taxation in the form of taxes forgone, as a rough approximation to the annuity rates paid by a Western state for domestic borrowing, then we reach the conclusion that the Ottoman state borrowed at extremely high rates in comparison with the West.

ESHAM[65]

Another disastrous war in 1774 obliged the Ottoman state to, once again, reform its financial system. With the introduction of the *esham* system in 1775, the Ottoman government was able to reduce its cost of borrowing from roughly 75 per cent to the range of 10–20 per cent.[66] But the real motive for introducing this system was to finance a war indemnity of 7 500 000 *gruş* to Russia.[67]

In comparison to *malikâne*, whereby the entire stream of revenue of a tax farm was auctioned off to the highest bidder for his lifetime, in *esham,* the tax farm was kept and managed by the state and the annual profit was divided into shares and each share was sold off. Once bought, the purchaser of a share, *sehm,* continued to receive the same annual profit share for his lifetime. Thus, what we have here is probably the first ever securitization by an Islamic state of the actual annual profit of a tax source, customs revenue.

This process of receiving the revenue for a lifetime was called *ber vech-i malikâne,* meaning, like *malikâne*. Based upon this, Yavuz Cezar has argued that the new system was inspired by the previous one. This argument should be taken with a grain of salt, because as we have seen, the European version of *esham* had been known in the West since the medieval era. Consequently, an institutional borrowing from the West is also possible. In any case, before passing judgement about the origins, it would be more appropriate to describe how the system actually functioned.

The initial steps to establish the new system appear to have been taken in 1758, when the Ottoman state decided to take over one of the most lucrative tax farms in the empire, the Tobacco Customs of Istanbul.[68] This tax farm had already been sold on a life-term basis to a group of *malikânecis*. So the state paid back to these people their original investments and evicted them. After taking over the tax farm, it was noticed that the tax farm generated an annual profit of one million *gruş*. In the year 1775, treasury officials began to discuss whether to resell the tax farm once again as a *malikâne*. Although the decision to do so was already reached, this time due to the difficult circumstances it was decided to apply a new method. This meant that the management of the tax farm would no longer be given to an entrepreneur. Instead, the tax farm was going to be managed by the state and the annual profit was going to be divided into shares and each one of these shares was going to be sold as *malikâne*, that is to say, on a life-term basis. Careful calculations had indicated that the tax farm would definitively generate at least a profit of 400 000 *gruş* annually. This figure was reached after deducting all expenses from the gross profit of one million *gruş* mentioned above. It was decided to divide this net profit figure into 160 shares. Thus each share was able to generate 2500 *gruş* net annual profit. Shares were offered for sale from April 1775 on. The price of each share, known as the *muaccele* as in the previous system, was determined to be 12 500 *gruş*. This meant that if all the shares were sold off, the treasury would receive two million *gruş*.

As a matter of fact, all the shares were sold. This was probably facilitated by the fact that the returns were guaranteed by the state[69] and the shares were divided into smaller fractions. Successful marketing of *esham* shares led to the extension of the new system. This was done by incorporating ever more tax farms into the system.

It must be noted that of the three tax-collection systems considered so far, that is, *iltizam*, *malikâne* and *esham*, the last one was the most similar to the European forms of domestic borrowing explained above. Indeed, the original *esham* shares issued together with special documents, *berats*, attached and registered to a specific person, came closest to the Flemish *lijfrenten*, annuities paid for life. But when *esham* began to be issued without the *berat*, it became a *de facto* bearers' share. This made it very similar to the Flemish *erfelijk renten*, payable in perpetuity. The transition from *esham* for the life of the investor to *esham* without *berat*, i.e., for several lives, made this instrument very popular and at the same time reduced the cost of borrowing to the state from 18–19 to 8 per cent.[70]

Looked at from the perspective of Islamic law, both types of *esham* shares, despite the returns guaranteed by the state, were not usurious. The first type, that is, those issued with *berat* and registered to a specific person (lender), were not usurious because of the uncertainty of the lifespan of this individual. Because of this uncertainty, it was not even clear if the purchaser of a share, *sehm*, would enjoy a profit or suffer a loss at the end of his lifespan. But more importantly, both types of *esham* were not usurious, because they were not structured as loans. In a usurious loan the borrower has the obligation to return the principal borrowed at a certain date together with the interest. But since the borrower (government) was not obliged to redeem *esham* shares, they were not loans.[71] Redemption of these shares was entirely at the discretion of the government. Consequently an *esham* share (*sehm*) did not constitute a loan, and according to Islamic law also, 'if there is no loan there is no usury'. This is because *riba*, usury, occurs when the creditor receives a predetermined and in the loan contract a clearly stipulated excess over and above the loan at a predetermined date.[72]

To sum up, in the field of public finance, the Ottoman state had a very significant disadvantage: throughout the sixteenth and the seventeenth centuries its cost of borrowing, compared with the European states, was huge. More precisely, with the *iltizam* system, the Ottoman state was not even borrowing but merely delegating the right to collect taxes to the private enterprise. The Ottomans took the first step towards public borrowing with the introduction of the *malikâne* system in 1695, when tax farms were delegated to the *malikâne-cis* on a lifetime basis. But true public borrowing was initiated in the year 1775 with the introduction of the *esham* system, about half a millennium later than Western Europe.

Meanwhile, able to borrow from their own public huge amounts, exceeding at times their gross national products (GNPs) by 200 per cent, at very low costs, some European states spent these funds to finance wars. In this way, domestic borrowing became a crucial component of European warfare and national survival. Post-Glorious-Revolution England, where the rule of law prevailed, was the champion of domestic borrowing during the late seventeenth and eighteenth centuries, and could defeat absolutist France time and again.[73] It cannot be an accident that first independent Holland and then the Post-Glorious-Revolution England, both expert public borrowers, were the rising stars of the seventeeth- and eighteenth-century Europe in terms of gross domestic product per capita. Absolutist France and Spain and the rest of the continental Europe, where public borrowing took place under less reliable conditions, were lagging behind.[74] These domestic borrowing trends were reflected upon external borrowing a century later. In the period 1869–70, England could borrow 24 270 000 sterling, while France only 16 600 000, Spain 6 735 000 and the Ottoman Empire 5 000 000.[75]

RIBA IN PUBLIC FINANCE

At this point a simple question comes to mind: why did the Ottomans wait for so long, until the late eighteenth century, to introduce the *esham* system? Indeed, as we have seen, *esham*-like systems were widespread and had a very long history in Europe. Therefore, Ottomans must have been aware of their existence. Introducing such systems would have reduced their borrowing costs greatly. The first point that comes to mind is the Islamic prohibition of interest. Indeed, payments of regular annuities for a lifetime, or particularly in perpetuity, appear to be usurious. But a closer look into the European *renten* would reveal that just as they were permitted by the Pope himself, they would have been permitted by Muslim jurists as well. For this point we need to look at just what constitutes *riba*, rate of interest, from the perspective of Islamic law.

First of all, *riba*, usury, is defined as a predetermined surplus over and above the loan. Moreover, the following three conditions must be jointly fulfilled for a transaction to constitute *riba:*

1. excess or surplus over and above the loan capital to be returned to the lender;
2. determination of this surplus in relation to time with a definite date of redemption;
3. stipulation of this surplus in the loan agreement.[76]

Uncertainty of the lifespan of the person, who purchases an *esham* share, that is, *sehm*, eliminates the certainty of a surplus occurring and therefore violates all three conditions. Moreover, lack of any stipulation obliging the state (borrower) to redeem the *esham* eliminates the basic characteristic of the loan and violates the first and the third conditions. We therefore conclude that *esham* were not usurious. Thus, since *esham* were not usurious, interest prohibition could not have been an impediment for the introduction of domestic borrowing to the Ottoman economy. Since a detailed study of the other possible reasons of the belated introduction of domestic borrowing to the Ottoman economy has been made elsewhere, this analysis will not be repeated here as it is not directly relevant for this book.[77]

Finally we need to say a few words about negotiability. Indeed, if *esham* is to be modernized and used as an alternative to the very popular but dubious *sukuk* in modern Islamic finance, it is essential that each share must be fully negotiable. This is because, as we have just noted, the state or a corporation, issuing *esham* shares may, but is not obliged to, redeem them. Consequently, the public would purchase these shares only if the borrower regularly paid the annuities without failure and the shares were fully negotiable. Full negotiability can be achieved only if:

1. the instrument of credit is made payable to the bearer;
2. transfer of the instrument by written endorsement to a third party is permitted without the consent or the knowledge of the original debtor, that is, the principal;
3. the bearer must have the legal right to sue the original debtor or the earlier assignees, in his own name, for full payment, and to enforce a legal claim for damages;
4. his legal claim must supersede anyone else's named in the bill.[78]

To conclude, it is to be hoped that these historical non-usurious instruments of public finance will inspire modern financial engineers to develop new instruments of public borrowing in conformity with the basic teachings of Islam. It is expected that particularly the modernized *esham* would fulfill the need felt by the rising middle classes in the Islamic world for a fixed return, yet *riba*-free instrument. Moreover, fully negotiable modern *esham* can also be used by the central banks of the Islamic world for open market operations aiming to control the money supply in the economy. In short, this *riba*-free and fixed return instrument promises to become a very important instrument of Islamic finance in the future.

NOTES

1. This transaction is referred to under several terms in modern literature: domestic borrowing, public borrowing, internal debt, etc.
2. Kardavi, *İslam Hukuku'nda Zakat,* pp. 56, 83.
3. Karaman, '*Zakat*', s. 496. Al-Kardavi has argued that non-Muslims should also be obliged to pay *zakat*. *İslam Hukuku'nda*, p. 107. But this is a minority opinion.
4. Erkal, *İslam'ın Erken Döneminde*, p. 67.
5. Karaman, '*Zakat*', p. 498.
6. Erkal, *İslam'ın Erken Döneminde*, p. 113. Obviously, the *zakat* of merchandise, which could easily be counted by officials at the customs, must always have been collected by state officials. Othman's decree refers to the merchandise kept in warehouses, the exact amount of which can be known only to the individual merchant.
7. 9: 60.
8. Whether an Islamic state can impose extra-Qur'anic taxes has been debated for a long time. Neither the Qur'an nor the *ahadith* provide any clue. Imam Malik has ruled in favour subject to the condition that the tax revenues are needed to defend the Islamic state against an attack. See Kahf, 'Taxation'.
9. Sayın, *Tekâlif Kavaidi*, p. 96.
10. Furat, *Kufe Ekolü*, pp. 226, 251.
11. 59: 7.
12. Inalcık and Quataert, *An Economic and Social History*, p. 106. This source reflects the Hanefite view. According to Imam Malik, however, since *sawad* lands were conquered by force, they became waqf property. Thus, they were made waqf land for the whole Muslim community. For more details on this, see Taher, *Islamic Culture*, p. 202. Since the territory in question, Iraq and Syria, both ended up being controlled by the Hanefite Ottomans, however, the Hanefite interpretation found application.

13. Hoffmann, 'Interdependencies Between the Military and the Economy'.
14. Demirci, 'İkta', pp. 46–7.
15. Ibid., p. 45. Also see Çizakça, *Comparative Evolution*, p. 139.
16. Morimoto, *Fiscal Administration*, p. 232.
17. Çizakça, *Comparative Evolution*, p. 138.
18. Çizakça, *Comparative Evolution*, p. 140.
19. Çizakça, 'The Economy', forthcoming. Profit rates were strictly controlled by the Ottoman state.
20. Çizakça, '*Gharar* and Risk Aversion', forthcoming.
21. Çizakça, *Comparative Evolution*, p. 146.
22. Çizakça, *Comparative Evolution*, pp. 147–8.
23. Udovitch, *Partnership and Profit*, pp. 242–3.
24. The Ottoman budget deficit of 12 million *akçe*s in 1660 exploded to 247 million *akçe*s shortly after the Vienna campaign. Çizakça, *Comparative Evolution*, p. 144.
25. Genç, 'Malikâne', p. 516.
26. This process will be explained in greater detail below.
27. That is, 10 per cent of the original auction price, the *muaccele*. Genç, 'Malikâne', p. 516.
28. Genç, ibid., p. 517.
29. Ibid., p. 517. An exception was made for the daughters of the sultan and they were permitted to continue purchasing *malikâne* shares.
30. Genc, ibid., p. 517.
31. Ibid., p. 517.
32. In the year 1692–93 the budget deficit stood at 262 217 191 *akçes*. Three years after the establishment of the *malikâne* system the deficit was reduced to 63 560 888 *akçes* despite the fact that the long war against Venice, Austrian Habsburgs, Poland and Russia was continuing unabated. In 1701–2 there was a surplus of 111 866 873 *akçes*. See Cizakca, *Comparative Evolution*, p. 144 and Genç, 'Osmanlı Maliyesinde *Malikâne* Sistemi', pp. 231–92.
33. North, 'Institutions and the Performance of Economies', p. 26.
34. Hanna, *Big Money*, p. 41.
35. Bayındır, 'Menkul Kıymetleştirme', pp. 260–61.
36. Munro, 'Medieval Origins', pp. 507, 510.
37. It has been announced in 2007 by no less an authority than Sheikh Mohamed Taqi Usmani, who heads the Accounting and Auditing Organization for Islamic Financial Institutions (AAOIFI) that currently 85 per cent of all *sukuk*s are not fully *Shariah* compliant. See *Islamic Finance News,* 18 April 2008: 7. Therefore there is an urgent need to redesign this instrument.
38. Actually, earlier and simple forms of domestic borrowing emerged in the first quarter of the seventeenth century, when the Ottoman state began to demand an increasing share of the *iltizam* auction prices in advance *prior* to the start of the collection year. The state was in fact using the future tax revenues as security for borrowing. See; Özvar, 'Fiscal Crisis'.
39. As it will be clear below, these annual payments did not constitute usury.
40. Munro, 'Medieval Origins', p. 504.
41. Munro, 'The Usury Doctrine'.
42. Munro, 'Medieval Origins', p. 523.
43. I deliberately do not use the term 'interest rate' here. This is because the rates on annuities were not usurious and therefore not identical to interest rates.
44. Macdonald, *A Free Nation,* p. 77.
45. Munro, 'Medieval Origins', pp. 514, 525.
46. Conditions of full negotiability are discussed below.
47. Munro, 'Medieval Origins', p. 537.
48. Roughly corresponding to the North-West of modern Belgium and the South-West of the Netherlands.
49. Munro, 'Medieval Origins', p. 519.
50. Martinez, 'Dette publique', p. 37.
51. Macdonald, *Free Nation*, p. 97.

52. The Japanese interbank interest rate reached zero rate of interest already in 1999. Japan was followed by several other western nations during this crisis. On July 30, 2010 the London interbank offered rate on three month dollars was fixed at 0.46563 per cent. See for details Uwe Vollmer and Ralf Bebenroth, 'Policy Reactions'.
53. Macdonald, *Free Nation*, p. 123.
54. Munro, 'Medieval Origins', p. 559.
55. Ibid., p. 559.
56. Ibid., p. 561.
57. The Genoese and the Venetian ducats were of the same weight and fineness. See Spufford, 'Coinage and Currency', p. 590. This is confirmed by Pamuk, *Osmanlı İmparatorluğu'nda Paranın Tarihi*, p. 65. Also see Prather, 'The Ducat'. The revenue of the Ottoman state for 1509, as revealed by that year's budget, stood at 1 326 144 Venetian ducats. See Özvar, 'Bütçe Harcamaları', p. 204, table 48.
58. Only as late as 1785 could the Ottoman state borrow up to half of the annual revenue of its Central Treasury at the cost of 15 to 19 per cent. But then its debts rapidly increased in response to wars. The shift from lifetime annuities to two-lifetime annuities was caused by the desperation of the state to increase its revenues in 1849, shortly before the Crimean war. Genç, 'Esham', pp. 378–9.
59. Peter Baum, 'Annuities', and Boone, *Urban Public Debts*, passim.
60. Obviously not all states managed their public debt prudently. Failure to do so led to state bankruptcies, particularly in Spain and France.
61. Çizakça, *Comparative Evolution*, p. 143. For more details on these tax farms see Çizakça, 'Tax-farming and Financial Decentralization'.
62. When these rates were exceeded, a mechanism for complaint existed. On this see Majer, *Das osmanische Registerbuch der Beschwerden*, and Faroqhi, *Coping with the State*.
63. Çizakça, *Comparative Evolution*, pp. 140–45.
64. Ibid, p. 166.
65. *Esham* is the plural of the Arabic word *sehm*, which means a share.
66. Genç, 'Esham', p. 376.
67. Ibid., p. 377.
68. Cezar, *Bunalım ve Değişim Dönemi*, s. 81.
69. The state guaranteed a minimum return per share. If the aggregate profit of a tax farm unexpectedly increased, then the state issued new *esham* shares and sold them to the public. I owe this point to Genç.
70. Çizakça, *Comparative Evolution,* p. 186; Munro, 'Usury Doctrine'; Genç, 'Esham', p. 379.
71. Genç, 'Esham', p. 377, 379. When the state failed to sell sufficient number of *esham*, after the 1800s, it began to assume the responsibility to redeem them thus rendering *esham* usurious.
72. Al-Qusi, *Riba*, p. 122.
73. North and Weingast, 'The Evolution of Institutions'. North and Weingast inform us that after the Glorious Revolution in 1688, when the rule of law was firmly and indisputably established in England, the Crown could borrow GBP17 million at 3 per cent rate of interest. This is in sharp contrast to the pre-1688 figures of at the most GBP1 million at 6–30 per cent rate of interest.
74. Pamuk, 'Batı Avrupa İle Karşılaştırmalı Çerçevede Osmanlı Devleti'nde Kişi Başına Gelir'.
75. Al, *Ondokuzuncu Yüzyılda Ülke Riski*, s. 25.
76. Al Qusi, *Riba*, p. 122.
77. For this, the reader is referred to Çizakça, 'The Economy', forthcoming.
78. Munro, 'Medieval Origins', pp. 546–55.

7. Voluntary redistribution of wealth (the waqf)

> Some regard it as a proof that moral considerations can never guide business enterprise, that the opposing pulls and pressures of God and Mammon can never be reconciled.[1] Once again the challenge is whether the walls of separation between profit motivated activities and charitable or welfare oriented activities can be demolished. If it is the same people who make profits in business as well as make charitable endowments and give away part of their wealth to the needy, can we envisage institutions that accommodate profit motive and serving social goals within the same framework? Does history offer any clue? Do we have contemporary examples?[2] (Prof. Dr Nejatullah Siddiqi)

I intend to answer the challenging questions asked by Professor Siddiqi in this and the next chapter. In this chapter I will focus on 'does history offer any clue?' and in the next one, 'do we have contemporary examples?'. Meanwhile I might add that the answer to all three questions is a resounding and definitive 'yes'!

Islamic capitalism encourages accumulation of wealth with low taxes and by imposing no upper limit on profits. But at the same time, Muslims are ordained to acquire only the legitimate, not the maximum profit. Thus, while there is no upper limit on profits, it is essential that these profits are earned through legitimate means.[3] Once wealth is accumulated with the instruments described in the previous chapters, Muslims are ordained to redistribute this wealth voluntarily. It is believed that those who redistribute their wealth voluntarily shall be rewarded in the hereafter perpetually, while those who do not shall be punished. Islamic economic history indicates that waqfs, rather than *zakat*, were the most important institutions for voluntary redistribution of wealth.[4]

Charitable foundations are known in the Islamic world as waqf or *habs*. Whereas the latter term is used primarily in North Africa and has also entered into French language, the former is known, with slight variations, in the rest of the Islamic world and has entered into English. The word waqf (pl. *awqaf*) is derived from the Arabic root verb *waqafa*, which means to cause a thing to stop and stand still. A second meaning is charitable or even philanthropic foundations.[5] For Western readers the traditional waqf can also be described as an unincorporated, non-profit trust. Although some pre-Islamic civilizations were aware of waqf-like structures, the origins of Islamic waqfs as we know them today are traced back to a *hadith*. This *hadith* is known as *Thawab ba'd al Wafah* (reward after death):

> Abu Hurairah reported Allah's messenger as saying: When a person dies, all his/her acts come to an end, but three: recurring (ongoing) charity, or knowledge from which people benefit, or a pious offspring, who prays for him/her.[6]

It has been argued that a waqf can combine all these three acts. Indeed, a waqf established as a *kulliyah*, can combine all these three.[7] At the centre of a waqf-*kulliyah* stands a mosque and whenever the faithful pray in it, the founder of the waqf is considered to have provided ongoing charity. A waqf-*kulliyah* can also provide free food for the poor, another very clear charity. In the school/university of the waqf, knowledge is produced and disseminated. The process of knowledge production in the university can be considered as a *mudaraba* (capital–labour partnership). Indeed, the waqf founder provides the livelihood of scholars, who work and produce knowledge. The *thawab* generated by scholars, in the form of knowledge from which people can benefit, is then shared between the scholars and the waqf founder, who provided for their livelihood. Like any *mudaraba*, there are risks in this arrangement as well. Loss occurs here in the form of harmful or wrong knowledge. Finally, the management of the waqf can be granted to the pious offspring, who, it is assumed, would pray for the soul of the founder. There are also other *ahadith*, which explain how a waqf should actually function.

This institution, whereby a privately owned property, *mal* or corpus, is endowed for a charitable purpose in perpetuity and the revenue generated, usufruct, is spent for this purpose, stands out as one of the great achievements of Islamic civilization. All over the vast Islamic world, from the Atlantic to the Pacific, magnificent works of architecture as well as services vitally important to the society such as education, health and many others have been organized, financed and maintained for centuries through this system. At least one eminent historian has argued that the waqf even replaced *zakat* for financing the Islamic society and that although *zakat* continued to legitimize a government's tax collection, it was no longer the material foundation for most 'specifically Islamic concerns. Private waqf foundations largely took its place in this role'.[8]

Historians have established that the Islamic waqf law was borrowed by Europeans during the crusades. An excellent example is Merton College of Oxford University, established in 1264. It is generally accepted that Merton College represents a threshold in the evolution of European colleges. The Merton foundation became a respected model in England and was imitated by the Peterhouse Foundation, Cambridge University. It has been argued that the endowment deed of Merton College was in such conformity with the Islamic waqf law that it would have been approved in the Islamic world by any learned judge.[9]

According to Abu Yusuf and Imam Muhammad, the two great Hanafi jurists, when a privately owned property is endowed and is made the corpus of a waqf, it becomes *Allah*'s property. Such a conversion of property usually takes place as a pious act in order to obtain *Allah*'s approval and to be nearer to Him. In societies where property rights are not fully respected, waqfs also provided property owners security against confiscations. For normally, in an Islamic society no revenue-seeking ruler would dare confiscate what belongs to *Allah*! Consequently, many waqfs with sound and sufficient endowments have survived for considerably longer than half a millennium and some even for more than a millennium.[10]

Notwithstanding this, the history of waqfs is a turbulent one. For centuries, the fate of this institution was closely linked to the fates of the states under which they functioned. Failing states and desperate revenue-seeking rulers had always a lust for the rich, waqf-controlled assets. This provocation could have been curbed somewhat had waqfs paid taxes to the state. But there were no uniform rules on this, while the Central Asian waqfs paid taxes to the state depending upon their fiscal status before their establishment, neither the Malikite waqfs of Muslim Spain nor the Hanafite Ottoman cash waqfs of Bursa paid any taxes. More specifically, the Malikite Andalusian waqfs paid their revenues to the *bayt al-mal* but not to the state treasury. Consequently, throughout Islamic history waqf–state relations have remained difficult. While, on the one hand, the Sultans established some of the greatest waqfs with their own property, on the other, the state often violated the property rights of waqfs, particularly if they were not legally sound. Nowhere in this long history, however, did the waqfs experience the universal and deliberate destruction that was inflicted upon them during the nineteenth and twentieth centuries, a fact which points to Western imperialism or Westernization as the culprit. Usurpation of waqf properties started under Western pressure and continued, even after Islamic countries gained independence, under the indigenous modernists.

CATEGORIES OF WAQFS

There are several categorizations of waqfs. If the revenue generated is spent entirely on charity/philanthropy, such a waqf would be known as waqf *khayri*. If the revenue is spent for the family members of the founder, this would be waqf *ahli* or *khas*. In mixed waqfs revenue would be shared between charity and family members. Since in the latter two cases, when the family of the founder becomes extinct the waqf is transformed into a waqf *khayri*, Islamic law accepts all the three types. Indeed, in view of the sharp demographic cycles caused by enemy attacks, epidemics, earthquakes and other natural disasters as well as the pre-industrial low life expectancy, it did not take long before family waqfs were transformed into *khayri* waqfs. The sharp distinction made between charitable and family foundations is a Western concept. Islamic law considered every family waqf as a potential *khayri* waqf and treated it as legitimate.

The waqf is also categorized according to duration. Hence there is a perpetual waqf and a temporary waqf. The latter is validated only by the Malikite jurists, who also allow the usufruct waqf, waqf *al-manafi* such as a waqf of a rental property for the duration of the rent agreement. All other schools consider waqfs as potentially perpetual institutions.

Yet another categorization pertains to the way the corpus is utilized. In the case of direct waqfs, the endowed property itself is directly used by the beneficiaries, such as the waqfs of mosques, books, weaponry etc. In the case of indirect waqfs, however, the corpus, usually in the form of real estate or cash, generates revenue and it is this revenue which is used for the original purpose of the waqf. The exact nature of the corpus leads to still another categorization: the real estate or cash waqfs (*awqaf al-nuqud*). When the corpus is a movable property, such waqfs are also known as the waqfs of movables.

REAL ESTATE WAQFS

Traditional real estate waqfs functioned in a simple manner. They were either endowed in urban areas, where their corpus would be in the form of residential buildings, shops, bath-houses or other rent-yielding urban property, or in rural areas in which case their corpus would be in the form of cultivable land. In the latter case, the land in question would be cultivated through share-cropping, *muzara'a*, with a certain share of the produce going to the land owning waqf and the rest to the peasant.

Frequent fires or devastating earthquakes constituted a serious danger for urban real estate waqfs. When that happened, and the corpus of the waqf was destroyed, the waqf simply failed to function. That is, deprived of its revenue, it could not continue to support the charity for which it had been endowed. The solution found was the *ijaratayn*. The word *ijaratayn* simply means double rent. In this system, in case of a disaster, the tenant pays a large lump sum, *mu'ajjal*, sufficient to restore the building, and at the same time continues to pay the waqf his regular annual rent. Due to the extraordinary circumstances, he is granted a rental agreement of the building on a long-term basis, *ijara tawilah*. Most recently, researchers have discovered that the *ijaratayn* was also used to obtain credit from the waqf system.[11]

As for the rural waqfs, the most serious problem they faced was one of legitimacy. As it is well known, *conditio sine qua non* for any waqf is that its original corpus must be privately owned. Consequently, privately owned lands could legally be made into waqf but not the state-owned lands. With some exceptions like Algeria, this principle was generally applied and therefore in most of the Ottoman realms arable land could not be turned into waqf land by their cultivators, who possessed mere usufruct rights but not complete ownership, *raqaba*, which was retained by the state. In the Algerian Tell, however, about one-third of land was privately owned and therefore could be made waqf. In most of the Ottoman Empire, 90 per cent of all arable lands were placed under the state ownership following Caliph Omar's *sunnah*, explained above. This obviously constituted a difficult problem for establishing waqfs with land as their corpus. But the same problem existed in all Islamic states and empires in varying degrees.

It has been argued that during the early Fatimid period, Muslim rulers tried time and again to confiscate the waqfs and to treat them as lands belonging to the state. This tendency reached its climax under the Ottoman ruler Mehmed II, who tried in the 1470s to 'sultanize' all arable lands including the waqfs. He recognized only orchards, vineyards and plantations as private property. The Ottoman system of land tenure was clearly based on the assumption that arable lands belonged in principle to the state.

As a result of these legal complexities, we have waves of centralizations followed by restorations of the waqfs. Indeed, until the nineteenth century, centralization policies were often followed by decentralization. What makes the nineteenth- and twentieth-century centralizations unique is the fact that they proved to be lasting. Since most of the modern states of the Islamic world did not reverse these policies during the twentieth century, waqfs all over the Islamic world remain firmly centralized and controlled by states. Overwhelmed by state control and bureaucratic impediments, waqfs in most Islamic countries have lost their previous importance and dynamism. Modernist states in the Islamic world have also not hesitated to confiscate waqf properties. The most dramatic violation of the waqf property rights, however, occurred in 1954, when all the Ottoman cash waqfs were abolished and with their confiscated capital, the Bank of Waqfs (*Vakıflar Bankası*) was established in Turkey. The long-term consequences of undermining the waqf system for the Islamic world will be dealt with below.

CASH WAQFS (THE ORIGINS)

When a waqf is established with cash capital, it is called a cash waqf. Such a waqf is managed by investing its corpus and channelling the returns to charity. The earliest origins of these waqfs are traditionally traced back to Imam Zufar's *fatwa*, who was asked a question about the permissibility of making cash endowment in the eighth century. The Ottomans began establishing cash waqfs from the fourteenth century on.[12]

The position of the Hanafi School on cash waqfs, which governed the Ottoman practice, can be summarized as follows: the whole issue can be traced back to Imam Muhammad al-Shaybani. His ruling applies and the Hanafi School declares waqfs of movables as valid subject to a generously interpreted custom. The step from here to the cash waqfs was taken by the fifteenth- and sixteenth-century Ottoman jurists, foremost among them Ebussuud, who served as the *Şeyhülislam,* the highest religious office of the empire. Ebussuud argued that Imams Abu Yusuf and especially Muhammad support the waqf of movables subject to custom. Cash is a kind of movable and therefore can be justified, along with other movables, on the basis of already established custom, as the corpus of a waqf. Finally, it was acknowledged that the cash corpus should preferably be invested through *mudaraba*, as suggested by Imam Zufar.[13]

In Istanbul, of the 2517 waqfs established in the period 1456–1551, 1161 (46 per cent) were cash waqfs, and in the smaller city of Bursa, there were 761 cash waqfs during the eighteenth century.[14] Cash waqfs' popularity inevitably led to a controversy, which has been already well documented and therefore will only be briefly summarized here.[15]

One of the basic arguments of those who opposed the cash waqfs was based on a seemingly powerful point: once endowed, the capital of a waqf belongs to God. But while investing this capital, whether in the form of a *mudaraba* or simple loaning, the cash endowed is inevitably distributed to the borrowers or entrepreneurs. But what belongs to God, the opposition argued, cannot be distributed to third persons.[16]

It should be noted, however, that only the right to utilize the waqf capital, the usufruct, was distributed to the borrowers, not the ownership. The ownership was protected by hefty collateral, usually in the form of the borrower's house. This Ottoman arrangement was known as *istiglal*.[17] How a typical Ottoman cash waqf practising *istiglal* functioned can be summarized as follows: a wealthy person (founder) goes to the court and declares his intention to establish a cash waqf. Once permitted, he makes cash endowment and then the cash waqf is established.

The essence of an Ottoman cash waqf was to invest the capital endowed (corpus) and to channel the returns thus generated to charity. Investment occurred in the form of sale/lease back and resale. *Istiglal* was designed such that the borrower (B1) first sold his house to the waqf and obtained in return the capital he needed. The borrower[18] usually kept this capital in his possession for a year. Meanwhile, he asked the waqf for permission to stay on in his house. This permission was granted on the condition that the borrower becomes a tenant and pays rent for as long as he kept the capital in his possession. When the borrower returned the capital he had borrowed and repurchased the leased asset, usually after a year, the deed of his house was returned back to him.[19]

For the waqf, the borrower's house had two functions: it served both as collateral and a source of rent income during the period, when its capital was loaned out. The borrower, on the other hand, was able to raise cash by utilizing his real estate. In this way, a passive asset (real estate) was transformed into cash.

The rents paid by all the tenants/borrowers were pooled and this pool constituted the total annual profit of the cash waqf. After the management expenses were deducted from the total rent, the remainder was then channelled to the charity declared in the endowment deed. Some waqfs were prudent enough to allocate part of their total rent income for enhancing their original capital, corpus. The bulk of the waqfs that enjoyed longevity, i.e., survived for more than a century, were those that enhanced their original corpus. Finally, it has been observed that waqfs contributed to each other.

The cash waqf controversy lasted from 1545 to 1586, when finally a consensus could be reached.[20] Based upon this consensus, cash waqfs were definitively legalized by the order of the reigning sultan, Murat III. Such a sultanic order was necessary, because even the *fatwa* of the *Şeyhülislam* was not binding on the judges of the empire: only a decree from the sultan could have that effect.[21] It is noteworthy that the consensus could be reached only after the death of Çivizade, one of the main opponents of cash waqfs.[22] The rate of return of the capital invested by cash waqfs was also determined by the *fatwa* of Ebussuud. This rate was 15 per cent and was approved by the sultan. Those trustees who demanded higher returns were to be punished by long prison sentences.[23] It should be noted, however, that the period 1545–86 was marked by high inflation. Thus the 15 per cent permitted rate of return must have simply aimed at protecting cash waqfs' capital. Indeed, the Istanbul price index based upon food prices had increased 53 per cent from 1547 to 1586.[24] Thus, even the permitted 15 per cent rate of return appears to have failed to protect endowed capital of cash waqfs.

At this point the following question becomes inevitable: how come, despite the fierce debate among the jurists, these waqfs were tolerated by the Ottomans? There is a simple answer to this question: due to the enormously important role they played for Islam. Indeed, Islam spread to South-East Europe, an ocean of Christianity, thanks to these waqfs, which financed and maintained all the pertinent institutions.

As for the Shafi'ite school, the stance taken by this school on the waqf of movables is based upon the ruling by Imam Shafi'i that the waqf of anything is valid from which profit can be derived while its original endures. Imam Shafi'i, like Abu Yusuf and Muhammad, ultimately approves of the waqf of movables subject to custom. Moreover, on the issue of custom he is almost as flexible as Muhammad al-Shaybani, for he has introduced the concept of *istishab*. *Istishab* pertains to the existence of a thing established by evidence. Thus, a practice once proved to be widespread may be presumed to be both ancient and continuing. The relevance of *istishab* for cash waqfs is that their ancient and probable existence during Imam Zufer's time, and their widespread and definitive existence in Ottoman lands between the fifteenth and twentieth centuries, render them valid for the Shafi'ites today.

Imam Shafi'i's ruling that endowment of any moveable is valid subject to the preservation and non-consummation of the corpus, has been accepted by the Malikites as well. Furthermore, it is well known that Imam Malik had approved the waqfs of horses and arms (movables) based on tradition. Two *fatwas* stated in the *Mudawwana* are even more directly related to the question of cash waqfs. Two cases have been put to Malik, the first concerns a cash waqf and the second, a simple donation. Malik has ruled that the annual return generated by the cash waqf should be subject to the payment of *zakat* while he has exempted simple donation from this obligation. The fact that he has not objected to the cash waqf itself, but has merely specified its relation to the *zakat*, that is, his silence, indicates that he has approved of this specific type of waqf. Moreover, the Malikite position as explained by the fourteenth-century jurist Khalil that 'there is effectively no transfer of property right if the property returns to the donor's possession during the year, whether as rent, passive possession, the donor's clandestine return to the property or even his presence there as a guest'[25] actually solved a major problem of the Hanefite cash waqfs. This was the problem of transferring the endowed cash (*Allah*'s property) to a third person. Hanefite Ottoman cash waqfs avoided this problem by lending their cash for only a year and thus solved their problem through the Malikite permission.

Imam Ahmad ibn Hanbal also accepted the Shafi'i condition that the endowment of any movable is valid providing that the corpus of the waqf is not consumed and preserved.

THE BIRTH OF THE WAQF OF STOCKS

As already explained, the history of waqfs is dominated by waves of centralizations to be followed by decentralizations: A process of centralization to be followed by confiscations initiated by a powerful, revenue-hungry ruler was often followed by a policy of rehabilitation introduced by a weaker ruler, who needed the support of the waqf sector. During the nineteenth and the twentieth centuries these cycles came to an end and waqfs all over the Islamic world remain firmly centralized and controlled by the state.

A silver lining on the since long-accumulating clouds over the waqf system appeared at the beginning of the twentieth century. This was the *fatwa* obtained by an Indian Muslim jurist, Suhrawardy, on the validity of the waqf of stocks. Suhrawardy asked the help of the Ottoman Field-Marshall Ghazi Muhtar Pasha, former governor of Egypt, for a *fatwa* from the *Mufti* of Egypt. Hasan Fehmi Bey, Secretary to Ghazi Muhtar Pasha, asked the following to the *Mufti*:

> What is your opinion concerning the following case? An Indian of the Hanafite sect makes a waqf of government securities, stocks and bonds known amongst Europeans as *rente* or of shares in trading companies, the practice of which has been recognised in our time in certain countries. Will such a waqf be valid and permissible in India if it is recognised in Turkey for instance …?[26]

Answer (Written on 9 Muharrem 1326 A.H. (1908), *fatwa* no. 167):

> Now, as to shares in trading companies, their waqf is of the nature of waqf of *musha'*. Now that you know that the waqf of movables is valid according to Muhammad you should have also regard for the conditions laid down by him, e.g., that they should be divided (not *musha*), when they are capable of division, and that they should be delivered to a *mutawalli* even though they do not satisfy the condition of perpetuity, '*ta'bid*'. Finally you should know that the language of the jurists here show some leaning towards taking special recognised practice, *'urf khass*, into consideration. This is one of the views of the school and it is a proper view, since the language of the dedicators is based on their special practice, *'urf* ….

Thus, the *Mufti* of Egypt hesitated only on the question of whether the practice in Turkey can be taken as binding for all Muslims. But his final words, 'you should know that … jurists here show some leaning towards taking special recognised practice, '*urf khass*, into consideration', make clear that custom in one Muslim country would be respected by the others.

It is also quite interesting that the suitability of the European '*rente*' was asked to the *Mufti*. This leads us to conclude that not only was the medieval European Permanently Funded Public Debt alive and well at the beginning of the twentieth century, but that it was used by Muslims as an instrument of waqf capital. Since the *Mufti* did not object to the usage of this instrument, we can deduce that he was fully aware that these Western instruments were not usurious.

To be on absolutely safe ground, Suhrawardy requested Hasan Fehmi Bey ask the *Mufti* of Alexandria the same question as well.

Answer by Muhammad Bakhit al-Muti'i, the Hanafi jurist of the University Mosque of al-Azhar, Mufti of Alexandria:

> These shares etc., are all included under the term movables and the pertinent rule is as follows: 'the waqf of movables as accessories to land is valid without any difference of opinion between Abu Yusuf and Muhammad. If the waqf of such movables be made independently (not as accessories to land) then Abu Yusuf rejects it, but Muhammad accepts subject to custom, *ta'amul*. This opinion has been adopted by the majority of jurists of various countries as stated in the *Hidayah*, the *Is'af*, and in the *Zahiriyya*. Moreover, it has been stated in the *Mujtaba* on the authority of the *Siyar* that according to Muhammad it is valid to make a waqf of movables unrestrictedly and according to Abu Yusuf only when there is *ta'amul*. Therefore, when a practice has arisen as to making a waqf of these securities and shares, their waqf is valid, especially as they are of the nature of coins, dirhams and dinars. Now we find in the *Manh*: as a practice has arisen in our days in Turkey and other countries of making waqf of dirhams and dinars, they come under the dictum of Muhammad in accordance with which is the fatwa as regards movables in which there is *ta'amul*... Since the *ta'amul* of the Muslims as regards to these things is based on the rule of recognised practice *urf*, whereby analogy is disregarded on account of the saying of the Prophet, 'Whatever is good in the sight of Muslims is good in the sight of Allah' as reported by Ahmad. That is why it is laid down in the *Mabsut*, 'What is established by usage, *'urf*, is like what is established by express text'. And God knows best.
>
> (Signed) Muhammad Bakhit al-Muti'i

Two points attract our attention in this *fatwa*: first, Bakhit al-Muti'i was aware of Imam Muhammad's permission regarding the waqf of movables whether there is established custom or not, hence his statement, 'according to Muhammad it is valid to make a waqf of movables *unrestrictedly*'; and second, based upon *Mabsut* by al-Sarakhsi, one of the most respected sources in Islamic jurisprudence, he gives custom an eminence approaching that of the Qur'an and the *sunnah*.

The Shi'ite position regarding the waqf of stocks is revealed by a *fatwa* given by Sheikh 'Abd Allah al-Mazandarani, the Celebrated *Mujtahid* of Karbala in 1907. Question:

> What does the great *Hujjat al-Islam* and the refuge of mankind, may his shadow extend, say in connection with the religious point in law that, if several persons form a joint-stock company and purchase a property at a fixed price and divide it into a number of shares of equal value, for instance some purchase 10 shares and some 20 shares and so on, each having a different number of shares, so that the annual profit may be divided proportionately amongst the share holders according to the number of shares they hold. To explain this point more clearly: hundred men purchased a bazaar, the total value of which is divided into 1000 shares, of 100 rupees each, so that each share holder may receive the annual profit in proportion to the number of shares he holds. For instance Zayd has got ten ... shares. Whether Zayd can make a waqf of his own shares, so that the principal may remain as it is and the income may be spent for a specific purpose. Whether such a waqf, according to the Shi'ah Law is valid or not? It is hoped that your holiness may write your opinion on this

point based upon the trustworthy writings of the learned predecessors and endorse it with your seal.

Answer:

In the name of God the Most High. The Shi'ahs in general and the majority of the Sunnis belonging to the four schools and others (with the exception of a few ordinary men whose views on the subject are out of the way) hold that *Musha'* waqf is valid. Numerous authentic traditions from the imams, peace be on them, have been handed down respecting *Musha'* charity, *sadaqah*, which clearly lay down that *by sadaqah is meant either* waqf *itself or that* waqf *is the most obvious kind of it*. Therefore, *the validity of such a* waqf *on account of its being owned by a joint-stock company cannot be questioned* [italics are mine]. And as possession is the condition for validity of a waqf, therefore the donor must hand over the property either to him for whose benefit the waqf is made, or to the *mutawalli*, exactly in the same way as he would have done to a purchaser to whom he had sold his share. In the case of waqf he must give possession to the *mutawalli*. If he constitutes himself the *mutawalli*, he must act according to the deed of waqf and must consider his possession as that of a *mutawalli* and not that of an owner. If he has made a waqf of *Musha'* property and given possession, the waqf is valid and binding. If he has not given possession, he may revoke the waqf during his lifetime. If the dedicator dies before giving possession, the waqf is null and void.

God is the all knowing.

11 Shaban, 1325 A.H.

Seal of the Mujtahid

I certify the seal marked A on the margin of this paper to be that of Sheikh Abdullah Mazandarani, the celebrated Mujtahid of Najaf, who made the same in my presence this 28th day of September 1907.

Signed. M.H.M... British Vice-Consul

Karbala, 28th Sept., 1907[27]

The importance of this *fatwa* cannot be emphasized enough, for not only does it confirm the validity of the waqf of stocks for the Shi'ites as well, but it also informs us about what must have been an unusual way of establishing such waqfs in the year 1907, that is, through joint-stock company shares. First, the reader may be surprised by the idea of using joint-stock company shares as the corpus of a waqf. After all, joint-stock companies are known to be a Western invention.[28] Consequently, we face the problem of establishing a waqf with essentially a Western financial instrument.

It is quite clear from the text of the *fatwa* that this did not bother the *Hujjat al-Islam*. For, like the *Mufti* of Egypt, he probably considered a joint stock company similar to a *musha'* waqf. *Musha'* is the term used for properties that have not been divided among the various owners. A joint-stock company would indeed be considered as a *musha'* on the grounds that although its physical capital would be undivided, hence *musha'*, its cash capital can be clearly divided into shares. Endowment of a property owned jointly by numerous individuals has constituted a lively debate among the jurists. The crux of the problem boils down to the *conditio sine qua non* of any waqf that only a privately owned property can be endowed. The problem of the jointly held property is that its true magnitude and boundaries are not known. Consequently, most jurists agree that before being endowed, the property must be divided among the owners and each owner's share clearly defined. Endowment of a share is permitted only after this process.[29] This is the reason why the *Hujjat al-Islam* insisted that the founder:

> Must hand over the property either to him for whose benefit that waqf is made, or to the *mutawalli*, exactly in the same way as he would have done to a purchaser to whom he had sold his share.

Actually, the *Hujjat al-Islam* could have solved the problem from another perspective as well. He could have considered a joint-stock company as a synthesis of *inan* and *mudaraba,* which would have also led to an approval.[30]

It should be added that the waqf of movables was permitted by the Article 61 of the prerevolutionary Iranian *Civil Code*,[31] while the Islamic Republic has permitted waqfs whose capital, corpus, is constituted of cash and stocks (Cabinet Decree no. 95270, dated 17 May 1986, Article no. 44).

Finally, waqfs are considered to have judicial personality. Indeed, Islamic law treats them as if they were human. Consequently, they are allowed to sell, purchase, be a debtor and a creditor, sue and be sued. They have all the characteristics of a judicial person.[32]

Thus, remarkably, the approval of the waqf of stocks has occurred quite early, at the very beginning of the twentieth century. From an evolutionary perspective, this was a decisive moment in the history of waqfs. Why this is so will become clear in the next chapter.

FROM WAQFS TO UNIT TRUSTS

Unit trusts are a form of collective investment that allows investors with similar investment objectives to pool their funds to be invested in a portfolio of securities. During the eighteenth century trusts merged with joint-stock companies and helped save Europe, particularly England, from one of the most destructive financial crises of history – the South Sea Bubble. This merger of trusts with joint-stock companies resulted with the birth of unit trust funds. All of this is relevant for this book on Islamic finance for two reasons: first, the English unit trust funds have evolved from two distinct business forms, the company and the trust. Both of these business forms have their origins in the world of Islam, where the former is known as *Shirkat* and the latter as waqf. Consequently, the resulting European merger in the aftermath of the South Sea Bubble crisis in the 1720s and the emergence of the unit trust fund is highly relevant for Islamic finance. Moreover, this is not a mere theoretical suggestion. For Islamic unit trust funds have recently started to flourish in the Gulf and Malaysia, indicating a borrowing back of an originally Islamic institution from the West. Thus, this section will explain the historical roots of this important phenomenon and aims to give a better perception of what the modern unit trust is. The modern Islamic unit trust and how it functions will be explained at the end of the next chapter.

Thanks to Monica Gaudiosi's pioneering work, it is now generally established that the Islamic waqf constituted the origin of the Western trust.[33] It is also probable that the European company may have, at least partially, evolved from the classical Islamic partnerships as well.[34] With these common origins, it is therefore not surprising that the trust and the company closely interweaved in history. In fact, investment companies in England and Scotland are still called 'investment trusts'.[35] Another reason why we should not be surprised by the close encounters between the two forms is that they both segregate investors from managers. This is a necessary characteristic of any collective investment vehicle. That the company does this well is obvious. Less obvious is the fact that the trust also fulfils this need. It will be remembered that the traditional Islamic waqf is established by entrusting the corpus of the waqf earned by an individual to a *mutawalli* or a trustee. The waqf or the trust thus segregates investors from managers by the reason of its ability to segregate the title and management of the corpus from its beneficial enjoyment.

While at many points in European history the trust and the joint-stock company competed for popularity among investors, there were also many instances where they complemented and aided the development of the other. At the early stage of the development of a company in England, when the concept of judicial personality was restricted by the state, it was the trust which enabled the company to hold properties. This occurred when the so-called deed of settlement company was used to overcome the objection by the English state to the corporate form.[36]

The joint-stock company emerged when the so-called regulated company, which was a loose association of merchants, also known as a merchant guild, began to utilize the partnership techniques borrowed from the Muslims.

Originally, each member of a regulated company traded on his own account and the liability of each was separate from the company. A charter was usually obtained from the state in order to gain monopoly privileges for trade conducted overseas.

When partnership techniques came to be utilized in similar fashion to the Islamic multiple *mudaraba* by a regulated company, or a guild of merchants, the guild became a joint enterprise of all members. Transformation of a loosely knit guild of merchants into a joint-stock enterprise of all members was a necessary step in view of the great risks of transoceanic trade.[37] But the line between corporate and unincorporated societies continued to be blurred at this period. Nor was there any distinction drawn between the status of a joint-stock company and a partnership. Shares could be transferred without regard to whether the company was incorporated or not. The shares of the English East India Company, for instance, were widely traded by way of auction in the same way as the East India commodities.[38]

In short, there was an extreme gap between commercial practice and legal theory. Much like the Islamic finance today, in the heyday of English finance also, merchants and capitalists were looking forward and inventing one new financial instrument after the other, while the law was following these dynamic developments with a substantial gap.

The next important step in the evolution of unit trusts occurred when the share market collapsed after the South Sea Bubble burst in 1720. Litigation followed. Since it had been difficult to obtain the permission to incorporate joint-stock companies, neither entity nor owner shielding could be provided and all the assets of all partners were in danger.[39] Moreover, the Bubble Act passed in 1720 had prohibited the establishment of a corporation without a charter granted by the state. This meant a *de facto* prohibition imposed on unincorporated companies.

It was at this point in time that trust (waqf) came to the rescue of investors. When the court was asked to determine the rights of members of the company, it resorted to the concept of trust, which was well known in England ever since the thirteenth century. The advantage of the trust was its ability to resolve issues involving property rights. The courts began to regard companies, even though unincorporated, to be the trustee of the members of the company. The status of directors of the company was held to be that of the trustees.[40]

These developments led businessmen to the use of trust to achieve the corporate objective. The result was the emergence of the deed of settlement company as a new business vehicle. The deed of settlement company was simply a use of the trust to establish joint-stock corporations without having to appeal to the King or Parliament – a very expensive and time-consuming affair without a guaranteed result.[41] The deed of settlement company represented a successful merger of the ancient trust and the joint-stock corporation. Thus, despite the restrictive Bubble Act, the incorporated joint-stock company as it had existed before the Act had been successfully revived. A deed of settlement usually appointed directors and managers of the company, defined the number of shares, the method of transfer, the mode of calling of general meetings of investors and their rights at such meetings. Later on, provisions were also introduced that held each shareholder to be liable only to the extent of his shares, or investment. As it will be remembered, this is one of the most important characteristics of an Islamic *mudaraba* or *Inan*.

The importance of trust in all this lies in the fact that the common law had laid down that an unincorporated group could not own property as a group. Without properties, however, a company would be severely restricted. The problem was solved by treating the company as a trust and its directors as trustees. Indeed, the relevant provision stated that 'the trustee shall stand possessed of the properties in trust for the company and shall apply and dispose of the same in such manner for the benefit of the company as the board of directors shall from time to time direct'.[42] In similar fashion to the traditional waqf or trust, trustees could not take decisions. In waqf or trust, decision making power was vested in the original founder and trustees were merely there to implement his decisions stated in the deed of trust. In deed of settlement company also, trustees were passive and decisions were made by directors.[43] In trust (waqf) as well as in deed of settlement company, the main function of the trustees was to keep the property in trust. What to do with this property was clearly stated by the founder in trust (waqf) or by directors in deed of settlement company.

To sum up, the trust as a part of the deed of settlement played an important role in avoiding the severely restrictive Bubble Act. It sustained the continued growth of the company form for a century until the Act was repealed in 1825, which would otherwise have been severely suppressed. Company disputes during this difficult post-crisis period were largely resolved by judges by resort to trust concepts. What the trust ultimately supported was the joint-stock concept formed before the Bubble Act. The deed of settlement company was thus an offspring of the joint-stock company and the trust (waqf). It has been considered as the most important development in the history of both company law and trust principles.[44]

The deed of settlement company evolved during the twentieth century into the American mutual funds and the British unit trust. Both emerged shortly after the 1929 crash. It has been claimed that the first unit trust was launched in the UK in 1931 by M&G. A derivative of this form was the so-called fixed trust, with a fixed portfolio for a fixed lifespan. The first example of this form was the First British Fixed Trust, which held the shares of 24 leading companies in a fixed portfolio that was not changed for 20 years. By 1939 there were around 100 trusts in the UK, managing funds in the region of GBP80 million.[45] In 2009, it estimated that there are more than 79,000 unit trust funds in the world.[46]

Another interesting recent development can be observed in Britain. This is the emergence of some British law firms to establish waqf-like structures in order to attract Arab capital.[47] Aware of the similarities between the classical Islamic waqf and the British trusts or foundations, these companies are trying to persuade high net worth Arabs to establish their waqfs in Britain according to the British trust or foundation law. The heavy irony of all this is that those who used to be the arch enemies of waqfs in their colonies have now changed their minds.[48] They have modernized their trusts and foundations and are now asking the Muslims to establish their waqfs with them.[49] Unless the now independent Muslim states reform and reintroduce their waqf laws, high net worth Muslims will certainly be lured to places like Jersey. When this happens, waqf will become just another instrument for recycling petro-dollars. The basic points of how the classical waqf system has been improved in some Muslim countries and how these reforms may spread to the rest of the Islamic world will be explained in the next chapter.

NOTES

1. Kuran, *Islam and Mammon*.
2. Siddiqi, 'Islamic Banking and Finance', vol. 13, No. 2, p. 23.
3. Hasan, 'Theory of Profit', p. 8.
4. Hodgson, *The Venture of Islam*, vol. II, p. 124.
5. Whereas historians generally do not distinguish between charity and philanthropy, sociologists refer to charity for local and ephemeral social responsibility and to philanthropy for long-lasting, definitive and even global efforts to eradicate human problems.
6. Muslim, *Sahih Muslim, bab 3, hadith* 14.
7. The word *kulliyah* means universal, general or complete. When used in the context of a waqf, it means a self-sufficient and perpetual entity that provides vital social services, primarily education, research and health financed by the revenue generated by the other units of the waqf.
8. Hodgson, *The Venture of Islam*, vol. II, p. 124.
9. Gaudiosi, 'Islamic Law of Waqf', pp. 1231–61.
10. Crecelius, 'Introduction'.
11. Kaya, 'Kredi Kaynaği', passim.
12. Döndüren, *Vakıf Meseleleri*, p. 95.
13. Çizakça, *Philanthropic Foundations*, pp. 37–38.
14. Barkan and Ayverdi, *Istanbul Vakıfları Tahrir Defteri*, p. XXX and M. Çizakça, *Comparative Evolution*, p. 132.
15. Mandaville, 'Usurious Piety', pp. 289–308.
16. Mandaville, 'Usurious Piety', p. 305.
17. Fast forward five centuries: recently the *Jeddah Fikh Academy* rejected *istiglal*. Yet the Accounting and Auditing Organization for Islamic Financial Institutions (AAOIFI) permitted the most important transaction of *istiglal* during its meeting on 15 January 2007 in Bahrain. The exact wording of the AAOIFI permission (item 5) is as follows: 'It is permissible for a lessee in a *sukuk al-ijarah* to undertake to purchase the leased assets when the *sukuk* are extinguished for its nominal value.'
18. The maximum number of borrowers observed in the Bursa Ottoman court registers was 20. See Çizakça, 'Cash *Waqfs* of Bursa'.

19. An interesting case of an Ottoman cash waqf is given by Güler. This was the cash waqf established by Amber Aga bin Abdullah, a palace official, who endowed one-third of his property (320 000 *akçes*). The income generated by the investment of the capital was to be sent annually with the *surre* to Madinah and daily 2 *akçes* were to be paid to the *Naib-i Harem* to oversee the recitation of the Qur'an by 15 readers each of whom was to be paid 2 *akçes* per day. They were to recite a *juz* a day of the Qur'an. In the year 1666, 23,447 sikke floris were distributed to 1102 people to recite the Qur'an in Mekka and Madinah. For details, see Güler, *Haremeyn Vakıfları*, pp. 131–2.
20. Main points of the opposition led by Imam Birgevi were the following: (1) cash waqfs impede the application of the law of inheritance; (2) if the founder changed his mind and wanted to revoke his waqfs, he would not be permitted; (3) the endowed cash is invested through *bay al-ainah*, which has been considered as *makruh* by the Prophet. See Döndüren, *Günümüzde Vakıf Meseleleri*, 1998, p. 94. Probably, in response to these objections, Ottoman cash waqfs began to apply the sale/lease-back/resale method described above. This has been approved not only in 1586 by an Ottoman *ijtihad* but also most recently by the AAOIFI in 2007. The AAOIFI decision of course refers to the *sukuk al-ijarah*, which also employs the sale/lease-back/resale method. Hence the similarity between the Ottoman cash waqfs and the *sukuk al-ijarah*.
21. Mandaville, 'Usurious Piety', p. 298.
22. Demir, *Osmanlı Hukuku'ndaki Yeri*, p. 164.
23. Ibid., p.173.
24. Pamuk, *500 Years of Prices and Wages*, Table 2.1, p. 48.
25. Shatzmiller, *Women's Property Rights*, p. 57.
26. Suhrawardy, 'The Waqf of Movables', p. 371.
27. Çizakça, *Philanthropic Foundations*, pp. 40–41. The fact that the *Mujtahid* used the office of the British Vice-Consul as a notary public, rather than the traditional Islamic court, in itself, is interesting.
28. The first Ottoman joint-stock company was the *Şirket-i Hayriyye*, established on 17 January 1851. This was a shipping company operating along the Bosphorus. For details, see Aslantepe, *Nostalgia for Ottoman Bonds and Shares*.
29. For conflicting positions of the Malikite and Hanafite schools (particularly Abu Yusuf), see Akgündüz, *Vakıf Müessesesi*, 1988: 134–5.
30. Sanusi, 'The Concept of Legal Entity', pp. lxv–lxxv.
31. Lambton, *Landlord and Peasant in Persia*, p. 231.
32. Sanusi, 'The Concept of Legal Entity'.
33. Gaudiosi, 'The Influence', passim. See also Çizakça, *Philanthropic Foundations*, pp. 8–15.
34. Udovitch, 'At the Origins' and Çizakça, *Comparative Evolution*, ch. 2.
35. Sin, *The Legal Nature*, p. 7.
36. Ibid., p. 7.
37. Why this particular evolution did not take place in the Islamic world has been recently explained. See Çizakça, 'Was *Shari'ah* Indeed the Culprit?'. A derivative of this idea led to the establishment of the Bank of England in 1694 for the purpose of lending to the government the capital subscribed by members. Members were in effect making investments, the return for which was the interest promised by the state. It was the same idea that formed the basis of the South Sea Company.
38. Sin, *The Legal Nature*, p. 11.
39. Such permissions were granted usually by the Parliament or by the King and were difficult to obtain. A great advantage of the corporation is that it provides both 'owner shielding', limited liability for members, and 'entity shielding', limited liability for the company itself. In the former, the personal assets of an individual partner are protected from the creditors of other partners and in the latter those of the corporation. For more details on this, see Hansmann, 'Law and the Rise of the Firm', pp. 1337–43.
40. Sin, *The Legal Nature*, p. 12.
41. Ibid., p. 13.
42. Ibid., p. 15.
43. Trustees began to have broad investment powers in later periods. Ibid., p. 20.

44. Ibid., p. 18.
45. www.wikipedia.org/wiki/unit_trust.
46. *Islamic Finance News*, 23 October 2009, p. 16.
47. Anderson, 'Waqf and Jersey Foundation'.
48. On the details of how this change occurred, see Çizakça, Demokrasi Arayışında, p. 180.
49. For full details about the Anglo-French hostility towards the waqfs, see Çizakça, *Philanthropic Foundations*.

Part IV

Islamic capitalism and finance today

8. Waqfs of stocks

In some Muslim countries considerable advances in modernizing the classical waqfs have been achieved. It is important that these achievements are fully explained so as to facilitate their dissemination all over the Islamic world. There is no doubt that, just as observed throughout European history, first identifying the best practice and then borrowing it, if necessary, with further improvements, constitutes a crucial element of economic development.[1]

THE *MODUS OPERANDI*

The Islamic world borrowed the concept of joint-stock corporations from the West during the nineteenth century, and this led to a synthesis of this Western invention and the traditional cash waqfs. The outcome of this synthesis, approved in the early twentieth century, is the waqf of stocks. Full details of this approval were presented in the previous chapter. The *modus operandi* of these waqfs can be summarized as follows. A waqf of stocks is established when a wealthy individual endows his shares for a charity. These shares belong to a multitude of incorporated joint-stock companies so as to form a portfolio and diversify risks. When these shares are endowed in the form of a waqf, the latter becomes a recipient of the profits generated by the companies. The exact amount of profits (or losses) to be distributed to the waqf depends on the number of shares endowed. It is generally expected that the losses that are made by some of the companies are compensated by the profits of the others. In any case, since the companies are managed professionally, a loss-making manager cannot stay on and would be replaced by another. Thus, under normal circumstances, the waqf of stocks would regularly and continuously receive dividends from the companies whose shares it possesses.

The waqf spends a small part of this revenue on administrative expenses and, possibly, on property investment. But more importantly, the waqf creates an emergency fund with the purpose of utilizing it in case one of the firms whose shares it possesses enhances its capital. If this is the case, the waqf resorts to the emergency fund and participates in the capital enhancement process so as to keep its shares at a constant ratio to the total number of shares of the firm in question. The bulk of the annual dividends, however, are spent for the charity for which the endowment had been made in the first place.

As a result of this East–West synthesis, the traditional Ottoman cash waqfs have been radically transformed and improved. Ironically, this happened not in the pious Ottoman Caliphate but in the fiercely secular Turkish republic. What the Turkish waqfs have achieved can be summarized as follows.

First, Imam Zufer's ruling that the corpus of a cash waqf should be invested through *mudaraba*, a condition which could not be applied in the past, became a reality. This is because *mudaraba* is practically identical to equity investment.

Second, when the corpus of a waqf is formed with corporate shares, the waqf of stocks enjoys the dividends and is no more obliged to lend its corpus as credit. Put differently, unlike the old waqfs, the new waqf is not obliged to invest its corpus to generate revenue but becomes a passive recipient of the profits generated by the associated companies. Consequently, the problem of *riba* completely disappears. This is because, once again, unlike the old waqfs, the waqf of stocks earns its revenue not by lending its capital through the dubious *istiglal*, but by the profits generated by the firms whose stocks it owns. The nature of profit has also changed. When profits are based not on quasi-credit-*riba* transactions, as was the case with traditional cash waqfs, but on actual production of the partner firms, *riba* is completely eliminated and the profits become similar to *mudaraba* profits.

Third, the information asymmetry problem is also solved. Once the endowment is invested in some joint-stock companies by purchasing their shares, the responsibility of investing this capital is transferred from the waqf trustees to the managers of these companies. The waqf freed from this responsibility starts free-riding on the investment decisions of the professional managers. In this way, the waqf begins to benefit from the dynamism of the companies it partially owns and can respond to the challenges and opportunities of the times. It is no longer governed by the decisions of founders taken centuries ago.[2] The will of the founder, however, still prevails in that the trustees of the waqf of stocks obey his directives in *spending* the revenue of the waqf. Put differently, the waqf of stocks is governed not by the investment but by the charity decisions of the long-deceased founder.

A waqf of stocks is not entirely risk free: the companies whose stocks it possesses may fail. The waqf, however, can diversify/minimize such risks by carefully forming a portfolio of various partner company stocks. In such a portfolio it is expected that losses will be compensated by profits.[3]

Fourth, waqfs of stocks permit multiple endowments to be pooled. Latest research has shown that the new Turkish waqfs of stocks have, on average, 35 founders.[4] This is not to say that endowment pooling is a speciality of the modern waqf of stocks. Under specific conditions of good governance a whole population may be persuaded to create endowments and to pool them in one major foundation. This was the case in eighteenth-century Ottoman Algeria, where traditional real-estate waqfs were pooled.[5] Nor is endowment pooling specific to the Islamic world. Indeed, the Chinese *Shantang*, 'charity halls', can be traced back to the 1590s and were formed by a multitude of persons often belonging to the same lineage and contributing regularly cash towards charity.[6] But the most striking example of endowment pooling has just occurred in the USA, where Warren Buffet has donated US$37 billion to the Bill and Melinda Gates Foundation. This may well be the biggest ever endowment pooling in the history of global philanthropy and Mr Buffet's donation exceeds even the US$31 billion that Mr Gates himself had originally donated to his own foundation.

The *modus operandi* of a multiple founder waqf can be summarized as follows. A multitude of founders pool their capital (in Turkey in order to accumulate at least half a million US$). They then entrust this capital to a waqf. The trustee/*mutawalli* of this waqf is responsible for generating revenue. This is usually done by selling services such as health or education in the form of private hospitals or schools/universities. After deducting the expenses, the profit generated is ploughed back to enhance the original capital. Obviously, a part of the services are provided to the needy as charity. These waqfs try to find a reasonable balance between their for-profit and not-for-profit activities.

It is probably in response to these advantages that ever since the early twentieth century the waqfs of stocks have been approved in Iran, Egypt, Lebanon, India, Pakistan, Bangladesh and, of course, Turkey. Malaysia seemed to be getting ready to jump into this bandwagon belatedly when the *Fatwa Committee of the National Council for the Religion of Islam* confirmed the legality of cash waqfs at its 77th meeting on 10–12 April 2007.[7]

Successful examples of waqf of stocks have already emerged. Based upon the Waqf Law of 1967, some powerful waqfs have been established in Turkey with shares of joint-stock corporations. These waqfs of stocks organize and finance some of the top universities and hospitals in the country. Of these, the Koç Foundation, established by the late Vehbi Koç, had a market value of more than one billion US dollars in 2004, comprising shares of companies belonging to the Koç Holding.

THE TURKISH WAQF REFORM AND THE KOÇ FOUNDATION

A visit by the late Vehbi Koç, probably the greatest businessman Turkey ever produced, to the USA soon after the Second World War, appears to have been the new beginning.[8] Vehbi Koç was already well aware of the traditional Islamic waqfs. His forefathers had established the *Ibadullah vakfı* in Ankara and his father had served as the trustee.[9] Thus, well acquainted with the traditional Islamic waqfs, he was quick to appreciate the enormous strides made by the American trusts. The opportunity to observe these trusts in action arose during business negotiations with the Ford Motor Company. When he visited a hospital run by the Ford Foundation for a check-up, he was convinced that the traditional Islamic waqf should be modernized.

By 1951 he began seriously to consider the idea of setting up a philanthropic foundation along the American lines in Turkey. It was at this time that he began to 'bang his head' against the French-inspired Civil Law and its extension in waqf affairs, the 1935 Waqf Law prevalent in Turkey. Soon it became obvious that a modernization of the waqf system could only be realized by a completely new law. It was at this time that Vehbi Koç, together with Aydın Bolak, a conservative Member of Parliament, began a series of meetings with the greatest legal authorities of the country. The problem was referred to the Institute of Private Law at Ankara University, Faculty of Law, headed first by Professor Esener, and then Professor Tandoğan, where the complex legal problems of combining Islamic traditions with the latest developments in the West were discussed.

One of the most important items to be considered was the tax exemption to be granted to the waqfs as well as to those who made donations. When the draft bill was submitted, it encountered fierce resistance. The chief opposition came from Hikmet Çetin, at that time a young socialist at the Department of Finance. Çetin expressed his opposition succinctly: 'the philosophy of central planning does not allow any person to perpetuate his name using revenue due to the state'. Notwithstanding such opposition, the reformers prevailed and the bill became law with full tax exemption granted.

The 13 July 1967 Law (no. 903) which was amended several times, introduced the following:

(a) The will prescribed in the foundation deed is not changeable.
(b) The Civil Tribunal is authorized to register the waqf and to give it a judicial personality.
(c) The word 'establishment', *tesis*, used exclusively in the Turkish Civil Code, is replaced by the word '*vakıf*' (Article 3).
(d) No waqf can be created that opposes the law or national interests, supports current politics, a certain race or community.
(e) Providing that 80 per cent of their revenues are reserved for public purposes, the waqfs *can* be exempted from taxation. This exemption can only be granted by the Council of Ministers (Articles 4 and 5).
(f) The control of these institutions is directly vested with the General Directorate of Waqfs.
(g) The annual profit of a waqf is to be added to the original capital of the waqf stated in the waqf deed and is reported at the beginning of each calendar year to the inspectors (Article 81).
(h) A multitude of persons, associations and even the state can create a waqf.

(i) A waqf is now allowed to establish a company and allocate the latter's total profits, or a share thereof, to its own specific purpose.
(j) Establishment of a waqf has been simplified.
(k) *Istibdal* has been reintroduced (Article 80/a) and is applied subject to the decision of the court.

Some of these Articles deserve our further attention. Consider, first, item (c), where it is stated that the word '*tesis*' is substituted by the word 'waqf'. This Article may appear bizarre. But such was the hostility of the modernist republican government to waqfs that it was prohibited to use even the word *vakıf* in the Turkish Civil Code and the Code of Commerce. Thus Article (c) once again legitimized the usage of this ancient term.

Item (e) rules that providing a waqf reserves 80 per cent of its revenue for public services, it *can* be tax exempted. The word 'can' is deliberately italicized here, for reservation of 80 per cent of the revenue does not automatically ensure exemption, which must be approved by the Council of Ministers, in reality quite a difficult procedure.

Item (g) restores and breathes life into an age-old practice of the Ottoman waqf system. Indeed, the practice of adding the annual profit to the original corpus of the waqf was observed so meticulously that it can be found in all waqf inspection registers from the sixteenth to the nineteenth centuries.[10]

Items (h) and (i) are of such extreme importance for the future development of the waqf system that we shall comment on them separately below.

Item (k) is also interesting and indicates how modern lawmakers, aware of Islamic law, can reintroduce ancient Islamic principles in a far more direct and simple way. Indeed, *istibdal* was a highly controversial issue among the classical Muslim jurists. Yet the modern jurists who drafted the 1967 Law, circumvented these controversies and simply reintroduced this institution without any reference to the huge historical controversy. Article 80/A is very simple and can be translated as follows:

> properties of a waqf whose income does not suffice to meet its expenditure, or in case these properties do not yield revenue commensurate to their real value, may be exchanged with another more beneficial property (*istibdal*) or with cash (*ibdal*).[11]

Returning now to the items (h) and (i) above, the idea to enable a waqf to establish its own company was actually clearly pronounced already in 1963.[12] In the 1967 Law the idea is repeated and confirmed in a highly cryptic style. Item 5 B/6 merely states that the net profit of a company, *kurum*, is paid to the tax-exempted waqfs, in proportion to their contribution to its capital. Ambiguities have been eliminated by a decree published by the Ministry of Finance in the Official Gazette dated 28 July 1994. In the preamble of the decree it is stated offhandedly that the tax exemption granted to the waqfs is not granted to the companies that the former may establish, thus confirming that a waqf can establish a company or companies.[13] It is further clarified in Article V/3 that these waqf companies are subject to taxation and their accounts are to be kept separately from their waqf founders. After these companies pay their taxes according to the prevalent tax law, their net profit is then to be transferred to the founder waqf.[14] The previously stated Article 5B/6 of the 1967 Law, on the other hand, makes it clear that in the case where a company has been created by a multitude of waqfs, then its profits will be distributed to these waqfs in proportion to their original contribution to the company's capital.

An infringement was introduced with the Corporation Tax Law No. 199 on the donations by outside companies, that is, those not established by a waqf. The Law No. 199 limited donations to the tax-exempt waqfs by outside companies to a mere 5 per cent of the latter's profits.[15] In the USA, by contrast, 'the charitable contribution deduction for a corporation' is limited to 10 per cent of the corporation's pre-tax net income. For an individual the same ratio is as much as 50 per cent.[16]

To sum up, through a series of laws and decrees promulgated in 1963, 1967 and 1994, supply side capital pooling among the waqfs has been permitted in Turkey. The reader will notice that we had referred to 'supply side capital pooling' for the first time above when we were discussing the Ottoman cash waqfs. It will be recalled that these had pooled their resources and allocated a part of their annual profits to certain other waqfs. What Article 5B/6 has provided for is the modern version of this historical process.

The modern capital pooling differs from the historical one in the following:

1. Whereas the historical process was practised among several cash waqfs, the modern one is practised with several waqfs purchasing (*iştirak*) the shares of a company.
2. Although in historical capital pooling the contributed capital was simply absorbed by the receiving waqf and never returned, in the modern one, since the receiving party, the company itself, is capable of regularly generating a profit, it returns a share thereof to its owners; the waqf(s).

All in all, businesses owned by waqfs are subject to the following general rules: they do not have separate legal status and are considered merely as units internal to the founding waqf; tax-exempt waqfs are not considered to be businesses because they are in possession of profit-making enterprises, but waqfs that are not tax-exempt are considered to be businesses if they possess profit-making enterprises.[17] To all this we need to add that companies also are authorized to establish their own waqfs.

Thus we have a situation whereby a waqf(s) is creating its own company as well as a company creating its own waqf(s). In the former case, a waqf or waqfs pool their resources and create a company or companies. They also get a relative share of the profits of the companies they have created in proportion to their capital contribution. In the latter case, a waqf or waqfs are created by a company which allocates a share of its profits voluntarily to these. The *Diyanet Vakfı* constitutes an example of a waqf creating a multitude of companies or providing equity finance to already established companies,[18] while the Vehbi Koç Foundation is the best example of a huge conglomerate creating its own waqf.[19] The Vehbi Koç Foundation specializes in education. It has financed a highly ambitious school and a major university, while the *Diyanet*, like the *Tabung Haji* of Malaysia, is involved in the organization of the annual pilgrimage to Mecca and is represented in 700 localities by 90 000 religious functionaries.

The importance of these innovations cannot be emphasized enough. This is because, for the first time in the centuries-long history of waqfs, we have this institution at last provided with the means to benefit from the dynamism of companies. It will be recalled that notwithstanding Imam Zufar's prescription that cash waqfs should invest their capital through *mudaraba*, Ottoman cash waqfs had invested their capital through *istiglal*. Consequently, they were involved in quasi-interest transactions. In the post-1967 Turkish Republic, however, waqfs have become direct recipients of companies' realized profits. Thus, ironically, it is not the waqfs of Ottoman but rather of the staunchly secular Republican Turkey that applied, at long last, Imam Zufar's teaching.[20]

Moreover, we can also interpret these waqf–company relations as the rebirth of cash waqfs.[21] Thus, Ottoman cash waqfs destroyed in 1954 by being incorporated into the bank of waqfs, *Vakıflar Bankası*, have, like a phoenix, been reborn albeit in a radically different organizational structure and in a far more dynamic form. A recent decision declared by the General Directorate of Waqfs (GDW) on 6 August 1999 has carried this process even further. The directorate has now permitted waqfs to purchase shares of a company not even yet traded in the stock exchange. Purchasing such shares, moreover, has been left entirely to the discretion of the waqf managers. Reselling such shares, however, is more difficult and involves a complex procedure. This latest decision is an exciting development, which may pave the way for cash waqf–venture capital (*mudaraba*) linkages.[22]

The following excerpt, dictated by the late Vehbi Koç himself, in January 1969 and taken from the Deed of Trust of his foundation, The Vehbi Koç Foundation, explains why he had decided to establish his foundation as a cash waqf:

> Praise be to the almighty God, who with His Will enabled me to perform charitable works during my lifetime with pleasure, and granted me the means to continue

> *performing ongoing charity* after my death. In my belief that the Turkish Nation will continue to exist so long as the world endures ... and my wish being to establish this foundation in perpetuity, I have based this endowment on a commercial entity that will be able to adapt itself to the requirements of the day rather than on properties dependant on economic conditions and vulnerable to natural disasters. I have chosen to set up this endowment with the shares of *Koç Holding*. These are made up of numerous commercial and industrial enterprises, and are therefore less subject to risks. This foundation that I have established by the grace and kindness of God, I entrust, first of all, to my heirs and to their succeeding generations, to my business colleagues and to the Government of the Republic of Turkey. I call upon all my heirs, my close acquaintances, my business colleagues, my fellow citizens who may be involved in this Foundation, and the officials who will assume its administration, to accept this endowment as a bequest made to the Turkish Nation, to protect it, and strive with their best intention to achieve its original aims. I request the auditing authorities of the State and, when necessary, its authorised agencies, courts and judiciary, never to depart from the dictates of their conscience when making decisions, lest this foundation suffers harm and be diverted from its aims. I have brought this enterprise into being as a result of lifetime effort and sincere desire. I pray that God will regard it worthy of His Protection and grant it success.[23]

The late Vehbi Koç's personal statement reveals a number of important points. First, there is a deep sense of religiosity and gratitude to the Almighty for allowing him to continue being charitable even after his death. In other words, an awareness of the importance of *sadaqa jariya* and the Prophetic tradition mentioned above. After this, he makes this endowment in perpetuity.

This is followed by an explanation of why he has decided to organize his endowment as a waqf of stocks rather than a real estate one. His decision was based on the concern that real estate waqfs may be vulnerable to economic conjuncture and natural disasters. Since the shares of his holding are made up of numerous commercial and industrial estates, 'they are less subject to risks'. Here we observe a profound understanding of the way a waqf functions. Vehbi Koç seems to have been fully aware of the vulnerability of real estate waqfs to economic conjuncture. Such vulnerability has been demonstrated by Suraiya Faroqhi using the seventeenth century records of *Mahmut Pasha Vakfı*.[24]

Although there is no evidence as to how the Vehbi Koç Foundation would have fared under similar conditions, theoretically it may be argued that a conglomerate capable of penetrating into international markets should be better equipped in dealing with stagnation by diversifying its markets. Indeed, there are more than 100 companies in the Koç conglomerate with 40 000 employees and the total number of Koç Holding shares allocated to the foundation has been declared as 10 000.[25] These registered shares, each with a nominal value of ten million TLs, constitute 9.4 per cent of the total assets of the Koç conglomerate. In this way, the late Vehbi Koç has diversified the risks.

The second-generation members of the Koç family have continued to expand generously the assets of the foundation with further donations of their own. These individuals have donated a total of 21 funds. Consequently, the original 10 000 shares endowed by the late Vehbi Koç constitute now a mere 1.4 per cent of the total assets of the foundation in book value. At the end of 1993 the book value of the foundation's assets stood at US$120 million with an approximate market value of US$297 million. These increased to US$187 million and US$762 million respectively, primarily due to the superb performance of the Istanbul Stock Exchange in 1999. Ten years later, when the Koç Foundation celebrated its 40th anniversary on 17 January 2009, its asset value had reached US$1.2 billion. Its total spending on education, health, culture and the arts had amounted to US$600 million. The foundation had established 27 educational, six health and five cultural institutions.[26]

The foundation is entrusted first to the coming generations of his heirs; thus, this is essentially a family waqf in perpetuity,[27] and then to the business colleagues and then to the future governments of Turkey. The business colleagues were probably included with the view that if the heirs prove to be incapable individuals, the colleagues who run the Koç enterprises should interfere and manage the waqf with proper business perspective. Their inclusion in the deed would certainly enable them to have a say in waqf affairs. Inclusion of the government is also telling: Vehbi Koç had been an eye witness to the great destruction of the Turkish waqfs by the modernist republican state that took place between the 1930s and 1950s. Perhaps, by entrusting his endowment to the future governments of Turkey, he wanted to impose a moral obligation to the state. Finally, he feels the need for the prayer that 'God will regard it worthy of His Protection'!

We are given further important information pertaining to the investment of the foundation shares in the waqf deed. Article 7 of the Vehbi Koç Foundation Deed stipulates that all excess cash of the foundation that accrues to the waqf on an annual basis shall be converted into government bonds and kept as an emergency fund. These bonds shall be used when the Koç Holding exercises a capital enhancement. Should this process take place, the foundation shall participate therein, so as to maintain its relative share within the conglomerate. Should the emergency fund not suffice to maintain the foundation's share in the conglomerate, the Board of Trustees can allocate 20 per cent of the primary revenue of the waqf for this purpose. Should a process of capital enhancement not take place, the excess cash of the fund shall be invested in shares and bonds, preferably those of Koç Holding companies. We are informed, furthermore, that the waqf can also exercise *istibdal* subject to the approval of the Board of Trustees and the Court (Article 8).

Article 9 stipulates that a minimum of 80 per cent of the total revenue of the waqf shall be allocated to social and cultural services. A maximum of 20 per cent of the revenue shall be allocated to administrative expenses, emergency cash, and investments to buy properties for the waqf. It is well known that in history the trustees often usurped waqf revenues allocated for charity. Consequently, while in history charity/total expenditure ratio of waqfs has often declined, salary/total expenditure ratio has often either remained the same or increased at the expense of the former.[28] Vehbi Koç seems to have been either aware of these historical tendencies or was able to envisage them thanks to his great business acumen. It is also possible that he may have been simply remaining within the boundaries set by item (e) of the 1967 Law in order to qualify for tax exemption, in which case the credit for this insight should go to the drafters of the law.

Finally, we are informed that the Vehbi Koç Foundation was granted tax-exempt status by the Council of Ministers on 28 December 1968. Thus, Turkey owes to Vehbi Koç, Aydın Bolak and to the brilliant jurists who helped them, not only the great Koç endowment but also all the positive developments that took place in the waqf system after 1967.

The reader may wonder about the actual impact of these innovations introduced by the Law No. 903 on the Turkish waqf system in 1967. Nothing illustrates this impact better than the actual number of waqfs endowed. From the beginning of the Republic in 1923 to 1967 when the new law was promulgated, a time span of 44 years, merely 73 new waqfs had been established, whereas from 1967 until 1985, a time span of only 18 years, one observes 1877 new waqfs. From 1986 to 1996 more than 100 waqfs were established annually with the trend rising until it reached 439 new waqfs in 1996, a maximum.[29]

Defining the ‘new waqfs’ as those established after the 1967 Law, the number of these waqfs has been calculated as more than 4000.[30]

One of the most significant contributions of the 1967 Law has been observed in the field of education. By 1998, altogether 16 waqf universities had been established. Currently, there are more than 50 waqf universities in Turkey and their numbers are rising steadily. Some of these already enjoy an excellent reputation and are considered among the top universities of the country.

THE JOHOR CORPORATION (MALAYSIA)

Although Malaysia was the latest Islamic country to have approved the cash waqfs, a powerful waqf of stocks appears to be emerging in Malaysia. This waqf has been established by the Johor Corporation. First, a brief introduction pertaining to this corporation should be presented here. The Johor Corporation was established in the year 1968, by a special decree known as Enactment No. 4 of 1968.[31] The enactment states clearly in article three that this institution is a ‘body corporate’, with perpetual succession and the right to sue and be sued – in short a corporation with judicial personality, which can enter into contracts and acquire movable and immovable properties. Thus, the Johor Corporation is a truly corporate body in the Western sense. It has been possible to design it as a corporate body with judicial personality because Islamic law also recognizes this concept and does not object to it.[32]

Within its complex structure it also contains a waqf of stocks, or what we may also call an incorporated cash waqf. Moreover, since it is involved in public development projects, which it finances through *sukuk*, it will be argued here that the Johor Corporation is actually a remarkable synthesis of three very important institutions: the Western corporation, the Islamic waqf of stocks and *sukuk*.

Establishment as a corporation means that this institution was not established for a fixed period but can live perpetually, that is, it has its own life. When its highest officials die, it will continue to live on. Thus, the corporate body concept, a Western contribution, grants the Johor Corporation potentially a perpetual life. This is not to say that these advantages could not have been obtained within the framework of Islamic law. There is, in fact, a growing body of literature arguing that the concept of corporation actually exists in Islamic law as well. Moreover, it has been shown that certain Islamic partnerships are not necessarily liquidated immediately at the death of one of the partners. But modern businesses cannot be involved in the complexities and debates of Islamic law.[33] They need codified, simple rules within which to conduct their fast-moving daily affairs. This is provided by Western law.[34]

Once established as a corporation with its own judicial personality, the first step was to establish a fund. Federal as well as state repayable loans were transferred to this fund. With these funds, profits and cash flows generated through business operations over the years, the Johor Corporation established some 250 corporations. The total number of employment opportunities provided by these corporations has reached 54 000.[35]

Since the original capital of the Corporation had been provided by the state, the danger of powerful politicians interfering in the management of the Corporation was felt acutely. To avoid this problem, it was decided that any person who wishes to become a director of the Corporation must take an exam conducted by external readers in Britain. Tan Sri Dato' Muhammad Ali Hashim, the corporate CEO himself, had to take this exam!

In the year 2000, the Johor Corporation began to provide health services with a clinic managed by a member company, KPJ, specializing in health. In the year 2005, it was decided to establish a quasi-waqf of stocks, the *Kumpulan Waqaf An-Nur Berhad*. 'Quasi' refers to the fact that the original capital of the Johor Corporation had been provided by state funds and therefore the RM258 million worth of Johor Corporation shares donated to the Corporate waqf actually constitute public and not private funds.[36] In the year 2008, the after-tax dividends from all shares that were endowed totalled up to RM2.57 million, which constitutes a drop of 21 per cent from the total of RM3.23 million in 2007 due to the international financial crisis.[37]

We have here an excellent example of a modern waqf of stocks. This waqf has been established with the endowed shares of incorporated joint-stock companies and that it is incorporated in order 'to manage the assets and shares of companies of Johor Corporation, which have been endowed in accordance with the principles of *Shari'ah*'. The waqf itself 'is a company limited by guarantee and not having share issue'.[38] The guarantee is provided by the Johor Corporation. At the same time, the waqf is the trustee of the shares of the Johor Corporation donated to it and yet although incorporated, its own shares have not been issued. Consequently, it cannot be taken over by a hostile merger and its basic function as a trustee cannot be altered.

The capital of this waqf is enhanced regularly by external private contributions. Small amounts of such donations are being provided by the *qard hasan* recipients. If these persons succeed in establishing well-functioning businesses with the interest-free loans they receive, they pay their *sadaqa*s to the waqf. More importantly, certain corporations within the group have started to donate funds to the waqf. Both the KFC (food) and KULIM (palm oil), for instance, have donated RM500 000 each. Along the same lines, the private hospital chain of the Johor Corporation, the KPJ, provides RM2 million regularly to support the waqf clinics.[39] Another source of revenue is the annual membership fees. Indeed, waqf members not only receive no salaries, they even pay for the privilege. These persons oversee the management of the waqf and consider this a great honour and Islamic duty. There are altogether 1141 such members. Each one pays an annual fee of RM100 plus a one-time registration fee of RM50. The general manager of the waqf is directly responsible to them.

But the most important source of income is the dividends of altogether six companies whose shares have been endowed. Three of these companies are listed in the Kuala Lumpur Stock Exchange and three are unlisted.[40] The deed of endowment informs us that 70 per cent of the profit yielded by the shares of these companies will be allocated to Johor Corporation and when this is reinvested, the profit thereof shall accrue to the waqf. The remaining 25 per cent profits of the companies will accrue directly to the waqf and 5 per cent to the *Majlis Agama Islam Negeri Johor*, which is the primary religious authority in the state of Johor. Tan Sri Muhammad Ali bin Hashim, the Chief Executive of Johor Corporation, has expressed his intention of allocating all the shares of all the 250 companies of the Johor Corporation to the *Kumpulan* Waqf *An-Nur Berhad*.

The 25 per cent profits of the companies which accrue directly to the waqf are pooled in the so-called *fi sebilallah* fund. In the year 2008, RM200 000 was received this way. In addition to this, RM14 000 were received from various donations. This fund splits its expenditure into four main areas.

The first is microfinance.[41] Since financing is provided free of interest, it is deliberately called microfinance rather than microcredit. According to this project, officially started in June 2009, the waqf will provide microfinance to women, who will be trained and asked to market semi-finished foodstuffs produced by a member company of the Corporation. This is an imaginative combination of charity, microfinance/poverty eradication and sheer for-profit business. The charity is provided by the waqf in the form of interest-free *qard-hasan* loans. Thus, this is pure *Islamic* microfinance. Hundreds of women who will receive these loans will move up from poverty to the middle classes. Meanwhile, in this process they will market commodities produced by a member corporation and generate profits for it. Part of these profits will accrue back to the waqf and support its microfinance programme – *ad infinitum*. The food company will also facilitate the process by guaranteeing the return of the microfinance loans to the waqf. So far, since the fund started providing support from March 2008 to February 2009, out of the total of RM214 000 received, RM169 000 have already been disbursed to 63 microfinance recipients. The maximum amount disbursed per recipient is RM3000.[42] The loan repayment takes place within 24 months with a grace period of three months. So far, 98 per cent of the loans have been repaid. Each loan recipient pays only RM1 administrative fee irrespective of the amount borrowed. Presently, the entire microfinance operation is managed by merely a three-person team helped by the volunteering executives of the Corporation.

The second area where the fund spends its funds is to support the *imams* of various mosques. These *imams* are asked, in return, to provide guidance to the pilgrims during the pilgrimage. These persons go through a vigorous training, at the end of which they qualify as *mutawwifs*. A total of 2314 pilgrims have already performed the pilgrimage under the *Waqaf An-nur Mutawwid* scheme. It is planned to extend this programme to all over Malaysia, which will effectively bring the *Tabung Haji*'s monopoly to an end in this matter.[43]

A third area is health care. The fund has established eight clinics and a fully fledged hospital. Patients are charged only RM5 for the health service they receive. These waqf establishments have provided 82 261 medical treatments in the year 2008. Out of this total, 480 treatments were provided to the non-Muslims. The total number of treatments provided since the beginning of the services has reached 444 714. Out of this, 25 140 were provided to non-Muslims.[44]

The fourth area is the so-called Brigade waqf, which focuses on rescue work during emergencies. The Brigade receives help from the various corporations of the Johor Corporation. The Johor Land, for instance, builds shelters and trains search parties, KULIM provides transport equipment, KFC provides food, Sindora focuses on rehabilitation/cleaning and KPJ provides medical help.

The Johor Corporation also applies a most creative 'intrepreneur scheme'. High-level managers of the companies within the group who have proven their management abilities are allowed to own up to 25 per cent of the equity of the companies they run. Therefore, parts of the profits accrue to these intrepreneurs. The Johor Corporation plays the role of an incubator and provides all the administrative and other support that an inexperienced intrepreneur needs. The better known term entrepreneur is deliberately converted into 'intrepreneur' to emphasize the fact that most, but not all, of these individuals are selected from within the group. The advantage of this system is that the 'intrepreneurs' are allowed to run their companies and their earnings are directly linked to their performance, which affect the value of the shares they possess. Moreover, by allowing them to manage their companies, management continuity is achieved and information asymmetry problems are avoided.

The Corporation preferred this model after having observed that 80 per cent of start-ups fail after the first five years. It was therefore thought that intrepreneurs, who had already proven their talent within the group and provided with a wide variety of support that the entire group could provide, would have a better chance of survival. That this vision was right is demonstrated by facts and figures.

The scheme was introduced in the year 1999. In that year, two intrepreneurs were given the chance to acquire a maximum 25 per cent of the shares of their companies. Four more intrepreneurs were added to the scheme in 2001. These companies were, in short, a trading company, a bulk mailing company, a marketing company, and a parking company, and all were low-technology companies. Thus, unlike the American venture capital, Johor Corporation's intrepreneurial scheme does not focus on high technology. The link between the corporation and universities, where technology is produced, is not yet established. After the introduction of the share ownership scheme, the overall performance of the companies improved dramatically. Their combined turnover increased by more than 267 per cent to RM66 million in 2001 compared with only RM18 million in 1999. Their combined profit before tax also improved from a meagre RM0.4 million in 1999 to RM4 million in 2001. For the financial year 2007, the intrepreneur companies recorded an aggregated pre-tax profit of RM46 million on the back of RM511 million revenue. At the end of 2008, gross turnover had grown tremendously to almost RM500 million, aggregated revenue to RM577 million and profit level to RM48 million, proving the scheme's viability. By this time the corporation had already spawned and developed 65 intrepreneur companies. It has now targeted to increase this number to 200 by the year 2020. The existing intrepreneur companies appear to have successfully adjusted themselves to competitive markets. This is attested by the fact that although they could easily market most of their products within the group, they obtain 84.3 per cent of their aggregate revenue from open markets.[45]

Johor Corporation's intrepreneurship programme is not limited to nourishing potential intrepreneurs from within the group. It also includes acquisitions of the majority of shares of well-established companies outside the group. This is done by *Sindora Berhad*, the venture capital company of the Corporation. So far, six such companies have been acquired. These are not hostile takeovers. Usually, it is the intrepreneur of a successful company who applies to the Corporation. This is because such intrepreneurs who wish to expand their firms find it very difficult to do so with their own means. By joining to the Johor Corporation they immediately begin to benefit from the externalities that Sindora as well as its parent corporation can provide, such as networks, larger group markets, better leveraging possibilities, management consulting, etc. This was observed in the case of a small shipping company, whose owner agreed to sell 51 per cent of his shares to the Corporation. The money was used to buy much larger ships and, as a result, the company became a major international shipping company.

The Johor Corporation is also keenly aware of the importance of hands-off management, thus successful intrepreneurs are given full freedom to run their companies. The criteria for success are determined by the specific key performance indicators (KPIs) of each business unit set at the beginning of each year. Naturally, the process of determining the KPI is of great importance. To the extent that they are imposed from above, they will bear the risk of information asymmetry.

Finally, we should refer to the Pasir Gudang Development Project. Pasir Gudang was a small fishing village and has now been developed by the Corporation to be an important industrial town. In the year 1977, the Johor Corporation was vested with the power to manage the Pasir Gudang municipality. Until 2009 this municipality has been managed by the Corporation, but now it has become autonomous. Presently, only two persons represent the Corporation in the municipal council.

What makes this project particularly interesting is the first ever issuance of municipal bonds by a Malaysian local authority. The claim, however, that this is 'the first ever global issuance of a municipal bond based upon *Shari'ah* principles'[46] is not correct. This is because the first ever *Shari'ah* compliant municipal bonds were issued 859 years ago by the Genoese.[47] Yes, *Shari'ah* compliant municipal bonds issued by Christians! The reader will note here that we are referring to the PFPD of medieval Europe discussed previously. Since these bonds were approved by the Pope, they were not usurious – hence the claim '*Shari'ah* compliant municipal bonds issued by Christians'.

What makes the Johor Corporation so relevant for this book is that it aims to 'fully integrate Islamic values into modern capitalist corporate practice'.[48] It therefore provides an excellent example of modern Islamic capitalism in action.

THE MANNAN MODEL (BANGLADESH)

Professor M. A. Mannan has recently introduced a new model of cash waqfs.[49] This is the case of the Social Investment Bank, a three-sector banking model operationalized since 22 November 1995 in Dhaka, Bangladesh. This bank floated the cash waqf certificate as a financial instrument in 1997. The three sectors are a formal incorporated bank, a non-formal bank focusing primarily on microinvestment and microenterprises and finally a voluntary banking sector focusing on cash waqf certificates. Thus this institution represents a synthesis of the Western corporation with cash waqfs as well as microfinance.

Mannan argues that issuance of cash waqf certificates and thus collecting cash from the public breaks the age-old monopoly of the rich for waqf establishment. Now, indeed, for the first time small savers can contribute to the establishment of a waqf. Mannan's Social Investment Bank constitutes a striking improvement upon the multiple founder cash waqfs discussed above, in the sense that theoretically the number of cash waqf certificate holders can now be infinite. Indeed, each certificate is issued in terms of a small denomination worth Tk.1000 (US$21 only). It is therefore affordable to a large section of the population. Moreover, to make contributions even more affordable, cash certificates can also be purchased in instalments.

The difference between the two institutions lies in the nature of the contributors. Those who contribute to a multiple founder waqf are founding members and they have voting power in the waqf management board. Cash waqf certificate holders, however, have no voting power and after identifying the purpose of the waqf they want to contribute, they entrust its management to the bank.

When a person purchases a cash waqf certificate, he actually makes a perpetual deposit in the cash waqf deposit account of the Social Investment Bank Ltd. Since the deposit cannot be withdrawn, the bank has the freedom to invest it in long-term projects. Thus the bank acts as the trustee of the cash waqf certificate holder. The latter has the freedom to choose the purpose of his waqf. Each certificate theoretically represents a separate waqf. But for ease of management, certificate holders are encouraged to designate one of the 32 purposes identified by the bank. The certificate holder, however, can insist on another purpose. Providing this purpose does not contradict the *Shari'ah*, it is obeyed by the bank. The cash waqf account is granted the highest profit rate generated by the bank. The original capital invested remains constant (unless additions are made) and only the profit generated by the bank with the endowed cash is spent for the purpose identified by the certificate holder. If any part of the profit is not spent, it is automatically added to the original capital endowed.

The numbers of cash waqf accounts have increased from a mere 21 in 1997 to 215 in 1998 and then to 367 in 1999. In 1997 merely 39 Taka were deposited. This increased to 1249 the following year and then to 2763 in 1999. This impressive growth trend appears to have been sustained. The balance sheet of the Social Investment Bank Ltd as of 31 December 2007 informs us that the cash waqf fund had increased to Tk.16 536 499 at the end of 2006 and to Tk.19 003 600 at the end of 2007.[50]

It seems that the basic idea of the Mannan model, that is, expanding the number of founders infinitely, is catching up. Indeed, in addition to the Johor Corporation model just explained, Malaysia is in the process of experimenting with several models of waqfs of shares. Seven State Islamic Councils are quite active in this and have established such waqfs. Interested persons buy shares at a modest price of RM10/US$3 and then donate their total outlay to the State Islamic Council with the purpose of the welfare of Muslims. Since this is a waqf donation, the donors do not receive any dividends from the investment of this amount. State Councils have opened up these schemes to corporations as well. It has been reported that the experiment is still at its infancy and the response of the public, though substantial, is not yet disclosed.[51]

ECONOMIC ROLE OF THE WAQFS

In sum, waqfs of stocks will probably dominate the future of the waqf system. This is because, unlike real estate waqfs, which cannot raise their rents in tandem with inflation and gradually lose their capital, waqfs of stocks can enhance their capital. Moreover, while the real estate waqfs tend to expand and gradually occupy huge areas, both urban and rural, they inevitably raise the question of opportunity costs. That is to say, are these resources being used most efficiently for the welfare of the society? Since real estate waqfs withdraw assets from private ownership, the most productive sector of any economy, they tend to reduce aggregate productivity. Waqf of stocks, by contrast, transfer endowed assets to incorporated joint-stock companies. Thus they not only channel resources to the efficient private sector and in this process enhance entrepreneurship but they also contribute to the aggregate productivity of the economy.

In order to fully understand the harm inflicted by the modernist policies directed against waqfs, the contribution of the waqf system to the economy must be acknowledged. The waqf system has provided throughout history a myriad of essential services such as health, education, municipal, etc., to Islamic societies. The system therefore contributes significantly towards that ultimate goal of so many modern economists: with the waqfs providing the bulk of the financial needs of the service sector, there would be a substantial reduction in the government's expenditure for provision of services. The reduction in government expenditure, on the other hand, would lead to a smaller budget deficit, which in turn would lower the need for government borrowing. A reduction in government borrowing would curb the 'crowding-out effect' and lead to a reduction in the rate of interest, consequently reining in a basic impediment to private investment and growth. It goes without saying that reducing the rate of interest, preferably to zero, would also be the ultimate goal of an Islamic government. To the extent that the waqf system contributes to the reduction/elimination of interest, it becomes an important tool for Islamic macroeconomics.

The waqf could fulfil these above-mentioned functions by voluntary donations made by the well-to-do. Thus, privately accumulated capital is voluntarily endowed to finance all sorts of social services to the society. At this point another extremely important function of the waqf becomes apparent: not only does it help reduce government expenditure and consequently the prevailing rate of interest and pave the way for growth, it also achieves another modern economic goal: a better distribution of income in the economy. Moreover, this improvement in the distribution of income would be achieved essentially through voluntary donations and the need for taxation is reduced.

Thus, the relatively low tax burden of Islamic capitalism must be considered within a broader picture that comprises the waqf system. Indeed, tax burden in an Islamic economy can be low because the bulk of the essential services should be provided by the waqfs. Tax revenues are earmarked primarily for defence. That this was not just in theory, but actually found application in past Islamic societies, is confirmed by the Ottoman budget studies.[52]

There are further implications: a lower tax burden means an enhancement in the consumers' and producers' surpluses and a diminution in the 'dead-weight cost of the tax'. Consequently, lower taxes would have a positive impact on aggregate production while at the same time reducing costs. Prices to the consumers would come down and pave the way for non-inflationary growth.

Moreover, the contribution of the waqfs to education and health must be reconsidered within the framework of the latest research. We have noted already that throughout history, schools, universities, hospitals and public kitchens have been organized, financed and maintained by waqfs. All of this means human capital. Research covering 192 countries has indicated that human capital explains no less than 64 per cent of the growth performance. By contrast, physical capital – machinery and infrastructure – explains only 16 per cent of growth. More specifically, global estimates show that 1 per cent increase in the share of the labour force with secondary education is associated with 6 to 15 per cent increase in the share of income received by the poorest 40 per cent. Thus education serves both growth and equity.[53] And throughout history it was the waqf system, which provided education and health in Islamic countries. There is no doubt that centralization and the damage inflicted upon the waqf system has been detrimental to the cause of these services in the Islamic world. It is clear that the state-provided education has not been a match for the waqf-provided one. At the very least, the waqf system is needed to supplement the state-provided education and health sectors.[54]

Presently, in the aftermath of the 1967 reforms, about 50 waqf universities have been established in Turkey. Most of them are mixed waqfs, that is, their capital is constituted of real estate and joint-stock company shares. Thus, they receive fresh injections of cash whenever their associated companies pay dividends. With these injections they finance research and expansion. Tuition fees, on the other hand, provide a steady stream of revenue and cover the salaries.

The positive impact of the waqfs on employment should also be remembered. Western countries, which abandoned their negative stance towards philanthropic foundations induced by the eighteenth-century European Enlightenment, once again began to support them during the twentieth century. The result was a significant increase in employment. The non-profit sector accounted for an average of 13 per cent of the net jobs added between 1980 and 1990 in France, Germany and the USA. In the USA, the non-profit sector accounts for 6.9 per cent of total employment.[55] Clearly, in addition to all the advantages mentioned above, the revival of the system would contribute to the problem of employment in the Islamic world as well. But in this process the greatest potential rests not with the traditional real estate or cash waqfs but with the waqfs of stocks. For it is the latter which combines the best of the Islamic waqf tradition with the best the West has to offer: incorporated joint-stock companies. As a result, the waqfs of stocks not only share the great dynamism of modern companies but also eliminate all doubts of *riba* and the problem of information asymmetry.

Finally, waqfs may also play a significant role in the democratization of Islamic countries. This is because waqfs constituted for centuries civil society institutions, *par excellence*, for the Islamic world. Indeed, established with private capital, which they often pooled, they were decentralized, autonomous decision-making units involved in local problems. It is quite possible that the incapacitating policies imposed on the waqf system for the last 200 years by the West, as well as the indigenous modernists, have deprived the Islamic world from its most potent democratic force. Thus, lack of democracy is not, as some believe, an outcome of Islam as a religion, but a consequence of the last two centuries of institutional and economic history.

ISLAMIC UNIT TRUST FUNDS

In this section we will examine how the historical unit trust concept which originated in the medieval Islamic waqf and evolved in the West, particularly in England, has now returned to the Islamic world and is flourishing in Malaysia and the Gulf.

An Islamic unit trust can be considered as an instrument of finance that has evolved from the waqf of stocks by merging with joint-stock investment companies. Unit trusts are a form of collective investment that allows investors with similar investment objectives to pool their funds to be invested in a portfolio of securities or other assets. A professional fund manager then invests the pooled funds in a portfolio which is constituted of forms of investment approved by the *Shari'ah*.

In similar fashion to the medieval ship shares, known in both the Islamic world and the West, ownership of the fund is divided into equal units of entitlement.[56] As the fund increases or decreases in value, the value of each unit increases or decreases accordingly. The number of units held depends on the unit purchase price at the time of investment and the amount of money invested.

The return on investment of unit holders is usually in the form of income distribution and capital appreciation, derived from the pool of assets supporting the unit trust fund. Each unit earns an equal return, determined by the level of profit distribution and/or capital appreciation in any one period.

Unit trust investors are typically those with savings to invest, who have neither the time nor the inclination to hold portfolios of direct investments or shares. Rather, they prefer to invest in a secure, reputable investment vehicle which suits their purposes. Unit trusts allow investors to have easy access to a wide range of investments not normally available to them.

As investors seek to maximize returns on their financial resources, unit trusts provide an ideal way for them to gain exposure to investments that, in the long run, should produce returns superior to cash savings and fixed deposit investments. Indeed, the returns for Islamic equity funds have averaged 26 per cent year-to-date.[57]

The downside of these potentially higher returns is of course the risk that accompanies the investment. In the short term, the certainty of investment returns of most unit trust products is less than those offered by fixed deposits. However, in the medium to long term (i.e. 3–20 years), unit trust investments generally provide better returns at acceptable levels of risk.

We have seen in the previous chapter that the merger of joint-stock companies and the trust had led to the emergence of the deed of settlement company. Evolving from the deed of settlement company, the deed constitutes the foundation stone of a modern Islamic unit trust. It spells out in detail how the scheme is to be administered, the valuation and pricing of units, the collection and distribution of income, the rights of unit holders, the rights and duties of the manager as well as the independent trustee, and the protection of unit holders' interest.

In Malaysia, the manager is obliged under the *Deed, Capital Markets and Services Act 2007* and *Guidelines on Unit Trust Funds* to administer the fund's scheme in an efficient and proper manner. The deed also provides for an independent trustee to be appointed for the unit holders. This person acts as the custodian for all the assets. His/her main responsibility is to ensure that the manager adheres strictly to the provisions of the deed, particularly with regard to the creation and cancellation of units, the investment of the fund, collection and distribution of income, proper record keeping and in upholding unit holders' interest.[58]

It has been claimed that the first modern Islamic equity fund, namely Arab–Malaysian *Tabung Ittikal*, was established in 1993.[59] At the end of August 2009, there were 478 Islamic unit trust funds amounting to 0.6 per cent of the total universe of 79 286 funds. In 2008 they merely held assets of about US$25 billion. Obviously, this is not a huge amount, particularly if compared to the private wealth in the GCC alone estimated at US$1800 billion.[60]

But the rate of growth of Islamic unit trust funds from 1993 to the present has been phenomenal. This is an exponential growth rate of 254 per cent with an average annual growth rate of 25 per cent. Malaysia has the highest number of Islamic funds launched, with 151 funds or 32 per cent of the market share. With respect to the assets under management, the funds amounted to US$27 billion out of a worldwide total of US$15.8 trillion. The highest year-on-year growth for assets under management was realized from 2004 to 2005 with 440 per cent rise from US$1.9 billion to US$10 billion. Funds registered in Saudi Arabia make up the largest group in terms of assets under management – US$15 billion or 54 per cent of the total. Saudi Arabia together with Malaysia contributed 60 per cent of the global Islamic assets under management.

In 2003, equity funds constituted almost 80 per cent of the total assets under management. Thus, it appeared in 2003 that equity finance, which is considered to be the nearest modern instrument to the classical *mudaraba* or *inan* partnerships and therefore entirely *Shari'ah* based, had at last triumphed. But the trend changed in 2005 when money market funds rapidly caught up. From 2006 to 2007 equity funds once again surged and dominated the market representing 57 per cent of the assets under management. The 2008 crisis reversed the trend once again with equity funds dropping significantly while money market funds increased, which indicates rising risk aversion among investors. By the end of August 2009, equity funds (US$11 696 billion) were slightly less than money market funds of US$12 903 billion.[61]

ISLAMICITY OF UNIT TRUSTS

At this point we need to investigate the reasons for this phenomenal rise of unit trust funds in the Islamic world. Indeed, why is it that this particular instrument has become so popular? This brings us to the question of the Islamicity of unit trust funds.

It has been argued that there is now an ageing generation of wealth creators in the GCC (Gulf Cooperative Countries) and MENA (Middle East and North Africa) regions. This generation wishes to preserve the family wealth for generations to come. As is well known, Islamic law of inheritance rapidly fragments the wealth of the family among a large number of inheritors. There are only two ways to preserve the family wealth without violating the *Shari'ah*. First is to establish a family waqf, known as waqf *ahli*, and the second is to give it as gift *inter vivos*. These are not mutually exclusive concepts. Often, making a gift *inter vivos* is considered as a precondition to establish a waqf.[62]

For such a gift to be valid under the *Shari'ah*, it is necessary that there must be a clearly defined proposal and acceptance. It is also necessary that the gift is *tamam* (complete) and that the recipient takes possession of it when the donor is still healthy and of sound mind. It is interesting that these conditions also apply to the Western trust, where they are known as the 'three certainties'. For a Western trust to exist there must be: certainty of intention, certainty of the trust property and certainty of the beneficiaries.

Alternatively, if a wealthy Muslim wants to preserve the wealth he has accumulated in his lifetime for generations to come, he could transform his wealth into a family waqf and put his most trustworthy and able offspring in charge of this waqf as the *mutawalli* or the trustee. Establishing a family waqf not only preserves the wealth of the family and avoids fragmentation, it also allows the most able offspring to manage the family wealth on behalf of the whole family. The founder can appoint other members of the family as beneficiaries and instruct the trustee to pay them a certain percentage of the revenue generated by the waqf properties annually.

Thus, the person who wishes to establish a waqf actually can do so either according to the Islamic law or, in former British colonies, according to the trust law. Due to historical reasons, the French civil law prevalent in the former French colonies is more hostile to waqfs than the British law.[63] Recently, in Bahrain, trusts laws have been passed that are very similar to the Trust Law that was first passed in Jersey in 1984.[64] Thus, Western trust laws are penetrating into the Islamic world and it has become imperative to determine whether these laws are in conformity with the *Shari'ah*. We have already seen above that the waqf and the trust have common origins in medieval Islam. But trust law that is now penetrating the Islamic world is the result of centuries' long evolution in the West. Determination of the Islamicity of these has therefore gained new urgency.

To start with, in both cases when the founder establishes a waqf or a trust, the nature of the endowed assets are transformed. In the case of a waqf, they cease to be the private property of the founder and are considered to have become the property of *Allah*. In the case of the trust, however, they are considered to be the property of the trustee. This leads us directly to the question of selling or exchanging the assets endowed.[65] This is important because the assets endowed, or the units of a unit trust purchased, are traded regularly and frequently by unit trust managers. Whereas the trustee of a unit trust has the freedom to do so, selling or exchanging waqf assets is a complicated affair. Known as *ibdal/istibdal*, this transaction is one of the ten conditions that a waqf founder can empower himself or a *mutawalli*/trustee.[66] This is an important power that the founder can bestow upon himself. The importance of *ibdal/istibdal* lies in the fact that it embodies certain dynamism. By allowing the founder or the trustee to sell/exchange the waqf property the system is made responsive to market conditions.

Istibdal assumes great importance, particularly for those waqfs whose corpus is constituted of movables. Such waqfs achieve perpetuity, a *conditio sine qua non*, often by applying *istibdal*. Indeed, if we consider a cash waqf, the most relevant form of a waqf for a unit trust, and assume further that the government is planning to change the currency of the country or to frequently devalue it, *istibdal*, under such conditions, becomes a vitally important instrument to assure the perpetuity of the waqf. In the case of a unit trust, every time the manager sells some shares in the portfolio for profit and then buys others, he is in fact changing the portfolio and practising *ibdal/istibdal*.

It goes without saying that while a certain dynamism is indeed embodied in *istibdal*, this rule also embodies great potential for misuse, so much so that this instrument, essential for the survival of the institution of waqfs, has been used by its opponents to destroy it.[67] Meanwhile, we may note that wherever applied, this instrument has fuelled passions. This is understandable, for *ibdal/istibdal* allows the sale/exchange of a waqf property, which is supposed to belong to God and be perpetual. Behrens-Abouseif has even argued that the Ottoman occupation of Egypt was prompted by an illegal *istibdal* procedure, which attempted to sell the Al-Azhar complex.[68]

This brings us to the question of under what conditions *istibdal* would be legal. The answer is complicated by the fact that the four major schools of Sunni Islam do not agree on this problem. The Malikites, for instance, strictly prohibit *istibdal* in real estate waqfs with very few exceptions. But the Malikites are considerably less strict concerning the *istibdal* of the waqf of movables. The only condition they attach to such *istibdal* is that the movable corpus of the waqf should have been reduced to such a state that it has become impossible to fulfil the original purpose of the waqf because it is not generating sufficient returns.

The Shafi'ite position is even more stringent than that of the Malikites. In view of this, Behrens-Abouseif's above-mentioned argument that the attempted sale of the Al-Azhar had prompted the Ottoman Sultan to occupy Egypt, which in his opinion had become totally corrupt, can be understood better. For Shafi'ite law was the prevalent law in pre-Ottoman Egypt and selling any waqf property, let alone the famous Al-Azhar, should have been strictly prohibited.

The irony of all this was that the Ottoman Sultan belonged to the Hanafite School, which had the most liberal perspective on *ibdal/istibdal*. The Hanafite position on *ibdal/istibdal* can be summarized as follows: on the condition that the founder has formally allowed himself/herself or the trustee to practise *ibdal/istibdal*, led by Abu Yusuf, the majority of the Hanafite School permits it.[69]

Thus, in short, for an Islamic unit trust to function, it is absolutely necessary that when the founder establishes a waqf with the units of a unit trust he purchases, he specifically allows the manager of the unit trust to practise *ibdal/istibdal*. Actually, fears of jurists that *ibdal/istibdal* inevitably leads to corruption and that this transaction is like a sharp knife capable of cutting both for good and for evil appears to have been exaggerated.[70] In a fascinating article Miriam Hoexter has argued that the alleged direct linkage between *istibdal* and corruption should not be taken for granted. On the contrary, she has furnished solid evidence from the Algerian waqf registers that *istibdal* transactions were not only economically fair but also constituted a very profitable business for the Algerian *Harameyn* waqfs.[71]

Classical Muslim jurists were concerned over the potentially destructive impact of *ibdal/istibdal* primarily because they considered waqfs as perpetual institutions. By contrast, English common law has been against 'perpetuities' ever since the sixteenth century. This is because it was felt in the West that a trust that lasts for a very long time means that a *deadhand* or *mortmain* is in control of the trust property, which ends up being controlled from the grave of the founder. They thought that this becomes harmful to the society by keeping the trust properties out of the market for far too long. But recently the rule against perpetuities is being debated and in some states of the USA it has been abolished.

In short, we have here a curious situation: whereas Islamic law would prefer that a waqf established with units of a unit trust should survive in perpetuity, Western law tries to limit the duration of a trust to at the most 21 years after the death of the last identifiable individual living at the time the trust was created.[72] The definitive preference of classical Islamic law for a waqf to last for very long periods, even centuries, means that if a wealthy Muslim establishes a waqf within the framework of a unit trust company, it is understood that this would be for the long, even the very long run. Obviously, unit trust funds are not established for such long periods. But this problem can be solved by 'sell/exchange', *ibdal/istibdal*, and the capital invested in a particular unit trust can be reinvested in another.

This brings us to the concept of the revocability of a waqf. Indeed, what happens if a person, after establishing a waqf, changes her mind and wishes to revoke the waqf? With the exception of Imam Abu Hanafi, the founder of the

Hanafite School, most jurists of all schools do not permit a founder to revoke an established waqf. Imam Hanafi permits the revocation of a waqf based upon a *sunnah* of the Prophet as well as the possibility that the founder may face unforeseen financial difficulties.[73] Thus, if a Muslim establishes a waqf by purchasing units from a unit trust company, he should be able to revoke it only based upon Imam Hanafi's ruling. This may prove difficult, particularly for those not adhering to the Hanafite School. By contrast, trust law permits revocation without any hindrance.

Possibly the most important problem a Muslim would face investing in a unit trust concerns the question of whether a waqf founder can appoint herself as the beneficiary of the waqf's usufruct. This is important because most people invest in a unit trust for personal benefit. But the trust component of a unit trust renders it, in the eyes of Islamic law, a waqf and subjects it to the law of waqfs. Classical Islamic jurists have not reached a consensus on this issue. The majority of the Shafi'ite, Hanbelite and Malikite jurists do not permit a waqf founder to appoint herself as the beneficiary. The only exception is provided by the Hanafite School. But even among the Hanafites there is no consensus, while Imam Abu Hanafi and Abu Yusuf permit, Imam Muhammad al-Shaybani does not. There is substantial evidence in the Ottoman archives that if the founder appoints herself as the beneficiary for a lifetime, providing she makes it clear that after her death the waqf revenues shall be spent for the good of the society, this has been permitted.[74] Thus, this Hanafite solution facilitates the use of unit trusts as modern instruments of investment providing Muslims of all schools can resort to it.

To sum up, investing in a unit trust, which combines the elements of both multiple *mudaraba* and waqf, is a *Shari'ah* based financial activity. It goes without saying that the actual investment must be done in products permitted by the *Shari'ah*. The major problem is that some of the components of this investment procedure are not allowed by some Islamic schools. However, Imam Abu Hanafi, followed by the majority of the jurists of the Hanafite school, permitted them. So the problem for a non-Hanafite Muslim boils down to whether she would feel comfortable with the rulings of Imam Abu Hanafi. For a well-intentioned Muslim who finds herself in this difficult situation, Imam Al-Ghazali recommends that this person should study why a certain activity has been permitted by some jurists and not by others. The Muslim investor should then practise her own *ijtihad* and make up her mind.[75] Providing they take these steps, all Muslims can invest in unit trusts within the framework of Islamic law and enjoy the peace of mind that comes with the belief that they are involved in a *Shari'ah* based financial transaction.

Apparently by 1992, 4.88 million *bumiputras*, Malay Muslims, had already made up their minds and invested their savings by purchasing RM14.46 billion worth of various units.[76] By 31 May 2005 they had purchased 125 billion units from 35 Unit Trust Management Companies.[77] But this is the story, primarily of *Permodalan Nasional Berhad*, which manages 53.5 billion units for eight million investors and must be told from the beginning.[78]

PERMODALAN NASIONAL BERHAD (PNB) OF MALAYSIA

The PNB was incorporated on 17 March 1978, as a wholly owned subsidiary of *Yayasan Pelaburan Bumiputra* (*Bumiputra* Investment Foundation) known as YPB with a paid-up capital of RM100 million.[79] The PNB was established as part of an ambitious national programme to enhance the economic well-being of Malay Muslims. The discrepancy in the relative economic situation of the various races in Malaysia had led to a series of frightening riots during the 1960s and it was decided that only a comprehensive affirmative action programme improving the lot of the *bumiputras* could save the country from disintegration. Launched in 1971 by the then Prime Minister Tun Abdul Razak, this programme was called the New Economic Policy (NEP) and targeted a 30 per cent share of the economy for the *bumiputra*. The NEP had the declared goal that while the economic discrepancy between the *bumiputra* and the economically dominant Chinese would decline in relative terms, in absolute terms the share of the Chinese would increase. More specifically, the initial target was to move the ratio of economic ownership from the 2.4:33:63 ratios of *bumiputra*, other Malaysian, foreigner ownership, respectively, to the 30:40:30 ratios.[80] This was to be done by increasing substantially the *bumiputra* ownership of enterprises mostly at the expense of foreigner (British) ownership. To this end a requirement that all initial public offerings (IPOs) set aside a 30 per cent share for *bumiputra* investors was imposed with the Industrial Coordination Act of 1975, which empowered the Minister of Trade and Industry to impose this requirement before a licence was issued (or renewed) to a company.[81]

Two institutions, *Perbadanan Nasional Berhad* (*Pernas*) and the PNB played a decisive role in the fulfilment of these goals. The *Pernas* was incorporated during the height of the race riots in 1969 with a paid up capital of RM116 million and is controlled by the Treasury. It immediately started to acquire some of the most important publicly listed companies of the country, particularly those under the control of the foreigners. In this context British corporations of tin mining and rubber plantations were particularly important.[82]

Despite these important developments and the accelerated transfer of corporate assets to *bumiputras*, the actual 'individual *bumiputra*' share of the total *bumiputra* equity dropped sharply from 60 per cent in 1970 to 34 per cent in 1980. This occurred at a time when the *bumiputra* equity was increasing at

23.5 per cent per annum.[83] This could mean only one thing: individual *bumiputras* were reselling the shares allotted to them during the IPOs almost as soon as they were getting them in their possession. This was self-defeating and was undermining all the goals of the entire affirmative action programme. In fact, it was clear that the shares were being sold back to the Chinese. Thus, clearly there was now an urgent need to stop reselling the shares back to the Chinese by retaining them under Malay control and at the same time spreading share ownership among the *bumiputras* so as to make them partners in the growth of modern Malaysia.

PNB was considered a solution to this problem. The corporation would take the possession of the shares allocated to *bumiputras* at the IPOs. It would then sell them to *bumiputras* through the unit trust system. This meant that while the *bumiputras* would be buying the units, the actual shares would be retained by the PNB. Initially, the units had prices fixed at one ringgit, but from January 1991, in addition to the old system, some units began to have flexible prices determined by the market.[84] These changes were deliberately designed by the government so as to introduce *bumiputras* to the complexities of stock markets.

To facilitate PNB acquisitions, the government provided large grants and interest-free loans. Within the first year of its inception, the PNB invested in 21 companies, that is to say, bought their *bumiputra* allocated shares at rock bottom prices in accordance with the New Economic Policy. The shares acquired amounted to RM51 346 374. At the end of 1978, the total market value of these shares had appreciated by 42.9 per cent.[85]

The speed of PNB's expansion has been phenomenal. By the end of 1990, it held shares in 162 companies, 107 of which were publicly listed.[86] About ten years later, in 2001, the then Prime Minister Dr Mahathir Mohamad announced that the PNB held equities of more than 300 companies, thus had successfully doubled its portfolio of companies. It was able to do this by pooling more than RM36 billion in *bumiputra* investments and it was able to attract these savings by having paid so far RM31 billion in dividends. Another important component of the whole scheme was to utilize the shares obtained so as to empower certain *bumiputras* to enter into the board of directors of these companies. The long-term goal was to equip *bumiputras* with important business know-how.[87] By 2003, the PNB had eight million account holders, who had bought 40 billion units.[88]

Moreover, the PNB did not grow in isolation. The unit trust industry's net asset value (NAV) under management increased to RM98.5 billion in 2005, an increase of 16.3 per cent from 2004.[89] Of the total 134.8 billion units circulating in the economy at the end of 2005, the units managed by the PNB accounted for 38 per cent. Looked from the perspective of NAV, the PNB controlled 53 per cent of the NAV in the country with a total of RM51.8 billion.[90] Thus, over the years the PNB has successfully maintained its leadership position within the Malaysian unit trust industry.

To conclude, the New Economic Policy of transferring wealth to *bumiputras* by utilizing unit trust funds appears to have succeeded in increasing share ownership among the Muslims. Wealth in the hands of Muslims went from 4 per cent in 1970 to about 16 per cent in 2006. Since the overall wealth of the country also grew from a GNP per capita of RM1170 in 1970 to RM12 102 in 1997, it can be concluded that the overall macrogoal of the NEP of increasing the relative wealth of *bumiputras* while increasing the absolute wealth of all, appears to have been achieved. All of this was accompanied by a substantial decline of absolute poverty from 50 per cent to 6.8 per cent.[91]

It goes without saying that imaginative economic and financial institutions mentioned in this book fully supported by an equally imaginative and determined state have contributed enormously to this success story. It is no wonder that the financial services sector has increased its share in GDP from 9.2 per cent in 2000 to 11 per cent in 2008 and that presently more than 140 000 workers are employed by this sector in Malaysia.[92] In short, the recent Malaysian economic history is actually by and large the story of building Islamic financial institutions with the full support of the state.

NOTES

1. On the importance of this process in European economic history, see Jones, *The European Miracle*.
2. This constitutes a definitive reply to the nineteenth-century orientalists' accusations that waqfs are nothing but a 'dead hand', a 'mortmain'.
3. When the endowed capital of a waqf is invested to buy corporate shares (equity finance), this is identical to *mudaraba* financing. This is because in this waqf–corporate partnership the entire capital is provided by the waqf, which becomes the *rab al-mal*, the principal. If the corporation (*mudarìb*/agent) makes a loss, its shares lose in value and the loss belongs to the principal, the waqf. The complicated problem of a cash waqf making a loss and endangering its longevity has been considered by the sixteenth-century Şeyhülislam Ebussuud, who dismissed it saying: 'I say, it does not matter. It evens out in time.' See Mandaville, 'Usurious Piety', p. 299.
4. This situation emerged as a response by the Turkish philanthropists to the government rule that the minimum paid in capital of a new waqf should not be less than US$500 000. This rule made capital pooling the *conditio sine qua non* of waqf establishment in Turkey.
5. Hoexter, *Endowments, Rulers and Community*, ch. 1.
6. For more details, see Faure, 'Charity Halls'.
7. The exact wording of the *fatwa* is as follows: 'Berwakaf dalam bentuk wang tunai adalah dibolehkan di dalam Islam', meaning: 'In Islam performing waqf in the form of cash is allowed.'
8. Kıraç, *Anılarımla Patronum Vehbi Koç*, pp. 81–5.
9. *Twenty-five Years of Philanthropy*, p. 6.
10. Çizakça. 'Cash Waqfs of Bursa'.
11. Italics are mine.
12. Ballar, *Yeni Vakıflar*, p. 663.
13. In the original 1967 Law, profits of the companies attached to the waqfs were tax exempt. Thus this 1994 decree is actually an infringement.
14. Yener, *Dernekler-Vakıflar Kanunu*, pp. 249, 259–60.
15. Ballar, *Yeni Vakıflar,* pp. 461–4.
16. Salamon and Toepler, *Non-Profit Law*.
17. Ballar, *Yeni Vakıflar*, p. 990.

18. According to Diyanet Vakfi, *Faaliyet Raporu*, pp. 109–19, this waqf had established six different companies and owned 80 to 99 per cent of their equities. It also purchased the shares of various Islamic banks (Kuveyt-Türk Evkaf Kurumu and Ihlas Finans) and insurance companies. Such shares constituted 1–10 per cent of the total net asset value of these companies.
19. The waqf–company linkages are cemented at the Koç conglomerate by an exchange of executive officers: two persons appointed by the holding sit at the Executive Board of the Vehbi Koç Foundation and two persons appointed by the latter sit at the Executive Board of the holding. In addition to these two persons appointed by the holding, the following persons sit at the Board of Directors of the Koç Foundation: four family members, the CEO of the holding, two professors (one jurist), and the General Manager of Iş Bank.
20. On the near identity of equity finance and the historical *mudaraba*, see Çizakça, (1996). This is not to say, however, that the modern Turkish cash waqfs completely operate through equity finance. Some of them are secularized and purchase bonds and receive interest disregarding the Islamic prohibition. See on this Ballar, *Yeni Vakıflar*, p. 41.
21. Indeed, consider the following rulings of the *Yargitay*, the Turkish Supreme Court: 'The *corpus* of a waqf can be any economic asset' and 'A waqf cannot be established unless *cash* has been deposited into its bank account.' *Yargitay 18. Hukuk Dairesi,* E. 1996/ 9020, K, 1996/ 9680, T. 5. 11. 1996 and E. 1996/ 11548, K. 1997/ 205, T. 21. 01. 1997.
22. Çizakça, 'Awqaf in History', pp. 43–73, 60–67.
23. The Vehbi Koç Foundation, *Twenty-five Years of Philanthropy,* p. 1. I am grateful to my sister, Professor Dr Çigdem Kâgitçibasi, for sending me this important document from Istanbul. Italics are mine.
24. Faroqhi, 'A Great Foundation' pp. 281–4.
25. *Vehbi Koç Vakfi Resmî Senedi*, Article 4, p. 5. Rahmi Koç, the late Vehbi Koç's son, has informed this author that his father one day summoned his children and asked them if they have any objection to the allocation of these shares to the Vehbi Koç Foundation. When they replied negatively, a notary public, who was waiting in an adjacent room, was called in and collected their signatures. In this way Vehbi Koç prevented any potential second-generation litigation in the future.
26. TÜSEV, *Elektronik Bülten*, No. 18, January 2009.
27. Although its endowment deed (Article No. 17) provides a minimum income (six million liras p.a. adjusted for inflation) to the future generations of the Koç family in case they need it, the Vehbi Koç Vakfi is only theoretically a family waqf. Its primary focus is charity and provision for the family is insignificant. Traditional family waqfs, which focus entirely on the provision for the family, though perfectly legitimate as far as the classical Islamic jurisprudence is concerned, are prohibited by Article 322 of the Turkish Civil Law. This prohibition, a clear Western influence, is now seriously challenged for undermining the institution of family. Thus, the search for modernized family waqfs has started (Ballar, 2000: 310, 771–6).
28. Faroqhi, 1995, p. 285.
29. Aydın, et al., p. 34.
30. Büker, Aydın, Sağlam, p. 4 and Aydın et al., pp. 33–4.
31. *Johor Corporation Legislations* (Johor Bahru: Perbadanan Johor, n.d.).
32. Sanusi, 'The Concept', forthcoming.
33. On these debates see; Çizakça, 'Was *Shari'ah* Indeed the Culprit?'.
34. The *Majallah*, an Ottoman codification from the nineteenth century still continues to be the most important Islamic codification. Modern and improved codifications are urgently needed in Islamic jurisprudence.
35. Waqaf An-Nur Berhad, *Annual Report*, p. 8.
36. The details of this endowment are revealed as follows: 'This declaration of endowment (waqf) is made at the Puteri Pacific Hotel, Johor Bahru, Johor before: 1) Sohibus Somanah Dato' Haji Noh bin Gadot, the Mufti for the State of Johor 2) Dato' Haji Mohd Zaini bin Osman, Chief Executive Officer, Majlis Agama Islam Negeri Johor 3) Sohibul Fadhil Ustaz Haji Mohd Noh bin Kadri, Kadi for the District of Johor on Thursday, 3 August 2006. That I, Tan Sri Dato' Muhammad Ali bin Hashim... as the Chief Executive of Johor Corporation, have been given the power by the Board of Governors of Johor Corporation pursuant to the meeting held on 27 September 2005 and I hereby in this day of... 3 August 2006 of sound mind, in good health, willingly and without any force and coercion from any other parties,

on behalf of Johor Corporation expressly declare that the shares of the below named companies shall now be converted to endowment (waqf): 1) *Kulim Berhad*: 12 347 826 shares in the total value of RM142 million 2) *KPJ Healthcare Berhad*: 18 595 041 units of shares in the total value of RM45 million 3) *Johor Land berhad*: 4 318 937 units of shares in the total value of RM13 million. The shares certificates are attached herewith for the purpose of determining the recipients (mauquf) of the benefit. The above shares are owned by Johor Corporation at the net asset value of RM 200 million for Allah Ta'ala. The 100 per cent profit benefit from the shares of *Kulim (M) Berhad, KPJ Healthcare Berhad* and *Johor Land Berhad* which have been converted to endowment (waqf) shall be distributed 70 per cent to Johor Corporation, 25 per cent to *Kumpulan Waqf An-Nur Berhad* and 5 per cent to *Majlis Agama Islam Negeri Johor*. Thereafter, the 70 per cent profit to Johor Corporation if the same is being re-invested, the profit thereof shall be distributed according to the discretion of the *Kumpulan Waqaf An-Nur Berhad*. Henceforth, from this date onwards, the ownership of the said shares shall be released by Johor Corporation to *Allah Ta'ala* forever and I shall determine or hereby appoint the *Kumpulan Waqaf An-Nur Berhad,* in lieu of Johor Corporation to be appointed special *Nazir* for the said endowment (waqf) in accordance with *Shari'ah* laws/principles. *Majlis Agama Islam Negeri Johor* by signing this declaration shall not be burdened by any liabilities or claims made under any written laws. On the creation and the validity of the endowment (waqf) hereby created, I hereby place my signature hereunto before the witnesses' presence. **Allah is the Best Witness.** Signature of the (Founder) *Waqif...* Tan Sri Dato' Muhammad Ali Hashim. *Declaration of Endowment (Waqf),* Rule 7(2), No. (WKF)J5/1/61, district: Johor Bahru, date: 3 August 2006.'

37. *Annual Report,* p. 27.
38. Ibid., p. 15.
39. Currently the KPJ manages 26 specialist hospitals that include 20 hospitals in Malaysia, three in Indonesia, one in Bangladesh, and two in Saudi Arabia. During the year 2008, the KPJ recorded a RM 1.3 billion earning, which is a 9.1 per cent increase from 2007 despite the global crisis. *Annual Report,* p. 32.
40. The listed companies are; KULIM, KPJ Healthcare and Johor Land Corporation. The unlisted ones are Tiram Travel, TPM Management Sdn Bhd and Capaian Aspirasi Sdn Bhd.
41. I was informed about this project directly by Tan Siri Muhammad Ali Hashim on 6 May 2009 at an informal discussion.
42. *Annual Report,* pp. 24, 45.
43. *Annual Report,* p. 27.
44. Ibid., pp. 23, 37.
45. Johor Corporation, *Intrepreneur Development Programme*.
46. *Business Jihad* (Kuala Lumpur: Corporate Bureau, Malaysian Islamic Chamber of Commerce), p. 20.
47. Munro, 'The Medieval Origins', p. 514.
48. Hashim, *Waqf An-Nur,* p. 8. At the time of the publishing of this book, I learned that Tan Sri Dato' Muhammad Ali bin Hashim resigned from his position as the CEO of the Johor Corporation and retired. It remains to be seen if the corporation will continue along the path Tan Sri Hashim had opened up.
49. Mannan, 'Cash Waqf Certificate', 1999.
50. Mannan, 'Cash Waqf Certificate', 1999, p. 21; Internet: http://www.siblbd.com/html/annual_report.html.
51. Abdel Mohsin, *Cash Waqf, A New Financial Product* , p. 50.
52. Barkan, 'H. 933-934 Tarihli Bütçe Cetveli', and Erol Özvar, 'Osmanlı Devleti'nin Bütçe Harcamaları'.
53. United Nations Development Programme, *Arab Human Development Report,* p. 7.
54. Çizakça, 'Waqf'.
55. Çizakça, *Philanthropic Foundations*, p. 4.
56. Ship shares were known in the Islamic world as *qirat*, and in the West as *carati*. Based upon the etymological similarity between *qirat* and *Qirad,* it has been hypothesized that the concept of ship shares may well have evolved from multiple *mudaraba*. *Qirad* is the synonym of *mudaraba*. For more on this, see Çizakça, *Comparative Evolution*, p. 27.
57. *Islamic Finance News,* 23 October 2009, p. 16.
58. www.affinfund.com.my.

59. Laldin, *Fundamentals and Practices*, p. 111.
60. Hasan, 'Islamic Finance: What Does It Change?'.
61. *Islamic Finance News,* 23 October 2009, pp. 16–17.
62. Çizakça, 'Was *Shari'ah* Indeed the Culprit?', passim.
63. These reasons can be traced to the different routes taken during the process of modernization. See on this Himmelfarb, *The Roads to Modernity.*
64. *Islamic Finance in Practice,* p. 47. For the most recent Jersey law, see Anderson, 'Waqf and Jersey', passim.
65. Selling the assets of a waqf in order to buy other assets is known as *ibdal,* and exchanging these assets with others as *istibdal*. Akgündüz, *Vakıf Müessesesi*, p. 195.
66. Known as *shurut al-ashara* (ten conditions), these Hanefite conditions have been regularly stated in most Ottoman waqf deeds. Unless stated clearly to the contrary in the deed, the founder can exercise these rights only once. If the founder wishes to exercise these rights more than once, however, he/she must clearly state so in the deed. The founder can equip the trustee with similar powers as well. The ten conditions are as follows. First, 'expand–reduce'. This condition empowers the founder to expand or reduce a beneficient's allotment. Second, 'enter–expel'. With this condition, the founder empowers himself/herself to include someone not originally mentioned in the deed as one of the beneficiaries. 'Expel' refers to the opposite. Third, 'pay–freeze'. This refers to the founder's power to freeze or to resume payments to a certain beneficiary. Fourth, 'change conditions–change purpose'. This refers to the founder's right to change the conditions or the purposes originally stated in the deed. Fifth, 'sell–exchange' (*ibdal/istibdal*). For further details, see Çizakça, *Philanthropic Foundations,* pp. 16–18.
67. Akgündüz, *Vakıf Müessesesi*, p. 291.
68. Behrens-Abouseif, *Adjustment,* pp. 146–7. In historical documents *istibdal* is often used for both sale and exchange.
69. Akgündüz, *Vakıf Müessesesi*, p. 294.
70. Akgündüz, *Vakıf Müessesesi*, p. 296.
71. Hoexter, 'Adaptation', pp. 319–33.
72. Vallario, 'The Rule Against Perpetuities'.
73. Akgündüz, *Vakıf Müessesesi,* pp. 95–6.
74. Ibid., pp. 183–5.
75. Rıza and Karaman, *Gerçek Islam'da Birlik*, p. 333.
76. Gomez and Jomo, *Political Economy*, p. 35.
77. Permodalan Nasional Berhad, *The Fabric of a Nation*, p. 15.
78. Permodalan Nasional Berhad, *Annual Report, 2005*, p. 30.
79. Permodalan Nasional Berhad, *Annual Report, 1978*, p. 14.
80. Some 35 years later, in 2006, the 15.8:42.8:40 ratio was achieved. Thus, while the shares of the *bumiputras* could be increased substantially, this increase still fell short of the originally planned 30 per cent. Kadir Jasin, 'The NEP Was Not a Failure', *Malaysian Business,* 16–31 July 2009, p. 5.
81. Ariff, *The Malaysian Economy*, p. 21, and 'Malaysian New Economic Policy', www.wikipedia.org, 7 November 2009.
82. For details, see Gomez and Jomo, *Malaysia's Political Economy*, p. 32.
83 Ibid., p. 34.
84. Gomez and Jomo, *Political Economy*, p. 35.
85. Permodalan Nasional Berhad, *Annual Report, 1978*, p. 14.
86. Gomez and Jomo, *Political Economy*, p. 38.
87. Zakaria, 'Dr. M Launches Another PNB Unit Trust', p. 1.
88. Ruhanie and Mahavera, '*Amanah Saham Gemilang*', pp. 1, 4.
89. Permodalan Nasional Berhad, *Annual Report, 2005*, p. 21.
90. Permodalan Nasional Berhad, *Annual Report, 2005*, p. 31.
91. Ariff, *The Malaysian Economy*, p. 26. Also see 'Malaysian New Economic Policy', www.wikipedia.org.
92. *Epicentre, the MIFC eNewsletter*, 26 October 2009, p. 1.
93. Faure, *China and Capitalism.*
94. Ibid., p. 38.
95. For detailed arguments about how the *dhimma* substitutes for judicial personality, particulary with regard to the waqfs, see Zahraa, 'Legal Personality', p. 205.

APPENDIX TO CHAPTER 8

The Chinese *tang* and the Islamic waqf: A Comparison

Thanks to the small but highly informative book of David Faure published recently,[93] we are now able to make a comparison between the Chinese *tang* and the Islamic waqf. This section is put into an appendix as it may not interest those readers who are primarily interested in the origins and evolution of Islamic capitalism and finance. But in a country like Malaysia, where Chinese and Islamic cultures coexist, this comparison may be of interest.

The first remarkable feature of the Chinese *tang* is that it had corporate structure. This was thanks to the fact that a *tang*, which means an assembly hall of a temple, was dedicated to ancestors or deities. The ancestor or deity in the name of whom the *tang* property was held, therefore, assumed the character of a legal person.[94] So people who shared the same lineage or worshipped the same deities came together in a *tang*. There is a similarity here to the Islamic waqf, which is also dedicated to an abstract person, *Allah* (see the endowment deed of the Johor Corporation presented above). The *tang* holds property on the understanding that it is held for the maintenance of sacrifice to ancestor or deity, and therefore the property is considered to belong to the spirit to whom sacrifice is offered. Exactly the same abstract concept of property rights can be found in the Islamic waqf.

But the similarity ends there because, as explained above, the concept of fictitious (or abstract or judicial) personality is subject to debate in Islamic jurisprudence.[95] Modern Muslims, however, establish their waqfs as corporations, a crystal clear concept borrowed from the West, and avoid the ambiguities of Islamic law in this context.

The *tang* enjoyed an advantage vis-à-vis the historical Western corporation in the sense that, unlike the latter, it did not need a government charter. This advantage also existed for the pre-modern waqf. Anyone with some means could go to the local *kadi* and obtain a deed to establish a waqf. In the Islamic world, the need to obtain a permission from the central government emerged much later under the influence and pressure of Western imperialism.

The pre-modern *tang* and the waqf differed in that the former was established by a multitude of individuals belonging to the same lineage. By contrast, the traditional Islamic waqf was established by a single person. Thus, the *tang* was more similar to the modern Turkish multiple founder cash waqfs, which emerged in Turkey in response to the pressure of the republican government. It can therefore be argued that, with the exception of sultans and extremely powerful viziers, Islamic waqfs, in general, must have had less capital at their disposal than the *tang,* which could pool the resources of many people. With the invention of the multiple founder waqfs in Turkey and cash waqf certificates in

Bangladesh, however, the modern Islamic world appears to have overcome this initial problem. A quantitative comparison of the Chinese *tang* with the Islamic waqf from the perspective of capital accumulation has not yet been attempted.

The question as to why this near-perfect Chinese corporate institution did not develop further, so as to accumulate sufficient capital to finance a Chinese industrial revolution, has been answered by pointing out to the state that the Chinese imperial government jealously maintained its power to control large-scale trade and allowed merchants to conduct trade only as an imperial favour, in return for which, merchants were subjected to unspecified and arbitrary exactions in the form of 'gift'. Moreover, taxation was also unpredictable. In the Islamic world, particularly in the Ottoman caliphate, the negative impact of the state on private enterprise appears to have been at least equally serious. But since this has been already explained in detail above, it will not be repeated here.

9. The birth and evolution of modern Islamic banking

Never accept conventional bankers into the Islamic banking sector!

Dr Ahmad al-Naggar, the Father of Islamic Banking

INTRODUCTION

Recent research has revealed that the value of total global assets and assets under management of Islamic finance reached US$951 billion in 2008 and is expected to reach US$1 trillion by 2010 and US$1.6 trillion by 2012. These assets are expected to generate revenues of US$120 billion. Commercial banks accounted for 74 per cent of the 2008 figure, with investment funds, *sukuk*, other funds and *takaful* accounting for 10, 10, 5 and 1 per cent respectively.[1] Research has also shown that Islamic banks are growing more rapidly than the average banking sector in most countries. Indeed, the rate of growth of the Islamic financial services industry, as a whole, has exceeded 20 per cent annually since 2000. In 2005 this rate of growth of the assets held by Islamic banks (and windows) was 28.6 per cent. By contrast, during this period, the world's top 1000 conventional banks achieved an annual asset growth of just 6.8 per cent as of July 2009.

The sub-prime crisis affected the Islamic and conventional banking systems in very different ways. While the combined market capitalization of top ten conventional banks suffered a huge decline of 42.8 per cent, Islamic banks suffered merely a decline of 8.5 per cent for the period 2006–9. By the same token, while net profits of conventional banks fell dramatically from US$116 billion to a net loss of US$42 billion in 2008, net profits of Islamic banks increased 9 per cent from US$4.2 billion to US$4.6 billion in the same period. Moreover, five of the top ten conventional banks received government assistance to the extent of US$163 billion in aggregate. As at 2009, none of the Islamic banks needed any government rescue scheme.[2]

These observations, however, are subject to the following caveats. First, the size of the Islamic banks is a fraction of that of the conventional banks. The size of Islamic bank assets as a percentage of total bank assets was less than 1 per cent in 2008.[3]

There are currently more than 300 Islamic financial institutions (IFIs) spread across 51 countries, including the non-Muslim countries such as Australia, China, France, Germany, Hong Kong, Italy, Japan, Korea, Luxembourg, Singapore and the UK.[4] There are already five Islamic banks formally established and operational in the UK as at end 2009.

But meanwhile, it must be noted that modern Islamic banks, as originally envisaged[5] by Dr Ahmad Al-Naggar, have been going through a remarkable transformation. While on the asset side *mudaraba/musharaka* have been replaced by *murabaha* from the early days on, recently the liability side is also being transformed. These changes, particularly the recent ones of the liability side, are tantamount to transforming Islamic banks to conventional banks. This trend, however, is strongly resisted by the *Shari'ah* boards of Islamic banks as well as higher authorities. Evidence for these claims will be presented below.

But for now, it would be appropriate to expand this chapter by an explanation of the pillars of Islamic finance.

THE FIVE PILLARS OF ISLAMIC FINANCE

Probably inspired by the classical five pillars of Islam,[6] modern Islamic finance is also considered to be based upon five basic principles, pillars. These are as follows.

1. The ban on interest must be obeyed.
2. The ban on uncertainty or speculation: uncertainty in contractual terms and conditions is forbidden. But when all conditions and terms are known to all parties, risk-taking is allowed.
3. The ban on certain products must be obeyed.
4. Profit and loss sharing must prevail. Parties to a financial transaction must share in the risks and rewards.
5. Each financial transaction must refer to a tangible, identifiable underlying asset.

We will now observe how these five basic principles of Islamic finance are institutionalized.

ORIGINS OF ISLAMIC BANKING

Cash waqfs may well be considered as the very first banks in the Islamic world. These waqfs provided credit to numerous borrowers by utilizing *istiglal*, a form of asset-based finance, based on selling and buying back the same asset (usually the borrower's house). Through these transactions cash waqfs obeyed, if not the spirit, at least the letter of the law and provided capital to those who needed it without violating Islamic law.

But what was disbursed here to various borrowers was the original capital, corpus, of the cash waqf endowed by a single wealthy person. Consequently, the amounts transferred to borrowers could not be very large. For much larger amounts to be transferred to borrowers the liability/deposit side had to be transformed and capital had to be pooled, in short, an Islamic bank had to be created, a process which had to wait until the twentieth century.

The first step during the twentieth century was taken with the so-called *Sunduq at-Tawhir* affair. This *Sunduq* was an early twentieth-century savings fund, which yielded a fixed rate of interest. The rate was fixed by the Khedive of Egypt and 3000 depositors refused to take this fixed rate of interest. The case was brought to the Mufti Muhammad Abduh (d. 1905). He ruled that in no way can *riba* be accepted and that these moneys should be put to use through *istiglal* on the basis of *Sharikat al-mudaraba*. In other words, the Mufti was reiterating the classical Ottoman cash waqf combined with what Imam Zufar had suggested way back during the eighth century.

The Khedive Abbas II was naturally annoyed about these developments. So he appointed a board of jurists from the al-Azhar to revise the *Sunduq*'s case. A highly complicated and confused case emerged out of all this. But the following conclusions can be drawn.

1. On paper, a scheme was devised to transform the fixed interest originally planned into a *mudaraba* operation.
2. But the *mudaraba* does not seem to have been applied. This is revealed by the fact that returns did not exhibit a fluctuating trend.[7]

The *Sunduq*'s activities seem to have gone on in practice unperturbed. The whole affair was unimportant in terms of the money involved. But it started the twentieth-century debate over *riba* at the highest intellectual and institutional level. The debate continued to evolve in undivided India during and after the depression of the 1930s.[8]

In Egypt, the debate resurfaced in the late 1930s. This time the trigger was the drafting of the Egytian Civil Law by a committee headed by Abd ar-Razzaq as-Sansuri. The work had taken more than a decade and in 1949 the new Egyptian Civil Code passed into law.

In the previous Civil Code, Article 125/185 had already permitted an interest rate up to 8 per cent. The new Civil Code, against all expectations, continued to permit, in Article 227, an interest rate up to the maximum rate of 7 per cent. This led to a renewed debate.[9] These debates prepared the ground for a quantum leap that was to come soon.

This leap was achieved by Dr Ahmed Al-Naggar in 1963, when he established the very first modern Islamic bank. In recognition of this achievement Dr Ahmed Al-Naggar is also known as the 'Father of Islamic Banks'. Dr Al-Naggar established his Islamic bank in Mit Ghamr. This bank is referred to as the Mit Ghamr experience, Mit Ghamr being a small city in Egypt. Although the experiment had lasted merely four years and was closed by Nasser amid accusations of Islamic fundamentalism, the foundations of modern Islamic banking had been successfully laid down.

It is possible to find some of the basic principles of Al-Naggar's bank in Muhammad Baqer As-Sadr's writings. But to what extent Al-Naggar was influenced by As-Sadr is not clear,[10] as-Sadr's model guarantees the deposits. This is done by the bank offering a third party guarantee to the depositors. Since Al-Naggar had received his PhD in Germany, it has also been argued that he was influenced by the German *Sparkassen*. Nienhaus has argued that 'the fantastic plan to transform *fellahin*s to savers' was born in the seminars and classrooms of the University of Köln.[11] To this I should add that, during the two years I spent with Dr Al-Naggar,[12] I do not ever recall him having referred to his German academic background. Although he was certainly convinced that the poor could become savers, and in this he may well have been influenced by the German *Sparkassen*, his reference point was the classical Islamic jurisprudence.

The Mit Ghamr project had unexpected success. Confirming Dr Al-Naggar's views, savings deposits increased from 25 000 Egyptian pounds in 1963 to 125 000 in 1966. These savings account holders were not paid any interest, but they were eligible for small, short-term, interest-free loans for productive purposes.[13] They were allowed to withdraw their deposits on demand.

Investment accounts on the basis of profit sharing were also introduced.[14] During the same period, investment deposits increased from 35 000 to 75 000 Egyptian pounds. It has been documented that the bank had followed a cautious approach and rejected 60 per cent of loan applications in the first three years. This was because, according to Dr Al-Naggar, who wanted to introduce a saving culture to Egypt, a person became eligible for an interest-free loan only after demonstrating a reliable saving behaviour. Probably thanks to this philosophy, the default ratio was zero.[15]

As revealed in Figure 9.1, the liability/deposit side of Dr Al-Naggar's bank was basically a multiple *mudaraba*. Each depositor to an investment account was actually considered to be an investor, a *rab al-mal* of a *mudaraba* partnership. The bank acted as the *mudarib*/agent for all the depositors. When the bank generated a profit, about 80 per cent of it would be distributed among the depositors *pro rata*. The remaining 20 per cent would be taken by the bank as the *mudarìb*'s fee. Recently, some banks have extended the *mudarìb*'s fee up to 40 per cent of the distributable cash flows in order to create a reserve in case of emergencies. Thus, if the bank faces a liquidity shortage, it can simply waive its *mudarìb*'s fee so as to allow a higher remuneration to investment account holders.[16]

If loss occurred, it would be distributed between the investment account holders, in proportion to their capital contributions, as well as the shareholders. As it will be remembered, these are the basic conditions of a classical *mudaraba* partnership: while profits are distributed either according to the original capital contributed or as mutually agreed between the partners, loss accrues entirely to investors.

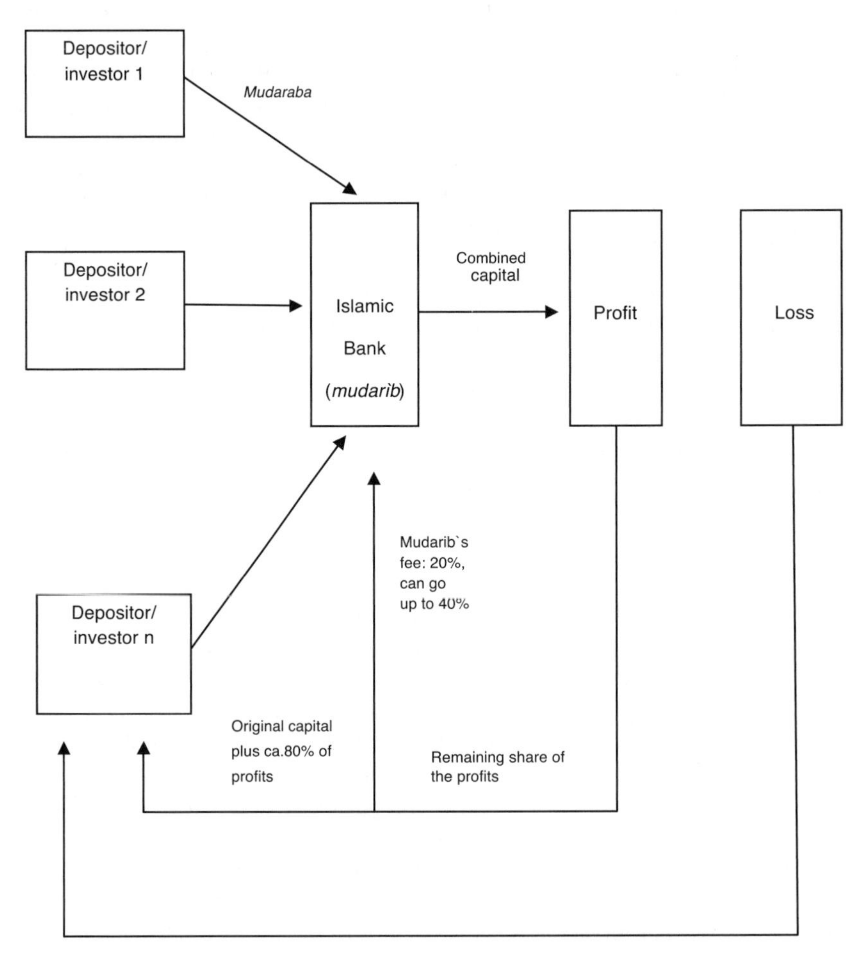

Figure 9.1 Islamic bank liability/deposit side (investment account)

But so far, this is only half of the story. The other half (asset side) pertains to the profit/loss sharing between the bank and the entrepreneurs it finances. Originally, it was envisaged by Dr al-Naggar that the bank would sign *mudaraba* contracts with these entrepreneurs. Thus, both the liability and the asset sides would be dominated by this partnership form. This structure was called the two-tier *mudaraba*.[17] Thus, whereas the term multiple *mudaraba* refers to the multiplicity of the depositor/investors depositing their savings with an Islamic bank, the term two-tier *mudaraba* refers to the entire structure of an Islamic bank combining both the liability and the asset sides, with both sides being dominated by *mudaraba* partnerships.

We might add here that in the asset side rather than the *mudaraba*, which Dr. Al-Naggar had originally planned, Islamic banks eventually came to prefer other instruments, primarily the *murabaha,* to finance the entrepreneurs. Indeed, the average share of profit and loss sharing (PLS) financing including both *mudaraba* and *musharaka*, during the period 2000–3, was a meagre 5.6 per cent, while the remaining 94.4 per cent was provided by *murabaha* and other deferred liability financing forms.[18] In the liability side, however, *mudaraba* was able to attract the savers who deposited their savings into the investment accounts with Islamic banks. Moreover, specialized *mudaraba* companies emerged particularly in Pakistan, where they were able to mobilize savers to deposit their savings with them. But they were less successful in finding suitable profitable outlets to finance with these savings.[19]

In short, the *mudaraba* partnership played an important role in the liability side and succeeded in attracting the savings of the masses. But, even this is being challenged and this ancient *Shari'ah* based partnership form practised by the Prophet himself is now being crowded out from the liability side as well. The details of this development will be given below.

THE *MODUS OPERANDI* OF ISLAMIC BANKING TODAY

Liability side of an Islamic bank is divided into two windows: demand deposits and investment balances. The model has 100 per cent reserve requirement for the demand deposits and no reserve requirement for the investment window. This is because demand deposits are *amanah* (trust) deposits and the bank may not use them as the basis for money creation through fractional reserves. Investment accounts are, however, invested with the full knowledge of the depositors that their funds are invested in risky projects and therefore no guarantee is granted. In Islamic banks investment account holders (IAHs) are a unique class of liability holders. They are neither depositors nor equity holders. Although IAHs are not part of the bank's capital they are expected to absorb all losses on the investments made through their funds.

Consequently, IAHs should not be subject to any capital requirements. But investments funded by current accounts carry commercial banking risks and should be subject to the same capital requirements. The complex problem of what should be included and what should be excluded from the capital adequacy ratio (CAR), has been clarified by the AAOIFI in 1998. In this statement it was suggested that first, the risk-bearing profit and loss sharing investment accounts should not be included.[20] Second, all assets financed by debt-based liabilities and own-equity should be included in the denominator of the CAR. Third, 50 per cent of PLSIA financed assets should be included in the denominator. The last measure is needed to cover for the possible losses arising from misconduct or negligence in investment activities. The AAOIFI proposal has been criticized on the grounds that risk-cushioned shareholders would push managers for excessive risk-taking in bad times and insufficient risk-taking in good times. This would naturally mean for the PLSIA holders that while their risks are amplified during bad times, too little risk would be taken in good times with the result that there would be lower returns on their investments. Moreover, since the AAOIFI proposal focuses on 'bank's own capital' risk measures, this gives managers and shareholders the incentive to shift even more risks onto the PLSIA holders. Favouring one party at the expense of the other would naturally violate the most important principle of Islamic banking – risk sharing. It has been argued that such an important violation has occurred due to mimicking the Basle solvency-oriented formulas. A true Islamic bank regulatory framework should have focused on protecting PLSIA holders from managers adopting inappropriate strategies (too much or too little risk-taking) in order to cater to the interests of the banks' shareholders.[21]

These different accounts with different liabilities provide the Islamic banker with a portfolio of investment funds, subject to the same capital requirements as are applicable to a fund manager.

An Islamic bank acting as a *mudarìb* faces a moral hazard issue: since it is not liable for losses to the PLSIA holders, it has an incentive to maximize the investments funded by the PLSIA holders and by attracting more PLSIA holders than it can have the capacity to deal with. This situation may call for greater capital requirement.[22]

Indonesia, Iran, Lebanon, Malaysia, Pakistan, Sudan, Turkey, UAE and Yemen have all enacted Islamic banking laws. But these laws do not always take into account the unique characteristics of these institutions. For instance, the Malaysian Islamic Banking Act (1993) refers to banking as 'lending business' and investment accounts are considered to be liabilities. In Iran, IFIs accept customer investments on the basis of *Wakala* contract, not the *mudaraba* contract as in other countries. The *Wakala* contract is on the basis of the agent receiving a fixed fee, not a share of profits like in the *mudaraba*.[23] In Saudi Arabia and Egypt no laws have been enacted to regulate the IFIs. They operate under the same laws governing conventional banks. Kuwait's sole IFI was licensed as a finance house, not a bank and supervised by the Kuwaiti Ministry of Commerce, rather than the Central Bank until 2004, when it came under the latter's supervision.

As for the overall assets controlled by Islamic banks, Malaysian Islamic banking assets amounted to about half of the total assets of Islamic banks operating in the GCC countries in 2004. Moreover, approximately 82 per cent of Islamic fixed income securities were issued out of this country. In 2006 Malaysia was reported to have become the largest Islamic banking market in the world, with an Islamic money market monthly volume of RM30–40 billion.[24] Moreover, research has shown that these Islamic banks are as efficient as any conventional competitor.[25] This is probably thanks to the fierce competition with the conventional ones. With competition so fierce, it is not surprising that banks achieve near equal levels of efficiency. In view of the great advantages enjoyed by the conventional system, the importance of having achieved more or less similar levels of efficiency for Islamic banks should not be underestimated. In Malaysia, the market share of the Islamic sector – exclusive plus Islamic windows of conventional banks – was around nine per cent in 2007. By 2010, it was planned to increase this to 20 per cent.[26]

Most recently, the fundamental structure of Dr Ahmed Al-Naggar's bank, described above, has been going through a transformation, particularly on the liability side. By utilizing instruments like the commodity *murabaha* and *tawarruq*, depositors are now being rewarded with fixed returns. Moreover, the very natures of investment accounts are now being changed. This is nothing less than transforming the depositor from the risk-taking *mudaraba* investor that he was in Al-Naggar's bank into someone who earns fixed returns for his deposits.

This transformation can now be documented thanks to the latest and still on-going research.[27] We are now informed that between 2004 and 2007 average deposit structure of 12 Islamic banks operating in Malaysia has undergone a significant change with the traditional *mudaraba* investment accounts declining and non-*mudaraba* accounts increasing. On average, the *mudaraba* deposits, which used to constitute 100 per cent of the investment accounts, are now reduced to 70 per cent and non-*mudaraba* deposits have increased from practically zero to 30 per cent. These non-*mudaraba* deposits are in the form of *wadiah* or *qard hasan*. Thus they appear to be deposits or loans for purely safe keeping without earning any return. But it is well known that depositors are paid so-called *hiba*s, gifts. Although definitive data are missing, we can surmise that these gifts are fixed returns benchmarked to the prevalent deposit rate of interest. Commodity *murabaha* and *tawarruq* contracts should also be considered within the non-*mudaraba* deposit category. Three Malaysian Islamic banks have transformed their liability side such that non-*mudaraba* accounts have now begun to dominate. Of these, Maybank Islamic's non-*mudaraba* accounts comprise 56 per cent, Public Islamic Bank's 80 per cent and AFFIN's 68 per cent of their deposits.[28] These arguments will be made clearer below, where commodity *murabaha* and *tawarruq* instruments will be explained in detail.

On the asset side, the bank disburses all the capital collected from investors to entrepreneurs. Originally, Ahmed Al-Naggar had thought that *mudaraba* or *musharaka* contracts would be signed between the bank and the entrepreneurs. This hope was shared by many scholars for two reasons. First, these contracts had been used by Prophet Muhammad himself, and therefore enjoyed great respect. Second, thanks to the basic characteristics of, particularly, the *mudaraba*, it was thought that Islamic banks disbursing their funds through this partnership would significantly enhance entrepreneurship.

The *mudaraba* enhances entrepreneurship in two important ways. First, since in this partnership the entire capital is provided by the capitalist partner, entry of a young entrepreneur without any capital of his own into business is made possible. Second, in case of loss, this young and penniless entrepreneur does not suffer pecuniary loss – he loses only time and effort. With entrepreneurship so enhanced, it was hoped further that the Islamic world would finally achieve its own industrial revolution. These hopes were shattered when it became clear that Islamic bankers stubbornly avoided signing *mudaraba*/*musharaka* contracts with entrepreneurs and preferred to utilize *murabaha* contracts instead.

There are a number of reasons why the Islamically most appropriate investment contract, the *mudaraba*, is shunned by Islamic bankers. To start with, there is uncertainty about the *ex post* rate of profit, and Islamic bankers who find themselves in serious competition with conventional banks, feel the need to pay their depositors rates of return at least commensurate with what the latter pay. To be able to guarantee this, they feel the need to use instruments with fixed returns. Moreover, uncertainty is aggravated due to asymmetric information, which gives rise to agency problems.[29] How to deal with such problems demands a specialized know-how and belongs to the realm of venture capital. Islamic bankers are not venture capitalists and it would be unfair to expect them to act like venture capitalists while at the same time subjecting them to all the pressures of short-term banking. If a bank provides financing to an entrepreneur with a *mudaraba* contract, it can receive from the entrepreneur the principal, if and only if the enterprise has achieved profits or broke even. In case of a loss, the bank would not be able to recover the principal. This is the essence of *mudaraba* and this situation does not constitute a default on the part of the entrepreneur. Moreover, the bank has no legal control over the actions of the entrepreneur, who has the complete freedom to run his enterprise. The primary difference between the Islamic *mudaraba* and venture capital (to be discussed below) rests in this issue of legal control. Whereas in venture capital, the venture capitalist can legally control the entrepreneur thanks to the shares he possesses, the Islamic bank has no such control over the entrepreneur. Since in *musharaka* contracts banks have better means to monitor the business they invest in, these contracts are more popular among the Islamic bankers. Indeed, in *musharaka* contracts all partners may concur with the management and banks hold direct voting rights.[30] Still another reason why *mudaraba* is shunned by Islamic bankers is that it is difficult to incorporate into these contracts a collateral clause. Furthermore, the problem of 'mis-match of funds' is also prevalent in *mudaraba* financing. Indeed, while most investment account holders deposit their cash on a short-term basis to Islamic banks, *mudaraba* investment yields returns in the long term. Finally, *mudaraba* investing, like its Western counterpart venture capital, is a highly specialized investment requiring close cooperation between the financier and the financed. Islamic bankers are neither equipped nor have the patience for this special and highly skilled form of investment.

Meanwhile, for some authors, it is not the legitimacy of deferred contract forms like the *murabaha* and its derivatives, such as the reverse *murabaha* or the *tawarruq*, that is the problem, but rather the extent to which they have come to dominate Islamic banking. There is a general consensus among scholars that this dominance will provide a cover for interest from the back door. While most scholars are very concerned about this, it is also acknowledged that deferred contracts enable Islamic banks to compete with conventional banks by bringing in assured income at lower risk.[31] In short, the desire to run the Islamic banking industry in compliance with the *Shari'ah* conflicts with the need to compete with the conventional system and the instinct to act like them. We will consider how these problems might be solved in Chapter 13.

THE MODERN *MURABAHA*

Thus, due to these difficulties, *mudaraba* is avoided and largely replaced by *murabaha* contracts. The application of the classical *murabaha*, described in Chapter 4, to modern Islamic banking is based upon two classical rulings:

1. Shafi'ite permission that a potential buyer can tell a seller 'buy this commodity and I will buy it from you at x per cent mark-up';
2. Malikite jurist Ibn Shubruma's ruling that the potential buyer's promise is binding.

The proposal to apply these *murabaha* concepts developed by the classical jurists to modern finance, thus replicating secured lending in a *Shari'ah* compliant manner, was made for the first time by Sami Humud in 1976.[32] This proposal inspired a *fatwa* at the First Conference of Islamic Banks convened in 1979 in Dubai. This *fatwa* was based on Ibn Shubruma's ruling that an Islamic financial institution may require its customer to sign a binding promise that he will purchase the financed commodity on credit with an agreed-upon mark-up once the bank buys it based upon his order. In the conference it was further concluded that the potential buyer's promise was legally binding on both parties based upon the Maliki ruling and religiously binding on both parties for all other schools. Moreover, it has been claimed that based upon the ruling of the Pakistani jurist M. Taqi Usmani, jurists allowed the mark-up to be benchmarked to conventional rate of interest.[33] This was considered *Shari'ah* compliant because of two risks: first, the risk of ownership between the two sales; and second, the risk that the property may be returned to the bank (as seller) if a defect is found therein.

In practice, however, the risk of ownership is made minimal by restricting the time period between the two sales to minutes if not seconds. Moreover, the cost of insurance against the risk of having to accept the returned defected asset can easily be transferred to the original seller.[34] The modern *murabaha* (mark-up sale to the one who ordered the purchase) which emerged from the rulings described above can be described as follows. A typical *murabaha* is a simple transaction between a bank and its customer, an entrepreneur who wants to borrow from the bank. *Murabaha* is also suitable for corporate customers borrowing large sums from each other and where transaction costs are sufficiently small.[35] Since a formal description of the *murabaha* by Bank Negara Malaysia will be provided below, it should suffice here to note that a typical *murabaha* contract drawn between an Islamic bank and a client would include the following: the product to be imported or bought by the bank, the mark-up to be charged, the mode of payment, that is, lump sum or in instalments and the statement to the effect that the bank accepts the commodity imported as collateral against the risk of default in payment by the client.[36]

As is well known, *murabaha* is the most frequently used and widespread instrument for modern Islamic finance. Moreover, new instruments are derived from it nearly every day and they are often misused. Misuse of such an important instrument and its very rapid evolution inevitably led to a reaction by authorities. The most recent and serious reaction came from the Shari'ah Advisory Council of Bank Negara Malaysia. Called *Shari'ah Parameter Reference 1: Murabaha*, this important document was announced by the Central Bank of Malaysia on 28 August 2009. This is a welcome development and will lead to a standardization of the *murabaha* contract not only in Malaysia but, in all probability, in much of the Islamic world as well. As the name of the document suggests, this is only the very first of such documents. Bank Negara has announced that similar documents aiming to standardize *ijara*, *mudaraba*, *musharaka*, *istisna'* and *wadiah* are in the pipeline as well. Some of the more important points of this 37-pages-long document can be summarized as follows,[37]

1. In modern Islamic finance *murabaha* is utilized as a mode of asset financing. The purchase price is a marked-up price, which is made known before the transaction. Islamic financial institutions (IFIs) executing the *murabaha* are expected to furnish the purchase orderer with full and correct information on cost and profit. Therefore, *murabaha* is also considered a trust sale, where the buyer depends and relies on the integrity of the seller with regard to the cost and profit that the latter discloses to the buyer.[38]
2. *Murabaha* contract has also been applied for deposit taking by Islamic banks and issuance of *sukuk*. Thus the Bank Negara acknowledges that it is aware of these practices without, however, revealing its position yet vis-à-vis these practices. It is to be expected that as *murabaha* applications for deposit taking by Islamic banks spreads further, as referred to above, the bank will eventually issue another parameter on this practice. This is confirmed by another statement that 'any practice by the IFIs, which is not specified in the parameter can be conducted as long as it does not contradict the features outlined in the parameter'.[39] Thus, we are given the impression that the Bank Negara prefers first to observe the latest innovations in practice and then would issue another pertinent parameter on it.
3. In illustration no. 1 of the parameter, *murabaha* is explained as follows: 'A purchase orderer applies to an IFI for car financing. The IFI purchases the car from the supplier, then, sells it to the purchase orderer on a deferred payment basis. The difference between the purchase price paid by the IFI to the supplier and the sale price that the IFI is selling to the purchase orderer is a mark-up for the IFI...' In a typical *murabaha* transaction the supplier earns trading profit while the financier earns the financing profit through the mark-up.
4. From an operational perspective a *murabaha* involves four components: customer order with *wa'd* or promise to purchase; acquisition at known and mutually agreed cost; sale at mark-up; and deferred payment.[40]
5. Since *murabaha* is essentially a sale contract, its legality is deduced from the Qur'an as well as the *sunnah*.[41] Some jurists have allowed *murabaha* based on the following analogy: since the Prophet has approved the *tawliah* sale, which is based on cost price, the sale on mark-up should also be equally permissible. Determination of cost and making the cost known to the buyer are common in both the *tawliah* and the *murabaha* sale.[42]

6. *Murabaha* comprises several other features as well: price of *murabaha* sale; asset of *murabaha* sale; duty of full disclosure of cost and profit; and *wa'd*, promise to buy.
7. The mark-up has to be determined before the conclusion of the contract. Most importantly, *any* mutually agreed benchmark, including the conventional financial benchmark, such as the base lending rate (BLR), may be used to determine the mark-up.[43] This important clause is then confirmed further by illustration two as well as item no. 77 of the parameter, so as to leave no doubt.
8. Upon the acquisition of an asset and until the ownership is transferred to the 'purchase orderer', the IFI is liable for the asset. If the IFI wishes to protect itself against this risk, the insurance, *takaful*, cost may be added to the cost of acquisition.
9. If the purchaser learns from the supplier that the IFI has disclosed too high a price for the asset, the *murabaha* contract becomes null and void *ab initio* due to the failure of disclosing the actual cost price.[44]
10. The mark-up could be either a fixed amount or a percentage of the purchase price.
11. Assets to be purchased shall be assets which are in existence. Assets under construction are not eligible. Moreover, these assets must be legally owned and physically possessed by the IFI prior to the *murabaha* sale to the customer. Thus the parameter prohibits some of the most blatant abuses of *murabaha* sales.
12. *Shari'ah* compliant shares may be made as asset of a *murabaha* transaction.[45]
13. A *murabaha* sale shall not take effect between the same contracting parties on the same asset. The importance of this item will become clear below.
14. The promise by the 'purchase orderer' to purchase the asset from the IFI upon the latter's acquisition of the asset shall be binding on the 'purchase orderer'. This is based upon the 1979 Dubai *fatwa,* which we have referred to above. Thus the Bank Negara has now incorporated it into the *Shari'ah* parameter and standardized it.[46]
15. In the case of the death of the customer, the outstanding liability of the customer may be waived by the IFI. If, however, the waiver is not granted in the contract, then the IFI may claim the outstanding debt of the deceased from his estate.
16. If a customer defaults, he may be granted an extension to settle his debts, provided no additional charges on the financing amount are imposed. This clause stands in sharp contrast to conventional finance, where an extension of the period of repayment is usually associated with additional charges.

17. There are basically two types of assurances in a *murabaha*. The assurance at the *wa'd* stage is to ensure actual purchase of the asset by the 'purchase orderer' from the IFI, while the assurance at the *murabaha* contract stage is to ensure full payment of the selling price at maturity. These assurances may be in the form of a security deposit, a third-party guarantee, a pledge of an asset, cheques etc. But securities of non-*Shari'ah* approved companies such as shares of conventional banks shall not be accepted as collateral. The IFI may also demand from the 'purchase orderer' a security deposit, *hamish jiddiyah*, to compensate against possible losses in the event that the 'purchase orderer' breaches the promise, *wa'd*. This deposit may be treated as part of the payment of the agreed selling price and hence is not refundable.[47]

THE COMMODITY *MURABAHA* (ORGANIZED *TAWARRUQ* OR REVERSE *MURABAHA*)

Currently a more complicated version, the 'commodity *murabaha*' is increasingly being used. This is also known as organized *tawarruq* or reverse *murabaha*. The origins of these instruments can be traced back to the classical *sharikat al-wujuh*, partnership of good reputations, also known as the *sharikat al-mafalis*, partnership of the penniless, described in Chapter 3. Both names denote a situation whereby two merchants who have lost their capital seek to re-enter into business by buying a commodity on credit with deferred price and selling this same commodity to third parties with spot price, for cash. When they sell the commodity for cash, they obtain the capital that they need to re-enter the market. They can then use this capital for further investment and profit, with which they then pay their debt to the original seller. They can do all this thanks to their good reputation, hence the name *sharikat al-wujuh*, partnership of good reputations.[48]

It must be noted, however, that the classical *wujuh* was characterized by ignorance in the sense that the original merchant from whom the commodity was bought with deferred payment did not know the merchant to whom the *wujuh* partners have sold on spot basis. Classical jurists have permitted these transactions, primarily for the reason that they enable merchants who have lost their capital to re-establish themselves. Ibn Taymiyya and his star student Ibn Qayyim, however, have rejected it on the grounds that it disguises *riba*.

Though inspired by the classical *wujuh*, a typical modern commodity *murabaha*, or *tawarruq*, operates somewhat differently.[49] First of all, ignorance of the transacting parties observed in the classical *tawarruq* disappears. Modern *tawarruq* is known as organized *tawarruq*. Indeed, the modern version is based on commodities traded on the London Metal Exchange. In Malaysia they are also based on crude palm oil, which has been officially endorsed by the Shari'ah Advisory Council of the Central Bank of Malaysia on 28 July 2005.[50] The modern *modus operandi* of a *tawarruq* or commodity *murabaha* can be described as follows.

1. Islamic bank buys commodity on the spot from broker A.
2. Islamic bank sells this commodity to client using *murabaha* on deferred basis (cost plus profit).
3. The client sells the metal to broker B on spot basis and obtains the cash he needed. Alternatively, the bank sells the metal on behalf of the client to the broker, obtains the cash and hands it to the client.
4. The client makes periodic payments to the Islamic bank to cover the deferred price.[51]

Needless to say, interest-based transactions can be (and are in fact) generated through such cycles. All these transactions occur within a few hours, if not minutes, and in most cases neither the borrower nor the lender actually takes possession of the commodity.[52] While this may be so, commodity *murabaha*, as well as other similar deferral contracts, are allowed on the ground that 'time has a share in price'.[53] But this permission notwithstanding, the overwhelming use of such contracts are disquieting. This is confirmed by recent advice given by Dr Zeti Akhtar Aziz, the Governor of Bank Negara Malaysia, to Islamic banks to voluntarily curb the use of such fixed-return instruments.[54] If this advice is not heeded, it would be reasonable to expect a stronger interference by Bank Negara.

Recently, three juristic councils examined the modern *tawarruq*. The *Fiqh Academy of the Organization of Islamic Conference* in Jeddah, Saudi Arabia, forbade it in April 2009. The *Fiqh Academy of the Muslim World League* in Mecca, Saudi Arabia issued two rulings. The first ruling, issued in October 1998, permitted it subject to the condition that the customer does not sell the commodity to its original seller. In December they focused more directly on the *tawarruq* as practised by Islamic banks today. Their verdict was negative and they also forbade it.[55] In brief, the Mecca Academy prohibits *tawarruq* where any of the following occur: there are effectively only two parties and no real, unconnected, third party; there is a concealed buy back; the transaction is a 'trick' with an embedded fixed return. Finally, the AAOIFI issued its *Shari'ah* Standard 30, where the correct way of doing *tawarruq* was explained. Some critics of the Mecca ruling have argued that it contravenes the AAOIFI permission. This is simply not true, for while the Mecca ruling prohibits the non-permissible elements in organized *tawarruq*, the AAOIFI *Shari'ah* Standard 30 explains the correct way of doing things. In short, there is no contradiction and the rulings actually complement each other.

According to the AAOIFI's *Shari'ah* Standard 30 the correct way of doing *tawarruq* would be as follows. First, there would have to be three real and distinct parties, namely Customer A, Seller 1 and Buyer 1. There would also be two distinct and unconnected sales, Sale 1 and Sale 2.[56] Let us consider Sale 1 first. Here Customer A buys metal on deferred payment from seller 1. Customer A must take the real possession of the metal. As for Sale 2: Customer A sells the same metal to Buyer 1, who is a genuine third party and the metal actually moves from the warehouse of Seller 1 to Buyer 1. The key question that the authorities ask is whether the metal actually moves from the warehouse of Seller 1 to that of the Buyer 1.

Why this is so important can be explained by examining a hypothetical case. Assume that at 10 a.m. on 10 September 2009, Seller 1 books four tons of aluminium for a deferred sale at US$2500 per tonne to Customer A, for US$10 000. Half an hour later Customer A takes the hypothetical possession of the metal without, however, ever seeing the metal. He simply receives a certificate indicating that his consignment is placed in a warehouse. Customer A then sells the same metal to Buyer 1, for, say, US$8000 spot price. Another half an hour later, at 11 a.m., according to the netting facility, four tonnes of aluminium are netted off between the storage facilities of Seller 1 and Buyer 1, without the metal ever needing to move at all.

In reality, of course, the *Shari'ah* Standard 30 as described above is never implemented, since there exists prior agreement between the two parties, Seller 1 and Buyer 1, with the metal never leaving the warehouse of the Seller 1, who actually keeps the metal in his possession as collateral to ensure that the deferred payment is fully paid. The whole point of the exercise is that customer A receives US$8000 and pays back at a future date US$10 000, with the metal serving the role of a veil disguising the rate of interest.

With the metal never leaving the original warehouse, there is nothing to prevent Seller 1 from engaging in multiple transactions of similar nature in the same day. Thus, he can hold 100 tonnes of metal in his warehouse valued at, say, US$2.5 million and yet conduct *tawarruq* transactions amounting to, say, US$25 million or more. If so, the situation becomes eerily similar to the concept of fractional reserve banking in the conventional system.[57]

To address these problems, Saudi banks changed their tactics and ensured that all their transactions were genuine sales and purchases, with the corresponding transfer of commodity risks. They also began to emphasize that all commodities used in *tawarruq* transactions are bought and sold in domestic markets with real merchants delivering the goods. But these new methods have been dismissed by El-Gamal as simple measures of increasing the transaction costs. El-Gamal refers to Ibn Taymiyya, who ruled that what is permitted and what is prohibited cannot be determined by the increased costs.[58]

The concerns explained above were seriously considered by the Bank Negara Malaysia as well and *tawarruq* is now described by the *Shari'ah* Parameter Reference 1 as follows: '*tawarruq* is a series of sales where a person sells a good to another person on credit basis and the latter sells the purchased goods on cash to another third party who is not the former'.[59] Thus sale and buy-back transactions between two fully informed persons (organized *tawarruq*) are now made, if not impossible, at least more difficult.

Recently, a new development potentially with vast consequences has emerged. This is the commodity *murabaha* being used on the liability side for deposit mobilization. Obviously, while this transaction is perfectly legal, in reality it enables a depositor to an Islamic bank to bypass the standard investment account procedure. As will be recalled, when a person makes a deposit in a standard investment account with an Islamic bank, this is actually a *mudaraba* transaction. If the invested amount is lost, the bank under the normal circumstances is not held responsible and the depositor/investor loses his deposit. This is precisely why depositors to investment accounts are considered actually not as depositors but as investors. Applying commodity *murabaha*, as described above, actually transforms the liability side of the Islamic bank normally dominated by multiple *mudaraba*s into fixed return yielding conventional deposits. It will be argued here that to the extent that these commodity *murabaha*s replace the original investment accounts, this is tantamount to transforming Islamic banks into conventional banks on the liability side. We have already noted above that this process is well on its way and in some banks non-*mudaraba* accounts have already reached from 56 to 80 per cent of total deposits.

The *modus operandi* of deposit mobilization through commodity *murabaha* can be summarized as follows.

1. Client buys commodity on spot basis from broker A.
2. Client sells the commodity to Islamic bank using *murabaha* on deferred basis (cost + profit).
3. Islamic bank sells the commodity to broker B on spot basis and obtains the cash (actually the deposit of the client).
4. Islamic bank makes the payment to the client of the deferred and higher price upon maturity.[60]

Once again, the whole point of the exercise is that the Islamic bank receives cash (deposit) and pays it back to the depositor with a mark-up.

Thus, commodity *murabahas* are beginning to dominate both liability and asset sides of Islamic banks. In the liability side, they are increasingly being utilized to collect deposits and, in the asset side, to invest them with entrepreneurs. Consequently, it would not be wrong to claim that the original design of Dr Ahmed al-Naggar has been substantially altered and Islamic banks have been brought closer to their conventional peers.[61]

THE BBA

Bai' Bithaman Ajil (BBA) is another form of *murabaha* and used to be popular, particularly in Malaysia. This is also known as cost plus *murabaha* in a credit sale setting,[62] whereby payment is made in instalments sometime after the delivery of goods. BBA differs from *murabaha* in that it is used for long-term financing and the seller is not required to disclose the profit margin that is included in the selling price.[63] The BBA is also considered as a form of *Bai' inah* sale. The latter is a series of sales where a person sells a good to another person on credit and the latter subsequently sells back the goods to the former on cash basis at price lower than the initial credit sale.[64] These transactions involve the sale and buy back of the same commodity between two persons, and by utilizing cash or deferred payments with a mark-up actually come very close to conventional credit transactions. If they do not violate the letter of the Islamic law, they violate its spirit.

In a BBA transaction, the bank first buys a commodity or property from a customer, who is the seller under a property purchase agreement (PPA). The purchase price is paid immediately or at agreed times to the seller. This is the first leg of the transaction and the bank has now become the owner of the property. It then sells the property back to the customer under a PPA. The sale price comprises the bank's purchase price plus its profit computed for the deferred period. This sale price must be a single price – it is not allowed to have different sale prices at different times. The bank has the freedom to determine the sale price. How the bank reaches this price is its own concern and the buyer cannot inquire about it. Bargaining between the bank and the buyer, however, is allowed.

On 18 July 2008, the BBA has been prohibited by a Malaysian court, with potentially vast consequences for the Malaysian Islamic banking industry. This has led ISRA, a sub-unit of INCEIF,[65] to organize a dispute resolution conference on the legality of BBA. In this conference the High Court Judge Justice Datuk Abdul Wahab Patail's ruling has been studied in detail. The judge had ruled that since some of BBA contracts were structurally faulty, defaulters need not pay more than the original capital that they had received, thus depriving banks of their profits. The judge had argued that the BBA contract is neither a genuine contract nor a genuine sale. He then reasoned, 'If it is a loan transaction, it involves interest. The so-called profit element in the contract is actually interest. And interest is prohibited in Islam. Therefore, you cannot recover the profit and can only recover the principal.'[66] In the seminar the judge was criticized on the grounds that 'he has applied the rules without modification. The rules were made in 1980 before Islamic banking was introduced in Malaysia in 1983. And they have not been amended to accommodate the principles of Islamic banking. Yet the judge has rigidly adhered to them'.[67] Moreover, the judge has been criticized for not having taken into consideration earlier precedence which have allowed BBA transactions as legal. He has also been criticized for failing to take into consideration the vast potential impact of his rulings on the Islamic banking industry and economy. Finally, the bank, Arab-Malaysian Finance Bhd, was urged to take the case to the Court of Appeal. In short, the case is not yet closed. Yet serious doubt has been cast on BBA transactions in Malaysia. In all probability, even with a positive ruling by the Court of Appeal, BBA transactions will probably lose their original appeal.

THE *SHARI'AH* CONVERSION TECHNOLOGY

Still another controversial financial strategem that is emerging is the so-called *Shari'ah* conversion technology. This refers to wrapping a non-*Shari'ah* compliant underlying into a *Shari'ah* compliant structure. The purpose of the exercise is to bring to the Islamic investor returns from investments that are not compliant with the *Shari'ah*.[68]

The process begins with the purchase by the Islamic investor of *Shari'ah* compliant assets. In most cases, this involves purchasing metals through commodity *murabaha*. Through such contracts the bank can offer apparent *Shari'ah* compliance and fixed returns of, say, 4–5 per cent. Then to give the investor the ability to enhance the returns, the bank arranges to swap the returns from the *Shari'ah* compliant transaction with returns from another investment. This it does by means of a promise, *wa'd*. What the promise says is that at maturity, generally three to five years, the parties promise to swap their returns. The Islamic bank then takes the further step of protecting the principal invested by the Islamic investor.

The benefits to this investor are obvious: the principal is protected, the returns will almost certainly be at least 4–5 per cent (from the *Shari'ah* compliant investment) and there is the strong likelihood that the assets in the other basket will outperform the *Shari'ah* compliant investment. Moreover, the Islamic investor is told that the investment is completely *Shari'ah* compliant. This is despite the fact that the returns come from the other non-*Shari'ah* compliant investment by means of the stratagem employing a promise to exchange returns. By this means the unwitting Muslim investor actually participates in a non-*Shari'ah* compliant investment. Moreover, the money that is paid into an investment employing this strategem is used to finance non-*Shari'ah* compliant investments and some of the money will certainly go to bonds, debt instruments, derivatives etc. Thus the investor's money, even though it remains in *Shari'ah* compliant contracts, is actually put to work in ways that are clearly not *Shari'ah* compliant. Much of the fees in this process are earned by the non-*Shari'ah* compliant institutions.

The danger in all this is that the swap mechanism could spell the end of the need for authentic Islamic products. Why, indeed, should a bank bother to spend all that extra money and time to make a *sukuk* securitization, when for less money and time it can simply offer conventional bonds and then use the 'mechanism' to appear to sanitize the money and satisfy the investor that his investment is *halal* and lawful. At a very fundamental level this swap technology attempts to make *haram halal*. *Shari'ah* boards must be extremely careful when considering these techniques.

These cases indicate the dynamic nature of Islamic banking. New instruments claiming to be *Shari'ah* compliant are constantly invented by practitioners. These are then subjected to scrutiny by the authorities. Such close examination then paves the way along which the industry develops.

There are currently two well-known such authorities, the *Accounting and Auditing Organization for Islamic Financial Institutions* (AAOIFI) and the *Islamic Financial Services Board* and several other *fiqh* boards. To these might be added the *Shari'ah Advisory Council of Bank Negara Malaysia* established in May 1997. The AAOIFI was established in accordance with the Agreement of Association signed by Islamic financial institutions on 26 February 1990, in Algeria. It was registered on 27 March 1991 in the State of Bahrain (now Kingdom of Bahrain) as an international autonomous not-for-profit corporate body. AAOIFI is responsible for developing accounting, auditing, ethics, governance and *Shari'ah* standards for the international Islamic banking and finance industry. In addition, AAOIFI contributes significantly to the professional development for the industry. AAOIFI is supported by over 160 institutional members from around 40 countries. As for the *Islamic Financial Services Board* (IFSB), this was established by eight countries consisting of Malaysia, Indonesia, Iran, Saudi Arabia, Pakistan, Sudan, Bahrain and Kuwait in a meeting held in Kuala Lumpur on 3 November 2002.

It must be recognized that the asset side of Islamic banks is dominated by BBAs or *murabaha* financing because these are financial instruments which minimize bankers' risks. Indeed, the bank and the merchant agree on the mark-up, the commodity is imported and the bank knows exactly what it will earn out of this transaction. Bankers accustomed to guaranteeing rates of return in the conventional banking sector find this form of financing quite attractive.

Ahmed Al-Naggar was convinced that *murabaha*'s ever-increasing popularity was caused by conventional bankers' 'invasion' of Islamic banks. According to Al-Naggar, these otherwise excellent managers were so much conditioned by conventional banking methods and were so risk averse that it was a Herculean task to convince them of the merits and potential of *mudaraba/musharaka* financing. For this reason he advocated until his death that conventional bankers should not be admitted into the Islamic banking sector. To achieve this, he established in 1982, with the help of Prince Muhammad al-Faisal of Saudi Arabia, the *International Institute of Islamic Banking and Economics* in the Turkish Republic of Northern Cyprus. The task of this institute was to train Islamic bankers not conditioned by conventional banking methods. When Prince Muhammad was forced to withdraw his support after two years, the project had to be abandoned. Islamic banking has been dominated by conventional bankers and the instrument that they prefer, the *murabaha* and its derivatives, ever since.

The *murabaha* is preferred by Islamic bankers coming from the conventional sector primarily for its similarity to the conventional banking instruments. This similarity played a vitally important role during the Islamization of a conventional system. When in Sudan a presidential decree was issued in 1984 directing all conventional banks to stop interest based transactions with immediate effect, this sudden change forced the banks to adopt the nearest Islamic alternative instrument. This was the *murabaha*, which soon constituted 90 per cent of their operations.[69]

Another reason why commodity *murabahas* are increasingly being used in the liability side at the expense of profit sharing investment accounts is that banks fear the latter may trigger liquidity shortage. To avoid this, they feel obliged to be more liquid. Indeed, it has been shown that the average liquid-to-total assets ratio for Gulf Co-operation Council based Islamic financial institutions rated by Standard & Poor's was 30 per cent in 2007, compared with 18 per cent for GCC based conventional peers. This extra liquidity, naturally, has an opportunity cost. That is to say, instead of investing and earning extra profits with this cash, IFIs are obliged to keep it for rainy days. Some IFIs are able to repo their funds with their central banks, but this is not yet a widespread practice.[70]

It must be emphasized that, though similar to a loan in practice, *murabaha* is not a loan contract and therefore does not constitute *riba*. The main difference between a loan and a *murabaha* is that whereas the former is a cash–cash transaction, the latter is an asset–cash transaction. As medieval European jurists used to say, '*ubi non est mutuum, ibi non est usura*', which means 'where there is no loan there is no usury'.[71] Another difference between an interest bearing loan and *murabaha* is the financial ownership of property. Thus the collateral is usually the product in question itself. This is what makes a *murabaha* transaction different from the Western toxic bonds: here a claim is created against a real asset with a short-term maturity and relatively low risk.

Indeed, in case of *murabaha*, no money is loaned but a specific asset is bought for the client to ensure that the financing is linked to an asset. Furthermore, whereas in a loan the financier is exposed to credit risk only, in *murabaha*, he is first exposed to the price risk when the product is acquired for the client, and then again, before the client decides to purchase the product. The client retains the right to decline to take delivery of the product. Thus the bank exposes itself to certain risks and trades with a certain asset. Sudanese Islamic banks, particularly, are known to apply these rules diligently.[72]

Moreover, whereas *murabaha* is a sale contract in which the price is increased for deferment of payment, *riba* is an increase in the amount of a debt for deferment. In *murabaha* the mark-up is not stipulated in terms of a time period and in case a client fails to make a deferred payment on time, it does not increase from the agreed price owing to delay.[73]

Still, the practice of using the prevalent interest rate as a benchmark to determine the *murabaha* mark-up has been criticized. Islamic banks answer these by stating that a benchmark, which would indicate what the rate return is in the economy, is needed.[74]

In short, *murabaha* is based on the permissibility of charging a credit price that is higher than the spot price of an asset. This price mark-up mimics the benchmark, i.e., the conventional interest rate. It is clear that this instrument is not the same as credit loans and they are a far cry from the toxic loans as practised in the West. But it is also clear that to the extent that Islamic banks deviate from the classical rules and in their haste to maximize profits avoid actual purchase and resale of commodities, they approach *riba*.

RESERVES IN ISLAMIC BANKING

After the profits are generated, they are subjected to certain deductions before they are allowed to accrue to the depositors (Figure 9.2). The first deduction from the gross profits is made to the Profit Equalization Reserve. The next deduction is the *mudarìb*'s fee ranging between 20 to 40 per cent, which is what the bank obtains in return for its services. Finally, there is the Investment Risk Reserve. This reserve also serves the same function as the others just mentioned. The IRRs are set aside by Islamic banks after allocating the *mudarìb* fee.[75]

Standard & Poor's has recently expressed both a concern and relief regarding these. The concern is related to the reliance of these banks on profit-and-loss-sharing investment accounts. Standard & Poor's is concerned that in this era of recession, Islamic banks may fail to distribute profits to the holders of these accounts commensurate with the deposit interest rates paid by conventional banks. Yet, at the same time, it has expressed relief that Islamic banks have created these buffer reserves mentioned above and that they can transfer sufficient funds to their depositor/investors not to lose them to the conventional competition.[76]

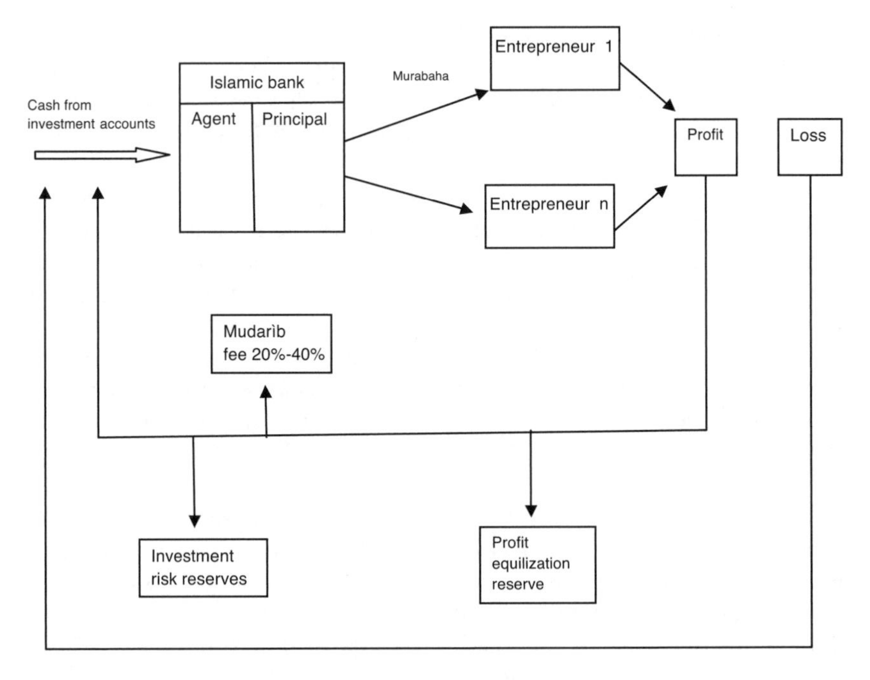

Figure 9.2 Islamic bank (asset side)

It is doubtful if Standard & Poor's argument about returns paid to investment account holders is a legitimate concern. Although serious research is needed about motives of these depositors/investors, we can surmise that for most of these people Islamic motives are very important. If so, they may be prepared to settle for less return if they are properly informed by the IFIs. If this is so, then the problem may boil down to one of communication and persuasion, rather than paying returns commensurate with those provided by conventional banks.

Despite the reserves mentioned above, if an Islamic bank faces a more serious liquidity shortage, it can have recourse to central bank funds. Obviously, if it has excess cash, it can also deposit them with it. In Malaysia, Bank Negara utilizes commodity *murabahas* for liquidity absorption and injection into the Islamic banking sector. The *modus operandi* for liquidity absorption can be summarized as follows.

1. Bank A having excess liquidity buys commodity from broker A on cash basis at spot price.
2. The bank then sells the commodity to Bank Negara Malaysia on deferred price (cost plus profit).
3. Bank Negara pays to bank A on deferred basis, at mark-up price.

4. The Bank Negara Malaysia appoints bank A as an agent to sell the commodity (net off).
5. Bank A sells the commodity on behalf of Bank Negara.
6. Bank A credits the proceeds to Bank Negara (placement).[77]

Obviously, more or less the same mechanism can be used for liquidity injection as well. The *modus operandi* for this transaction, that is, injecting a bank facing liquidity shortage with cash, can be summarized as follows.

1. Bank Negara purchases the commodities from broker A on cash basis. The ownership of the commodities is transferred to Bank Negara.
2. Bank Negara sells the commodities to the bank facing liquidity shortage on deferred price (cost plus profit) to be paid later.
3. The bank sells the commodities to broker B on spot at the original cost price, thus, in fact, obtaining the cash it needed.
4. On maturity date the bank will pay to Bank Negara the value of the commodities with deferred price.

As we have seen above, such extensive usage of *murabaha* and organized *tawarruq* throughout the industry at all levels was always a cause for concern. Therefore, though expected, when these transactions were declared illegal by the highest *Shari'ah* authorities, the industry was still shocked. What makes the situation particularly difficult is the extent to which these instruments are used in interbank liquidity operations. Consequently, the industry has started to fight back and challenge the ruling. Akram Laldin, a member of Bank Negara's *Shari'ah* Board, has issued a statement that organized *tawarruq* is actually *Shari'ah* compliant.[78] Still others have argued that *tawarruq* should be permitted on the grounds of *maslaha* (public interest).[79] In short, it seems *tawarruq* will go and be replaced by another instrument yet to be born. But in view of its widespread application and importance, this will not be so easy and without a fight.

The reason why these transactions are called, confusingly, sometimes commodity *murabaha* and sometimes *tawarruq* is that both of these instruments are usually contained in the same transaction. For instance, when a commodity is bought with ready cash on spot price and then sold off to another party at a higher price with deferred payment, this is a commodity *murabaha* transaction. On the other hand, when a commodity is purchased for a deferred price and sold off to a third party for a spot price so as to obtain cash, this is *tawarruq*[80] (or the historical *wujuh*).

There are many other contract forms practised by the contemporary Islamic banks. These forms, altogether, constitute a minority. On average *murabaha* (41 per cent) has been the first choice of Islamic banks, followed by *musharaka*

(11 per cent),[81] *mudaraba* (12 per cent), *ijara* (leasing) (10 per cent) and others (26 per cent).[82] Thus, equity based financing is seriously lagging behind trade financing. It has been argued that *mudaraba* and *musharaka* are underutilized due to high monitoring costs, information asymmetry and moral hazard problems. Islamic banks do not wish to spend their limited resources on monitoring expenses. This reluctance is probably due to their already high costs. As it will be remembered, these high costs are incurred due to the high wages of a limited number of *Shari'ah* experts and the low profits explained above. If so, then it is possible that Islamic banks have already entered to the following vicious circle: high costs prevent Islamic banks from taking care of monitoring costs and the reluctance to do so forces them to avoid equity financing and into trade financing, which is potentially less profitable and incurs higher costs.

Another important deviation from the theory is a lack of firewalls separating deposits of demand accounts from investment accounts and the funds of equity holders. In reality all funds are mixed, which creates problems for regulators.

CONCLUSION

To sum up, modern Islamic banks are facing tough challenges from the conventional sector. They are under pressure to provide their depositors rates of returns commensurate with what the conventional competitors provide. Moreover, they are forced to promise them quasi-fixed returns. In order to fulfil these needs and to avoid any potential mismatch of funds and liquidity shortages, they are forced to apply, in the asset side, fixed return instruments. All of this boils down to applying a bewildering variety of *murabahas* and *tawarruqs* in both the liability and the asset side. Now both of these instruments are permitted and can be traced back to the classical age of Islam. Thus, in essence, they are not new inventions. But their modern applications differ significantly from the historical origins. Utilizing brokers, who exist in name only in some obscure London office, commodity transactions are concluded without actual sales ever taking place and assets ever reaching the purchaser. Moreover, sale transactions are concluded at such speed using modern communications technology that these transactions approach dramatically to *riba*. In short, interest prohibition is not violated and the letter of the law is obeyed but its spirit is violated.

On the positive side, three great achievements of Islamic banks should be mentioned here. First, Islamic bankers have transformed non-banking Muslim societies into banking societies. Before the advent of Islamic banking Muslim savers had only two choices: either disregard the rules of their religion and be involved in conventional banking by depositing their savings with them or stay out of banking altogether. With the emergence of Islamic banking, Muslims' savings are now channelled to the banking sector and are injected into the economy.

Second, Islamic banks have succeeded to channelize savings of the masses for major projects. Without banking, these savings could not have been injected into the economy and financing major investments would have been nearly impossible. Even the traditional cash waqfs could not have fulfilled this task, as their capital pooling capacities were quite limited. But, together with the modernized cash waqfs (Mannan Model) as well as Islamic Unit Trust Funds, Islamic banks are able to channel modest savings of the masses to major projects.

Third, Islamic bank–central bank transactions utilizing commodity *murabaha*s and *tawarruqs*, as described above, have paved the way for monetary policy being implemented by central banks while still remaining within the *Shari'ah* framework. Application of *Shari'ah* compliant monetary policy will become more clear in the next chapter, where we will focus on *sukuk*.

Meanwhile, we must be aware that there are risks looming on the horizon. To the extent that Islamic banks' operations imitate conventional banking, Muslim savers may become disillusioned and begin to withdraw their savings. This is known as the *Shari'ah* risk. An equally great risk pertains to the conventionalization of Islamic banking. Indeed, to the extent this takes place, and the risk and return characteristics of conventional banks are replicated, this will dilute the distinctiveness of Islamic finance. This is important because it can expose Islamic banks to the same destabilizing forces inherent in the conventional system. It is significant that these dangers have been clearly acknowledged by a high level body of Islamic finance in their latest meeting in April 2010.[83]

Therefore, there is a huge need to introduce completely *Shari'ah* compliant, or even better, *Shari'ah* based instruments to evaluate the needs of these savers. One such instrument that can be utilized both by central and Islamic banks may well be the modernized *esham*. The Ottoman *esham*, as it will be remembered, was a completely *riba*-free, fixed return yielding instrument. Based upon the securitization of the revenue of a government owned asset, it provides fixed returns. Fully negotiable *esham* shares can be purchased by central as well as Islamic banks. If the former, they can be used for open market operations to control the aggregate money supply. If the latter, Islamic banks can use them to pay their depositors fixed returns. In either case, because they have simpler structures, they can be used at a lower cost than the currently used instruments and at the same time avoid *Shari'ah* risks.

NOTES

1. Hasan, 'What Does It Change?', fn. 15; Task Force on Islamic Finance, *Islamic Finance and Global Financial Stability*, p. 28.
2. Task Force on Islamic Finance, *Islamic Finance and Global Financial*, p. 34.
3. Task Force on Islamic Finance, *Islamic Finance and Global Financial*, p. 37.

4. Task Force on Islamic Finance, *Islamic Finance and Global Financial Stability*, p. 28–30. Also see Hesse, Jobst and Solé, 'Trends and Challenges in Islamic Finance', p. 175, fn. 1.
5. As a multiple *mudaraba* on the liability side and series of *mudaraba* and *musharaka* investments on the asset side.
6. To pronounce the *kalima*, daily prayers (the *namaz*), fasting during the *ramadan*, to pay the *zakat*, to go to the pilgrimage.
7. Mallat, *The Renaissance of Islamic Law*, p. 285. The surest way to distinguish between interest or quasi-interest and profit/loss sharing trends in the long run is that whereas the former exhibits a relatively fixed trend fluctuating within a narrow margin, the latter fluctuates significantly, thus reflecting genuine long run profits and losses.
8. Hasan, 'Islamic Banking at the Cross-Roads', p. 12.
9. Ibid., p. 288.
10. For details of the latter's model, see Mallat, *The Renaissance of Islamic Law*, pp. 340–45.
11. Nienhaus, *Islam und Moderne Wirtschaft*, p. 233.
12. During 1982–84 at the International Institute of Islamic Banking and Economy in the Turkish Republic of Northern Cyprus.
13. Thus, in fact, Dr Al-Naggar had also laid the foundations of another institution that came to be known as microfinance in the future.
14. Iqbal and Molyneux, *Thirty Years of Islamic Banking*, p. 37.
15. Ahmed, 'The Evolution of Islamic Banking', p. 21.
16. Standard & Poor's, *Outlook 2008*, p. 30.
17. Hasan, 'Crossroads', p. 15.
18. Ibid., p. 19.
19. Ibid., p. 16.
20. Profit/loss sharing investment accounts are of two types: restricted PLSIA and unrestricted PLSIA. In the former, the depositors have the right to determine the investment type. The statement does not distinguish between the two types.
21. Venardos, *Islamic Banking and Finance,* pp. 102–3.
22. Iqbal and Mirakhor, *An Introduction to Islamic Finance*, p. 260.
23. Iqbal and Mirakhor, *An Introduction to Islamic Finance*, p. 272, fn. 6.
24. Venardos, *Islamic Banking and Finance*, p. 160.
25. Hassan, Mohamad and Bader, 'Efficiency of Conventional vs. Islamic Banks', p. 60.
26. Hasan, 'Crossroads', p. 18.
27. Ahmad, Abubakar and Yazid Isa, '*Practices and Issues of Risk Management*'. I am grateful to the authors for allowing me to refer to their yet unpublished paper.
28. Ibid.
29. Hasan, 'Mudaraba As a Mode of Finance', p. 50.
30. Venardos, *Islamic Banking and Finance*, p. 107.
31. Hasan, 'Crossroads', p. 21; Çizakça, *Türk Finans Kesiminde*, pp. 178–9.
32. El-Gamal, *Islamic Finance*, p. 18.
33. El-Gamal, *Islamic Finance*, p. 67. El-Gamal does not give any reference where Taqi Usmani has approved of this. Elsewhere, regarding the *sukuk*, Taqi Usmani has made it clear that he does not approve of benchmarking expected profits to the prevalent rate of interest. See his 'Sukuk and Their Contemporary Applications', http://www.muftitaqiusmani.com/ArticlePublication.aspx, p. 7.
34. El-Gamal, *Islamic Finance*, p. 67.
35. For more complicated commodity *murabahas* utilized between banks, see Schoon, 'Application of Islamic Products', p. 25.
36. Iqbal and Mirakhor, *An Introduction to Islamic Finance*, p. 6.
37. Shari'ah Advisory Council of Bank Negara Malaysia, *Shari'ah Parameter Reference 1*.
38. Ibid., p. 37.
39. Ibid., p. 3.
40. Ibid., p. 5.
41. 2:282. Consider also the statement of the Prophet as narrated by Hakim: 'The best earning is what man earns with his own hands and from permissible trade.'
42. *Shari'ah* Advisory Council, *Shari'ah Parameter*, p. 6.

43. Ibid., p. 8.
44. Ibid., p. 18.
45. Ibid., p. 22.
46. Ibid., pp. 26–7.
47. Ibid., p. 32–4.
48. For further details about profit and loss division in this partnership, see Udovitch, *Partnership and Profit*, p. 81.
49. The Fiqh Academy of the OIC in Jeddah forbade *tawarruq* as it is practised today by Islamic banks in its 17th session held in December 2003. For details of the ruling, see El-Gamal, *Islamic Finance*, p. 72.
50. Dusuki, *An Old Skeleton*, p. 228.
51. Mokhdar, 'Commodity *murabaha* and *Sukuk* Pricing', p. 6.
52. El-Gamal, *Islamic Finance*, p. 69; Haneef, 'Liquidity Management', pp. 7–8.
53. In Arabic, 'lil zamani hazzun fil thaman'.
54. See on this Hasan, 'Commodity *Murabaha*'.
55. For full details of the ruling, see ibid., p. 72.
56. Khan, 'Why *Tawarruq* Needs To Go', pp. 17–22.
57. Ibid., p. 18.
58. El-Gamal, *Islamic Finance*, p. 73.
59. Bank Negara Malaysia, *Shari'ah Parameter Reference 1*, p. 1.
60. Mokhdar, 'Commodity *murabaha* and *Sukuk* Pricing', p. 6.
61. Research yielding quantitative evidence for this view, based upon actual numbers and magnitude of commodity *murabahas* in both liability and asset sides, is in its infancy. To my knowledge, the best yet incomplete evidence so far has been provided by Nor Hayati Ahmad et al. mentioned above. This important research is not yet completed and its conclusions should therefore be viewed with caution.
62. El-Gamal, *Islamic Finance*, p. 18.
63. Iqbal and Mirakhor, *An Introduction to Islamic Finance*, p. 91.
64. Bank Negara Malaysia, *Shari'ah Parameter Reference 1*, p. 1.
65. ISRA (International *Shari'ah* Research Academy for Islamic Finance), INCEIF (Formerly: International Center for Education in Islamic Finance, now: Global University in Islamic Finance). Both institutions are in Kuala Lumpur and sponsored by Bank Negara.
66. ISRA, *Dispute Resolution in Islamic Banking*, p. 19. For the complete judgement, see pp. 163–92. The exact wording of the court is as follows: 'where the bank purchased directly from its customer and sold back to the customer with deferred payment at a higher price in total, the sale is not a *bona fide* sale, but a financing transaction, and the profit portion of such *Al-Bai' Bithaman Ajil* facility rendered the facility contrary to the Islamic Banking Act 1983.' Ibid., p. 191. The court also ruled that the BBA violated the Banking and Financial Institutions Act 1989, as well.
67. Ibid., p. 156.
68. DeLorenzo, '*Shari'ah* Conversion Technology'.
69. Iqbal and Molyneux, *Banking and Financial Systems*, p. 154.
70. Standard & Poor's, *Outlook 2008*, p. 31.
71. Munro, 'Medieval Origins', p. 523.
72. Mirakhor and Zamir, *Introduction to Islamic Finance*, p. 97, fn. 3.
73. Mirakhor and Zaidi, 'Profit and Loss Sharing Contracts in Islamic Finance', p. 52.
74. Mirakhor and Zamir, *Introduction to Islamic Finance*, p. 6.
75. Standard & Poor's, *Outlook 2008*, p. 30.
76. Standard & Poor's, *Islamic Finance News*, 13 March 2009, p. 21.
77. Bank Negara Malaysia, *Annual Report '07*, p. 87. For a slightly different and simpler version, see Dusuki, *Old Skeleton*, p. 229.
78. Froozye, '*Tawarruq*: *Shari'ah* Risk or Banking Conundrum?'.
79. Khnifer, 'Maslaha and the Permissibility of Organized Tawarruq'.
80. As defined by AAOIFI *Shari'ah* Standard No. 30. I am grateful for this information to Shabnam Mokhtar of ISRA/INCEIF.

81. Early books of *fiqh* consider business partnerships as *shirka*. But modern scholars have preferred to use the term *musharaka* for a broader concept representing *shirka* and *mudarabah*. Iqbal and Mirakhor, *An Introduction to Islamic Finance*, p. 97, fn. 5. As we have seen above, classical sources refer to partnerships formed by partners contributing different amounts of capital also as *inan*.
82. Ibid., p. 150. The balance sheet of the Bahrain Islamic bank has revealed that *murabaha* deposists are ten times greater than *mudaraba* deposits. Iqbal and Mirakhor, *An Introduction to Islamic Finance*, p. 119. Among the 'others' *musharaka mutanakisa* particularly stands out. This is a home financing product based on the joint-ownership concept, whereby the Islamic bank and the customer contribute their respective shares of the capital and acquire a property according to a mutually agreed, predetermined ratio at the beginning of the contract. The bank then leases the property to the customer who undertakes to incrementally acquire the full ownership from the bank over an agreed period. Once the customer fully acquires the bank's share of the property, the partnership comes to an end with the customer becoming the sole owner. For more details, see Task Force on Islamic Finance, *Islamic Finance and Global Financial Stability*, p. 21–2.
83. Task Force on Islamic Finance, *Islamic Finance and Global Financial*, p. 37.

10. Borrowing from the public: *sukuk*

BY WAY OF INTRODUCTION, A PERSONAL ANECDOTE

In the year 1991, shortly after Operation Desert Storm ended the occupation of Quwait, I received a phone call from the late Muazzam Ali of the *Institute of Islamic Banking and Insurance*, London, asking me whether I can prepare a paper on the origins and evolution of Ottoman public borrowing. This paper had to be ready in two weeks' time and presented in Lahore, Pakistan, to no less a person than His Royal Highness Prince Muhammad bin Faisal of Saudi Arabia. Two weeks later I ended up in Lahore and delivered my paper to His Highness, in person. The private seminar was attended also by six Pakistani professors, all *Shari'ah* experts. My presentation covered more or less an early version of the same topics presented in Chapter 6. After explaining the classical Ottoman instruments of public finance, *iltizam* and *malikane*, we focused on *esham*. The presentation lasted about two hours, which was followed by a rigorous critique by the Pakistani professors. The essence of the discussion was whether *esham* was usurious. They were claiming that it was and I was disputing their claims. At one point, I felt like being the spokesperson of the long deceased Ottomans!

When the seminar finally ended, I was able to tell His Highness how impressed I was of his interest in Ottoman public finance. He was amazed by the naivety of my comment and patiently explained that after the Operation Desert Storm Americans had sold all the war material they had brought to Saudi Arabia to the Saudi government. Thus the Saudi budget, which had traditionally enjoyed a surplus, overnight plunged into a substantial deficit.[1] This led to a difficult situation whereby an Islamic state had to borrow, and this it had to do without resorting to *riba*. The Prince had correctly thought that this problem cannot be a new one and that the Ottoman Caliphate also must have faced it at the time of its decline. He had then wondered if the Ottomans had been able to solve this problem and whether it would be relevant to the current situation – hence the invitation I received. When I asked him if he thought that a modernized version of the Ottoman *esham* could contribute to solving his country's current problem, he responded in a princely fashion and said 'I disagree with those who disagree with you'. Apparently, although the Prince was convinced himself, he could not convince the Saudi government, which continued to address its budget problem through conventional means.

The brain storm I had that day in 1991 in Lahore with His Royal Highness and Pakistani professors was probably the first of its kind in the twentieth century. Because, in a world totally dominated by Western finance, we were discussing whether it would be possible to solve a serious current public finance problem of an important Islamic country. Moreover, we were doing this by referring to Islamic economic history and trying to link it with the present. The outcome of the discussion was immaterial; its importance lies in the fact that it took place at all. After all, this brain storm was probably the first of its kind trying to apply the *Shari'ah* to modern public finance via economic history at the presence of a prince very high in the Saudi royal hierarchy.

THE DILEMMA OF AN ISLAMIC STATE

All states, Islamic or otherwise, at all times, have huge expenditure and need money. Nearly always, taxes collected do not suffice for expenses. Therefore, most states experience budget deficits. These deficits are usually covered either by extra taxation or by reducing the expenditure. A third method is government borrowing from the public, a process known as domestic borrowing. Such problems are universal.

But Muslim countries face a particularly great challenge for two reasons:

1. The taxes that an Islamic state can legitimately impose are rather limited.
2. Interest prohibition renders domestic borrowing difficult.

The taxes that an Islamic state can legitimately impose on the population are, indeed, rather limited. This is because the Qur'an mentions only a few taxes by name: primarily, *zakat*, *jizya* and *kharaj*. Scholars argue that since only these taxes are specifically stated in the Qur'an, any other tax must be illegitimate. Therefore, imposing extra taxes not specifically stated in the Qur'an is problematic.

The taxes that are stated in the Qur'an are all direct taxes and, more often than not, they do not suffice for a state that must protect its people from external aggression and provide essential services. Indirect taxes based on consumption are not considered as legitimate. Actually, all taxes are viewed within the general rule that taking property is forbidden. Taking property even in the form of taxation and by the state is therefore considered undesirable and viewed with suspicion.[2]

Since protection of property, *hifz al-mal*, is considered to be one of the primary functions of the *Shari'ah*,[3] any state that imposes extra taxes that are not specifically mentioned in the Qur'an risks being considered as violating the property rights of Muslims and confronting the *Shari'ah*.

On the other hand, abolishing the indirect taxes not specifically mentioned in the Qur'an would deprive the state of substantial revenue. This would weaken the state and may even lead to its destruction. This is exactly what happened during the early nineteenth century in Morocco. Much influenced by the Wahabite movement, the sultan Moulay Sulayman of Morocco abolished all taxes considered to be illegal. The only tax that the people had to pay now was the *zakat*. The *kharaj* that had been imposed on Muslim peasantry was also abolished. In the cities, all indirect taxes on trade, like tolls and market fees, were also abolished. To govern with these reduced revenues, the sultan reduced his expenditure by reducing the size of the professional army to just 2500 men. The result was a serious depletion of military power, which led to the loss of independence and French occupation in 1912.[4]

The opposite case is imposing extra taxes, maintaining them in the long run and providing a reasonable security for centuries, is represented by the Ottoman caliphate. What legitimacy the Ottomans lost by charging these extra taxes was probably compensated when they applied their power to roll back the crusaders to expand Islam in Europe and to protect Muslims of the Indian Ocean from the Portuguese aggression.[5]

CHALLENGE TO CONTEMPORARY ISLAMIC STATES

So, we have the following basic questions: how does an Islamic state, in our times, obey the basic teachings of Islam and enjoy legitimacy without sacrificing security? Is there an inevitable trade-off between these two concerns, or can security needs and legitimacy be combined? Does the *Shari'ah* provide us with any clue as to how and under what conditions the imposition of extra taxes would be legitimate?

A partial answer to these questions has been provided by Imam Malik. He permitted the imposition of extra taxes subject to the following conditions:

1. If the regular revenues are depleted.
2. Defence expenses exceed tax revenues.
3. Taxes are imposed temporarily.
4. Taxes are imposed not to exceed genuine needs.
5. Taxes are levied on the rich only.[6]

Although the Ottomans were Hanefite and therefore not bound by the conditions imposed by Imam Malik, they nevertheless seem to have acted within these conditions. For instance, fighting three, sometimes four, front wars during the sixteenth to seventeenth centuries, and facing serious budget deficits particularly after 1683, they legitimately imposed taxes based on the second condition. Whether they violated the third condition is not so clear. This is because they initially imposed extra taxes, *imdad-ı seferiye*, as an emergency measure to finance their wars and then made them permanent on the grounds that they were perpetually in war to defend Islam. They obeyed the fifth condition, and imposed differential rates of taxation upon three different categories of wealth.

LEGITIMATE SOURCES OF TAXES

Monzer Kahf mentions seven legitimate tax sources. These are: *Kharaj*, *jizya*, revenue of public enterprises, fees and voluntary contributions, equity finance and public debt.[7] *Kharaj* and *jizya* are both discriminate direct taxes imposed on non-Muslims. Although they have been applied for centuries, in this age of universal human rights, they have become irrelevant. This is also because any imposition of taxes based on religion would immediately invite a backlash against millions of Muslims living as minorities in non-Muslim countries. Such a policy would also lead to a further deterioration of the already tense relationship between the Islamic and non-Islamic worlds. There is therefore a need to look for other alternative sources of revenue.

Public enterprise revenues are also irrelevant, because these enterprises, more often than not, make losses. Fees and voluntary contributions are also problematic, because fees suffer the same question of legitimacy as taxes. Voluntary contributions have also little scope. This is so, because waqfs were traditionally the most important avenue through which voluntary contributions were channelled to charity. But due to the massive destruction inflicted upon the waqf system throughout the Islamic world, voluntary contributions can increase only if waqf systems are thoroughly reformed. Until this is achieved, we should not expect much from voluntary donations either.

Equity finance, that is, financing development projects by selling their shares to the public, remains a feasible idea. During the 1980s the revenues to be generated by the First Bosphorus Bridge in Istanbul as well as several hydroelectric dams were sold to the public in this way. Actually this is not typical equity finance because the ownership of the asset remains with the state. Shareholders obtain not the ownership but merely the right to share the revenue generated by it. Each shareholder receives annually a share of the revenue generated in proportion to the nominal value of the shares he possesses. Since the amount of revenue to be generated is uncertain, this is a system of profit and loss sharing and the annuities paid do not constitute *riba*. The state redeems the shares according to a fixed schedule. The details of this system will be discussed below under the section *Revenue Participation Scheme* (GOS).

Of the six possible and legitimate public finance instruments so far discussed, I consider public borrowing and debt with the greatest potential for generating revenue. Indeed, we learn from European history of public finance that a small European city-state like Genoa was able to borrow in 1509 with a cost of borrowing merely at 2.8 per cent, more than five times the amount of the annual revenue of the Ottoman Central Treasury for the same year.[8]

By the same token, about 200 years later, the post-Glorious-Revolution England was able to borrow 17 million sterling at three per cent interest. England used these funds to finance its wars and defeated France time and again to emerge as the super power of the nineteenth century.[9] Thus, domestic/public borrowing is without any doubt a powerful instrument. The challenge for Muslim countries is how to do it without violating the prohibition of *riba*. We will look at this problem first in history and try to determine how it has been tackled in the past.

PUBLIC BORROWING IN THE ISLAMIC WORLD

If we look at much of the pre-modern Islamic world, we do not observe domestic borrowing. What we observe, instead, is tax farming, that is, privatized tax collection. But this was a very costly system of revenue collection. For instance, at the beginning of the eighteenth century, about 75 per cent of the Ottoman taxes collected went to middlemen. Thus the cost of tax collection to the Ottoman state, that is, cost in the form of taxes forgone, was 75 per cent.[10]

With the introduction of domestic/public borrowing, that is, *esham* system initiated in 1775, the Ottoman government was able to drastically reduce its cost of borrowing to the range of 10–20 per cent. At the same time, the amount of revenue it could raise increased by at least seven-fold.[11] Very briefly, the system worked as follows: the annual profit that a tax source yielded was divided into shares called *sehm* (pl. *esham*). Investors paid a lump sum to buy each one of these *esham*, shares. In return, the investor was guaranteed annual revenue for as long as he lived. In a way, the system was similar to the personal retirement pensions of today in the sense that after having fulfilled all the conditions, a retired person receives a monthly income for the rest of his life.

To sum up, in the field of public finance, Muslim states had a very important disadvantage: from the birth of Islam until the late eighteenth century (1775), for more than a millennium, not only did these states not practice domestic/public borrowing, but their cost of tax collection, in comparison to the European states, was simply huge.

This situation had very important consequences. First, European governments able to borrow very large amounts at low costs were able to convert their fiscal power to military power. Second, borrowing large amounts from their public made these governments sensitive to the needs and demands of their public. It has therefore been argued that public borrowing has played an important role in the emergence of capitalism and democracy in those heavily indebted countries. This is because public borrowing in the long run ultimately determines the very structure of a political system. A government that borrows from the public, usually merchants, is forced to become sensitive to their needs and begins to apply more liberal economic policies. This usually leads to democracy or at least to quasi-democracy and capitalism.[12] Third, developments just described lead to a virtuous circle: as the executive branch in a country begins to be controlled by a democratically elected parliament, government revenues per capita increase significantly.[13]

MODERN PUBLIC BORROWING IN THE ISLAMIC WORLD

To the extent that the above arguments made for European economic history apply equally well to the Islamic world, we can presume that *Shari'ah* based instruments developed for domestic/public borrowing may well play a hugely important role in the future of Islamic countries – well above just fiscal concerns. *Sukuk* is just such an instrument for public borrowing in the modern Islamic world and constitutes 11.7 per cent of the total global *Shari'ah* compliant assets[14].

The following are the basic features of *sukuk*:

1. *Sukuk* certificates represent undivided shares in ownership of a particular project.
2. The *sukuk* must not contain any guarantee of *sukuk* capital (AAOIFI recommendation).
3. The *sukuk* must not contain any guarantee of a fixed profit or profit based on a percentage of the capital. *Murabaha* and *ijara sukuk* are exempted from this ruling.
4. The *sukuk* must not contain any statement of obligation from the issuer's side that it will buy back *sukuk* for a nominal price. The issuer may make a promise to buy back the *sukuk* at a market price, or a mutually agreed price, at maturity.[15]

According to the Standard and Poor's Rating Services, the potential market for Islamic financial services is about US$4 trillion. Of this, the global *sukuk* market at the end of 2007 exceeded US$90 billion in value and is expected to top the US$100 billion mark by the end of 2009.[16] The total issuance in 2007 accounted for roughly a quarter of conventional securitization in emerging markets. It is expected that the total *sukuk* issuance will pass the US$150 billion mark by the end of 2010.[17] *Sukuk* issuance increased by 49 per cent in 2005, 153 per cent in 2006 and 79 per cent in 2007.[18] Despite the global economic down-turn, the first seven months of 2008 saw *sukuk* issuance worth US$11.1 billion. This was followed by US$9.3 billion in 2009 for the same period. The 20 per cent decline is due to the global economic slow-down and the resulting steep fall in oil prices. Malaysia has taken the lead and issued 54.2 per cent of all the new *sukuks* during 2009 to be followed by the Saudi issuers who contributed by 12.7 per cent and the UAE with 13.6 per cent.[19] The cumulative total *sukuk* issuance has reached US$100 billion in 2009. Thus, all in all, the global crisis had the effect of slowing down the *rate* of growth of *sukuk* issuance but not the process of growth itself.[20]

The recent approval of the Malaysian Parliament of a law that gave the National *Shari'ah* Advisory Council of the Bank Negara legal status as the final arbiter in matters related to *Shari'ah* compliance, is expected to enhance the rate of growth in the near future by increasing investors' confidence in the products issued in Malaysia.[21] These expectations were confirmed in 2009, when 78.1 per cent of *sukuk* issued in the second quarter were issued by the South-East Asian countries; Malaysia (60.3 per cent) and Indonesia (17.8 per cent), to be followed by the Middle East; Bahrain (16.4 per cent) and Saudi Arabia (3.8 per cent).[22] The relative dynamism of Malaysia may have been caused, at least partially, by the more diversified nature of Islamic finance in that country. Indeed, while the Middle Eastern market relies heavily on banks, the Malaysian market is diversified into institutions such as pension funds, *takaful* market, banks and individual investors. There are important implications of this. When there is a heavy reliance on banks, as is the case in the Middle East, long term is not emphasized. Banks cannot buy assets beyond five years because they have to match deposits with investments[23] – this is the well-known 'mismatch of funds' problem that has discouraged Islamic banks from *mudaraba* investments in the first place. Since most bank deposits are of short term nature, the Middle Eastern market is also dominated by such investments.

In the same context, the creation of the Saudi *sukuk* market within the *Tadawul*, the Saudi Stock Exchange, is also considered as a positive step for the global *sukuk* market. This is because lack of liquidity has always been a major obstacle in the further development of *sukuk*. Investors faced serious difficulties to close their positions and free up liquidity. The recent Saudi development should further enhance the market.[24] But the largest exchange in the world for *sukuk* is the NASDAQ Dubai, where 20 *sukuk* worth US$16.45 billion have been listed on the exchange.[25]

A major difference between the contemporary and the historical forms of public borrowing is that the modern public borrowing has become dominated by corporations. Indeed, on 31 July 2008 only 8 per cent of the global *sukuk* issuance was originated by sovereigns, 6 per cent by financial institutions and a huge 86 per cent by corporations. In short, private corporations began to dominate modern public borrowing in the Islamic world.[26] But this has changed dramatically in response to the *sukuk* failures of private sector caused by the global crisis. Indeed, in the second quarter of 2009, a total of 42 *sukuk* came to the market out of which 30 were government debt.[27] This leads us to conclude that the relative ratio of corporate to sovereign *sukuk* issuance depends on the economic conjuncture and confidence in the market.

It is also interesting that *sukuk* issuance is no longer limited to the Islamic world. 48 per cent of recent sovereign issue was subscribed for by conventional investors, including 24 per cent by institutional investors, 11 per cent by fund managers and 13 per cent by central banks. Thus *sukuk* constitutes a very clear case of a genuine Islamic contribution to world finance.[28]

Non-Muslims are also beginning to participate making *sukuk* a truly global modern instrument of public borrowing.[29] The first European *sukuk* was the Saxony-Anhalt *sukuk* issued in 2004. Of these contenders, Britain is probably one of the most serious. *Her Majesty's Revenue and Customs* has already published (in June 2008) two documents, both of which reveal the depth of the consultation the government has conducted with experts in the field. In 2010, Britain issued a USD 10 million *sukuk*. Britain has removed all tax barriers in its Finance Act to a UK corporate issuing Islamic bonds. It is also planned that the *sukuk al-ijara* method will be preferred. The French government has also introduced tax changes and introduced a concept of trust law into its existing civil law system. It is expected that the French state will soon issue a sovereign *sukuk*. German and Italian governments are also expected to join the bandwagon.[30]

The preference for the *sukuk al-ijara* mode actually follows a new general trend. This trend emerged in response to the doubts expressed by some *Shari'ah* scholars about the legitimacy of *sukuk al-mudaraba and musharaka*. Since *mudaraba* and *musharaka* are known to be the purest *Shari'ah* based forms of investment, these doubts expressed may be surprising. The problem was that in practice the *sukuk al-mudaraba* and *musharaka* issuers, in order to market their bonds to investors, committed themselves to repurchase the bonds from the holders using predetermined values. But this commitment guarantees an investor's capital, which seriously deviates from the classical *mudaraba* and is prohibited by the *Shari'ah*. Indeed, under this guarantee the investment is transformed into a loan and the returns become *riba*. It was because of these concerns that the President of the AAOIFI *Shari'ah* Board Sheiykh Taqi Usmani declared that 85 per cent of the current *sukuk* were *Shari'ah* non-compliant. Since by a statement that followed this declaration the AAOIFI approved the *sukuk al-ijara*, a shift towards the *ijara* structure has been observed in 2008.[31] On 31 July 2008, *sukuk al-ijara* constituted 54.3 per cent of all global *sukuk* issuance. It is expected that all the interested Western governments mentioned above will issue their sovereign *sukuks* in the *ijara* form as well.

At this point it might be appropriate to investigate why *sukuk al-ijara* is considered *Shari'ah* compliant. To start with, *sukuk al-ijara* is essentially a rent contract. There are two parties to this contract, the owner of a rentable asset (lessor) and the person who rents (lessee). When the contract is signed, while the ownership of the asset continues to reside with the owner, the lessee obtains the right to use the asset. This right is known as the usufruct and the lessee pays a rent for this right. All Sunnite schools agree that since the ownership of a leased asset resides with the lessor, he has the right to sell the asset, providing the new owner honours the rent (*ijara*) contract signed between the previous owner and the lessee. The Hanbelites add that the new owner deserves the rent for the rest of the *ijara* period.[32] Although this looks like stating the obvious, it is nevertheless important for modern securitization of the leased assets because it facilitates the negotiability of the *ijara* bonds. Moving from renting a single asset as described above to renting one whose ownership is shared by many is but a small step. This can be done either by each owner leasing his owned share of the asset, or it can be leased by all owners together in one contract and under the same conditions. The *sukuk al-ijara* contract is not restricted to a specific term. It can be set to short, medium or long term as long as the asset in question remains in existence and renders its usufruct for duration of the contract whatever that may be. It is also possible to rent an asset for one year renewable on a permanent basis.[33] Obviously, for a rent contract to be valid, the rent as well as any annual increments and how these increments are to be calculated must be known.

When leased assets are transformed into financial assets, the idea of an *ijara* bond is born. This transformation is done through securitization, which means putting a certain income-generating asset as a base of, or a guarantee for, the issuance of securities that are financial assets. Both the ownership of an asset and the *ijara* contract should be documented.[34] These documents can then play the role of securities and thereby become financial assets. The OIC *Fiqh* Academy has ruled that:

(a) any combination of assets can be represented in a bond, and
(b) this bond can be sold at a market price providing that the assets represented by the bond are physical assets and financial rights.[35]

Based upon the above, *ijara* bonds have been defined as follows:

> The *asset Ijara Bonds* are securities of equal denomination for each issue, representing physical durable assets that are tied to an *ijara* contract as defined by the *Shari'ah*.[36]

These assets represent leased assets without implying any relationship between their owners. For instance, any asset that yields a regular stream of income to a government can be securitized and be represented in bonds and owned by thousands of different bond holders. Each one of these bond holders individually and independently presents her bonds to the government or a company and collects her share of the periodic rent. In other words, a bond holder is not an owner of a share in a company that owns the rented asset but simply a sharing owner who only owns one-thousandth or more of the asset or its usufruct as the case may be. It is possible to issue *ijara* bonds entitling the bond owner to the outright shared ownership of the asset or its usufruct.

In its simplest form, the *ijara* bonds are based on a leased asset and the conditions of the lease are stated on the title of the lease document itself. This title becomes the bond and can be traded in the market. If we are talking about an expensive asset like, say, an aircraft, it would be difficult to find individual buyers for such an asset. To facilitate this transaction, the aircraft is securitized and, say, one thousand bonds (titles) are issued whereby each title or bond represents the ownership of only one-thousandth of that asset that is leased. The bond entitles its owner to one-thousandth of the periodical rental that is determined in the *ijara* contract.

Since *ijara* is obviously going to become the dominant *sukuk* form, we will focus in this book only on the *sukuk al-ijara*. An interesting development, however, has occurred in Bahrain, where a luxury real-estate development corporation Villamar@the Harbour issued in May 2008 a *sukuk al-musharaka* worth US$190 million. While in itself interesting, this model is not expected to spread since *mudaraba*/*musharaka* are equity-based techniques and cannot generate the quasi-fixed returns associated with *sukuk al-ijara*.[37]

On the other hand, in England, the sale/lease back/resale transactions associated with a typical *sukuk al-ijara* have been analysed from the perspective of tax burden. Assuming that if a typical *sukuk al-ijara* takes place in England subject to the current laws prevalent in that country with a building worth more than GBP500,000, the Stamp Duty Land Tax (SDLT) would reach 8 per cent. Furthermore, the SPV[38] would be subject to the corporation tax at 28 per cent on the gain made. By contrast, for a comparable conventional transaction, that is, the owner issuing a conventional bond secured on the building, there would neither be SDLT costs nor corporation tax related to the disposal of the building.[39] Britain is now considering how to change its tax system to make the country more *sukuk* friendly. Malaysia has already done this by declaring all *sukuk al-ijara* profits tax exempt providing the transaction has been approved by the authorities.[40]

Returning now back to the global *sukuk* trends, the GCC and Malaysia are at the forefront of the global *sukuk* market, with Saudi Arabia in the third place.[41] Indeed, in the first half of 2008, issuers from the first two countries accounted for three-quarters of total *sukuk* issuance. The predominance of the GCC and Malaysia[42] is primarily due to the support they receive from the authorities. By contrast, the Islamic bond market in Turkey, where early modern Islamic public borrowing instruments were invented centuries ago, is constantly impeded by a secularist and hostile establishment. The Turkish market has begun to become active only recently, where the very first KFH *murabaha* and *ijara sukuk* worth USD 100 million was issued in 2010 and was over-subscribed by 45 per cent.

To date, the world's largest *sukuk* transaction was issued in Malaysia (US$4.8 billion) by Binariang GSM, a Malaysian telecom giant owned jointly by T. Ananda Krishnan's Usaha Tegas Sdn Bhd and its affiliates. This was followed by four very large *sukuks* issued by the Saudi Basic Industries Corporation, Aldar Properties, Nakheel Properties and the Dubai Electricity and Water Authority for a cumulative US$4.2 billion.[43]

*Sukuk*s are participation certificates against a single asset or a pool of assets. Just as in conventional securitization, a pool of assets is built and securities are issued against this pool. *Sukuk* is similar to a conventional bond as it is also a security instrument that provides a predictable level of return. But it differs from a bond in that whereas a bond represents pure debt of the issuer, a *sukuk* represents a creditworthiness risk of the issuer or an ownership stake in a well-defined asset.

More precisely, credit risk of a *sukuk* is either 'asset-backed' or 'asset-based'. If it is asset-backed, the credit risk is linked to the asset. But if it is linked to the issuer, then it is known as asset-based. In such asset-based *sukuk*, the *sukuk* holders rely on the obligor for repayment of the principal and return. By contrast, in an asset-backed *sukuk*, *sukuk* holders rely on the assets, that is, their claims are secured by the ownership of the underlying asset. However defined, *sukuk* is now acknowledged as the fastest growing segment of Islamic finance.[44] *Sukuk* instruments, however, suffer from the following basic shortcomings: First, they involve, depending upon the exact structure, about seven to ten different transactions. They have therefore high transactions costs. Second, since each transaction is subject to taxation, they also incur high tax costs. Third, even more importantly, since issuers had created a fixed income for investors by promising to buy back the assets underlying *sukuk* at their face value on maturity, irrespective of whether the assets made or lost money, some scholars had doubts whether such *sukuk* were 100 per cent *Shari'ah* compliant. As we have seen, these doubts surfaced by a striking comment of the Chairman of the *Shari'ah* Board of the Accounting and Auditing Organization for Islamic Financial Institutions, Sheikh Muhammad Taqi Usmani, when he observed in November 2007 that 85 per cent of the GCC non-*ijara sukuk* are not *Shari'ah* compliant.[45] Fourth, due to the doubts concerning their *Shari'ah* compliance, they fail to attract high net worth pious Muslims and cannot fulfil the true potential of the market. In what follows, I will submit a model which, in my opinion, overcomes both of these shortcomings, high transactions costs and *Shari'ah* incompatibility. Fifth, Islamic transactions often face a competitive disadvantage against conventional bond issues in terms of cost efficiency. Each new issue incurs higher levels of legal and documentation expenses as well as distribution costs. Contract standardization is expected to reduce this problem. Sixth, due to the shortage of good-quality bonds in the market, most investors hold to their *sukuk* till maturity. Consequently, secondary market activity is low, which in turn reduces liquidity and increases transaction costs. The solution to this problem probably lies in an increase in the supply of *sukuk* and the development of a secondary market for retail investors. Seventh, notwithstanding the claims of some, *sukuk* issuance is not immune to global economic fluctuations. Issuance had fallen by 54 per cent in the first half of 2008 (1H08) compared to 1H07. In 1H08, the total number of *sukuk* issued was 61, compared with 111 in 1H07 and 77 in 1H06.[46]

The earliest modern *sukuk* probably emerged in Jordan. In 1978 Jordan Islamic Bank issued *muqarada* bonds with the permission of the Jordanese government. The 1981 *Muqarada Bond Act* followed. But due to lack of proper infrastructure and transparency in the market this *sukuk* is not considered to be a success story.[47]

According to the Resolution No. 30, 5/4 of the Council of the Islamic Fiqh Academy, *muqarada* (or *mudaraba*) certificates are investment instruments, which allocate the *muqarada/mudaraba* capital by floating certificates as evidence of capital ownership, on the basis of shares of equal value, registered in the name of their owners, as joint owners of shares in the venture in proportion to each one's share therein.[48]

Turkey and Malaysia both claim to have issued the first successful modern *sukuk*s – Malaysia in 1983 and Turkey in 1984. While the slightly earlier Malaysian Government Investment Issues exhibited a very slow development,[49] the Turkish GOS scheme designed by the Özal government was highly dynamic and deserves special attention. But, in the long run, while the secularist-Muslim democrat conflict in Turkey eventually began to impede the Turkish *sukuk* market,[50] the Malaysian *sukuk* industry, enjoying full government support, eventually shot ahead of Turkey. In what follows, I will first discuss the Turkish Revenue Participation Scheme and then focus on the First Malaysian Global *Sukuk*, which heralded the massive expansion of the *sukuk* industry in Malaysia in the following years.[51]

THE TURKISH REVENUE PARTICIPATION SHARES (GOS)[52]

The GOS was introduced by the conservative government of Turgut Özal in Turkey by the Law No. 2983 in the year 1984.[53] The scheme started on

2 December 1984 initially with the sale of the First Bosphorus Bridge's revenues. The total nominal value of the shares was TL10 billion and they were sold out within one hour! This was followed on 7 January 1985 by the sale of Keban dam's revenues. The total nominal value was TL40 billion and the shares were sold out within half a day.

The law served several purposes. First, since the scheme was designed *riba* free, it aimed to attract the hitherto untapped savings of devoted Muslims to the economy. These shares were indeed *riba* free, because they were designed as government bonds with flexible rates of return reflecting the actual performance of the asset. Second, the law declared clearly that the GOS system aimed at enhancing savings by yielding sustained and reliable returns to the savers. Third, it was also planned that with the enhanced savings attracted to the scheme, additional funds external to the budget would become available for the state to invest in major development projects. Fourth, it was thought that these shares, directly linked to the actual performance of specific and impressive projects, could be marketed better than the standard government bonds. Fifth, since the returns were flexible and could be determined by the government at half-year periods, it was thought that, unlike the standard government bonds with fixed rates of return, the returns of GOS shares could be brought down when inflation is successfully reduced. Thus, although investors were guaranteed rates of return above the prevalent rate of inflation, the government could adjust GOS rates to the inflation and reduce its overall costs. The scheme was to generate no profits; it was designed purely as a revenue sharing system.[54]

The model worked as follows: a state-owned asset, say the first toll bridge over the Bosphorus, was incorporated into the system and a certain part of its revenue was reserved for payments to shareholders. The GOS shares were issued against this asset and matured in one to three years. These were bearers' shares and could be linked not only to a specific asset or project but also to several projects. In that case, they were referred to as 'group shares'.[55]

Each GOS share had two sections, the bond and the attached coupons. The bond contained the following information: the name of the asset, the nominal value of the bond, the date when the bond would mature and so on. Each coupon would indicate to a specific payment period and shareholders could claim their dividends for a specific period with the coupon of that period. The percentage of the total revenue to be distributed to investors would be determined up-front by the TKKOK, a government agency.[56] This would be done for each share issuance. The TKKOK would also determine the prices of the commodities or services produced by the asset. In doing this it was understood that it would take into consideration the need to provide sustained and reliable returns to the investors exceeding the prevalent annual inflation rates.[57]

At the end of this period the purchaser was paid back his initial investment plus his share of a certain percentage of the annual revenue of the bridge. Thus, the GOS shares were short- to medium-term instruments yielding uncertain returns.[58] Uncertainty was due to the fact that dividends reflected the overall performance of the asset, which in turn depended on economic circumstances. They were therefore definitively *riba*-free.

Pınar Akkoyunlu has followed the performance of these shares in the following years from the press. This has revealed the following information: in December 1986, two years after the issuance, it was reported that while during these two years the average rate of inflation was 86 per cent, the Bosphorus GOS shares yielded 125 per cent returns thus exceeding the rate of inflation by 39 points. It was declared by the authorities that GOS shares were the most profitable way to invest one's savings.[59] Throughout this period high inflation and the inevitable devaluations of the Turkish currency played havoc with savers' plans. To remedy the situation it was decided to issue GOS shares indexed to hard currencies like the German mark and the US dollar. This was explained to the public by announcing that when savers purchase these hard currency GOS shares, their investment shall be protected from any devaluation by adding compensatory payments to their usual returns.

The excellent performance of the Bosphorus Bridge GOS shares did not last and in April 1987 the government paid only 19.33 per cent return for a six-month period. Investors immediately responded by converting their shares to cash. It was then that the government, aiming to attract this cash, responded quickly and issued bonds indexed to hard currencies. These hard currency government bonds yielded high returns and succeeded to eliminate hard currency black markets.

Meanwhile, the poor performance of the Bosphorus Bridge shares made it difficult for the government to issue new shares based upon the Karakaya dam. It has been reported that hard currency bonds have crowded out the capital market and savers channelled their savings to these instruments.[60]

Probably in an effort to revitalize the interest in GOS shares, the government declared in January 1988 that the 1987 performance of the Bosphorus bridge has been excellent and that the savers will be paid 108 per cent for the A group bridge shares and 96 per cent for the B group shares. The performance of the Keban dam was also apparently excellent and the A group dam shares yielded 70.42 per cent net revenue for six months. The six months' rate of return for the B group shares yielded as much as 85.25 per cent. The press also reported that the Keban dam shares yielded such high returns thanks to the latest increases in electricity prices and accused the government of deliberately transferring capital from the electricity-consuming public to the GOS share owners.[61] Government authorities, on the other hand, rejected any deliberate wrong doing and insisted that it was the high rates of inflation which made increases in electricity prices reaching to 30 per cent inevitable. As for the

Bosphorus bridge, the totally unexpected increases in the amount of traffic using the bridge was behind the huge rates of return.

To reach a general conclusion about the profitability of GOS shares is very difficult. This is because each project has yielded different returns. Moreover, profitability was also affected by the time of the share purchase, which changed for each investor. Notwithstanding these general comments, we can observe cyclical trends. Indeed, while the early shares had been made deliberately very attractive, shares issued subsequently were not. The public responded immediately to such fluctuations and adjusted its investments.

The following actual examples should demonstrate how the scheme functioned in reality. Consider first the B group Bosphorus Bridge shares. Owners of these shares were paid their dividends twice a year in January and July. In the period January–June 1988, the bridge yielded TL22 667 722 784. 16 per cent of this revenue was to be reserved for the owners of GOS shares. This amounted to TL3 626 835 645 and was paid out in July 1988. Since altogether TL5 billion worth of shares had been issued, the amount distributed to the share owners was 72.53 per cent. As for the next six months period of July–December 1988, the revenue generated amounted to TL21 818 537 868. Out of this, 16 per cent or TL3 490 966 059 were distributed. Thus, out of the total revenue of TL44 486 260 650 generated by the first Bosphorus bridge in the year 1988, a total of TL7 117 801 704 were distributed to the GOS shareholders. Since originally TL5 billion worth of shares had been issued by the state, this amount constitutes a return of 142.34 per cent.[62] In short, the state ended up paying considerably more to the share owners than what it collected from them. The rate of inflation for the year 1988 was 69.7 per cent. Thus, on average, GOS shares yielded 72.64 per cent annual *real* rate of return to their owners.

On 12 March 1989, Professor Bülent Gültekin, the former head of TKKOI, criticized the system by arguing that the GOS scheme was the most expensive domestic borrowing system ever in the history of Turkish public finance.[63] He was answered by his predecessor, Kaya Erdem, that before passing a definitive judgement about the GOS scheme, it is necessary to consider what has been achieved with the capital borrowed from the public. He said the money was used to build other hydroelectric dams which contributed immensely to the economy. Thus, he argued, a cost-benefit analysis would reveal that the benefits would exceed the costs despite the claims made. Looked with hindsight, Professor Gültekin was right, the GOS was certainly an expensive method of finance. But Mr Erdem was also right as he referred to a very important principle of domestic/public borrowing in general: in the long run all such borrowing boils down to what the government does with it. Providing the borrowed funds are used for productive investment that generates greater revenues in the long run, then even expensive domestic/public borrowing schemes make sense.

This view seems to have been accepted, because on 22 May 1989, the government decided to issue new GOS shares based upon the first and the second Bosphorus bridges, and five new hydroelectric dams. It was decided that 5 per cent of the total revenue of these assets would be reserved for the new scheme.[64]

On 27 December 2006 the government announced its intention to reintroduce the GOS shares. The new shares would be made fully negotiable in secondary markets so as to enhance their liquidity. A major reason why the older shares had been difficult to sell for the government was that secondary markets were not yet fully developed then.[65] Despite this statement, however, apparently no new shares were introduced. In January 2009, I had the opportunity to ask the Governor of the Turkish Central Bank, Mr Durmuş Yılmaz, about the fate of the system and was informed that it was gradually discontinued by paying out the promised dividends and redeeming the principals.[66] He informed me further that no new GOS shares had been issued and the Turkish state was now generating sufficient revenue to finance its investments directly out of the budget. Moreover, the Build Operate Transfer (BOT) was now the preferred method of finance for major projects.[67]

Apparently the timid response of the Governor was reflecting the government's low profile approach. It is now common knowledge that the Turkish government had prepared a new draft law to completely reorganize and reactivate the earlier GOS system invented in the 1980s but withdrew the bill from the parliament in order to avoid a new conflict with the secularist establishment.[68] The latter objected to the GOS due to their Islamic character and viewed them as further Islamization of the economy. This objection was countered by the Union of Participation Banks[69] in Turkey by pointing out that *sukuk* is a viable and desirable alternative to privatization, particularly for those state-owned assets not suitable for privatization. Since the state-owned assets are leased for the long term and then returned back to the state, *sukuk* avoids any legal conflict concerning the privatization of state-owned assets. Moreover, since the returns generated for investors do not constitute *riba*, savings of the conservative Muslims remaining hitherto outside the circulation are channelled back to the economy.[70]

However, this was not to be the end of the GOS system in Turkey. Because soon after I had the above discussion with the Governor of the Central Bank, the Prime Ministry Treasury Office announced that new government bonds indexed to government revenues were to be issued on 28 January 2009.[71] These bonds were called GES (*Gelire Endeksli Senet* – bonds indexed to revenue). They were essentially the same as the earlier GOS with minor differences. Apparently rather than passing a new law, the government preferred to issue these bonds with minor adjustments.

Like the earlier GOS, the GES also were linked to the revenues of government-owned assets, this time the Turkish Petroleum Company, the Airports Management Authority and so on. More specifically, the GES returns were indexed to the revenues generated and actually deposited to the treasury by these state-owned enterprises. These assets had performed very well in the previous five years and the percentage of their net revenues to be securitized had increased from TL129 million in 2003 to TL230 million in 2007.[72]

They were to mature three years later on 1 February 2012 with 12 payment instalments in between. In order to avoid the fluctuations observed with the earlier GOS, the GES were to generate returns for their owners within a band of minimum and maximum returns. These returns were based on the estimates of the revenues to be generated by the assets. These estimates for the budgets of 2009, 2010 and 2011 have been officially declared.[73] The minimum annual return compounded was to be 15.68 per cent and the maximum 17.52 per cent for shares issued in TLs. For US$ shares these values were to fluctuate between 6.14 per cent and 6.46 per cent. These were estimates and it was announced that they could be increased further if the actual returns were to be realized at higher levels. For TL shares, 90 per cent of the dividend payments were guaranteed. This guarantee was 95 per cent for the US$ shares. The total nominal value of the shares to be sold to the public was to be TL1890 million (US$1171 million). The shares were to be issued in two groups in TLs and US$s and reflected a percentage of the revenue to be generated by these assets. The shares were to be negotiable and could be traded in the Istanbul Stock Exchange as well as the bond markets.

Actual coupon payments to be paid to each investor every three months were to be calculated as follows: the revenue share allocated to the programme out of the total amount of actual revenue to be generated by the assets was to be divided by 18 900 000, the total number of GES shares issued, multiplied by the number of GES shares held by the investor. Each GES was to have TL100 nominal value.

Despite the attractive returns promised, the Turkish Treasury has been able to raise merely a quarter of the US$1171 million targeted. This is despite the fact that Professor Hayreddin Karaman, a leading *Shari'ah* scholar in Turkey, has approved these instruments.[74] Poor marketing appears to have been the main reason for this failure. Indeed, fearing secularist backlash, the Turkish government failed to promote the GES not only domestically but also globally – it has not dared to call the GES scheme with its proper and globally accepted name, *sukuk*. Moreover, the fact that the GES returns were indexed to the revenues to be generated by some state economic enterprises may have failed to attract international investors who prefer fixed returns. Thus this Turkish case demonstrates clearly the importance of marketing for *sukuk* issuance.

THE FIRST MALAYSIAN GLOBAL *SUKUK*

When I heard some years ago that the Malaysian government had issued an instrument called *sukuk* and that this was an Islamic instrument for public borrowing, I presumed that this represented a further evolution of the first public borrowing ever practised in the history of Islamic public finance. I was convinced of this until 2005, when Saiful Azhar Rosly published his *Islamic Banking and Financial Markets*. When I read this book, I realized that this new instrument was an unintentional synthesis and a modernized version of the Ottoman *esham* and the cash waqfs. Put differently, although from the perspective of institutional evolution the *First Malaysian Global Sukuk*, indeed, represents a synthesis of the two earlier Ottoman institutions, the *esham* and the cash waqfs, its designers were unaware of them. Indeed, it is clear that all the transactions of the First Malaysian Global Sovereign *Sukuk* as described by Rosly, from transaction (1) to (10), can be found in the Ottoman cash waqf and *esham*. Let's start with the *modus operandi* of an Ottoman cash waqf. The numbers in parentheses correspond to Prof. Rosly's numbers depicting transactions of the Malaysian *Sukuk*.

1. Ottoman cash waqf corresponds to the Malaysian Global *Sukuk* Inc., or to the SPV (special purpose vehicle). The borrower (Malaysian government) requests a loan from the waqf. Waqf demands collateral. Borrower sells his asset, usually his house, to the waqf and gives the deed to the waqf. Thus the ownership of the asset is transferred to the waqf.
2. In return for the deed, which also fulfils the function of collateral, the waqf pays to the borrower the capital he had requested. The borrower requests permission to continue to use his asset (to live in his house) and pay rent.
3. In the next section (*esham*).
4. In the next section (*esham*).
5. Waqf agrees and leases the house to its previous owner.
6. Borrower starts paying the rent and thus becomes a tenant of the waqf.
7. In the next section (*esham*).
8. When the borrower (government) is ready, he returns the cash he had borrowed. In return for this cash, a resale transaction occurs and the waqf sells the asset back to the borrower.
9. The deed of the house, collateral, is returned to the borrower.

Rent income received from the time the first transaction took place until the last one constitutes the profit of the waqf, which it spends for the original purpose of its founder.

So far, with the exception of three transactions, 3, 4 and 7, we have identified a one-to-one correspondence between the transactions of the Ottoman

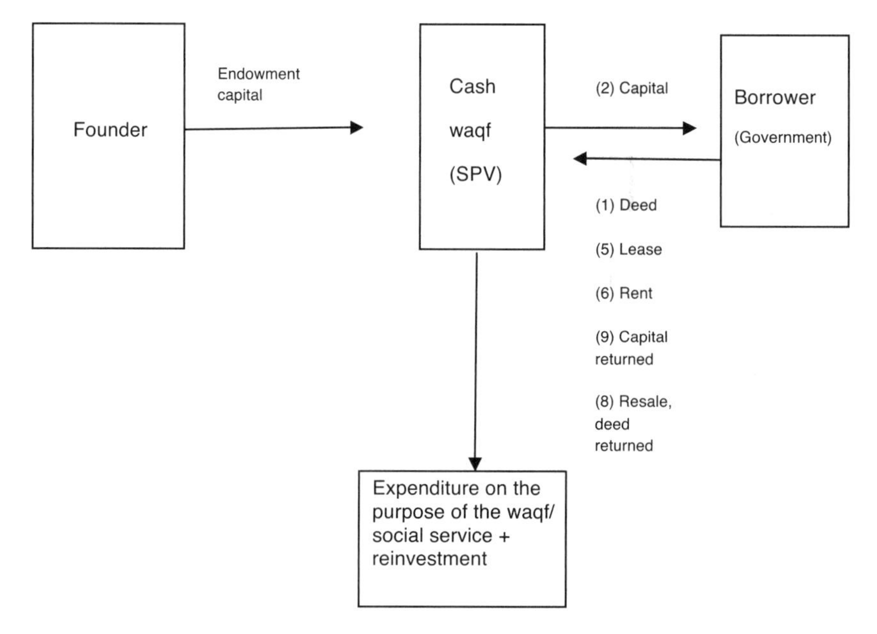

Figure 10.1 The Ottoman cash waqf revisited

cash waqf and the First Malaysian Global Sukuk. These three remaining transactions can be found in another Ottoman institution, the *esham*.

As the reader will remember, the *modus operandi* of the Ottoman *esham* was as follows:

1. The government identifies a tax source generating a regular annual profit.
2. This annual profit is then securitized and is divided into equal parts. Each part is called a *sehm*. *Sehm* means a share, its plural is *esham*.
3. These *esham* are then sold to investors. This transaction corresponds to the SPV selling *sukuks* to investors in Malaysia.
4. Investors pay in cash for these certificates. Each *sehm* certificate authorizes its owner to collect a commensurate share of the annual profit yielded by the asset. In the case of the Ottoman *esham*, this asset was the annual profit of a specific tax source. In the case of the First Malaysian Global *Sukuk*, it was the revenue of a composite pool of assets worth US$600 million.
5. Annual profit of the tax sources, annuities, were then paid to the *esham* owners regularly.

In the case of the Ottoman *esham,* these annuities were paid for the lifetime of the *sehm* owner. Occasionally, the Ottoman government redeemed them. But it

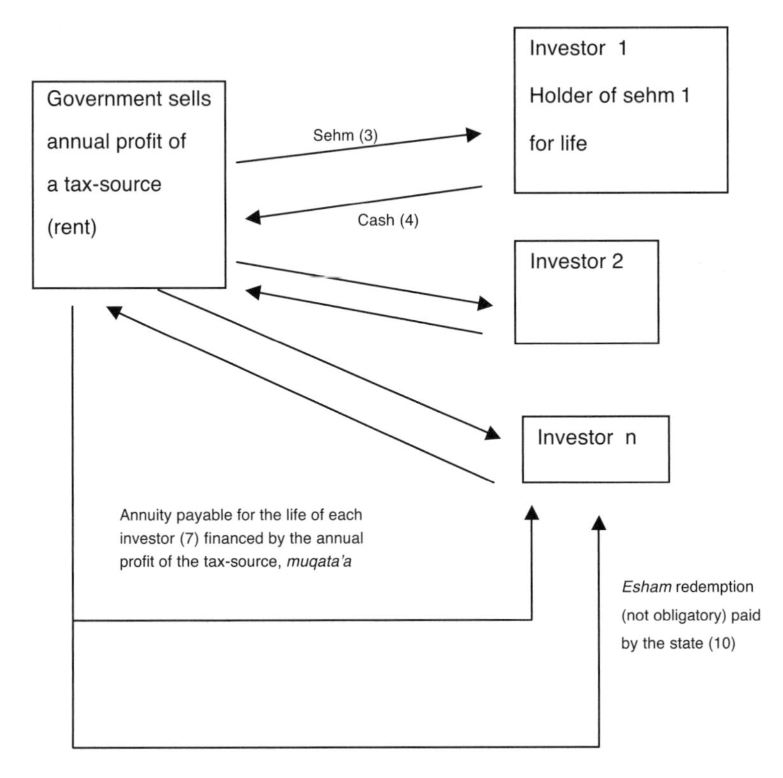

Figure 10.2 The Ottoman esham *system*

was not obliged to do so. In the case of the Malaysian *Sukuk*, there is definitive redemption.

While we were discussing with His Royal Highness the possibility of government borrowing according to Islamic principles, that is, a sovereign *sukuk*, and trying to discover historical precedents in Lahore, the Shell MDS Sdn Bhd, a Malaysian company, had already issued the first ever corporate *sukuk* of RM75 million for a tenure of five years and another RM50 million with an eight year maturity. This was followed in 1991 by Sarawak Shell Berhad with its RM600 million guaranteed *musharaka* financing. In short, the Malaysian private sector had already discovered Islamic bonds and started using it.[75] This was followed by an explosive growth. By the year 2007, the *sukuk* market reached a volume of US$24 billion.[76]

But this growth was not without problems. The *Shari'ah* scholars from the Gulf Cooperation Council (GCC) countries severely criticized *sukuk* based upon the securitization of *Bai' Bithaman Ajil*. Another critique also came from Iran, where the design of the Malaysian *sukuk* based upon *Bay al-Ainah* was declared unacceptable by Ali Salehabadi, a scholar and the president of the *Securities and Exchange Organization of Iran*.[78] The *Malaysian Securities Commission* reacted to all this and issued a guideline in 2004 for issuing *sukuk*. As a result, a great increase in non-debt *sukuk* has been observed in 2007, amounting to 58 per cent of the market's total issuances. This ratio increased to 83.6 per cent by the first half of 2008. If we consider this in combination with Sheikh Muhammad Taqi Usmani's comment in November 2007 that 85 per cent of the GCC non-*ijara sukuk* are not *Shari'ah* compliant, we reach the conclusion that Malaysia has gone further in the issuance of *Shari'ah* compliant *sukuk* than the GCC.[78] To a large extent this was achieved by the establishment of the *National Shari'ah Advisory Council* of Bank Negara Malaysia on 1 May 1997.[79] The idea of having a *Shari'ah* advisory body attached to a central bank so as to have substantially more clout than the usual advisory bodies is beginning to find acceptance. This is confirmed by the recent decisions of Pakistan and the UAE to establish similar institutions.[80]

The first Malaysian sovereign *sukuk* was issued in 1997 by the *Khazanah Nasional Berhad,* the Malaysian government's investment arm and was based upon the *murabaha* and *bay' al-dayn* concepts.[81] In 2006, the *Khazanah* introduced the industry's first ever equity-linked *sukuk* (US$750 million). From the Islamic perspective, this was a far more respectable instrument as it utilized a *musharaka* structure linked to the performance of Malaysian Telecom shares. The claim 'industry's first ever equity linked *sukuk*', however, may be contested by the Turkish GOS shares described above.[82]

In 1999 *sukuk* made up only a meagre 6 per cent of the total corporate bonds issued. This ratio shot up to 76 per cent in 2007. In 2002, Malaysia went international and issued the first international sovereign Islamic *sukuk*.[83]

Every sovereign *sukuk* has essentially two components: first, generation of a regular annual revenue by a government-owned asset and second, securitization and sale of this revenue (profit) to the public.[84] The first component of the Malaysian sovereign *sukuk*, generation of profit, is similar to the Ottoman cash waqf and the second component, securitization of this profit, to *esham*.

In the Malaysian case, a special purpose vehicle (SPV) was created with the purpose of raising the US$600 million fund. The *sukuk* were issued by this institution, which has legal personality. The SPV corresponds to the Ottoman cash waqf. Moreover, this correspondence is not accidental. For it has been argued that for all practical purposes the SPV can be regarded as a non-profit trust. Indeed, the trust structures for which there is special provision in English law are widely used for cross-border *sukuk* issues.[85] Since Malaysian law has been derived from English law, with comparable provision for trusts, this has facilitated the development of a *sukuk* market in Kuala Lumpur. Elsewhere, I have already shown that the medieval English trust had been originally borrowed from the Islamic world.[86] Thus we have here a fascinating case of institutional borrowing across civilizations and centuries: the English borrowing of the Islamic waqf during the crusades, incorporation of the classical Islamic waqf concept into the medieval English law under the name 'use' or 'trust', the Malaysian borrowing of the originally Islamic trust from the English law and finally the Malaysian application of the concept of trust in *sukuk* in the form of SPV! Consequently, there is nothing surprising about the structural similarity of the Malaysian SPV and the Ottoman cash waqf – they both have their origins in the classical Islamic waqf.

But the relative ease with which the originally Islamic waqf/trust concept has been applied to the SPV of a *sukuk* should not mislead us. Financial engineers often complain that in many Middle Eastern jurisdictions, which apply the French civil law, it is very difficult to form *sukuk* SPVs.[87] I would like to advise these financial engineers that instead of trying to impose Anglo-Saxon trust concept in Muslim civil law countries, they should resort to the classical Islamic waqf accepted and respected in all Islamic countries. But this necessitates a modern codification of Islamic law.[88]

The SPV applied an *al-ijara* contract based upon sale plus lease-back, which we observed clearly in the Ottoman cash waqfs explained above. In the Ottoman case, a borrower sold his house to the waqf, transferred its ownership and after that was allowed to continue living in his house but had to pay rent. In the Malaysian case, the government sold to the SPV a hospital complex and the ownership of these properties were transferred to the SPV. The government then rented back these properties, which continued to function as before with the only difference that the Malaysian state was now paying rent for these facilities. These rental payments were collected by the SPV and then passed on to the investors or securitized. This part is similar to the Ottoman *esham*, where investors, purchasers of *esham* shares, were paid their annuities with the proceeds of the tobacco customs of Istanbul. Owners of *esham* shares were paid fixed returns and these returns were guaranteed by the state. If the actual returns were less than the promised rates, the state compensated the difference. But if the actual returns were greater than what was promised, then the state simply securitized further and issued additional shares. In Malaysia the rent paid by the government to the SPV fulfilled the same function as the rent paid by the Ottoman borrowers to cash waqfs – generating profit for the SPV/waqf. It is understood that the Malaysian government shall buy back the property at the expiration of the lease term and pay SPV in cash. This money will then be used by the SPV to pay the investors and the *sukuk* certificates shall be redeemed. After the redemption the SPV no longer has a role to play. Consequently, it is wound up and ceases to exist as a legal person. The SPV is a very convenient instrument. Being a trust/waqf, it faces none of the risks associated with a bank and is bankruptcy remote, hence is attractive to both the issuers and the investors. Not surprisingly, it is applied in the overwhelming majority of *sukuk* issued to date.[89]

Having made a comparative analysis of the historical Ottoman and the modern Malaysian institutions of sovereign borrowing, let us now examine the *modus operandi* of the First Malaysian Global Sovereign *Sukuk* step by step as depicted by Professor Saiful.[90] Numbers reflect Professor Saiful's depiction of the steps of the *modus operandi*.

1. SPV purchases the hospital and other assets from the government for US$600 million and the ownership is transferred from the Malaysian state to the SPV.
2. The government receives the cash.
3. The SPV issues *sukuk* certificates to investors worth US$600 million.
4. Investors pay to the SPV US$600 million and purchase the shares.
5. Meanwhile, the government rents the assets it once owned and sold to the SPV. The Malaysian government now becomes a tenant of SPV for these assets.
6. The government starts paying the rent to the SPV.
7. The SPV transfers these rents to investors. Thus investors receive regular rental income as a reward for their investment.
8. The SPV resells the assets for US$600 million back to the state.
9. The state pays US$600 million to the SPV.
10. The SPV transfers US$600 million to investors and redeems the *sukuk* certificates. The certificates are returned to the SPV.

The end result is that the Malaysian government has used its otherwise passive assets to borrow a large amount of cash in return for which it was prepared to pay rent. Meanwhile, it might be noted that a rent contract is considered by the *fiqh* authorities as a sale contract by which, not the asset itself, but its usufruct is sold over successive periods. Thus, normally, there is no doubt about the legality of an *ijara* contract. The securitization of leased assets and thus their transformation into financial assets, *ijara bonds*, is also permitted.[91]

There are, however, some problems stemming from the determination of the amount of rent. A major criticism of such *al-ijara*, lease back, types of *sukuk* is that the rate of return is usually based upon the London Inter-bank Offer Rate (LIBOR). This is of course an interest rate and disturbs everybody concerned. There is therefore a great need for alternative benchmarks. It has been suggested that real rather than monetary indicators should be used for sovereign *sukuk* and company performance indicators for corporate *sukuk*.[92]

SUKUK IN DUBAI

The First Malaysian Sovereign *Sukuk* is generally known as the first ever international sovereign *sukuk* issued in modern times. It was soon followed in October 2004 by a much greater one issued by the Government of Dubai for the Department of Civil Aviation worth a massive US$1 billion. This was originally planned at US$750 million but was oversubscribed by nearly 60 per cent. 78 per cent of the investors were banks, 9 per cent were government agencies, 7 per cent were insurance and pension funds. 73 per cent of these investors originated from the Middle East, 16 per cent from Europe and 11 per cent from Asia. This transaction was known as the largest *sukuk* issued so far.[93]

But soon a much larger *sukuk* was launched in January 2006 by the Dubai Ports, Customs and Free Zone Corporation (PCFC). The original issuance was US$2.8 billion, which was increased to US$3.5 billion in response to the strong demand. This *sukuk* was structured as a convertible *sukuk* in the sense that up to 30 per cent of the *sukuk* could be redeemed into PCFC shares if an Initial Public Offering (IPO) proceeded within two years of the launch. This convertible structure is also known as *musharaka sukuk* and was issued to transform the PCFC into one of the three largest port operators in the world. It is considered as the first *sukuk* to be convertible into equity upon an IPO. It has been argued that this *sukuk* was targeted at Islamic investors interested in the thriving IPO market in the Middle East – hence its structure as equivalent of a pre-IPO convertible bond.[94]

SUKUK IN BAHRAIN

In the year 2001, the *Central Bank of Bahrain* launched a so-called *salam sukuk*, which ended up being a hugely popular liquidity management tool for regional financial institutions.[95] But first, a few words to explain the *salam* contract.

The essence of the *salam* contract is the future delivery of an asset with the full price paid in advance. What makes *salam* different from the better known *murabaha* is that in the former the payment for the commodity traded is made in advance. The problem with a *salam* contract is that it violates the prohibition of *gharar* (ambiguity). Not to be labelled as *gharar*, a transaction must have deliverable commodities, which must clearly exist and must be owned by the seller. Although *salam* sale violates these conditions it is permitted based upon Prophetic tradition. It is argued that the Prophet had allowed it on the basis of necessity, *darrura*. The structure of the modern *salam sukuk* launched by the *Central Bank of Bahrain* is coupled with a unilateral undertaking, *wa'd,* promise, by the bank. The *modus operandi* is as follows:

1. At time t_1, the Government of Bahrain sells a specified commodity of aluminium (x_1) to the investors (*sukuk* holders) for delivery in 90 days for a price, p_1. This is a *salam* transaction.
2. The *sukuk* holders appoint the Government of Bahrain as their agent to market the specified aluminium at the time of delivery.
3. The Government unilaterally undertakes to sell in 90 days ($t_2 = t_1 + 90$ days) the specified aluminium x_1 to a third party user for a price p_2, which is equivalent to p_1 + rate of return.
4. The proceeds of the sale conducted by the Government are then transferred to the investors.

It has been argued that the returns on the *salam sukuk* reflect the market returns available on short-term treasury bills. Obviously, this particular *sukuk* is entirely inspired by the Western treasury bills and constitutes a very different category from the *sukuk al-ijara* with its own structural evolution.

There are basically two risks in this structure: credit risk (counter party default risk) and market risk with regard to the delivery of the commodities in the future. The counter party risk essentially translates into sovereign risk on the Government of Bahrain. The same is true for the market risk (the promise by the Government of Bahrain to sell the aluminium at a given price at the date of delivery) also transforms the market risk into sovereign risk on the government.

SUKUK IN GERMANY/THE NETHERLANDS

In 2004 another very interesting *sukuk* was issued. The offering was merely €100 million. But what makes this *sukuk* interesting is the fact that it has been issued by a European authority, *Stichting Sachsen-Anhalt Trust*. Saxony-Anhalt is one of the new states of the reunified German Federation and its debts are guaranteed by the whole German Federation. Consequently the *sukuk* received AA-rating by Standard & Poor's and AAA by Fitch. The SPV was registered in the Netherlands as a *Stichting*, foundation, which corresponds, once again, to the Islamic waqf! The registration in the Netherlands was due to the more favourable securitization law in that country, particularly from the perspective of taxation. Choosing a Dutch foundation as the SPV has made the *sukuk* competitive with respect to the municipality tax. The *sukuk* holders will receive a variable rent benchmarked to the EURIBOR for a period of five years. After the repayment, the Ministry has the option of using the SPV for a second time for a new issue.

This is the first euro-denominated *sukuk* offering issued by a quasi-sovereign issuer. It has been argued that this has paved the way for corporate issuers to tap the *sukuk* market. Moreover, 67 per cent of the deal was distributed in Europe, thus introducing Islamic finance to that continent, particularly to Germany, where Islamic finance is little known. From the issuer's perspective the transaction was important for having successfully raised funds from the Middle East, thus recycling petro-dollars. The holders of the certificates owned the usufruct of certain properties for a five-year period. In 2004, Saxony-Anhalt issued a €100 million five-year bond. The bond was priced plus one basis point six month EURIBOR (European Interbank Offered Rate), which was chosen as the benchmark. Citibank was chosen as the lead manager and Kuwait Finance House as the co-lead manager. The *Shari'ah* Board of Citi Islamic Investment Bank certified the *sukuk* from the *Shari'ah* perspective. Assets underlying the *sukuk* were a certain number of buildings. The deal was fully subscribed with 60 per cent of the issue sold to the GCC investors and other 40 per cent sold in Europe. All of these examples constitute the *sukuk al-ijara* variety.

To sum up, asset-based *sukuk* fulfils the following economic functions: first, it provides limited liability in the sense that the *sukuk* issuer's liability is limited to the value of its assets, thus reducing the probability of bankruptcy. Second, it provides a second benchmark for the interest rate paid on bonds. Third, it substitutes for the difficult process of privatization of state economic enterprises in countries which otherwise would be too slow to privatize. Fourth, and most importantly, it allows the state as well as private corporations to borrow large amounts of capital by securitizing their otherwise idle assets. In this way, savings of the masses are channelled to major projects while at the same time, particularly in the case of *sukuk al-ijara*, the interest prohibition is not violated.

INSTITUTIONAL BORROWING OR REINVENTING?

Since we have identified all the ten transactions of the First Malaysian Global Sukuk in the historical Ottoman cash waqfs and *esham*, we are justified to consider the modern *sukuk* as an evolution from these origins. Actually, the remarkable similarity between these historical and modern institutions should not surprise us. After all, as Prince Mohammad had correctly guessed, the Ottomans were facing the same challenge as any modern Islamic government faces now – how to borrow from the public without violating the interest prohibition. Consequently, if modern solutions to this problem are similar to those found by the Ottomans centuries ago, this is only natural – the same problem demands the same or similar solution. The only difference between the Ottoman *esham* and the First Malaysian Global *Sukuk* is that the former was simpler in that it was a mere instrument of securitization. The latter is more complicated because it first generates revenue and then securitizes it. But the above argument simply repeats itself here. Indeed, the revenue generation segment of the First Malaysian Global *Sukuk* is also very similar to another Ottoman institution – the cash waqf. This similarity should also be considered quite normal.

If a historical institution reappears centuries later in a modern form, there can be only two possibilities: institutional borrowing from historical forms, or reinventing. Reinventing occurs because, as Ronald Coase, a Nobel Laurate in economics, once said, 'institutions spring into being when there is a need for them'.[96] I have been able to learn directly from Dr Zeti Akhtar Aziz, the Governor of *Bank Negara Malaysia*, that the First Malaysian Global *Sukuk* was reinvented by highly paid and specially commissioned financial engineers. Thus, there was a need for this institution, global *sukuk*, and it 'sprang into being'. But this emergence took the form of reinvention of an institution actually known for centuries and was, therefore, needlessly expensive. The high cost was the result of not only the very high wages of financial engineers but also the *fatwas* that had to be obtained as well as the time it took to design the instrument. Had historical forms been modernized instead, Ottoman *fatwas* could have been utilized at near zero cost and actual designing could have been made at a much shorter time, resulting in radical cost savings.

CONCLUSION

To sum up, we observe the following. First, the *sukuk* market is not immune to the global credit crunch. Indeed, as liquidity has disappeared from global markets, the prices of existing *sukuk*, particularly the dollar-denominated ones, fell sharply and the yields have increased as a result.[97] Second, small and medium-sized *sukuk*, particularly in Malaysia, have not slowed. Third, should the trend toward mega-*sukuk* continue in the GCC, this region will emerge as the market leader in *sukuk*. Fourth, it seems, Malaysia will be able to maintain its leadership only by extending its *sukuk* issuance to regions beyond South East Asia and by beginning to finance megaprojects. For instance, had the Turkish Istanbul–Izmir motorway, costing US$5 billion, been financed by a Malaysian organized *sukuk*, Malaysia would have been able to double its total 2008 *sukuk* issuance obtained from 54 issues and shot ahead of the GCC with this single project.[98]

Obviously, explaining in detail all the varieties of *sukuk* is beyond the confines of this book. Indeed, according to the AAOIFI there are 14 different ways of structuring *sukuk*. But so far only seven types have been observed in practice. These are *ijara*, *musharaka*, *mudaraba*, *murabaha*, *istisna*, *salam* (presale of future delivery of goods) and *manfa'a* (selling the usufruct of assets). After the AAOIFI statement, which confirmed the most important characteristic of *sukuk al-ijara*, the sale and lease-back, but condemned the rest, the relative importance of the most frequently observed forms, the *sukuk al-mudaraba* and *musharaka* declined rapidly. This is natural, because issuers always seek the less controversial structures in order to attract as many investors as possible. Moreover, compliance with the AAOIFI standards is optional but they are required in some countries such as Bahrain and the UAE. From 2007 to 2008, while *sukuk al-ijara* maintained its leading position, *sukuk al-mudaraba* declined by 68.6 per cent and the *sukuk al-musharaka* by 83 per cent.[99] As a result, the relative weight of *mudaraba* and *musharaka* in the *sukuk* industry has started to exhibit the same downward trend that has been observed in Islamic banking and *takaful*. It is for this reason that I have focused here primarily on *sukuk al-ijara*.

It is appropriate to conclude this chapter by referring to the salient characteristics of the Islamic *sukuk* and how they differ from the conventional methods. This is necessary because the entire current debate as well as, in all probability, the debates of the future will ultimately be decided by referring to these essential principles.[100]

1. The essence of *sukuk*, as actually the whole of Islamic finance, is sharing. In the specific case of *sukuk*, the holders of the *sukuk* certificates should share in the profits of the enterprises financed or in their revenues. This is in sharp contrast to the conventional system, where depositors are allowed to earn merely the prevalent deposit rate and it is the owners who earn the real profits.
2. *Sukuk* constitutes the ideal way for channelling the modest savings of the Muslim masses for major projects or for public finance. While the former may be achieved by the Islamic banks as well, there is no other Islamically viable instrument for the latter (public finance). In this context it might be added that *sukuk* provides some of the advantages of the privatization of state-owned economic enterprises without the difficult problem of transferring the ownership of these enterprises, originally financed by tax payers, to certain individuals. This is because *sukuk* allows the purchasers to share the profit/revenue or the usufruct of a state economic enterprise without transferring its ownership.
3. To the extent that secondary markets develop, *sukuk* would also provide the means to the masses to convert their *sukuk* shares into cash. It is therefore imperative that the governments do their utmost to develop these markets.
4. On the assumption that the secondary markets develop, *sukuk* also provides an excellent opportunity for Islamic banks and financial institutions to manage their liquidity. Indeed, when these have excess liquidity, they can simply purchase *sukuk*, and when they are in need of liquidity they can sell them at the secondary markets.

5. By allowing all participants to share in the real profits, *sukuk* also fulfils another major Islamic economic goal: the equitable distribution of income in the society and ensures that wealth circulates on a broad scale and does not remain the exclusive domain of a handful of wealthy persons.[101]
6. *Sukuk,* like the rest of Islamic finance, faces a grave danger. This is the tendency of the issuers to make them compatible with conventional bonds so as to facilitate their acceptance in both Islamic and conventional markets. This results in confusion and dilution between the two systems. To clarify this confusion we need to remember the following. First, conventional bonds do not represent ownership on the part of bond holders; they merely document the interest-bearing debt owed to the bond holders by the issuer. Second, when interest payments are made to conventional bond holders, the amount of interest is determined as a percentage of the capital invested and not as a percentage of the actual profits. Third, conventional bonds guarantee the return of principal at maturity, regardless of whether the enterprise has generated a loss or a profit. The issuer is not obliged to return anything exceeding the principal invested plus the rate of interest. Actual profits earned by the enterprise accrue entirely and exclusively to the issuer. By contrast, legitimate Islamic *sukuk* does not guarantee the capital invested[102] but, in return, compensates the *sukuk* holder by enabling him to participate in the true profit/revenues (or loss) of the enterprise. This is the most important characteristic that distinguishes Islamic *sukuk* from conventional bonds.

This most important characteristic, however, remains in theory. In actual practice, virtually all of the *sukuk* issued today guarantee the return of the principal to *sukuk* holders at maturity, in exactly the same way as conventional bonds. This is accomplished by means of a binding promise to repurchase the assets represented by the *sukuk* at the stated price at which these were originally purchased by *sukuk* holders. Consequently, *sukuk* assume the same characteristics as conventional interest bearing bonds as they do not return to the investor more than a fixed percentage of the principal benchmarked to the prevalent interest rate while at the same time guaranteeing the return of the invested capital at maturity.[103] This percentage is by no means linked to the expected real profits of the enterprise but to the prevalent rates of interest in the market. Under normal circumstances, this rate would be substantially lower than the expected returns from the actual profits of the enterprise. In short, all incentives should be based on sharing the actual expected profits (or losses) and certainly not on the prevalent rate of interest. By the same token, all measures to compensate *sukuk* holders for rates of returns less than the prevalent rates of interest such as loans, purchasing *sukuk* assets at face value upon maturity etc., are also illegal.[104]

One common explanation provided by the *sukuk* issuers who violate so blatantly the well-known principles of Islamic finance is the need to obtain the approval of the conventional rating agencies. Such approval, they argue, cannot be obtained unless some mechanisms are used to guarantee the return of the principal to investors. Islamic financial institutions needing to obtain the approval of rating agencies that operate under conventional principles constitutes a serious institutional problem. There is therefore an urgent need to create Islamic rating agencies that rate financial institutions according to Islamic principles. Such agencies have already been established. Both the IFSB and the AAOIFI perform rating services.[105] But to what extent these institutions operate as *bona fide* rating agencies and what difficulties they face, need to be studied carefully. Put bluntly, if these agencies function as *bona fide* rating agencies, why do the market players need to obtain endorsements from conventional agencies? Is this primarily a marketing problem, or are there other factors involved? Finally, is *sukuk al-ijara* the best instrument for public borrowing? Wouldn't modernized and fully negotiable *esham* and improved revenue participation shares be better instruments in view of their simplicity, therefore lower costs as well as *Shari'ah* compliance?

NOTES

1. The deficit problem had already emerged in 1988, when the usual annual oil revenue of about US$100 billion plunged to US$21 billion due to oil price fluctuations. The Saudi government was then forced to follow the trend started first by Bahrain and followed by Oman and Kuwait in 1986 and decided to issue treasury bills. *New Straits Times*, 2 January 1988, p. 19. This must have exacerbated the already existing tension between the conservative Islamic hierarchy and the government. Hence the Prince's desire to find a permanent and definitive solution to this public finance problem which became far more serious after the Gulf war.
2. Kahf, 'Taxation Policy', p. 118.
3. Consider the following quotation concerning the *maqasid al-Shariah*: 'The very objective of the Shari'ah is to promote the welfare of the people, which lies in safeguarding their faith, their life, their intellect, their posterity and their wealth. Whatever ensures the safeguarding of these five serves public interest and is desirable.' In Chapra, *Islam and the Economic Challenge*, p. 1.
4. Fritschy, 'Indirect Taxes and Public Debt', pp. 51–75.
5. On the Ottoman support for Indian Ocean Muslims, see İnalcık and Quataert, *An Economic and Social History*, pp. 20, 328, as well as Casale, 'The Ottoman Administration of the Spice Trade, pp. 170–98.
6. Kahf, 'Taxation Policy', p. 119.
7. Kahf, 'Taxation Policy', pp. 120–2.
8. Çizakça, 'The Economy: 1453–1606'.
9. North and Weingast, 'The Evolution of Institutions'. See also Dincecco, 'Fiscal Centralization', pp. 48–104.
10. Çizakça, *Comparative Evolution*, ch. 5.
11. Genç, 'Esham', p. 376.
12. Macdonald, *A Free Nation Deep in Debt*, p.6. The term 'quasi-democracy' here refers to the semi-democratic arrangements of medieval European city-states in, particularly, Flanders

and the Italian Quadrelateral, that is, the most important city-states of Genoa, Milan, Florence and Venice.
13. Dincecco, 'Fiscal Centralization', passim.
14. Zeti Akhtar Aziz, 'Enhancing the Resilience', p. 8.
15. Mohamad, 'Ground Rules', in Securities Commission Malaysia, *Sukuk*, p. 42.
16. Standard & Poor's 'Chief Drivers Behind Islamic Finance's Global Expansion', p. 4; Standard & Poor's, '*Sukuk* Market Picks up Pace Despite Gloomy Conditions', p. 19.
17. Hesse et al. 'Trends and Challenges', p. 176.
18. Bi, 'Islamic Capital Markets', p. 13.
19. Zeti Akhtar Aziz, 'Enhancing the Resilience', p. 10.
20. Standard & Poor's, '*Sukuk* Market Grows Despite Roadblocks (part 1)', *Islamic Finance News,* 11 September 2009, p. 15. See also Zeti, A. Aziz, 'Enhancing the Resiliencies', p. 10.
21. The Malaysian National *Shari'ah* Advisory Council was established on 1 May 1997 as the highest *Shari'ah* authority on Islamic banking and *takaful* in that country. See Venardos, *Islamic Banking and Finance,* p. 147.
22. www.cpifinancial.net, IBF 809 Issue 44, 27 August 2009.
23. *Islamic Finance Asia*, 27 August 2009.
24. Standard & Poor's, '*Sukuk* Market Grows Despite Roadblocks (part 1)', *Islamic Finance News*, 11 September 2009, p. 15.
25. www.cpifinancial.net, IBF 809 Issue 44, 27 August 2009.
26. Standard & Poor's, '*Sukuk* Market Picks up', p. 19.
27. www.cpifinancial.net, IBF 809 Issue 44, 27 August 2009.
28. Iqbal and Mirakhor, *An Introduction,* pp. 178–81, 186.
29. According to S&P, entities located in more than 15 countries, predominantly non-Muslim, had expressed interest in *sukuk*. See '*Sukuk* Issuance to Exceed RM 69 billion This Year', *Malaysian Reserve*, 15 September 2008. Details of a German *sukuk* are provided below. In July 2008, the Mizuho Corporate Bank of Japan arranged a syndicated *sukuk* worth US$ 3.85 billion for a Saudi mining project. See on this www.cpifinancial.net/v2.
30. Bi, 'Islamic Capital Markets', pp. 13–14; IFIS, *IFIS Global Sukuk Market, H2. 2010 Report*, 2010, p. 8..
31. Reference is made here to the by now famous paper of Sheikh Taqi Usmani, which was circulated towards the end of 2007. The Sheikh criticized the *mudaraba* and *musharaka sukuk* structures on the grounds that the credit on the *sukuk* was based on the credit-worthiness of the provider of the purchase undertaking and not on the assets underlying the *sukuk*. See on this www.nortonrose.com/knowledge/publications/2008. The basic structure of the *sukuk al-ijara*, the sale and lease-back, on the other hand, has been approved by the AAOIFI in its 15 January 2007 meeting (Decision number 5). The exact wording of the decision is as follows: 'It is permissible for a lessee in a *sukuk al-ijara* to undertake to purchase the leased assets when the *sukuk* are extinguished for its nominal value, provided he (lessee) is not also a partner, *mudarìb* or investment agent'. See also Al-Amine, '*Sukuk* Market', 2008.
32. Kahf, 'Use of Assets', p. 79.
33. Ibid., pp. 78–9. There is historical evidence for this: the Ottoman *esham*, though not strictly rent contracts, were issued on life term basis in the late eighteenth century. Latest on-going research by Ali Akyıldız appears to indicate that these terms changed and became shorter over time. Moreover, both Ottoman and Iranian waqfs could be leased on a long-term basis. Iranian waqfs were rented out for 99 years and on the lapse of this period a new lease for the same period was issued on payment of one year's revenue. See on this and the so-called *ijareteyn waqfs* Çizakça, *Philanthropic Foundations*, p. 147.
34. The Qur'an, 2: 282.
35. Decision no. 5 of the 4th Annual Plenary Session of the *OIC Fiqh Academy* held in Jeddah on 6–11 February 1988. See Kahf, 'Use of Assets', p. 81.
36. Kahf, 'Use of Assets', p. 82.
37. Nadim Khan and Paul McViety, 'Scholarly Debate'. See also '*Sukuk* Issuance to Exceed RM 69 Billion This Year', *Malaysian Reserve*, 15 September 2008.
38. Special Purpose Vehicle in charge of organizing the whole transaction.

39. Amin, 'The UK Tax Law', p. 16.
40. Ram Ratings, 'Malaysian Sukuk', p. 19.
41. Kawach, 'GCC *Sukuk* Issues', 24 July 2009.
42. Global Investment House, '*Sukuk* Market – Down But Not Out', p. 16.
43. Standard & Poor's, '*Sukuk* Market Picks up', p. 18.
44. The AAOIFI has provided the following alternative definition of *sukuk*: '*sukuk'* are certificates of ownership of a pool of underlying assets, in which the certificates are of equal value, issued with the aim of using the mobilized funds for establishing a new project, developing an existing project, or financing a business activity as per their respective shares'. Securities Commission Malaysia, *Sukuk,* pp. liii, lvii, 24.
45. Nadim Khan, 'Scholarly Debate'. Sheikh Muhammad Taqi Usmani's comments were followed by a AAOIFI advisory, which strongly advised issuers to legally transfer the ownership of assets to bondholders. In a nutshell the advisory insists that the assets must be tangible rather than cash flow. The advisory is now being hotly debated with at least one Islamic banker urging his colleagues not to take it seriously. See Mukhtar and Aziz, 'Is AAOIFI Irrelevant?', p. 9.
46. '*Sukuk* Issuance Hit By Global Credit Conditions', *The Edge Financial Daily*, 15 September 2008. But despite this setback, Standard and Poor's still expects that *sukuk* issuance will reach US$ 20–25 billion in 2008. See on this Standard and Poor's, '*Sukuk* Market Continues to Grow Despite Gloomy Global Market Conditions', p. 2. In 2010 domestic issuances alone reached USD 37.4 billion in SEA. See, *IFIS, 2010 Report*, p. 7
47. Iqbal and Mirakhor, *An Introduction to Islamic Finance*, p. 176.
48. For further details, see Securities Commission Malaysia, *Sukuk*, p. 43.
49. Ibid., p. 176.
50. On the details of this ongoing conflict and a proposal for a settlement, see Çizakça, *Demokrasi Arayışında Türkiye*.
51. While the latest bunch of Turkish GES bonds issued in January 2009 totalled a mere US$1.171 million, in Malaysia as of February 2008, there were 36 *Shari'ah* compliant funds (out of 533) with an asset size of US$5.2 billion. For these figures, see T.C. Başbakanlık Hazine Müsteşarlığı, *Gelire Endeksli Senetler Tanıtım Klavuzu*, s. 2, and, Mukhtar and Aziz, 'Is AAOIFI Irrelevant?', p. 9.
52. GOS is the abbreviation of *Gelir Ortaklığı Senetleri*, which can be translated as Revenue Participation Shares.
53. The government body, which organized this scheme and issued the shares was the Public Housing and Partnership Directory, known as TKKOI (*Toplu Konut ve Kamu Ortaklığı İdaresi*).
54. Akkoyunlu, 'Esham Sisteminin Günümüzdeki Uzantısı', p. 76. Also see www.millenniumbank.com.tr/digermenkul.aspx.
55. Bakanlar Kurulu, *Kamu Ortaklığı Fonu Yönetmeliği*, madde 6.
56. Ibid., madde 9–10.
57. Ibid., madde 14.
58. Ibid., pp. 76–85.
59. Ibid., p. 78.
60. Ibid., p. 78.
61. Ibid., p. 79.
62. By comparison, six months savings accounts yielded between 51 and 70 per cent in 1988. See ibid., p. 81.
63. Professor Gültekin was almost correct. During the eighteenth century the approximate cost of borrowing for the Ottoman economy in terms of revenue forgone to the middlemen was 76 per cent. For details, see Çizakça, *Comparative Evolution,* pp. 165–6.
64. Akkoyunlu, 'Esham Sisteminin', p. 85.
65. http://hurarsiv.hurriyet.com.tr/goster/haber.aspx?id=5680898&tarih=2006-12-27.
66. For details of the principals redeemed in the period 1988–1993, see Akkoyunlu, '*Esham Sisteminin Günümüzdeki*'. p. 81.
67. Indeed, in June 2009 it was announced that a new 420km motorway linking Istanbul to İzmir via a 3 km long bridge crossing the Bay of İzmit would be financed by the BOT

method without burdening the government budget. The estimated cost of the project is US$5 billion. Had this project been financed by GOS or GES (Turkish *sukuk*), it would have put Turkey almost on par with the United Arab Emirates, where during the first three quarters of 2009 ten *sukuk*s were issued totalling to US$5.3 billion. See on this Kawach, 'GCC *Sukuk* Issues', p. 24.

68. The bill was called *Kamu Varlıklarının Kullanılması Suretiyle Kamuya Finansman Sağlanması Hakkında Kanun Tasarısı*.
69. Due to secular legislation Islamic banks are called Participation Banks in Turkey.
70. Saylan, *Kira Sertifikası Sistemi*, 2009.
71. T.C. Başbakanlık Hazine Müsteşarlığı, *Basın Duyurusu, Sayı*, 2009.
72. T.C. Başbakanlık Hazine Müsteşarlığı, *Gelire Endeksli Senetler Tanıtım Klavuzu*, p. 2.
73. For details, see ibid., p. 5.
74. Kuwait Finance House, *Islamic Finance Research*, 16 February 2009, p. 6. Karaman, 'Gelire Endeksli Senetler', *Yeni Şafak*, 15 February 2009.
75. Kamil, 'Introduction to *Sukuk*', p. 21. Also see Securities Commission Malaysia, *Sukuk*, p. x.
76. Task Force on Islamic Finance, *Islamic Finance and Global Financial*, p. 31.
77. *Bay al-Ainah* refers to the sale of assets on cash with spot price and the repurchase of the same asset by a higher deferred price. As long as the first transaction is not conditioned upon the second, such sales are approved. But if at the beginning the seller strikes a deal with the buyer to repurchase the property at a higher price, the transaction is rejected by the majority of jurists. Ali Salehabadi, 'A Jurisprudential (*fiqh*) Survey on the Design of Malaysian Islamic Bonds', in Salehabadi, *Essays on Islamic Finance*, pp. 34–7.
78. Kamil, 'Introduction to *Sukuk*', p. 22.
79. Venardos, *Islamic Banking and Finance*, pp. 158–65.
80. Parker, '*Sukuk*', pp. 146–7.
81. Laldin, 'Islamic Financial System', p. 230.
82. Securities Commission Malaysia, *Sukuk*, p. x.
83. This honour, indeed, belongs to Malaysia, because the Turkish Revenue Participation Scheme, though earlier, was limited to the Turkish capital market alone. Globalization initiated by Malaysia was followed by the State of Qatar, which issued a *sukuk* worth US$700 million in 2003. This was followed in the same year by an issuance of the *Islamic Development Bank* worth US$400 million. Rosly, *Critical Issues*, p. 473.
84. Obviously, securitization can only take place if the state-owned asset generates regular/reliable profit.
85. Wilson, 'Innovation', p. 173.
86. Çizakça, *Philanthropic Foundations*, pp. 8–12.
87. Ali, 'Legal Certainty for *Sukuk*', pp. 96, 105.
88. The first and last codification of the Islamic law was the Ottoman *majallah*.
89. Wilson, 'Innovation', p. 175.
90. Rosly, *Critical Issues*, p. 475.
91. Kahf, 'Bridging the Budget Gap', passim.
92. Wilson, 'Innovation', p. 171.
93. Haneef, *The Sukuk Market*, p. 6.
94. Abdullah, 'Regulatory Issues', in Securities Commission Malaysia, *Sukuk*, pp. 80–2.
95. Farook, 'Capital Market Instruments', in Securities Commission Malaysia, *Sukuk*, pp. 163–8.
96. Coase Theorem as interpreted by Kindleberger, in Kindleberger, *A Financial History*, p. 206.
97. Global Investment House, '*Sukuk* Market – Down But Not Out (Final Part)', *Islamic Finance News*, 6 March 2009, pp. 20–1.
98. In 2008, Malaysia raised US$5.5 billion from 54 issues and just managed to pass the UAE, where US$5.3 billion were raised from ten issues. Thus the average issue in Malaysia is about US$100 million and in the UAE US$530 million. For further details, see Global Investment House, '*Sukuk* Market', p. 17.
99. Global Investment House, '*Sukuk* Market', p. 19.
100. In what follows, I have benefited from Mufti Muhammad Taqi Usmani, 'Sukuk and Their Contemporary Applications', http://www.muftitaqiusmani.com.

101. Qur'an, VII: 59.
102. Usmani, 'Sukuk and Their Contemporary Applications', http://www.muftitaqiusmani.com, p. 8.
103. Usmani, 'Sukuk and Their Contemporary Applications', www.muftitaqiusmani.com, p. 4.
104. Ibid., p. 7.
105. Task Force on Islamic Finance, *Islamic Finance and Global Financial*, p. 33.

11. *Takaful* (Islamic insurance)

Insurance, particularly life insurance, is a highly controversial subject in Islamic economics. In this chapter we will analyse this debate and briefly explain how contemporary Muslims have come up with solutions. But first, we need to provide a historical background of this important institution.

HISTORICAL BACKGROUND

The concept of insurance has a long history in the Islamic world and it is known as *takaful*. This word is derived from the Arabic word *kafala*, which means to guarantee. The origins of this institution can be traced back to the pre-Islamic customs of the Arab world where tribal wars were very common and tended to perpetuate. When a member of a tribe was murdered by a member of another, revenge had to be taken and hatred and revenge continued generation after generation. This is because when a tribe lost a member it could retaliate by killing any member of the other tribe. Thus, murder committed by one put the entire tribe into danger. The concept of *kafala* solved this problem and was therefore absolutely important for the survival of the social fabric.

When a member of a tribe committed a murder, this led to one of two consequences. Either a tribal war would break out to avenge the death of the tribal member or a settlement would be reached by paying blood money known as *diyah*. This blood money that was used to compensate the loss of life came from the tribal fund. The fund was collected from among the members. Each member donated a certain amount into the fund. Once the donation was collected, no refund was allowed. Although the fund was used mainly to settle compensation in cases of tribal disputes, it could also be used as a ransom to free a member of the group from captivity. The practice was known as *al-aqilah*, which actually means the paternal relatives.[1] This pre-Islamic custom was approved by the Prophet and included in the first constitution.[2] It has been argued that during the period of the second Caliph, Omar, the government encouraged Muslims to practice *al-aqilah* nationwide.[3]

Al-aqila and the concept of *takaful* provided the following benefits for Arab tribes. First, it reduced bloodshed. Second, it replaced individual responsibility with collective responsibility of the tribe. Third, it reduced the financial burden of the individual by transferring it to the group. Fourth, it developed a spirit of cooperation and brotherhood among the tribe members.

The practice of paying compensation in terms of blood money can be found in the Qur'an.[4] Islam helped to reduce the severity of punishment and the terrible consequences of the pagan custom of revenge by adopting and improving the pre-Islamic custom of compensation for the relatives of the victim.

As it is well known, Muslims successfully linked and maintained the two most important world-economies.[5] These were the Indian Ocean and the Mediterranean world-economies. Arab sailors, particularly from the Hadramaut and Yemen, brought products of the Malay world via the Arabian Peninsula to the Mediterranean. They were able to sail across the Indian Ocean with relative ease. Transoceanic sailing would not have been possible without providing some maritime insurance. Although we are not informed about the details of such insurance it was most probable that the principles of *al-aqila* and mutual help were applied in maritime commerce as well. Very probably, based on the principal of helping one another, *taawun*, ship owners contributed to a fund prior to starting their voyage and used it to compensate any of them who incur losses. The essence of this practice can also be found in the Qur'an.[6] Indeed, by working as a group in facing the risks or dangers the burden becomes much lighter and the bigger the size of the group the lighter is the burden.

During the fourteenth to seventeenth centuries a Sufi order, the *Kazeruniyya,* was active in the port cities of the Malabar Coast of India and in China. The order apparently functioned as a kind of maritime insurance company. The order drew its strength from the tomb of a Sufi saint, Abu Ishaq Ibrahim Ibn Shahriyah, whose blessings were considered as protection against the perils of sea voyages. The system worked as follows: merchants before embarking on a voyage by sea specified the amount they pledged to pay to the order if they arrived safely to their destination. Upon the arrival of the ship, the order's agent came on board and collected the amount specified on the note from all the passengers. How these funds were utilized to assist merchants in need is not clear. But we are informed that the order itself had shares in ships. Apparently, such ships were better protected by the order. The *Kazeruniyya* started to lose its importance during the seventeenth century, when it began to be replaced by Western insurance companies which began to operate in the Indian Ocean basin.[7]

Two *fatwas* issued by the well-known jurist Muhammad Abduh between 1900 and 1901 legalized insurance for Muslims. The first one considered the relationship between the insurer and the insured as a *mudaraba* relationship and the second one as a waqf life insurance.[8]

It is this cooperative spirit on the part of the whole group to mutually share the burden of any of its members which is reflected in modern *takaful*. What is at stake here is mutual coverage of accidental loss by the community exposed to a common danger. The underlined principle of modern mutual insurance is that the individual members themselves are the insurers as well as the insured. This principle was certainly in application in the tribal relationships discussed above.

MODERN *TAKAFUL*

Based on the above, the principles of modern *takaful* are as follows: policy holders cooperate among themselves for their common good, every policy holder pays his subscription to help those that need assistance, losses are divided and liability spread according to the community pooling system, uncertainty is eliminated with respect to compensation, a member does not derive advantage at the cost of others.

Essentially *takaful* is a cooperative insurance where members are those who face the same risk or danger of incurring losses and who willingly contribute a certain sum of money which will be used to compensate those members of the group who incur such losses. Whether as in the case of ancient Arab tribal custom or a group of merchants sailing across the Indian Ocean, every member of the tribe faced the same danger of being inflicted harm by another tribe or the elements.

In conventional insurance, when the insured has incurred a loss, the company will pay or cover the losses incurred. If, however, nothing happens during the period under cover, the company takes all the money or premium that has been paid up front. The insured does not get any benefit except protection as stated in the policy. Conventional insurance has been prohibited in the ninth declaration of the second session of the *Fiqh Academy of the Organization of Islamic Conference*. In Malaysia, *fatawas* from Perak and Trengganu (1974), Kelantan (1975) and Malacca (1980) have forbidden life insurance and urged for the creation of a fully Islamic system.[9] But this is by no means a unanimous opinion. A well-known scholar Mustafa Al-Zarqa had permitted conventional insurance of all kinds until his death. More recently, in 2004, the Grand Mufti of Egypt, Dr Ali Jum'ah, permitted all types of insurance.[10]

Muslim jurists argue that while the objective of the conventional insurance is good, the manner it is being conducted in is not *Shari'ah* compliant. The first objection is the presence of the element of chance, *al-Gharar*, taken by the company. The second objection is the element of gambling, *al-Maisir*. The insured is prepared to lose the premium if the risk does not materialize. But if the risk materializes, he will get much more than the premium he has paid for and this is considered as gambling. The third objection is *riba*. It is argued that conventional insurance companies invest the funds accumulated in their companies in interest-based instruments. Of these three objections, the easiest part is the third one. By simply investing the *takaful* fund in noninterest-bearing instruments this objection can be overcome. The question as to how to avoid the first two objections of ambiguity and uncertainty is more difficult.

All in all, the concept of insurance is one of the most controversial topics in modern Islamic finance. The jurists who have passed judgements on the topic have been categorized into three groups:

1. Those who have permitted insurance providing it is free of any element of interest. We have already mentioned Shaikh Muhammad Abduh, who had given probably the earliest approval. Other prominent jurists and academicians including, Mohammad Nejatullah Siddiqi, M.A. Mannan and no less a figure than the late Ayatullah Khomeini are also in this group.
2. Those who accept general insurance but reject life insurance policies because these contradict the Islamic law of inheritance.
3. Those who totally reject the institution on the grounds that it involves interest, gambling and uncertainty (*riba, maisir* and *gharar*). Some jurists in this group have also expressed their objection on the grounds that there is no express authority from the Qur'an regarding insurance. Others have felt that insurance actually contradicts the principle of *tawakkul*, that is, putting one's trust in the Creator. There are even some who argue that life insurance means insuring one's life against death.[11]

These arguments have been refuted on the grounds that an Islamic insurance policy is not based upon *riba* but on *mudaraba, wakala* and waqf, all permitted instruments. The last two arguments, that is, *tawakkul* and insuring one's life against death are rejected because every Muslim knows perfectly well that nothing can insure against death.[12] Muslims put their trust in Allah but by buying an insurance policy they are merely trying to provide some protection and comfort for their loved ones when death comes. The similarity between gambling and insurance has been rejected by Mustafa al-Zarqa on the grounds that the gambler always tries to defeat other fellow gamblers and gains material advantage at their expense. Indeed, their loss becomes his gain. But parties to an insurance transaction are bound together in a spirit of cooperation against future loss.[13]

Islamic takaful must be based on the principle of *ta'awun*, that is, mutual assistance with participants agreeing to mutually compensate each other for specified losses. Based on this understanding, a fund can be created from the contributions of each member on the basis of donation or *tabarru*. Based on these principles of *ta'awun* and *tabarru* the company then simply becomes the operator who invites people facing the same risk to form the group. The company is not selling a policy as such, which will give rise to the prohibited elements of uncertainty and gambling. Rather, the company is merely an operator who makes arrangements for the group to come together and not only agree to contribute to the fund but at the same time agree to donate at least part of the fund to any member of the group who has suffered a loss. Thus the company does not own the fund and the ownership of the fund remains with the policy holders or participants as they are called by the *takaful* industry. Since the company is not the owner of the fund, it does not take risk. The risk belongs to the participants who are mutually covering each other. The company is only a trustee or an agent acting on behalf of the participants to manage the operation. As a manager of the *takaful* business, the company is like an entrepreneur or *mudarìb* whil the participants are the provider of capital, *rab-al-mal*s as in the case of a multiple *mudaraba* partnership. Consequently the loss belongs to the capital providing participants while profits are shared between the participants and the *takaful* operator at a pre-agreed ratio.

The *tabarru*, donation, on the other hand, gives the company a waqf-like characteristic. Participants make this contribution for the benefit of fellow participants without any intention of earning any profit for themselves. It is this non-profit characteristic which makes the insurance company approach the waqf. Venardos has even argued that it is the *tabarru*, which actually Islamizes the *takaful* company and makes it different from the conventional insurance companies.[14] I tend to disagree and would like to argue that rather than the *tabarru*, which can be found in Western insurance as well, it is the *mudaraba* element which is unique about the *takaful*. This is because participants of a conventional insurance are also prepared to forego their investments for the benefit of other participants hit by some disaster. What makes *takaful* really different from the conventional insurance is the idea of profit sharing (*mudaraba*) between the *takaful* company and the participants.

Basic differences between the conventional and the Islamic life-insurance modes have now been formally stated.[15] First and foremost, a conventional life insurance is based on the elements of *riba*, whereas *takaful* is free from it. Second, in a conventional life insurance policy, the nominee(s) is an absolute beneficiary(s).[16] In *takaful*, however, the nominee(s) is not an absolute beneficiary but a mere trustee, who receives the benefit over the policy and distributes it among the heirs of the assured according to the *Sharì'ah*. This has been confirmed by the National Council of Muslim Religious Affairs in Malaysia, which issued a *fatwa* in 1979 to the same effect.[17] Third, in the case of a conventional life insurance policy, if the assured dies at any time before the maturity of the policy, the nominee(s) is entitled to recover from the insurer the whole amount stated in the policy. If the assured is still alive upon the expiry of the policy period, he is also entitled to the whole amount agreed in the policy plus interest, dividends and bonus subject to the company's policy. By contrast, in *takaful*, if the assured dies before maturity, the beneficiary(s) is entitled to the whole amount of paid premiums, the bonus and dividends according to the company's policy, a share of the profits made over the paid premiums plus a donation from the company's charitable fund according to the financial status of the beneficiary. This means that if the beneficiary has a sound financial position, the donation will be small, but if he is in financial stress, the amount can be larger. This is considered as a form of mutual support towards the welfare of the needy and is based upon a Qur'anic injunction.[18] If, however, the assured is still alive at maturity, he is entitled to the whole amount of paid premiums, a share of profit made over the paid premiums according to the principle of *mudaraba*, bonus and dividends according to the company's policy. Fourth, in a conventional life insurance, the payments for the agents are paid out of the assured's paid premiums, whereas under the Islamic model of a life insurance policy, the agents work for the company and thus should be paid by the company itself. This means that the payment for the agents could include a share of profits made over the paid premiums, plus dividends and bonus according to the company's policy.[19]

Modern *takaful* industry has been envisaged in four different models. First, is the *mudaraba* model just described. The second is the *wakala* or agency model. The third is the modified *mudaraba* model and fourth is the *wakala* waqf model. It is interesting to note that just like in Islamic banking and *sukuk* industries, in the *takaful* industry also the *mudaraba* model is abandoned. Today the *takaful* industry is dominated by the *wakala*. This is probably due to the fact that the Shari'ah Committee of the Islamic Development Bank has objected for the *takaful* operator to take any percentage of an underwriting surplus in *takaful* because an underwriting surplus is not supposed to be a profit and the *takaful* operator is not permitted to take on underwriting risk as this would contravene the fundamental principle of *takaful*.[20] This principle, as it will be remembered, was the ancient *al-akilah* custom whereby it was the paternal relatives of the culprit alone, who shared the compensation, *al-diyah*, to the victim's family.

THE *WAKALA* MODEL

The *wakala* model is currently the most commonly used model in most countries. Although the *takaful* companies which were established in the 1980s employed the *mudaraba* or the modified *mudaraba* models, the newly established companies during the last four to five years have chosen to employ the *wakala* model.[21] Here, we will therefore focus mainly on this model.

Wakala, which means agency, employs the *shari'ah* principle of providing a service for a fee. In this model, the *takaful* operator acts as the agent on behalf of the participants. The operator is paid a pre-agreed management fee but he does not share in the underwriting surplus. The proceeds from the underwriting surplus are ploughed back into the fund. Any liabilities for the risks underwritten are borne by the fund and any surplus arising from there belongs exclusively to the participants. The operator is not liable for any deficit of the fund and is paid a management fee as it is not the owner but only a custodian of the *takaful* funds. This is also known as the *wakala* fee and is calculated as a percentage of the contributions paid. The Islamic Financial Services Board (IFSB) has declared that the *wakala* fee must be pre-agreed and expressly stated in the *takaful* contract. It is expected to cover the total sum of management expenses and distribution costs. Thus the *takaful* operator will enjoy profits if the *wakala* fee it receives is greater than the management expenses incurred. The operator does not directly share the risk borne by the *takaful* fund or any of its surplus/deficit.[22]

In addition, some versions of the *wakala* model also permit the *takaful* operator to receive part of his remuneration as agent in the form of a performance related fee as an additional incentive. A performance-related fee is related to the underwriting surplus. The IFSB has stated that there is no need from the participants' perspective for any underwriting surplus.[23]

The IFSB has also warned against the possible emergence of the following problems. First, there is no clear mechanism by which the *takaful* participants can control the *takaful* operator. After all, it is the shareholders and not the participants who appoint the management. Second, it is also possible that the shareholders may have commercial interests that may conflict with the interests of the participants. The demarcation of the rights and obligations between the *takaful* operator and the participants necessitates a clear segregation of the participants' funds from the shareholders' fund. Third, such clear separation of ownership and control may raise agency problems – specifically, information asymmetry and misalignment of the incentives of the principal and the agent. Fourth, since the *takaful* operator answers to two sets of principals and is appointed and instructed by the shareholders, it would be more inclined and be under pressure to favour shareholders rather than the participants. More specifically, it is feared that the *takaful* operator representing the shareholders will maximize value for the shareholders. This is notwithstanding the fact that the operator has similar fiduciary duty to the participants. The lack of representation for the participants and the prevalent asymmetric information may give ample room for the maximization of value for the shareholders at the expense of the participants. In view of the above potential problems, the IFSB has recommended that the participants should be given voting rights at the *takaful* operator's general meetings. Having made this recommendation, the IFSB, nevertheless, is aware that effective governance by participants can still be difficult to achieve. After all, experience with mutual in conventional insurance suggests that such governance becomes more difficult as a company reaches a certain size. In such situations management *de facto* becomes autonomous.[24]

To combat inadequate representation of the participants, the IFSB has introduced the following principles:

1. *Takaful* operators shall have in place an appropriate governance structure that represents the rights and interests of *takaful* participants.
2. The *takaful* operators shall adopt and implement procedures for appropriate disclosures that provide *takaful* participants with fair access to material and relevant information.
3. The *takaful* operators shall ensure that they have in place appropriate mechanisms properly to sustain the solvency of *takaful* undertakings.[25]

FAMILY *TAKAFUL*

This is another type of *takaful* with basically three aims: to encourage participants to save regularly, to invest their contributions in Islamically approved ways and to provide protection to the participants or their heirs. This is a fixed period *takaful* but it does not carry a fixed sum. The amount of benefits a participant will receive at maturity depends on the maturity period itself, the amount of contributions that he has made and the profits, if any, from the investment of his contributions. The Takaful Company of Malaysia offers participants three maturity periods to choose from: 10, 15 and 20 years.

The money paid by the participant goes into two different accounts, the Participants' Account (PA) and the Participants' Special Account (PSA). The PA, into which the larger proportion of the participants' money is paid, is a form of savings and investment account. Money paid into the PSA, on the other hand, is in the spirit of *tabarru*, a charitable donation to help fellow participants in times of hardship. This can also be considered as similar to the donations made to traditional cash waqfs. The total amount deposited into this account depends on whether some members die before the maturity of their plans. If all members survive the year, the entire PSA contribution remains in this account.

Money from both accounts is invested by the company on a profit and loss sharing basis in various enterprises. Profits generated from the investments of the PA accounts are shared between the company and the participants in a pre-agreed ratio. Profits generated by the investment of PSA funds, on the other hand, are used to beef up the fund.[26] This is similar to the profits of the traditional cash waqfs being ploughed back to the waqf to enhance its original capital.

The contract between the participants and the *takaful* company is based upon the multiple *mudaraba* partnership. Consequently, participants not only share the profits of the company but also the losses. In view of the difficulties this may cause, the *Committee on the Setting up of the Takaful Scheme* recommended that any loss should be borne by the company alone as part of its operating costs, to be paid from the following year's profits. This is obviously a departure from the well-known classical *mudaraba* principles and was introduced because of the possibility of losing potential participants from participating in the future.[27]

DEVELOPMENT OF THE *TAKAFUL* INDUSTRY

The very first modern *takaful* company, the Islamic Insurance Company Ltd was established in the year 1979 in Sudan. It was able to distribute profits to its shareholders at the rate of 5 per cent in the first year, 8 per cent in 1980 and 10 per cent in 1981. Following this success story other *takaful* companies were established in Jeddah (1979), Luxembourg (1983), Bahrain (1983) and so on.[28] Recently, *takaful* premium contributions have grown from US$1.4 billion in 2004 to US$3.4 billion in 2007. The largest global markets include Saudi Arabia and Malaysia, the latter being the largest market in Asia with contributions of US$0.8 billion.[29]

In Malaysia the grounds for the *takaful* industry were laid down in 1972 by the proclamation of the *fatwa* committee of the *National Religious Council* declaring that conventional insurance practices, especially life policies, were unlawful under Islamic law as they include elements of gambling, interest and uncertainty. Similar *fatwas* on the same issue were issued in most Malaysian states (Perak-Terengganu 1974, Kelantan 1975, Malacca 1980). These committees then called for the establishment of a fully Islamic insurance system. In response, the government set up a committee to study the implementation of the Islamic system of insurance. The committee completed its study and recommended the introduction of the *takaful* scheme of insurance. Based upon this recommendation, the Malaysian Parliament enacted the first *Takaful* Act in 1984.[30] The first Malaysian *takaful* company was incorporated and registered the same year. It is understood that the licence of a *takaful* company will be abolished if the company is found to violate any aspect of the Islamic law. Every Malaysian *takaful* company, just like any Islamic bank, has to have a *Shari'ah* Supervisory Council.

After about two decades, the industry has achieved unprecedented double digit growth rates for a number of years. The potential aggregate for *takaful* contributions worldwide is estimated to be at least US$20 billion. Notwithstanding these optimistic estimates, participants' contributions as of 2007 stood at merely US$2.2 billion, accounting for only 1 per cent of the USD3.7 trillion global insurance premiums. This amount represents 6.3

per cent of the total assets of the insurance and *takaful* industry in Malaysia. Although quite small, this percentage represents an increase of 11 per cent from the previous year. Thus, the Malaysian *takaful* industry has started from very modest beginnings but is growing at substantial rates.[31]

Moreover, the *takaful* industry is also quite small in comparison to Islamic banking industry as well. The *takaful* sector grows at a relatively slower pace than the *sukuk* market, which is growing at about 40 per cent per annum. It is also estimated that up to 20 per cent of the *takaful* revenues originated from non-Muslim customers. Currently there are more than 250 *takaful* operators worldwide. Established conventional players in the UK, USA and Germany are now beginning to establish *takaful* and *re-takaful* companies within their groups. In Malaysia, there were eight registered *takaful* operators by 2008. Total *takaful* contributions in 2007 were at least US$99 million, an increase of 36 per cent from the previous period.[32]

Currently *takaful* players are relatively small with the largest *takaful* company having total assets of only US$3 billion. Although Muslims account for at least 22 per cent of the world population, *takaful* contribution in Muslim countries constitutes only 1 per cent of the total global insurance premium. As far as Malaysia is concerned, Dr Zeti Akhtar Aziz, the Governor of *Bank Negara Malaysia*, has estimated that the Islamic banking and *takaful* industry would contribute at least 20 per cent of the Malaysian banking and insurance market by 2010. This should be viewed within the overall goal of epitomizing Malaysia as a global Islamic financial hub.[33]

As Malaysia progresses towards this goal, various components of the Islamic financial sector begin to provide mutual support. The rapid growth of the *sukuk* market, for instance, has become a key supporting factor in the development of the *takaful* industry. The availability of *sukuk* investments has helped meet the needs of *takaful* operators, who previously did not have sufficient options to invest in Islamic financial instruments. Islamic banks are also providing help in marketing *takaful* products. This is attested by the fact that in 2004 and 2005 there was a sharp switch of business from that marketed by the direct channel comprising the branch network of *takaful* operators towards indirect marketing via *bancatakaful*, that is, marketing through Islamic banks. Indeed, business via direct marketing formed 61 per cent in 2004 and fell sharply to 44 per cent in 2005, whereas business via *bancatakaful* increased from 7 per cent in 2004 to 20 per cent in 2005. This shift also implies a win–win proposition for all stakeholders, that is, the customer, the bank, the *takaful* operator and the regulator. This shift appears to have been deliberately planned by the *Bank Negara Malaysia*, which introduced regulatory requirements for *bancatakaful* in 2005 with the primary aim of ensuring that customers benefit directly from the efficient cost structures. In order to ensure this, the *Bank Negara* had also required in 2004 that the Islamic banks offer *takaful* as the first choice in protection.[34]

But there are problems which need to be overcome. Consider, for instance, the lack of re-*takaful* support. Adequate support from strong re-*takaful* companies is vital for the *takaful* sector in managing risks. Currently there are about ten to fifteen re-*takaful* companies available to support over 250 *takaful* operators worldwide. Currently most *takaful* and even the re-*takaful* operators have to depend on conventional re-insurers. *Bank Negara Malaysia* is now inviting strong and qualified applicants to make Malaysia their centre for re-*takaful* activities. This invitation appears to have been well received. Indeed, by 2006, several powerful international re-*takaful* entities were already established in the Labuan International Offshore Financial Centre.[35] These are BEST Re, *Takaful* Re, Converium, Hannover Re and Munich Re.[36]

NOTES

1. Billah, *Applied Takaful*, p. 6.
2. Hamidullah, *The First Written Constitution,* Article 3, p. 55.
3. Billah, *Applied Takaful*, p. 8.
4. 2: 178, 4: 91, 5: 48.
5. Reference is made here to the concept of world-economy as developed by Braudel and Wallerstein.
6. Qur'an: 5: 3.
7. Billah, *Applied Takaful*, p. 9.
8. Ibid., p. 10.
9. Hooker, 'Fatawa in Malaysia', p. 99.
10. El-Gamal, *Islamic Finance*, p. 149.
11. For a long list of scholars who have opposed life insurance on the grounds that it involves insuring one's life against death and a detailed refutation of these views, see Billah, 'A Model', pp. 294–5.
12. Every Muslim knows the verse 3: 185 saying: 'Every soul shall have a taste of death'.
13. Billah, *Applied Takaful*, pp. 74–7.
14. Venardos, *Banking and Finance*, p. 83, fn. 74.
15. Billah, 'A Model of Life Insurance'.
16. A nominee is the person designated by the policy holder to receive the proceeds of an insurance policy, upon the death of the insured.
17. Billah, 'A Model of Life Insurance', p. 291.
18. V: 2.
19. Billah, 'A Model of Life Insurance', pp. 291–2.
20. Islamic Financial Services Board, *Exposure Draft*, p. 3, fn. 7.
21. Alhabshi and Abdul Razak, 'Takaful: Concept, History, Development and Future Challenges of Its Industry', forthcoming. I am grateful to the authors for their permission to refer to their yet unpublished work.
22. IFSB, *Exposure Draft,* p. 4.
23. Ibid., p. 4.
24. Ibid., p. 8.
25. Ibid., pp. 12–22.
26. Mahmood, *Insurance Law in Malaysia*, p. 245.
27. Ibid., p. 246.
28. Venardos, *Banking and Finance*, pp. 82–3.
29. Task Force on Islamic Finance, *Islamic Finance and Global Financial*, p. 32.
30. Mahmood, *Insurance Law in Malaysia*, p. 244.

31. Nair and Chen, 'Malaysian *Takaful* Industry', p. 28.
32. Ibid., p. 28.
33. Bank Negara Malaysia, *Financial Sector Stability*, p. 150.
34. Ibid., pp. 29–30. Other significant channels are the agencies and the brokers.
35. For this and other very significant achivements of the Labuan International Offshore Financial Centre, see Zeti Akhtar Aziz, *Key-note Address at the Seminar on Labuan IOFC*, 2–3 May 2006.
36. Nair and Chen, 'Malaysian *Takaful* Industry', p. 31.

12. The *lembaga urusan dan Tabung Haji*: financing the modern pilgrimage

The *Tabung Haji* is one of the most successful institutions for financing and organizing the modern pilgrimage. This was confirmed in 1990, when it was awarded the Islamic Development Bank prize in Islamic banking for the services it has provided to Malaysian pilgrims. In this chapter we will explain not only its establishment but also the reasons behind its success. This information will be provided in the hope that other Islamic countries may also wish to establish similar institutions.

THE ESTABLISHMENT OF *TABUNG HAJI*

In December 1959, merely two years after the achievement of independence of the Federation of Malaysia, Ungku Abdul Aziz bin Ungku Abdul Hamid, a member of the royal family of the State of Johor and an economist at the University of Malaya, submitted a memorandum to the Ministry of Rural Development.[1] The Ministry referred the memo to the then Economic Advisor, Dato' O. A. Spencer, who advised that the plan outlined in the memo was sound. The memo was then referred to the Cabinet and a committee was appointed to examine it in detail.[2] The memorandum was also presented to Sheikh Mahmoud Al-Shahltut, Rector of Al-Azhar University of Cairo, during his visit to Malaysia in 1962. After his approval was obtained, the *Pilgrims' Saving Corporation* was incorporated and launched on 30 September 1963.[3]

THE MEMORANDUM

The memorandum, called 'Pilgrims Economy Improvement Plan' and presented in appendix I at the end of the *Command Paper*, starts with two verses from the Qur'an, verse 2: 196 and 5: 2, respectively.

> Perform the Pilgrimage and the *Umrah* for Allah

and

> Help one another unto righteousness and pious duty.

Thus with a very clever choice of these two verses, the cabinet members were reminded not only that every Muslim was ordained to perform the pilgrimage, but that they, the cabinet members, were also ordained to help them in this matter.

After this, it was stated that this was a plan to help Muslim pilgrims as well as the national economic progress. The memo then began to explain the *modus operandi*. It was envisaged that persons intending to save for the pilgrimage to Mecca would make small deposits with a Malayan Pilgrims Corporation, which would organize full pilgrimage facilities when the required amount is saved and when the participant wishes to make the pilgrimage. It was argued that the plan would have many advantages which would benefit small savers, particularly in rural areas, the national economy from the perspective of enhancing aggregate savings and the actual travel and living conditions of pilgrims during the pilgrimage.

To do all this, it was proposed that a *Malayan Pilgrims Corporation* be set up as a public corporation, which would mobilize pilgrims' savings and invest them. To facilitate entry to the system, it was proposed that any intending pilgrim could go to the nearest post office and obtain a Pilgrims Savings Book and thereby open an account with the corporation. All further deposits were to be made by means of special Pilgrims Stamps of denominations from 50 cents to US$100. The stamps were to be pasted in the Pilgrims Savings Book and every six or twelve months the book was to be sent by registered post to Headquarters of the Corporation for verification and addition of bonus. Bonuses were to be given to all depositors from the profits obtained on the investments of the corporation after operating costs were deducted.[4] When a member managed to save a sufficient amount, he would give not less than 12 months' notice of his desire to make the pilgrimage. During the entire pilgrimage, officers of the corporation would look after the participants.

It was expected that the participants would save small amounts ranging from US$1 to US$10 per month over periods ranging from 10 to 25 years. It was estimated that if the bonus was based on 3 per cent compounded annually, then the required amount of US$1500 would be obtained in 13 years if US$100 per annum were saved, or in 22 years if US$4 per month were saved.

Thus it is clear that the system was to be based on interest. Envisaged five years before the very first modern Islamic bank was established in Egypt, it is only normal that this Malaysian project should be based on interest financing. Ungku Aziz presumably thought that since the interest earned would be spent for financing the pilgrimage, this would be Islamically permitted. After all, modern Islamic finance was not yet born.

Ungku Aziz also envisaged that participants would deposit rather smaller amounts in the early period and larger sums in the last few years of their savings plan. He was thus reversing the well-known life cycle hypothesis, which claims that individuals dis-save towards the end of their lives. He seems to have anticipated that the *homo-Islamicus* would do the opposite in order to make sure that he/she accumulates the necessary amount for the pilgrimage before it is too late.

The cost of administration of the corporation was to be paid for out of profits from investments. Postal Department was also to be paid a fee for its services. A relatively small bureaucracy was thought to suffice for the task at hand.

Transferring an account to another person was permitted. More importantly, the scheme was also going to introduce life insurance. Since it was designed particularly for rural persons, combining the system with a life insurance, and insuring millions of peasants probably for the first time, was simply brilliant. The scheme was explained in the following very simple words:

> A husband could open an account on behalf of his wife. He may intend to make monthly deposits of US$5 which with bonuses would probably give him about US$1500 (the cost of the pilgrimage) in less than 20 years. Say, he dies five years after opening the account. If he had included the insurance scheme in his account then immediately the corporation would make available to his widow the full amount (US$1500) necessary for the pilgrimage.[5]

The plan was designed as a purely voluntary one and allowed individuals to make private arrangements for the pilgrimage if they so desire. It was also possible to participate only in the insurance without participating in the bonus scheme.

It has been argued that the biggest motive for savings among the Malays is that of saving for the pilgrimage. The scheme was therefore envisaged as a new institution that will not only help them to achieve their desire in a more efficient way but also to do so in less time and with less loss to themselves and to the national economy, particularly to the rural economy. Thus Ungku Aziz had envisaged the system primarily as a rural development project, which was inspired by the saving habits of Malay peasants. He had observed that these people often saved in stages. They keep surplus *padi*, which they turn into buffaloes. Then, buffaloes are sold to buy land. Finally, the land is sold to pay for the pilgrimage. Saving in the form of buffaloes can be risky because of animal sicknesses and there can be losses from the purchase and sale of buffaloes. Saving in the form of land can also be problematic because of fragmentation of farms, high rents etc. It is therefore desirable for people to be inculcated with the habit of saving in cash. However, cash can also be risky if hoarded in large amounts at home. Traditionally Malay peasants buried money in jars or kept them in bamboos or even in mattresses. They refused to save with the conventional banking system as they did not wish their pilgrimage to be tainted with *riba*. Ungku Aziz argued further that if this cash is safe with a corporation it would not get lost, burned or stolen and the members would also receive substantial bonuses. He estimated that a member saving US$4 a month would receive bonuses over US$500 in 22 years. Moreover, this corporation would also provide support to the pilgrims throughout their pilgrimage. It is often said that savings are very limited in the rural sector but in fact Ungku Aziz calculated that US$3 million are dispersed each year by pilgrims. He estimated that once this plan had been in operation for 20 years a fund of over US$20 million would be mobilized. This is a material benefit quite apart from the cultural benefit that the nation would gain by monetizing savings habits of the rural folk. The other benefit pertains to inculcating the habit of insurance among the peasantry. Ungku Aziz concluded his memorandum by requesting the establishment of a committee to study his plan.

This suggestion was accepted and the committee was formed to examine the plan in detail. The committee met seven times during the period 16 July 1960 through 24 January 1962. In these meetings the committee particularly focused on the present methods of savings and their effects in rural areas. It also examined alternative methods of savings being practised in the country. For instance, the Chinese *tontine* or Indian *kuttu* were examined.[6] Deposits held in commercial banks, post office saving banks, cooperative societies and provident funds were also considered. After due consideration given to all these different forms, it was concluded that most of these institutions were actually designed for urban populations. The branches of these organizations were simply inadequate to address the savings needs of the rural Malay population. Their operations were also too complex to be understood by these people. The committee therefore decided that it is indeed desirable to establish the proposed pilgrims' savings corporation. It then proceeded to examine the feasibility of such an organization. It recognized that the future well-being of the corporation will depend on the methods used to collect savings. It warned against possible corruption and misappropriation of funds. It thoroughly investigated the number of pilgrims and concluded that this number had increased from 3730 in 1958 immediately after the independence to 5795 in 1961. Moreover, most pilgrims were in the 40 to 60 age group. The average expenditure incurred by an intending pilgrim amounted to US$1650. It was also calculated that an average farmer could save not US$4 but US$5 a month (US$60 a year). To save US$1640 at the rate of US$60 a year would take an average farmer over 27 years. This is calculated when the principal does not earn interest or dividend. It would take him, however, 18 years if the sum saved earns a return at the rate of 5 per cent compounded annually.

The committee found that in view of the prohibition of interest, the investment of deposits was the key problem. Thus, the committee concluded that Islamic funds to be used for religious purposes cannot be lent in return for a rate of interest. The key problem therefore appeared to the committee whether under the limitations imposed by Islamic law the funds of the corporation could be invested so as to provide an adequate return. The corporation would have to invest its funds in order to produce a return sufficient to meet its operating expenses, provide for a reserve and maintain adequate liquidity to meet cash withdrawals by its depositors. Because of the interest prohibition, the committee considered the possibility of the proposed corporation investing the bulk of its deposits in the equity of public companies. It was thought that such investment of private individuals would be tantamount to participation in the economic growth of the country. Much depended on the capacity for economic growth in Malaysia. It was estimated that the corporation would accumulate investment funds at a substantial rate. It could indeed become in time one of the biggest sources of capital for equity investment in Malaysia. It was anticipated that the corporation would have US$10 000 available monthly for investment in its first year, rising to US$125 000 monthly in the sixth year. The ability of the Malaysian capital market to absorb such capital needed to be studied.

The next question was whether investment of the corporation funds in equities would produce sufficient annual yield to enable the corporation to pay its depositors. For this question rubber and tin shares were considered and it was concluded that they yield far larger returns in dividends than industrial shares. But the prices of these commodities fluctuated greatly depending upon the terms of trade, that is, the state of world rubber and tin markets. The risk of capital loss therefore was always present. Moreover, this risk would increase substantially during periods of economic depression. The committee concluded that the corporation could justifiably invest in equity shares and that the yields from these investments were sufficiently attractive.

The question about the withdrawal of deposits was also considered and it was thought that the corporation would be similar to a savings institution. Accordingly, deposits could be withdrawn only when a sufficient amount had been accumulated. This provision would have to be an essential feature of the corporation. Withdrawal of deposits could be permitted only in cases of extreme hardship.[7] The committee recommended that the corporation should maintain some of its assets in a liquid form in order to meet demands for withdrawal of deposits. It was suggested therefore that the corporation should seek the assistance of the central bank in working out a scheme whereby a reserve fund is created and invested, perhaps in the central bank itself in a form which is realizable at call and which does not stipulate a predetermined rate of interest. The committee furthermore advised that the corporation funds should be invested in three phases. The first phase would cover the first six years with investment of funds to be made in selected Malaysian shares, the majority being in industrials. The second phase would cover the funds received up to the eleventh year and a part of these funds may be used to invest in buildings. In the third phase, consideration could be given to investments in plantation, industrial and housing projects.

The committee recommended further that deposits in the proposed corporation should be fully guaranteed by government. Such a guarantee was considered to be necessary to attract potential depositors. It was thought unlikely that the corporation would have much success in attracting significant participation by intending pilgrims without such a government guarantee. The potential amount of deposits to be guaranteed was thought to be vast, increasing from US$120 000 in the first year to US$46 million in the 18th year.[8] It would be therefore very important for the government that the funds of the corporation would be profitably invested to produce a yield of between 5 per cent and 7 per cent a year at least. However, the committee thought it likely that the government might be called upon to honour its guarantee at a time of serious national or global depression. But overall it was thought that the corporation need not necessarily incur severe losses.

Regarding taxation, the committee recommended that the corporation can be regarded as a public religious trust[9] and as such it was recommended that the corporation should be exempted from income tax and stamp duty.

It was thought that yields from investments in equity shares would not be sufficient to meet administrative costs for the first six years of the corporate existence. The committee recommended therefore that the administrative costs of the corporation for the first three years should be met by a grant or an interest-free loan from the federation government and/or the state governments. Such costs were estimated to be about US$575 000.

The committee agreed that the corporation should establish a reserve fund as soon as possible, particularly if the government is to guarantee the funds of depositors. This reserve fund should be established and no bonus should be declared until such a fund is established.

This report of the Pilgrims Economic Welfare Committee was presented to the parliament by command of his Majesty The *Yang Di-Pertuan Agong* on 14 August 1962.

THE BILL

The bill, also known as the Malayan Muslim Pilgrims Savings Corporation Act, 1961, was to come into force by notification in the *Gazettee*. In brief, it promulgated the following: the Malayan Muslim Pilgrims Savings Corporation would be established as a corporate body and would enjoy perpetual succession. Put differently, the Corporation would possess judicial personality with indefinite life span and be able to sue and be sued.[10]

The Act also promulgated the establishment of a Malayan Muslim Pilgrims Savings Fund, which would be administered and controlled by the Corporation. This fund would consist of sums deposited by intending Malayan pilgrims, profits generated by the investments of the Corporation, property developments, gifts, donations, bequests, etc. The Corporation would be the sole custodian of the fund and was authorized to invest it.[11] In addition to this, a reserve fund was also to be established.[12]

The repayment of all monies deposited in the Corporation was to be guaranteed by the government.[13]

Members of the Board were to be paid salaries to be determined by the Minister. Decisions of the Board were to be taken by a majority of the members. The Corporation was allowed to borrow subject to the approval of the Ministry of Finance.

The money deposited by an intending pilgrim could only be withdrawn for the purpose of the pilgrimage. If the existing deposit was inadequate for the pilgrimage, the Board may 'before sanctioning such withdrawal, require the depositor to make cash payment... as the Board considers adequate'.[14] Thus, it is clear that the critique of the Chinese MP was not accepted. Indeed, *Tabung Haji* was considered to have a specific purpose and deposits entrusted could not be withdrawn at will as was the case with other financial institutions. In addition to the pilgrimage, only three other causes of withdrawal were to be accepted:

1. the death of the depositor;
2. illness or debility of the depositor which made it impossible for him/her to perform the pilgrimage;
3. permanent departure, emigration, from Malaysia[15]

The accounts of the Corporation were to be audited by the Auditor-General or other auditor appointed by the Board with the approval of the Minister. The Minister was to convey the audit report together with his comments to the House of Representatives 'to be laid on the table'.[16]

The Board was to declare a rate of bonus each financial year. This bonus was to be credited to the account of each depositor annually *pro rata* and would be calculated on the balance of each account on the last day of each month. It would then be credited to each depositor's account on 1 January for the year subsequent to that to which it relates. No bonus payments would take place until the reserve fund mentioned above (Article 6) has been established.[17]

To sum up, this was the Malayan Muslim Pilgrims Savings Corporation Act and the Corporation started its activities in the year 1963 with just 1281 members/depositors who had deposited RM46 610. Presently, *Tabung Haji* has more than five million depositors with total amount of deposits reaching US$2 billion. Since there are 12 million Muslims in Malaysia, this means one out of every three Malaysian Muslim saves with the *Tabung Haji*.[18]

ACTUAL FUNCTIONING

Tabung Haji does not have a formal archive. Therefore, conducting research about its establishment and the subsequent evolution to the present is extremely difficult. Notwithstanding this, it has been possible to obtain important information from the officials of the Corporate Communication Department of *Tabung Haji*. This will be presented below. Another useful source of information is the collection of back issues of the *New Straits Times*, the major newspaper of Malaysia.

On 17 April 1989 Director General of *Tabung Haji*, Haji Ahmad bin Haji Yeof Abdul Hamid, responded to an accusation that the bonus paid to the depositors was too low. From the Director General's explanation we deduce the following. More than 20 years after its foundation, *Tabung Haji* was adhering to the recommendation made by the Parliamentary Committee and investing the savings of the depositors in various economic activities such as industries, trade, plantations and property. Thus the Islamic prohibition of interest came to be strictly obeyed. From the aggregate profits generated, *zakat* and business expenses were deducted. The bonus to the depositors was paid from the remaining net profits. The rate of bonus was therefore a function of the actual profits generated. This rate was also subject to the approval of the Treasury. In 1987 *Tabung Haji* had made a net profit of MR64 million. In 1988 this was reduced to RM41.45 million. The reduction was due to the fact that in 1987 *Tabung Haji* had sold substantial amount of shares. Moreover, the deposits had increased by RM190 million during 1988, reaching to RM790 million.

It will be remembered that when Ungku Aziz submitted his memorandum in 1959, he had estimated that within the next 20 years the total funds mobilized by the *Tabung Haji* might reach RM20 million. Thus the RM790 million of deposits actually mobilized in 1988 represents almost 40 times the amount originally expected. In short, the *Tabung Haji* has far exceeded the expectations of its founder.

With so much capital available, there was a sudden need to invest this amount in long-term projects. This was not easy and took time. Meanwhile, the funds were placed in short-term investments, which yielded lower returns. The total amount of these short-term investments was RM223 million, of which RM200 million was in property.[19] Moreover, a substantial part of the deposits were spent for the construction of the *Tabung Haji* headquarters in Kuala Lumpur and did not yield returns. The construction of this building was rationalized with the argument that it would serve better the needs of depositors, whose numbers had reached 1.3 million in 1988.[20] The director further announced that these depositors received a net bonus rate of 6.5 per cent after *zakat* was deducted. The gross bonus rate was 9 per cent, which compared favourably with that paid by other financial institutions. The trend of net profits generated, after the deduction of *zakat* and other variables between 1987 and 1994, can be observed in Table 12.1.

The net bonuses are credited to depositors' accounts on 31 December of each year. Starting from 1 January 1986, these bonuses have been exempted from income tax. This is due to the payment of *zakat* by *Tabung Haji* on behalf of depositors.[21]

In 1989, participation in a long-term project was announced. This was the decision to participate in the Islamic Development Bank Unit Trust. The investment would amount to between US$1 million and 10 million[22] pending approval from the Ministry. The fund was expected to reach initially to US$100 million from the member countries and eventually expand to US$1 billion. Part of this fund was going to be invested in the five projects proposed by *Tabung Haji*.[23]

One of these projects was going to be a housing project comprising three-bedroom houses in Bangi near Kuala Lumpur. It was also announced that more such projects would follow pending permission to open up palm oil plantations to housing construction in areas near Kuala Lumpur.

Apparently, despite such projects, placing the ever-increasing deposits in profitable long-term investments continued to be a major problem. To remedy the situation, *Tabung Haji* decided to establish its own investment company, to be called *Syarikat Istimar Islamiah Bhd*. The primary aim of the company was to improve the economic situation of the Muslims in the country by addressing the unemployment problem directly. Another company, also established by *Tabung Haji*, the *TH Plantations Berhad*, focused on establishing and managing palm oil plantations.[24] Still another *Tabung Haji*-owned company, the *TH Travel and Services Berhad*, focused on organizing the travel needs of the pilgrims and serving them during the pilgrimage. The *TH Properties Berhad* focuses on property development[25] and finally, the *TH Technologies Berhad* focuses on construction, information and telecommunication industries.[26] In recent years other companies were established by *Tabung Haji* and presently there are 12 companies which it owns directly. All in all, the total amounts of investments have reached US$4 billion.[27]

Meanwhile, *Tabung Haji* had apparently become a major *zakat* collector. The amount of *zakat* collected by *Tabung Haji* from the depositors in the Federal Territory alone had reached RM265 474.[28] The bonuses are paid to depositors after the deduction of *zakat* and all other taxes. This relieves depositors from the inconvenience of tax filing and the pertinent bureaucracy. In recent years, net bonus payments have reached 8–9.5 per cent per annum. This is an excellent rate in a country with only 2 per cent inflation.[29]

Prior to the decision to directly establish its own investment company, *Tabung Haji* had already made long-term investments in the equity of 75 companies amounting to RM329 million. 48 of these were listed in the Kuala

Table 12.1 Tabung Haji'*s performance (RM)*

Year	Total number of depositors	Net profit	Bonuses paid	Bonus rate	Total deposits	*Zakat* paid
1963	1281				46 610	
1964	6566				816 146	
1965	14 403					
1966	22 516		66 880	3%		
1967	29 450		171 484	4%		
1968	34 929		310 181	5%		
1969	42 078		618 219	5.5%		
1970	54 520		772 080	5.5%		
1971	67 372		978 870	5.5%		
1972	91 300		1 398 591	5.5%		
1973	133 298		2 399 216	6%		
1974	215 927		3 252 513	6.25%		
1975	251 706		2 152 158	6.75%		
1976	267 190		3 582 327	7%		
1977	294 274		3 887 814	7%		
1978	324 889		4 762 237	7.5%		
1979	359 603		5 738 767	7.75%		
1980	411 172		7 467 638	8%		
1981	469 541		10 263 966	8.5%		
1982	535 934		12 672 638	9%		
1983	609 846		15 203 820	8%		
1984	743 223		34 471 005	8.5%		
1985	867 220		27 143 070	8.5%		
1986	994 880		27 661 236	8%		
1987	1 133 492	64	36 362 000	7%	600 m	2.3 m
1988	1 319 416	41.45	39 270 497	6.5%	790 m	
1989	1 532 199		55 694 821	7%		
1990	1 773 789	53.20	58.234 672	7 %		3.04 m
1991	2 052 581	84.1	73.339 626	8 %		
1992	2 200 202	102	83 510 283	8 %		2.88 m
1993	2 367 795	170.3	176 896 201	9 %		4.33 m
1994	2 536 582	214.8	178 949 855	9.5%		6.50 m
1995	2 737 567		236 498 812	9.5%		
1996	2 977 838		327 496 032	9 5%		
1997	3 189 570		440 397 919	9.5%		
1998	3 440 971		459 239 734	8%		
1999	3 708 283		543 087 899	8%		
2000	4 023 790		455 412 662	5.5%		
2001	4 328 942	336	322 220 949	3.25%		13.5 m
2002	4 534 318	368	346 034 960	3.5%		15 m

2003	4 718 888	414	411 471 626	4%		14.6 m
2004	4 906 917	500	482 156 577	4.3%		
2005	5 097 713	575	548 074 347	4.5%		
2006	5 248 561	641		4.75%	14 700	26 m
2007	4 432 986	1 050	1 051 154 023	7%	16 000	
2008	4 743 940		897 068 886	5%	17 100	
2009	5 086 378		n/a		23 000	

Sources: Data presented in this table are a compilation. While bulk the of it, the columns 2, 4 and 5 have been provided by the Corporate Communication Department of *Tabung Haji* on 15 September 2009, the rest have been obtained from the following sources: *New Straits Times*, 15 January, p. 9; 17 March, p. 7, 1988; 6 June 2007; 6 February 2008, p. 4; 3 September 2009, B2 and IRTI, *Tabung Haji as an Islamic Financial Institution*, pp. 35–37; *Malay Mail*, 11 February 2006, Mohamad Akram Laldin, 'Islamic Financial System: The Malaysian Experience and the Way Forward', *Humanomics*, vol. 24, No. 3, 2008, p. 221. www.bernama.com/finance/news/php?id=246765&vo=11, *Business Times*, 8 February 2005; www.nst.com.my/current_News/NST/Tuesday/Newsbreak/20080506150744/Article/Index/html. I am grateful to the officials of the Corporate Communication Department of *Tabung Haji* and my research assistant M. Muhaizam bin Musa for the data in columns 2, 4 and 5.

Lumpur Stock Exchange while 22 were not. Another five were subsidiaries of these companies.[30] From an Islamic perspective, such equity investments are tantamount to *mudaraba*/*musharaka* investments and therefore in total conformity with the *sunnah* of the Prophet. Moreover, there are some built-in controls to lead *Tabung Haji* away from dubious financial activities. Indeed, should the management be tempted to involve *Tabung Haji* in foreign exchange trading, it would have to inform the Minister in charge and the chairman.[31]

Equity investments reached RM7011 million and comprise 61 per cent of the total investments. By the year 2008, these equity investments have accounted for 67 per cent of *Tabung Haji*'s total earnings.[32] The corporation has over RM6 billion of investments in more than 100 listed and unlisted companies.[33]

As is well known, equity investments are nearly identical to *mudaraba*/*musharaka* financing. If so, then we get the impression that with equity financing constituting the bulk of its total investments, *Tabung Haji* deserves to be recognized as the most Islamically appropriate financial institution existing today. But we need to consider these observations with caution. Indeed, the very impressive equity figures of *Tabung Haji* may not have been the outcome of a deliberate policy to implement *Shari'ah* based finance but rather an outcome of the New Economic Policy (NEP).[34] The Malaysian NEP, an affirmative action programme already referred to above, was initiated in 1971 as a direct response to the race riots that took place on 13 May 1969. The purpose was to improve the economic well-being of the *Bumiputras*.[35] For this purpose, it was announced that any company that wanted to be listed in the Kuala Lumpur stock exchange had to have at least 30 per cent *Bumiputra* ownership. This policy has only partially succeeded in its original purpose and is now being gradually abandoned.[36] Thus the very high contribution of equities to the overall earnings of *Tabung Haji* may well have been caused by NEP, with many companies wishing to be listed in the Kuala Lumpur Stock Exchange donating or selling at rock bottom pre-IPO[37] prices up to 30 per cent of their shares to Islamic institutions, particularly to *Tabung Haji*, which is highly respected in Malaysia. The question as to whether *Tabung Haji* has been merely a passive recipient of shares or an active investor in equities must be searched separately – not an easy task in view of the lack of archives.

INVESTMENT ANALYSIS

We will now have a closer look at these investments. To start with, we need to acknowledge that 1995 was the turning point. This is because the former *Lembaga Urusan Tabung Haji* Act of 1969, also known as the LUTH Act 1969, was quite restrictive regarding *Tabung Haji*'s investments. This Act had regarded *Tabung Haji* primarily as a government body that handles the financial affairs of Muslims within the framework of the pilgrimage. It allowed *Tabung Haji* to invest the accumulated capital of pilgrims only in subsidiary companies it owns outright. *Tabung Haji's* investment activities in other companies were strictly limited.

In the year 1995, the LUTH Act 1969 was replaced by the *Lembaga Tabung Haji* Act 1995, also known as the LTH Act 1995. This Act permitted *Tabung Haji* to invest directly in companies. In order to take sound investment decisions, the Act also permitted the establishment of a committee known as the Investment Advisor Panel. The panel is responsible for advising the Board of Directors on their investment decisions. The Act also permitted in item 4(2) *Tabung Haji* to invest abroad without going through the Ministry of Finance. The structure and composition of this committee was changed several times. Currently the so-called *Panel Penasihat Pelaburan*, or the Investment Advisory Panel, controls and advises *Tabung Haji* on its investment decisions. The nine-member committee includes *Shari'ah* experts, accountants, corporate members and the representatives of Bank Negara Malaysia.[38]

Tabung Haji invests primarily in two different categories: subsidiaries which it owns and equities. The latter can also be categorized into two groups: listed and unlisted companies. The latter are primarily prearranged stock offers through the *Ministry of International Trade and Investment* allocated to *Bumiputras* as part of the New Economic Policy. The stock offers come from companies wishing to be listed in the stock exchange. *Tabung Haji* considers these stock offers and after a process of due diligence purchases or refuses to purchase them. Since these shares belong to companies not yet listed in the stock exchange, they are offered at what we may call the pre-Initial Public Offering (IPO) prices, which are significantly lower than post-IPO prices. In assessing these offers *Tabung Haji* considers several criteria such as whether the company in question is involved in *halal* business activities and products, the potential for growth, prices and finally the quality of the management team. Once decided to purchase, *Tabung Haji* gets involved in short- or long-term investments.

While long-term investments of *Tabung Haji* have increased by 79 per cent from RM1 248 307 131 in 1997 to RM2 235 485 684 in 2000, short-term investments have increased from RM516 736 690 to RM785 710 954, that is, by 52 per cent, in the same period. Thus, as should be expected from such a large institution, *Tabung Haji* is not in the market for a quick kill but prefers to invest its capital for the long term. At the same time, it has become risk-averse during the last two decades. This is attested by the fact that whereas in 1990 the ratio of unlisted to listed companies was 56 per cent, in the year 2001 it has declined to 36 per cent. Moreover, whereas the number of listed companies in the portfolio of *Tabung Haji* has increased by 452 per cent between 1990 and 2004, that of the unlisted companies has increased by a mere 41 per cent. Thus we can conclude that *Tabung Haji* invests primarily for the long term and prefers listed to the unlisted companies.[39] If we look at this picture from the perspective of book value, we note that book value of investments has increased from RM595 million in 1990 to RM3844 million in 2001. This is an increase of 546 per cent. If we look at the listed companies, their book values have increased from RM287 million in 1990 to RM1911 million, an increase of 565 per cent. The same ratio for the unlisted companies is only 367 per cent. Thus the conclusion that *Tabung Haji* prefers listed companies to the non-listed is also confirmed from the book value perspective.

When the shares it has obtained gain in value, *Tabung Haji* does not hesitate to sell them.[40] Moreover, it sometimes utilizes foreign investment banks to market the shares it holds overseas. This took place on 20 March 2007, when the *Credit Suisse Group* successfully placed out 40 million *MMC Corp Bhd* shares belonging to *Tabung Haji* to investors in Hong Kong.[41] It has been shown that *Tabung Haji* made 18.94 per cent profit from such equity trading, amounting to RM131.32 million.[42] But sometimes objections are raised and *Tabung Haji* can be impeded from taking purely rational business decisions. This is what happened when *Tabung Haji* wanted to list its lucrative subsidiary the *TH Plantations Bhd* in the Kuala Lumpur Stock Exchange. Arguing that a lucrative company belonging to Muslim pilgrims could be acquired by non-Muslims, certain members of the Parliament objected to this transaction and the Prime Minister was obliged to 'postpone' the decision. Eventually a settlement was reached whereby it was agreed that only 5 per cent, or about 9.8 million, of the more than 74 million shares of *Tabung Haji* subsidiary was earmarked for public subscription.[43]

Although equity finance is considered to be the *conditio sine qua non* of venture capital, it would be wrong to label these modest beginnings as such. Before doing so, we need to find out why exactly these shares were purchased and whether *Tabung Haji* intended to sell these shares with profit and thus make a typical venture capital exit. The type of support, if any, given to these portfolio companies is also of course very important. In any case, as we have seen, although some unquoted shares have been purchased, *Tabung Haji* is conservative and usually prefers to purchase shares of companies that are already listed in the Kuala Lumpur Stock Exchange. Indeed, in 1994 RM693 674 957 was invested in quoted shares and only RM190 941 737 in unquoted shares.[44] Thus, purchasing shares of unquoted companies, nurturing and bringing them to the Initial Public Offering (IPO) stage, i.e., venture capital financing, is at its infancy.

Thus, in short, this investment analysis yields a conflicting message regarding the involvement of *Tabung Haji* in venture capital. While on the one hand, long-term preference indicates a venture-capital-like activity, the relative preference for the listed companies over the unlisted ones may be interpreted as a certain reluctance for the riskier venture-capital type of investments. Consequently, the data at hand are inconclusive in this regard. Naturally, it would be most appropriate for an institution like *Tabung Haji*, with such high Islamic credentials, to establish its own venture capital company, or at least to purchase the shares of already established venture capital companies.

Tabung Haji invests its temporary short-term funds in Bank Islam Malaysia. In the case of a substantial short-term surplus for pilgrimage expenses, it invests this surplus in a Special Investment Account at a profit-sharing ratio of 75:25. As far as a normal surplus is concerned, funds are maintained in the current account and invested by the bank. In this case, the profit-sharing ratio of 70:30 is applied.[45]

By 1988, *Tabung Haji* had begun sending 25 000 pilgrims annually to Mecca. It had also rented three DC 10s for their transport.[46] These pilgrims had invested, on average, RM400 annually. In view of the prevalent inflation, *Tabung Haji* had urged the depositors in 1988 to increase their deposits to RM1000 annually.[47] One year later, in 1989, the number of depositors to register for the pilgrimage was expected to reach 32,000.[48] An ability to operate at such a large scale naturally provides economies of scale. Indeed, while the cost per Malaysian pilgrim stood at US$2300 in 2004, it was US$3200 for an Indonesian and US$5300 for a Singaporean pilgrim travelling roughly equal distances from neighbouring areas. This cost increased to US$2481 for a Malaysian pilgrim in 2007.[49] Since air fare and accommodation constitutes 80 per cent of this cost, in order to accommodate the ever-increasing numbers of pilgrims and to do so at a reasonable cost, *Tabung Haji* applied to the Saudi authorities and obtained the permission to build a 30-storey, 1650 room hotel in Mecca costing RM911 million.[50]

Tabung Haji is aware of the advantages of economies of scale and jealously guards its monopoly of organizing the pilgrimage. Indeed, any party which organizes Hajj transportation without the permission of the Board could be liable for prosecution and if convicted could be fined up to but not exceeding RM100 000 or sentenced to imprisonment for a period of not more than one year. These restrictions were, however, gradually relaxed and *Tabung Haji* began to issue licences to private companies to organize pilgrimage tours. But these companies are strictly controlled by the *Tabung Haji*, which frequently asks pilgrims who have gone to the pilgrimage whether they have been mistreated by them. Since the *Tabung Haji* has substantial power over these companies including suspending their licences and barring them from operating during the next pilgrimage season, this is no idle threat.[51]

1988 was also the year when a majority of the *Tabung Haji*-owned palm oil plantations were to be harvested for the first time. The expected profit in 1988 from this sector was RM13 million. The previous year this figure stood at merely RM6 million.[52]

The total value of assets held by *Tabung Haji* had reached RM915 million in 1989. It was hoped that annually 250 000 people would open new savings accounts and eventually all Muslims would register.[53] *Tabung Haji* planned to collect RM5.2 billion over the next decade from the depositors. This amount was hoped to be collected from four million depositors. At the end of 1990, the total number of depositors stood at 1.7 million with investments totalling RM1 billion.[54]

While the growth trend of deposits in the twenty-first century appears to have continued unabated and even accelerated, the number of depositors appears to have reached a plateau. By 7 May 2008 the total fund size reached RM17.1 billion.

The total amount of equity investments in private companies has reached RM6 billion.[55] Of these, one of the most important ones is its participation *in Bank Islam Malaysia Bhd. Tabung Haji* owns 51 per cent of this bank. Most recently, it was announced that the Bank Islam will go through a process of capital enhancement. It has been decided that *Tabung Haji* will maintain its level of ownership at 51.47 per cent by purchasing additional shares.[56]

For all these services provided to Malaysia, Islamic Development Bank awarded its Prize in Islamic Banking for the year 1990 to *Tabung Haji*. The reward was awarded for its successful mobilization of savings of Muslims and investing these savings successfully in an Islamic way. The highly innovative way by which it has motivated Muslims to save for their pilgrimage was also highly regarded. Mobilization of small savings and investing them in major industrial, commercial, agricultural and real estate projects and doing all this in conformity with the *Shari'ah* was considered as the primary reason for awarding the prize.[57]

In view of the above, the *modus operandi* of *Tabung Haji* can be depicted in Figure 12.1. On the liability side, the boxes D1–Dn denote deposits made by prospective pilgrims. Since these deposits are made annually, they can be considered as annuities. They are also considered as *wadiah*, that is, interest-free deposits for safe keeping. Depositors authorize *Tabung Haji* with an *al-wakala* document to invest their deposits. This is also known as *aqad izin*.

On the asset side, *Tabung Haji* has established 17 subsidiaries with direct investment of the deposits. After a period of trial and error, these subsidiaries have now been reduced to four and comprise companies specializing in travel, construction, plantations and property development. In addition to these subsidiaries directly owned, *Tabung Haji* also invests in already established

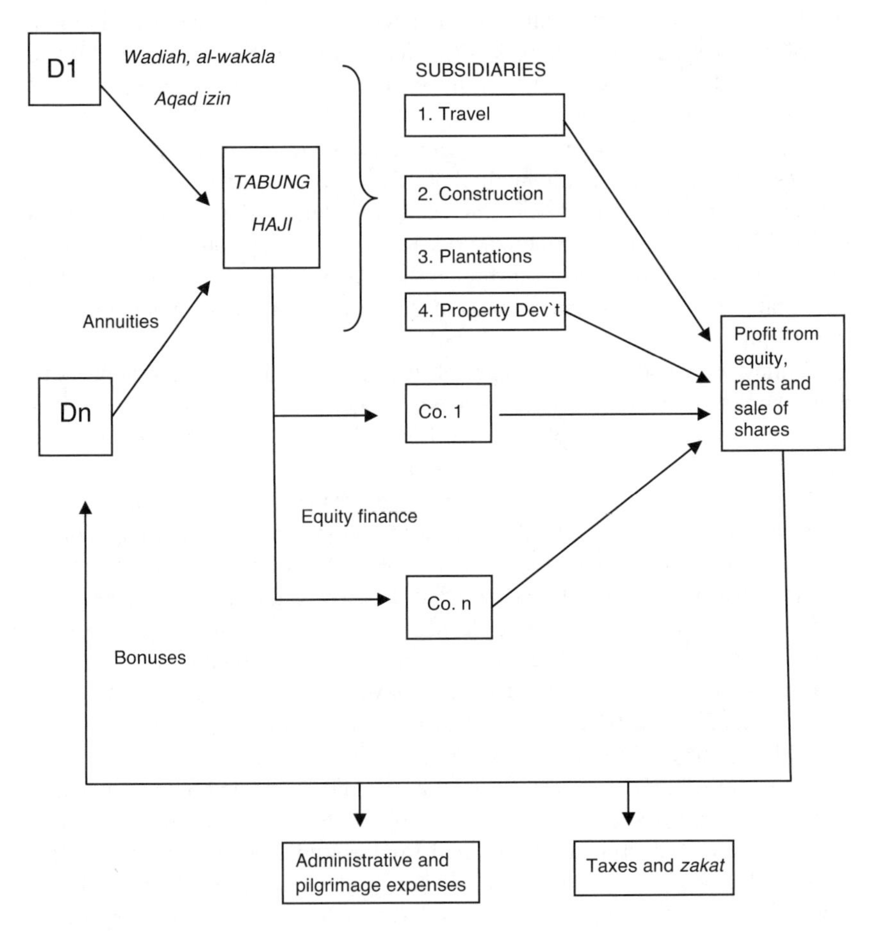

Figure 12.1 Tabung Haji

and usually listed companies. This is done through equity finance as already explained above. Profits from all these equity transactions as well as direct investments in the subsidiaries are pooled. Between 2002 and 2008, *Tabung Haji*'s earnings had recorded an average annual growth of 25 per cent.

After the *zakat* payments are made on behalf of the depositors at the rate of 2.5 per cent, we come to the administrative and pilgrimage expenses. This item, naturally, is the *raison d'être* of *Tabung Haji* and constitutes the most important expense item. All the expenses of sending hundreds of thousands of pilgrims to Mecca are included in this item. If, after covering all these expenses, a profit is generated, it is distributed to depositors as bonuses.

To conclude, starting with only RM46 610 deposited by its first 1281 depositors in 1963,[58] *Tabung Haji* has performed far better than the original expectations of the Royal Professor Ungku Aziz, its founder. In 1962 Ungku Aziz had estimated that the number of depositors would stabilize at 90 000 from 1982 onwards. In fact, the total number of depositors reached 535 934, a figure almost six times as great. Moreover, the total number of depositors never stabilized but continued to increase. In fact, it is now estimated that half of the Malaysian Muslim population, approximately eight million persons, will eventually become members.[59] By 2006 this figure had reached 5.24 million, a 57.8-fold increase since 1982. Ungku Aziz had further estimated that in its 25th year of existence, that is, in 1987, the cumulative total of deposits would reach RM51 300 000.[60] In fact, total deposits had reached RM600 000 000 in that year – a figure 11.7-fold greater than the original estimation. All of these indicate, without any doubt whatsoever, that when provided with a well-designed, efficient and transparent institution, Muslims respond extremely well and perform well above the original estimations.

When I informed Ungku Aziz that my calculations indicated that *Tabung Haji* had performed far in excess of his original estimations and asked his view on the subject, he responded saying that he had mixed feelings about it. While he was obviously pleased with the performance, he was disappointed with the fact that *Tabung Haji* had become just another profit-maximizing investment institution. He added further that his estimations were based on the assumption that *Tabung Haji* would channel all of its earnings to poverty alleviation. Instead, those who managed this institution have decided to transform the institution into a profit maximizer with the result that while, indeed, impressive profits have been realized, poverty alleviation among the pilgrims has been neglected.

To these powerful critiques by its very founder, I would like to add another one. The CEO of *Tabung Haji*, Datuk Ismee Ismail, is reported to have said that they have already invested RM2.3 billion on properties in Mecca and Medinah and that they have now started to survey investment opportunities in Europe.[61] It is difficult to imagine how *Tabung Haji* investments in European properties can improve the lot of Malaysian Muslims. Investments primarily in Malaysia, and if Malaysia is completely saturated for investment and better opportunities exist abroad, then at least in the rest of the Islamic world, should have priority over investments in the West. Moreover, in terms of the type of investment, equity investments should also have priority over real estate investments. The CEO's statement gives the warning made by Dr Ayman new credibility. Indeed, if *Tabung Haji* is primarily interested in real estate investments in Europe, obviously, our initial impression that they must have been involved in equity, therefore *mudaraba/musharaka* investments, can no longer be sustained. *Tabung Haji* seems simply to be interested in the safest possible investments even if this means the least benefit for Malaysian or other Muslims worldwide. It is to be hoped that *Tabung Haji* will enhance its institutional leadership in the Islamic world by boldly getting involved and spearheading venture capital in Malaysia as well as the rest of the Islamic world. Such a move would help eliminating poverty by creating entrepreneurs.

Poverty alleviation through enhancing entrepreneurship may not fit into Ungku Aziz's original concept, which favours redistribution of income to the rural poor. But venture capital combined with microfinance can be a powerful tool attacking poverty from above as well as from below. We will discuss this particular combination further below.

This chapter can be concluded with a final bit of information. In recognition of the enormous services he has rendered to Malaysia, the Royal Professor Ungku Aziz was offered the highest honorific title 'Tun' by three different Prime Ministers but declined to accept all as a matter of principle. This principle has recently been referred to by Abd Hamid and Joseph, who explained that Ungku Aziz has strong views on feudalism and considers the current Malaysian practice of using non-academic titles as a reflection of the lack of confidence in academic standing of those who use them.[62]

NOTES

1. Professor Aziz was the the Vice-Chancellor of the University of Malaya from 1968 to 1988. In recognition of his services to Malaysia, he was given the title of 'Professor Diraja' (Royal Professor) in 1978. He is the only academic holding this title in Malaysia.
2. Command Paper No. 22 of 1962, Federation of Malaya, Presented to the Parliament by the command of His Majesty the Yang Di-Pertuan Agong Ordered by the *Dewan Ra'ayat* to Lie Upon the Table, 14 August 1962, p. 1.
3. IRTI, *Tabung Haji as an Islamic Financial Institution, the Mobilization of Investment Resources in an Islamic Way and the Management of Haj* (Jeddah: IRTI/IDB, IDB Prize Winners' Lecture Series No. 4, 1995), p. 11. The Malayan Muslim Pilgrims Savings Corporation Act, 34/1962, was amended in 1967, 1969 and in 1982. See Mannan, *Islamic Socioeconomic Institutions*, 1996, Appendix I.
4. A *fatwa* from Kedah (1974) declared that these bonuses would be permitted on the grounds that they were profits from the *Tabung Haji*'s investments. Two years previously, another

fatwa from Kelantan had ruled that proceeds from any government agency such as the Post Office etc., are not permissible. See Hooker, '*Fatawa* in Malaysia', p. 99.

5. *Command Paper,* no. 22 of 1962, Appendix I, 'Pilgrims Economy Improvement Plan', p. 26.
6. During the parliamentary debate a Chinese MP, Enche' Lim Kean Siew (Dato Kramat) criticized Ungku Aziz's proposal on the grounds that it was inferior to the Chinese *tontine*. Accordingly, this was on the grounds that whereas a person participating in the *tontine* can borrow money from that bank on the promise that he will repay that sum and he may do so before he has finished paying to the bank, these rights were denied under the proposed plan. Siew, in short, criticized the proposal on the grounds that first, the depositor can only withdraw up to the amount of his credit and second, that the depositor could not withdraw his deposit unless he was able to prove to the Board his extenuating circumstances. See *Parliamentary Debates, Dewan Ra'ayat,* vol. IV, Fourth Session, part I, April 1962–December 1962 (First Parliament), pp. 1110–12.
7. Conditions for withdrawal were eventually relaxed. It is now permitted to withdraw deposits for a beneficial purpose once every six months. See IRTI, *Tabung Haji as an Islamic Financial Institution,* p. 14.
8. Apparently, the committee's expectations were far too cautious. In fact, total deposits reached RM816 146 in the second year.
9. It is interesting that the committee had referred to the Anglo-Saxon trust but not to its equivalent the Islamic waqf, which indicates to what extent the Malays had lost contact with Islamic tradition and institutions due to the British occupation. Rapid Islamization of the country after the independence may be considered a reaction to this situation.
10. *Command Paper No. 22 of 1962, Appendix VI,* p. 1, Article 3/2 and 4.
11. İbid., Article 5/2(a–f) and 3.
12. Ibid., Article 6/1–2.
13. Ibid., Article 8.
14. Ibid., Article 22/2–4.
15. Ibid., Article 23/a–c.
16. Ibid., Article 25/3–4.
17. Ibid., Article 27/1–2.
18. Rahman, 'Towards Islamic Banking', www.eldis.org/fulltext/rahman.pdf (2004).
19. *New Straits Times,* 17 March 1988, p. 7.
20. This number constituted 14 per cent of the 8.5 million eligible Muslim depositors in 1988. Thus, it took *Tabung Haji* 26 years to reach out to the 14 per cent of Muslims in Malaysia. This percentage was 15 per cent in the state of Perak. *New Straits Times,* 4 December 1988, p. 4
21. IRTI, *Tabung Haji as an Islamic Financial Institution*, p. 16.
22. RM2.7 was equal to US$1 in 1989.
23. *New Straits Times,* 22 June 1989, p. 4.
24. By 2008 this company possessed 28,730 ha of land. This is a small holding in Malaysian standards for palm oil production. *Tabung Haji* decided to increase the size of its palm oil estates by 50 per cent this year. This will make the company a medium-size palm oil producer in 2009. This company was listed in the Kuala Lumpur Stock Exchange in 2006. *New Straits Times*, 25 May 2007 and 14 May 2008.
25. The most important property development of this company in 2008 was the RM9.2 billion project in Negri Sembilan. *New Straits Times,* 28 April 2008.
26. The TH Technologies Sdn Bhd was incorporated in 1994 and is wholly owned by *Tabung Haji*. Its paid up capital was RM30 million and it has completed projects worth more than RM1 billion. *New Straits Times,* 9 June 2007.
27. Rahman, 'Towards Islamic Banking'.
28. *New Straits Times,* 1 November 1988, p. 9.
29. Rahman, 'Towards Islamic Banking'.
30. *New Straits Times,* 17 March 1988, p. 7.
31. *New Straits Times,* 27 December 2006.

32. A further 15 per cent was generated by dividends, 9 per cent by the currency market, 4 per cent by rentals, 3 per cent by *sukuk,* 2 per cent by 'others'. *New Straits Times,* 6 February 2008, p. 4.
33. Laldin, 'Islamic Financial System', p. 222; *Islamic Finance News,* 28 March 2008, p. 6. *New Straits Times,* 25 March 2008.
34. I am grateful for this point to Dr Tawfiq Ayman.
35. The Malay-speaking Muslims were the original peoples of Malaysia. Since they were primarily engaged in agriculture and bureaucracy, they were left behind by the commerce-oriented Chinese, who had been brought in by the British to work in the tin mines and rubber plantations and then moved on to trade.
36. By 2006, some 35 years later, the *Bumiputras* controlled merely 15.8 per cent of the shares of the companies listed in the stock exchange as opposed to 42.8 per cent by the non-*Bumiputras* and 40 per cent held by foreigners. See on this Jasin, 'The NEP Was Not a Failure', p. 5. On the reasons why the NEP is now being abandoned, see Majed, 'Removing the Clutches Slowly', pp. 9–10.
37. IPO: Initial Public Offering. This is discussed in detail in Chapter 15.
38. Çizakça and Musa, '*Tabung Haji* and Its Performance', forthcoming.
39. Ibid., forthcoming.
40. Naturally, sometimes losses are also observed. This was the situation with the troubled optical disc maker Megan Media Holdings Bhd. *Tabung Haji* had bought a 5 per cent stake in this company and has decided to sell it at a loss. *New Straits Times,* 5 July 2007.
41. *New Straits Times,* 21 March 2007.
42. Laldin, 'Islamic Financial System', p. 222.
43. *New Straits Times*, 12 October 2005; *Malay Mail*, 18 October 2005; Mohd Azlan Jafaar, 'THP Will Stay Under Muslim Control', *Business Times*, 13 October 2005.
44. IRTI, *Tabung Haji as an Islamic Financial Institution*, pp. 40, 43.
45. Ibid., p. 42.
46. It is estimated that within the decade 2003–2013, the Malaysian Airlines will earn RM1.5 billion for carrying the pilgrims. *New Straits Times*, 8 August 2008.
47. *New Sunday Times*, 17 January 1988, p. 6.
48. *New Straits Times*, 20 April 1989, p. 9.
49. Rahman, 'Towards Islamic Banking'. *New Straits Times*, 7 July 2007.
50. *New Straits Times*, 22 September 2008.
51. IRTI, *Tabung Haji as an Islamic Financial Institution,* p. 19; *New Straits Times*, 16 November 2009, p. 4.
52. *New Straits Times*, 15 January 1988, p. 9.
53. *New Straits Times*, 23 January 1989, p. 2.
54. The RM5.2 billion figure was to be collected from 250 000 new depositors each year over the next decade. *New Straits Times*, 2 November 1990, p. 10.
55. www.nst.com.my/Current_News/NST/Tuesday/NewsBreak/20080506150744/Article/index_html.
56. www.btimes.com.my/Current_News/Btimes/Articles/20090406203818/Article/.
57. IRTI, *Tabung Haji as an Islamic Financial Institution*, p. 7.
58. Çizakça and Musa, forthcoming; *New Straits Times*, 9 June 2007, p. 41.
59. Malaysia's current population is about 28 million. Roughly 60 per cent of this, 16 800 000, are Muslims.
60. For the original estimations of Ungku Aziz, see Appendix II of the CMD.22 of 1962. For the actual figures realized see the sources of table XII/1.
61. *New Straits Times*, 3 September 2009, p. B2.
62. Abd Hamid and Joseph, 'Ungku A. Aziz – A Man For All Seasons', p. 20.

Part V

Future of Islamic capitalism and financing

13. The Islamic gold dinar

Recently, there has been an increasing amount of publications, conferences, even a campaign, about the reintroduction of the Islamic gold dinar. The proponents of this idea, known as the *denarists*, particularly active in Malaysia, advocate that this country as well as the whole Islamic world 'urgently' return to the Islamic gold dinar.[1] They argue that if this return is achieved, many ills of modern economies such as rampant inflation, credit crunches, etc., which they associate with the present paper money system, would be solved. Some scholars also argue that since the Prophet used coins, it would be only appropriate for Islamic countries to transform their currencies into gold dinars. In short, what the *denarists* are doing is to propose an essentially historical system – coinage was the predominant form of currency throughout history – for the future. It is therefore only appropriate that we start the fifth part of this book on the future of Islamic capitalism and finance with this proposal of a common currency for the Islamic world.

FROM BARTER TO COINAGE

Let us start with the last argument that we should reintroduce the gold dinar because it was the *sunnah* of the Prophet. First of all, we need to understand what the overall purpose of the Prophet was when he condoned the use of coinage. The Qur'an as well as a number of *ahadith* make it perfectly clear that there was a divine plan to make Mecca the global hub of world commerce.[2] For this, the first task was to catapult the Islamic community from the age of barter to the age of monetized trade. The Prophet did this with two *ahadith*.[3] While barter was thus declared as a form of *riba*, trade with money was approved and encouraged. The Prophet used Byzantine and Persian coins. Authentic Islamic coins were introduced later.

Since paper money had not yet been invented during the Prophet's time, he couldn't have used such currency even if he had wanted to. Therefore we need to ask, would he have wanted to use paper money, if he had any choice? Let us imagine for one minute that the Prophet had the choice between coinage, containing gold or silver, and paper currency. Which one would he have chosen and on what basis would he have made his decision? It is my contention that he would have thought of the Qur'an and would have based his decision upon the inspiration he obtained from the Word of God. The Qur'an does not ordain Muslims to use this or that currency but does provide a powerful clue: the prohibition of the rate of interest. Obviously, it is based upon this clue that he would have tried to reach a decision. We now know, with hindsight, that while paper money fulfils the ultimate Islamic goal of zero rate of interest, coinage does not.

BRINGING DOWN THE RATE OF INTEREST

Now, fast forward 14 centuries: as it is well known, the Japanese interbank interest rate reached zero rate of interest in 1999. Japan was followed by several other Western nations during the latest crisis. On 30 July 2010 the London interbank offered rate on three month dollars was fixed at 0.46563 per cent.[4] Although this was obviously unintentional – indeed, none of these countries reduced their rate of interest to zero for religious or ideological reasons – they nevertheless inadvertently demonstrated that it is possible to bring into being an economy with zero rate of interest using paper money. The question boils down now whether this could have been achieved with coinage. This is doubtful because every coin has two different values, face value and intrinsic value. Face value, which we may call 'fiat value', refers to what is written on it and is determined by the power of the state which declares it legal tender, while the intrinsic value refers to the cost of producing the coin plus, more importantly, the value of the metal contained in it. The intrinsic value of the coin is thus primarily determined by the global commodity market, where equilibrium prices of gold or silver come into being.[5] Under normal circumstances, face value should be greater than or at least equal to the intrinsic value. But this is not always so as will be explained below.

Let us make three assumptions now. First, let us assume that a government with Islamic inclinations decides to reach zero rate of interest. This follows directly from the interest prohibition in Islam. Since most economists agree that interest rate is actually the price of money, interest prohibition means that this price should be zero. Assume further that gold coinage constitutes the currency of the country and the Central Bank is ordered to take all necessary measures to reduce the prevailing interest rate to zero, regardless of any macroeconomic consequences. Finally, assume that there is no gold standard – a realistic assumption since it is very unlikely that the rest of the world will also go back to coinage just because the Islamic world has.

My hypothesis, under these assumptions, is that whereas the Japanese Central Bank reached this level without any such intention with paper money, the Central Bank of an Islamic country using coinage as its currency cannot do so with all its good intentions. Indeed, the Central Bank can adjust all the macroeconomic variables under its control to reach its target of zero rate of interest but would find it extremely difficult, even impossible, to do so. This is because of the intrinsic value of the coinage, which is determined not by the Central Bank but by the global demand and supply for the metal that is contained in the coin.

The hypothesis that coins would always have a positive rate of interest is confirmed by monetary history. Genoa aside, where a 1 per cent rate of interest had been observed during the seventeenth century thanks to very special institutional factors, in general, historical rates of interest never fell below 3 per cent in economies using coinage. Indeed, a zero rate of interest has never been recorded throughout history in monetary systems using coinage.[6]

At this point we may ask if there is any *fiqhi* objection to the use of paper money. Some of the most respected classical Muslim scholars, particularly Mohammad al-Shaybani, Ibn Kayyim and Ibn Taymiyah, did not limit currency to gold and silver coinage only. Ahmad Ibn Hanbal ruled that there was no harm in adopting as currency *anything* that is generally accepted by the people. Thus, these scholars, among themselves, opened the way for Muslims of future centuries to utilize paper money. Leading contemporary scholars like Yusuf al-Qaradawi and Muhammad Taqi Usmani are also of the same opinion.[7]

There is a further complication: *ceteris paribus*, not only coins would always have a greater than zero price, that is, a positive rate of interest, their circulation in the economy would also be affected in the long run by the price trends of precious metals in world markets. We will have more to say on this below.

The mechanics of an inflow or outflow of gold into a country should also be considered. An inflow, ignoring reasons, would lead to inflation and an outflow to depression.[8] It is for this reason that in history most European nations were obsessed about ensuring that no gold would flow out of the country. Gold inflow, however, was encouraged as it expanded the economy. This Europe-wide doctrine was called *mercantilism* and was the cause of many wars between mercantilist nations. This is another very dangerous implication of introducing the gold dinar.

Ahamed Kameel Mydin Meera, who is the main proponent of the gold dinar, has argued that money creation would not be possible in a fully gold backed system. With money creation thus prevented, inflation too would be avoided.[9] This is pure theory and needs to be checked against historical evidence. Let us now observe, if indeed in history, currency systems based upon coinage have been able to keep money supply stable and therefore avoid inflation.

THE HISTORICAL EVIDENCE

If we study historical data, the first thing we note is that inflation was alive and well in the past. Indeed, throughout Europe, there was massive inflation in the period 1440–1760, with the most rampant inflation being observed in the late sixteenth and early seventeenth centuries. Therefore, the claim made by another denarist, Umar Vadillo, that '1400 years ago, a chicken cost one dirham. Today, it still costs one dirham'[10] invites incredulity. I do not know the details of Mr Vadillo's calculations, but since all serious works done by economic historians indicate otherwise, I have grave doubts. Indeed, during the period 1440–1600, sheep, candles, wine, beer, beef and wheat prices expressed in gold or silver coins exhibit a massive inflation all over Europe.[11] To give some examples; in Strasbourg, France, the average price index of rye went from 100 in the fifteenth century to 350 in the seventeenth. Meat went from 100 to 250. In Saxony, Germany, the two percentages were respectively 350 and 250.

It may be argued that the prices given above are European prices and therefore are not relevant for the Islamic world. In that case, we can look at prices in the Islamic world as well. Thanks to rich Turkish archives we are well informed about the Ottoman prices. Data collected from the waqf and palace kitchen books indicate that prices expressed in grams of silver reached their peak in Istanbul during the first quarter of the seventeenth century at approximately 80 to 100 per cent above their levels in the base year of 1489–90.[12] In this period two types of coins constituted the prevailing currency in the Ottoman economy; the gold *sultani* and the silver akçe.

The problem with the bimetallic system, where coins containing gold as well as silver circulated, was that the money supply was never fixed as Meera would like us to believe. On the contrary, money supply was subject to fluctuations both caused by chance discovery of gold or silver deposits as well as deliberate debasements. While money supply increased during the late sixteenth century due to the discovery of huge silver deposits in Potosi, South America, it continued to increase further during the next, seventeenth century, primarily by debasements.

Debasement occurs when a government, obliged to increase the money supply, mints new coins with lower metal content. Put differently, more coins would be cut from a given amount of precious metals. This is, of course, tantamount to increasing the money supply. Thus, money supply in a bimetallic system was by no means fixed. It fluctuated in tandem with the worldwide discovery of precious metal deposits as well as the need of the state for additional money and the consequent debasements. With money supply not fixed and tending to increase, it was natural that inflation would occur. There is solid evidence that, indeed, this was the case.[13] As explained above, data obtained from throughout Europe as well as the Ottoman Caliphate all tell the same story of rapid inflation. All of these countries were using gold or silver coins. Thus, we conclude, having gold or silver based coins as the currency of a country does not in any way provide a protection against inflation.

That not only the American silver from Potosi but also debasements were behind this inflation is demonstrated by numismatists, who have examined the precious metal content of European coins. They have informed us that all the main coins of Europe lost their silver or gold content. In the period 1440–1760 the coins of England, Russia, Germany, France, the Netherlands, Austria, Genoa, Venice and Spain were all debased and their precious metal contents were reduced – some drastically, some to a lesser extent. To give some specific examples: in this period even the pound sterling, the most stable currency in the world, lost 43.42 per cent of its equivalent weight in silver. The French livre tournois lost 82.68 per cent, the Genoese lira 72.98 per cent and the Dutch guilder 68.74 per cent.[14]

In case the reader wonders about the Islamic world, it should suffice to note that the Ottoman Asper (akçe) was one of the most frequently and drastically debased coins in Europe. In 1585–86 it was drastically debased and lost 44 per cent of its silver content. One akçe weighed 0.68 grams in 1584 and only 0.23 grams in 1689.[15]

Nor was debasement a special curse of the early modern period. It was observed throughout history. Consider, for instance, the original Roman denarius, which, by the way, gave its name to the Islamic gold dinar. The denarius was 95 to 98 per cent pure silver weighing 4.5 grams by the decree of Caesar Augustus in 15 BC. By the reign of Nero, its weight was down to 3.8 grams. By the second half of the third century, some 270 years after its initiation, it was merely 2 per cent silver.[16]

The most important universal reason for these debasements was warfare. When a government suddenly faces an external threat, it has to increase the number of men under arms and improve its armed forces – a very expensive affair. More soldiers, more and better arms all need to be paid in cash. If cash is in the form of gold or silver currency then the solution is to cut new coins from a given amount of precious metal. In the year 1585, for example, during the long war with Iran, the Ottoman government wanted to nearly double the money supply by ordering the mints to strike 800 *akçe*s from 100 *dirham*s of silver whereas the earlier standard had been 450 *akçe*s per 100 *dirham*.[17] Another important reason for debasement was the so-called seigniorage. This was the revenue received by the ruler during the debasement process.

GRESHAM'S LAW AND EQUATION

Governments desperate to increase the available money supply to cover their emergency expenses or pay their debts, however, faced a further difficulty with the coinage. This is the so-called Gresham's law and should be explained properly.

We start with the following equation:

$$FV = x + \frac{G}{TW}.P_g$$

where FV is the face value of the coin, x is the cost of producing the coin, G/TW is the ratio of pure gold to the total weight of a coin, and P_g is the global price of gold.

The left side of the equation shows the face value and the right side the intrinsic value of the coin. This is a precarious equality. As long as the face value of the coin is greater than or at least equal to the intrinsic value, there is no problem and the coin circulates in the economy without any problem. If, however, P_g increases in response to a worldwide increase in gold prices, then Gresham's law dynamics would be set in motion. This is best illustrated with the following numerical example. Assume that we are considering a gold coin with a face value of RM1000. Assume further that the cost of producing this coin is RM50. This coin, moreover, is 90 per cent pure gold. The global gold price is RM1000 per ounce. This would give us the following:

RM1000= 50+0.9 (1000)

RM1000>950

Thus, the face value of the coin is greater than its intrinsic value, and the coin circulates without any problem.

Now assume that the global gold price has increased to RM1200 per ounce. The equation now becomes:

RM1000<50+0.9(1200), or

RM1000<1130

Thus, the intrinsic value of the coin has now surpassed its face value. It pays every citizen to melt the coin he possesses, extract the pure gold it contains which he can sell in the market and obtain RM1080 (intrinsic value minus the cost of production). With the RM1080 he obtains, he buys another gold coin and makes RM80 profit, *ad infinitum*.

There would be two consequences of all this. First, the demand for coins would increase shifting the aggregate demand curve for money, $D_{m'}$, to the right. Second, the coins obtained by the speculators would simply disappear from the circulation – they would be melted away! This shifts the aggregate supply curve for money, S_m, leftward. Combining the first and the second shifts ($D_{m'}$ and $S_{m'}$) gives us the new equilibrium rate of interest, R_1. Thus, the rate of interest would increase in an Islamic country because of global gold prices – not a very desirable situation. Muslims obviously want to reduce the rate of interest, even to bring it down to zero. This is not only because of the need they feel to obey the Qur'an but also pure economics. Indeed, a substantial increase in the rate of interest, through its negative impact on investment and unemployment, can be deflationary and curb economic growth. These dynamics are depicted in Figure 13.1.

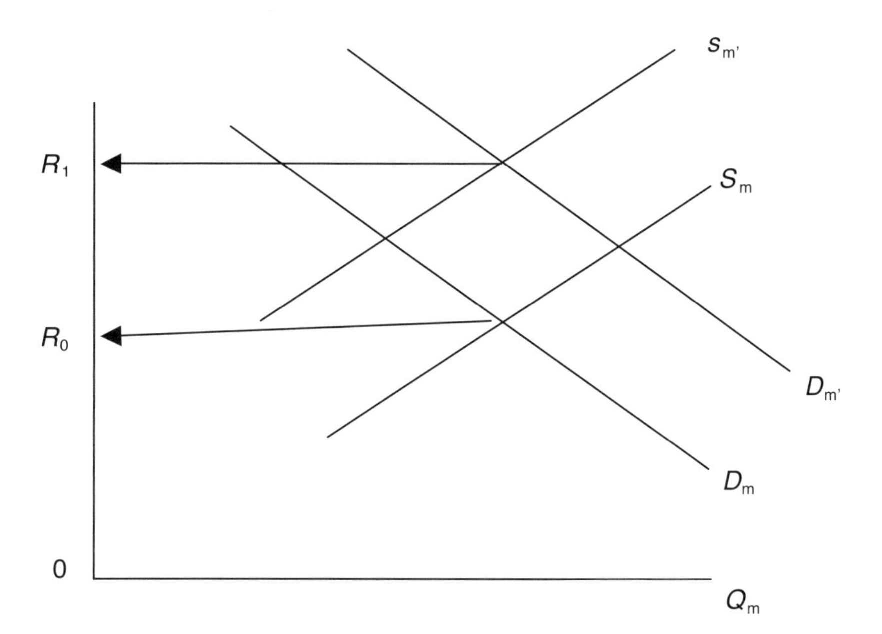

Figure 13.1 Gresham's law dynamics

The government, wishing to avoid a deflation, would have to respond to all this by increasing the money supply. In coinage systems, this is done by debasement, i.e., by reducing the gold content of the coin, or the *G/TW* ratio. The government does this by striking more coins from a given amount of pure gold. In short, the government issues new coins with lower gold content. But this too would put in motion the dynamics of Gresham's law.

Indeed, when the public realize that new coins with lower intrinsic value are being issued, they immediately would take out their old and better coins from the circulation and hoard them. Since the new coins issued would inevitably cause inflation and bring down the fiat value, the whole process would repeat itself and the old coins would be either hoarded or melted. Consequently, 'bad money' always drove 'the good' out. This is the famous observation made by Sir Thomas Gresham back in the sixteenth century. Known unfairly[18] as Gresham's law, it is expressed as 'bad money drives out the good', and means that issuing new and lower quality coinage is actually a self-defeating process. Indeed, new coins issued in order to increase the money supply to combat deflation or to cover the emergency expenses of the state, end up leading to the disappearance of the old coins altogether.

From the Islamic perspective Gresham's law has the additional harm that it encourages hoarding – a situation strongly forbidden by the Qur'an.[19] Furthermore, unless the amount of new coins issued is much higher than the old coins that disappear, the disappearance of the old coins means a leftward shift in the aggregate money supply, which would increase the rate of interest – once again, an undesirable situation for Muslims.

Another huge disadvantage of the gold dinar is that among all the Muslim countries only Indonesia is an important producer of gold – 6.6 per cent of the global production. Other Islamic countries are insignificant producers. This would put the Islamic world at the mercy of the significant producers (South Africa 11.8 per cent, the USA 10.4 per cent, China 8.9 per cent and Russia 7.2 per cent).[20] The Islamic gold dinar would give these countries quite a substantial leverage to play havoc with the monetary system of Islamic countries – if they so wish, the largest producers can collude and play with gold prices and therefore, indirectly, the rate of interest in the Muslim world using gold coins. If such speculations are possible, this would create a huge uncertainty – *gharar*.

Now, *gharar* is a complicated concept. But Ibn Taymiya has shown that in a transaction involving two or more partners, mutually agreed shared risks are permitted and constitute no *gharar*, risks unshared and imposed solely on one of the partners, however, are not permitted and constitute *gharar*. This can be considered as a corollary of the prohibition of *riba*.[21]

The reason why the Islamic gold dinar may be subject to *gharar* and might be prohibited is that any speculation by the major producers of gold would not harm them but would harm the Islamic world. Risks would not be shared fairly by all transacting partners but only by the Islamic world. This is *gharar* of the worst sort – because we are not talking about an ordinary risk but a massive risk that would put the entire monetary system of the Islamic world in danger.

CONCLUSION

We are now at a position to summarize the arguments presented above.

1. Combining the interest prohibition in the Qur'an with the rulings of Ahmad Ibn Hanbal, Muhammad al-Shaybani and Ibn Taymiya, some of the greatest classical jurists, we deduce the following position of Islam regarding money: anything that is generally accepted by the public can fulfil the role of money. Thus money is, primarily, a medium of exchange and not a commodity. The price of this money (interest) must be zero.
2. Economic histories of early modern Europe as well as the Ottoman Caliphate have vindicated that money, indeed, is not a commodity but a medium of exchange. Economic historians have observed throughout history that the precious metal content of coins in the long run has always been reduced. Thus there is a natural tendency for money to lose its commodity character, metal content, and to progress towards being a pure medium exchange. With the advent of paper money, the intrinsic value of money approached zero. With e-money, by which we transfer billions with the click of a mouse, it has become absolutely zero. Thus, the Islamic view that money is not a commodity but purely a medium of exchange is vindicated.
3. Japan as well as several other Western economies, though inadvertently, showed that with paper money it is possible to reach a state of zero interest rate – hence a zero price for money, Islamic position, is possible.
4. With coinage it would be much more difficult to reach this stage. This is because every coin has two different values. While the fiat value can be controlled by the Central Bank, the intrinsic value is beyond such control. Indeed, for the intrinsic value to be zero, the global supply of gold should increase at such a rate so as to completely balance the demand for it – not a very likely scenario. Consequently, a return to coinage would compel a country into a position where zero rate of interest cannot be achieved. This is an un-Islamic position and represents not progress but regress.
5. Throughout history governments have increased the supply of coinage through debasement. This supply could also increase when new gold or silver deposits were discovered. In short, the supply of coinage was never fixed as the *denarists* claim.
6. It follows then that with money supply constantly changing, coinage cannot avoid inflation – another *denarist* claim that must be discarded. For those who are worried about inflation in the Islamic world, the solution does not lie in the type of currency in circulation but in safe guarding central banks' autonomy from the pressures of unscrupulous and short-sighted governments.

7. Introducing the Islamic gold dinar, despite this pretentious name, is not only un-Islamic due to its worsening impact on the rate of interest, it is also of no practical value since it cannot control inflation.
8. Since the Islamic world is a minor producer of gold, introducing the Islamic gold dinar would create unshared uncertainty, and therefore *gharar,* at a massive scale. Islamic law prohibits *gharar.*
9. Finally, introducing a common currency for all Muslim countries accepted throughout the world is a noble idea, providing the currency in question is made of paper, not of gold or silver.
10. An Islamic currency accepted worldwide should not be imposed from above by some well-meaning academicians and governments but should be demanded by Muslims. This can only come about by massively increased trade among the Muslim countries. Let us remember in this context that even the European Union was originally established as a coal and steel union, then progressed into the European Common Market and then, finally, to the European Union. The common European currency, the Euro, was introduced much later. The priority for Muslim countries, therefore, should not be to introduce a common currency but, first, to increase trade among themselves and to do this, as much as possible, by using our own existing currencies. This should be followed by designing economic and political systems within the framework of the *maqasid al-Shari'ah*, to be discussed next.

NOTES

1. Ahamed Kameel Mydin Meera, *The Islamic Gold Dinar*, pp. 88–9.
2. Consider for instance: Qur'an: 2: 198, as well as Dawud: Book 10, *Kitab al-Manasik wa'l-Hajj, hadith* 1730.
3. Malik, Book 31 (Business Transactions), *hadith* 31.12.21; Muslim, Book 10 (Book of Transactions), *Hadith* 3861. These *ahadith* pertain to the exchange of poorer quality of a commodity with a better quality of the same commodity. Since barter is defined as the 'direct exchange of goods and services without any medium of exchange for settling payment', these *ahadith* actually prohibit barter. Thus, barter is not limited merely to exchanging apples for oranges. It also covers exchanging lower quality of dates for better ones as explained in the *hadith*. On the definition of barter see; Siklos, 'Barter', p. 242.
4. Uwe Vollmer and Ralf Bebenroth, 'Policy Reactions'.
5. Zubair Hasan, 'Ensuring Exchange Rate Stability'.
6. James Macdonald, *A Free Nation Deep in Debt,* pp. 77, 97. See also Manuel Sanchez Martinez, 'Dette publique', p. 37.
7. Muhammad Aslam Haneef and Emad Rafiq Barakat, 'Must Money be Limited to Only Gold and Silver?', *Journal of King Abdulaziz University: Islamic Economics,* 2006, vol. 19, no. 1, pp. 21–34. See also Muhammad Umer Chapra, 'Monetary Management in an Islamic Economy', *Islamic Economic Studies,* 1996, vol. 4, no. 1, p. 5.
8. Z. Hasan, 'Ensuring Exchange Rate Stability', p. 14.
9. Ahamed K. M. Meera, *The Islamic Gold Dinar*, p. 79.
10. James Hookway, 'Malaysians Go for Gold', p. 10.

11. Fernand P. Braudel and F. S. Spooner, 'Currencies, Precious Metals', pp. 474–9.
12. Şevket Pamuk, *A Monetary History*, p. 124. In the Ottoman silk sector I have observed price increases in the range of 100 to 300 per cent in the same period. See Murat Çizakça, 'Price History', pp. 533–51.
13. Fernand P. Braudel and F. S. Spooner, op. cit., pp. 378–486.
14. Ibid., p. 458.
15. Pamuk, *A Monetary History,* p. 122, 136.
16. Alan Pense, 'The Decline and Fall of the Roman Denarius', p. 213. See also Prodromidis, 'Diocletian's Price Edict', p. 578.
17. Pamuk, *A Monetary History,* p. 124.
18. The phenomenon was known as long ago as the fifth century BC.
19. 9: 34.
20. Z. Hasan, 'Ensuring Exchange Rate Stability', p. 18.
21. M. Çizakça, '*Gharar* in Public Finance'.

14. *Maqasid al-Shari'ah* and Islamic banking

ISLAMIC BANKS VIEWED FROM THE PERSPECTIVE OF *MAQASID AL-SHARI'AH*

What does the future hold for Islamic banks? Will they stagnate and become an unimportant component of Islamic capitalism or will they reform themselves with vigour and become predominant?

Whatever direction Islamic finance may take in the future, it must be in conformity with the *maqasid al-Shari'ah*, which has been defined as the 'purpose and wisdom behind the enactment of all or most of the *Shari'ah* rulings'. Laldin has correctly argued that current scholarship is obliged to focus on the way *maqasid al-Shari'ah* is related to modern financial transactions.[1] We will now look at modern Islamic finance from the perspective of *maqasid al-Shari'ah* and try to envisage how it might evolve in the future. A more comprehensive treatment of the *maqasid* will be provided in the final chapter. Readers who are not familiar with this concept might wish to read the first subsection of the last chapter first.

It is well known that the share of Islamic banks within the financial sectors of Islamic countries is generally very low. Indeed, in 1988, the market share of Islamic banks in Egypt, Kuwait and Sudan was, on average, 20 per cent. In Jordan and Qatar it was 10 per cent. More recently, in 2004, assets mobilized by the Islamic banks constituted 10 per cent of the Malaysian system, while deposits with the Islamic banks constituted 10.4 per cent of the market share. But Islamic bonds, *sukuk*, have done much better and constituted in 2003, 19 per cent of the total funds raised in Malaysia.[2] There is also a general consensus that this share must increase. But, as things stand, this is unlikely for three reasons. First, Islamic banks are increasingly being conventionalized. While during the last century only their asset side was dominated by *murabaha*, most recent research has shown that nowadays even the liability side is becoming dominated by commodity *murabaha* or *tawarruq*. There is also an increase in the amount of *wadias*. But these *wadias* are accompanied by *hibas*. Indeed, non-*mudaraba*/total deposits ratios in the liability side of some Malaysian banks have reached 56 per cent (Maybank); 68 per cent (Affin Islamic) and 80 per cent (Public Islamic).[3]

To be sure, these are all *Shari'ah* compliant instruments but they incur high costs and therefore lower profits. They are also benchmarked to the market rate of interest. Consequently, Islamic banks are now facing an increased *Shari'ah* risk. The more Islamic banks converge with conventional banks the greater is the risk that the public will become disenchanted with them. Thus, there is a great need to reform Islamic banks within the framework of *maqasid al-Shari'ah*.

Second, there is a confusion concerning the safety of deposits with Islamic banks. This is due to the fact that while investment accounts are, naturally, not guaranteed by the banks, deposit accounts, though guaranteed, do not effectively protect the real purchasing power of deposits against inflation.

Let us start with the essentials, *al-daruriyah*, of *maqasid al-Shari'ah*.[4] If we start with the notion of *hifz al-aql*, this can be related to the future of Islamic finance as the need to ensure transparency. *Hifz al-aql* means protection of the mind. The most important product of the mind is thought. This is related to modern finance as the need to make sound decisions. The *sine qua non* condition for sound financial thought and decision is transparency, which is the only way to avoid information asymmetry. Obviously, if lack of transparency leads to information asymmetry, sound decision making would become extremely difficult. Moreover, information asymmetry means that knowledge is not shared fairly among the concerned parties. This, in itself, is un-Islamic. Since Islam insists that profits, losses and risks must be shared, we can safely deduce that knowledge too must be shared. Consequently, a situation where one of the contracting parties has all the information and hides it from the other – a clear case of information asymmetry – actually violates one of the most basic principles of Islam. Therefore, the need to provide transparency so as to eliminate information asymmetry for Islamic banks of the future becomes an absolute *shari'ah* requirement dictated by *hifz al-aql*.

Hifz al-din, protection of religion, is also closely related to the future of Islamic finance. The *Shari'ah* imposes three profound conditions on modern finance and protection of religion means that these conditions must be absolutely obeyed in the future. The first one of these conditions is the prohibition of *riba*, the second one is the profit and loss sharing and the third one is to avoid hoarding and the consequent need to inject savings into the circular flow of income, or the economy.

The first condition is straightforward: *riba* must be avoided in both the liability and the asset side of the future Islamic banks. The currently used *shari'ah compliant* methods in the liability side are obviously not satisfactory as they have been adopted from conventional finance and are benchmarked to the prevalent conventional rate of interest. Thus, they violate, if not the letter, certainly the spirit of the *Shari'ah*. As we have seen above, their combined effect is one of conventionalizing Islamic banking, which is simply unacceptable. There is therefore an urgent need to protect the liability side from such violations. Very much the same concerns are also valid for the asset side.

The second condition implies that profit and loss sharing contracts should be preferred and applied whenever possible in both the liability and the asset sides and the third condition implies that savings should be injected into the economy by depositing them into Islamic banks. Currently savings are deposited into the liability side of Islamic banks in three different ways. First, we have the deposit accounts, which do not yield any return and are purely for safe keeping. These deposits are guaranteed by the banks. Second, we have the investment accounts. When a person deposits her savings into this account, she signs a *mudaraba* contract with the bank and is therefore considered an investor. We have already seen how profits are distributed between the holders of these accounts and the bank and how banks take precautions and create special reserves in order to avoid reflecting the losses on these depositor/investors.

The commodity *murabahas* and *tawarruqs*, which provide fixed returns, have no place in future Islamic banking. This is because, as we have seen, these methods have already been justly criticized by AAOIFI and the *Mecca Fiqh Academy*. We can safely assume that the more these methods are utilized, the stronger the critiques will become because although they are cloaked as trade, they are in fact loans benchmarked to the conventional interest rate and we know that they conventionalize Islamic banks. There is no doubt that eventually these methods will have to be discontinued. Let us now, therefore, focus on deposit as well as investment accounts and try to relate them to the *maqasid al-Sharia'ah*.

The three remaining essential *maqasid* conditions, *hifz al-mal*, *hifz al-nefs* and *hifz-al nasl* (respectively protection of property, self and the future generations), give us important clues for the future of these accounts. First of all, Muslims are ordained not to hoard their savings, which means that in the future every Muslim who is capable of having positive savings must either spend them directly or deposit them with an Islamic bank. The three conditions of the *maqasid*: *hifz al-mal*, *hifz al-nefs* and *hifz al-nasl*, actually dictate that they should be deposited. Indeed, whether they wish to protect their wealth, *hifz al-mal*, or to provide, say, for their old age (*hifz al-nefs*), or to provide for their children and grandchildren (*hifz al-nasl*), Muslims are obliged to deposit their savings into an Islamic bank. At the same time, these same *maqasid* conditions, particularly the *hifz al-mal*, also dictate that these savings deposited into an Islamic bank must be perfectly safe. This also means that these deposits must be protected against inflation. This is because, if these accounts are not protected against inflation, their purchasing power would diminish in the long run. Therefore, we reach the conclusion that savings/deposit accounts of Islamic banks should not only be fully guaranteed by the system, but should also be paid an annual inflation premium. The three essential conditions of the *maqasid al-Shari'ah*, together, make it quite clear that deposit protection emerges as a perfectly legitimate concern.[5]

Indeed, to demonstrate, assume that a wealthy individual has established a cash waqf for the welfare of his family as well as orphans. Assume further that he has made a substantial donation for this purpose and deposited his donation with an Islamic bank. The need to protect this deposit becomes a perfectly legitimate concern according to all the three conditions of *maqasid al-Shari'ah*. This prudent waqf founder might wish to split the capital of his waqf into two, with a substantial portion into the deposit account for purely safe keeping and another portion into an investment account for revenue generation. The first part deposited into a deposit/saving account must be fully guaranteed by the Islamic bank, and this guarantee must comprise not merely the principal but also an inflation premium.

Actually, all deposit accounts in all Islamic banks should be provided with a third party guarantee either by the state or by a national deposit *takaful* scheme. The latter demands that the *takaful* companies are thoroughly redesigned to fulfil this need. Assuming that there are no *Shari'ah* impediments, such a task would expand the *takaful* sector momentously. If, however, there are *Shari'ah* impediments, then the only alternative left would be a state guarantee, which would mean that, in fact, the deposits would be guaranteed by taxpayers. If such solid guarantees as well as inflation premiums are provided to the savings/deposit accounts, the dismally small share of Islamic banks would no doubt increase.

Actually, guaranteeing deposits by the Central Bank or another state institution[6] is an extreme measure resorted to during serious financial crisis. For normal day-to-day management of the financial sector, money market operations are utilized. In the conventional system, banks needing short-term liquidity borrow from each other, or ultimately from the central banks, at a fluctuating interbank borrowing rate. We have seen in Chapter 9 how the Malaysian Central Bank utilizes *commodity murabahas* and *tawarruqs* to inject money to banks needing liquidity (or to borrow from those with excess liquidity). The Malaysian system was established in 1993 and became the first ever Islamic Interbank Money Market. This was followed by Bahrain, where the Liquidity Management Center was established in 2002.

Most recently, Islamic banks in Pakistan finalized two interbank trading agreements – the so-called *interbank musharaka* and *interbank wakala,* in a move to develop a *Shari'ah* compliant interbank market. The former is a short-term arrangement where the banks are invited to invest in a special pool of assets on a pre-agreed profit sharing ratio agreed upon among the partners. The *interbank wakala*, on the other hand, is an investment management contract where the investor agrees to provide the Islamic bank with funds to invest in different assets. The Islamic bank would be, in effect, the investor's agent or *wakeel* and will be paid a fee for its services, while the investor receives the returns.

Probably in response to the criticism of the *commodity murabaha* and the *tawarruqs* by the AAOIFI and the Mecca Fiqh Academy, Dr Zeti Akhtar Aziz, the Governor of the Central Bank of Malaysia, is now reported to be pushing for the development of a broader range of Islamic financial market instruments including ones with equity ownership features.[7] In this context, the modernized versions of the definitively *riba*-free historical fixed return instruments such as the European PFPD or the Ottoman *esham* as well as the more recent Turkish Revenue Participation Shares can assume new roles and importance. For these instruments explained above would not only provide *riba*-free fixed or variable returns to the rising middle classes but also interbank money market facilities. The more diversified are such instruments, the more leeway the central banks would have to control the money supply. Such diversification would also facilitate Islamic banks to fulfil their responsibilities towards their depositor/investors.

If the liability side of future Islamic banks is to be dominated by fully protected and inflation adjusted savings/deposit accounts and high risk/high return investment accounts, we can expect that the asset side should also reflect this. Consequently, the fixed return yielding *murabaha* contracts in the asset side will probably continue to be important. For the inflation premium mentioned above will probably be paid by these contracts. This would be in harmony with the three essential conditions, *hifz al-mal*, *hifz al-nefs* and *hifz al-nasl* of *maqasid al-Shari'ah*. But we have to make absolutely clear that the overwhelmingly dominant position of *murabaha* contracts observed currently in the asset side violates one of the most important principles dictated by *hifz al-din*, profit and loss sharing. It is therefore absolutely necessary to increase the share of profit/loss sharing contracts in the asset side. This means a substantial increase in the number and volume of *mudaraba*/*musharaka* contracts.

INCREASING THE SHARE OF THE PLS ACCOUNTS: SOME PROPOSALS

There are a number of ways this goal might be achieved. Consider first, resorting to a selective tax policy. In order to encourage Islamic banks to use more *mudaraba* and *musharaka* in the asset side, governments may systematically reduce tax rates with respect to risk. Put differently, while the least risky *murabaha* transactions (and its derivatives) can be taxed fully, lower tax rates can be imposed on *musharaka* financing with higher risks. Any *mudaraba* transaction, the riskiest of all, can be made completely tax exempt.[8] It will be argued here that if such a selective tax policy is applied, Islamic banks would also try hard to set up venture capital windows and begin to apply *mudaraba* financing. Furthermore, such non-bank institutions as venture capital companies, unit trust funds and the like, which are set up to practise equity finance to start with, should also be taxed favourably or be completely tax exempt to the extent that their transactions approach to *musharaka/mudaraba* financing respectively. Since equity finance in general, and venture capital or *mudaraba* companies more specifically, are incubators in the sense that they create entrepreneurial companies, any tax revenue the state loses by applying the selective tax policies suggested above would be more than compensated by taxing the newly created entrepreneurial companies. It goes without saying that granting a tax holiday to these entrepreneurial companies during the first few years of their existence should also be considered seriously.

Profit distribution rules can also be utilized to encourage Islamic banks to utilize *mudaraba/musharaka* investments. As it is well known, most Islamic banks apply a ratio of 20/80 to distribute their profits. Put differently, they take in 20 per cent of the profits and distribute the remainder to the investment account holders. It will be proposed here that they should continue to apply the same ratios to the *murabaha* investments but should be given complete freedom as to how to distribute the profits obtained from *mudaraba/musharaka* investments. The importance of this proposal should be obvious if we note that while *mudaraba/musharaka* investments can be quite risky, they can also generate huge profits. Islamic banks should not be obliged to distribute 80 per cent of these profits, they should be permitted to keep as much of the profits of such investments as they wish as a reward for the risks they have taken. Presently, most central banks do not impose any conditions on Islamic banks on how to distribute their profits. But if such conditions are to be imposed in the future, it is to be hoped that this proposal will be taken into consideration.

Another reason why *mudaraba/musharaka* investments are avoided by Islamic banks is the so-called 'mismatch of funds' problem. This one refers to the fact that while savers invest/deposit their savings with Islamic banks for the short term, *mudaraba/musharaka* investments are usually long-term commitments. As we have seen in Chapter 9, Islamic banks have already recognized this problem and taken safety measures by introducing reserves. These are the profit equalization reserve, the investment risk reserve and the *mudarìb* fee. Having already introduced these reserves, Islamic banks cannot introduce further reserves. This is because each deduction made for a reserve is actually deducted from the depositor's profit share and constitutes a discouragement for future deposits. Attracting long-term funds to the liability side, therefore, assumes great importance. It is at this juncture that cash waqfs, once again, come into the picture.

Cash waqf deposits are long-term deposits *par excellence*. Consequently, we can argue that the greater the amount of cash waqf deposits in the liability side, the less need there will be to create reserves for the potential 'mismatch of funds' problem and the greater will be the profit shares that can be paid back to the depositors, which of course would in return encourage further deposits in the future. In short, a virtuous cycle would emerge. But to attract cash waqf funds to Islamic banks is not a simple problem. To start with, the public needs to be educated about the virtues of establishing cash waqfs. At the same time, the prevalent waqf laws need to be reformed. This is particularly so for Malaysia, where existing laws of most states render waqf establishment practically impossible by insisting that only a highly centralized *Majlis* can become the trustee for all waqfs.[9] Consequently, potential philanthropists who wish to establish waqfs, and run them personally, are strongly discouraged from doing so.

Still another problem pertains to management. Indeed, *mudaraba/musharaka* investments demand a totally different management approach than ordinary banking. Whereas the former involves a style of management that requires a very personal and often hands-on approach, for the latter a hands-off approach would suffice. Indeed, conventional bankers as well as Islamic bankers with conventional banking background are trained to detach themselves from the businesses of the entrepreneurs they finance. By contrast, *mudaraba/musharaka* investments demand a constant cooperation and support for the entrepreneur. Islamic bankers with a conventional mindset are simply not prepared for this sort of management.

One way out of this dilemma might be to recognize that we need two different institutions for two different needs. Short-term liquidity needs of trade and finance might be left to Islamic banks utilizing primarily various forms of *murabahas* and the like, while long-term growth needs might be left to specialized institutions of long-term finance, like the venture capital windows of Islamic banks, Islamic investment banks, Islamic unit trust funds, *mudaraba* companies or Islamic venture capital.[10] For the latter, obviously, specially trained managers are needed. At this point, should special institutions be created for training for such investment, Dr Ahmed al-Naggar's warning must be once again remembered: students admitted to these institutions should not have conventional banking background!

All of the above are proposals made by the present author. Let us now look at the proposals for securing financial stability made by the Task Force on Islamic Finance, in their April 2010 meeting. Their proposals are grouped together into so-called 'building blocks'.

The first building block refers to the establishment of comprehensive 'cross-sectoral prudential standards'. For this purpose the IFSB has issued a whole spectrum of prudential and supervisory standards which, in the Task Force's own words, 'constitute the equivalent of Basel II in Islamic finance'.[11] Thus, once again, conventional standards are taken as a standard.

The second building block aims at enhancing financial resilience and stability by developing a robust national and international liquidity infrastructure, which encompasses the potential for monetary policy and money market operations. In this context central banks are expected to provide the lender of last resort (LOLR) function and to provide liquidity to the market. To address this question, it is stated that the IFSB has established a High Level Taskforce on Liquidity Management.[12]

The third building block relates to the strengthening of the financial safety net mechanism as well as deposit insurance compatible with the *Shari'ah*. It is stated that deposit insurance, prudential supervision and the LOLR function all constitute part and parcel of the financial safety net arrangements. The Task Force thus confirms the importance of protecting the deposits mentioned at the beginning of this chapter but finds its actual implementation challenging. More specifically, according to the Task Force, deposit protection for the current/deposit account holders of Islamic banks does not constitute a problem, which can be addressed by the *takaful* companies. It is the depositor protection of the profit and loss sharing accounts that the Task Force finds difficult to address. Theoretically, of course, no such protection should be needed as the holders of such investment accounts are supposed to be considered as investors, not depositors to start with. But in reality, these 'investors' demand protection for their investments. The Task Force envisages problems in determining the fair value of these accounts that should be insured, the evaluation of the riskiness of the underlying assets, etc.

The fourth building block involves the development of a reliable crisis management framework such as bank insolvency laws. To offer this framework in a *Shari'ah* compliant manner is considered to be particularly challenging.

The fifth building block consists of accounting, auditing and disclosure standards for Islamic financial institutions.

The sixth building block refers to the development of the macro-prudential surveillance framework and financial stability analysis.

The seventh building block refers to the all-important problem already mentioned above, establishment of Islamic rating agencies. It is implied here that this function currently fulfilled by the IFSB and AAOIFI should be taken over by private independent agencies.

Finally, the eighth building block emphasizes the importance of developing human capital for the Islamic finance industry, which can function across multiple jurisdictions. Above all, it is recommended that future Islamic finance persons should recognize the theoretical merits of Islamic finance as espoused by the *Shari'ah*.

All in all, the Task Force has touched upon important points regarding, particularly, the Islamic banks and their resilience vis-à-vis possible crises of the future. But to what extent do these banks represent the future of Islamic finance?

NOTES

1. Laldin, *Fundamentals and Practices*, pp. 71, 77.
2. See on this Aziz, 'Developing Islamic Banks and Capital Market', pp. 168–9.
3. Ahmad, Bakar and Isa, *Practices and Issues of Risk Management*.
4. Other aspects of the *maqasid*, the complimentary, *al-hajiyah*, and embellishments, *al-tahsiniyah*, will not be considered here.
5. This is indirectly confirmed by Kahf, who has argued that 'a *Shari'ah* compatible fixed-return financial instrument is needed in an Islamic economy'. See his 'The Use of Assets *Ijara* Bonds', p. 75.
6. Such as the Turkish *Tasarruf Mevduatı Sigorta Fonu* (Savings Accounts' Insurance Fund). Although this fund was established in 1983, savings accounts in Turkey have been under state protection ever since 1933. Currently all deposits under TL50 000 (US$33 780) are under 100 per cent protection of the fund. When during the 2001 crisis some banks went bankrupt, the fund fulfilled its obligation. In return, it was given the power to confiscate assets of the failed banks. It has paid so far US$9 641 000 000 to the treasury.
7. Jacobs, 'Loughing All the Way to the Bank'.
8. Çizakça, *Türk Finans Kesiminde Sorunlar*, pp. 178–9.
9. On the problems of the prevalent waqf system in Malaysia, see Çizakça, 'The British Legislation', passim.
10. This idea is supported by Hasan. See his 'Mudaraba as a Mode of Finance', p. 50, where he suggests: '*inter alia* establishment of separate investment banks for providing long term finance to industry, leaving the business of meeting the short duration credit needs of trade and commerce to the conventional sort of Islamic banks'. He also proposes 'the launching of special programs to develop entrepreneurship among both the seekers and providers of credit for business on Islamic lines'.
11. For a complete list of these standards and their comparison with those of the Basel Committee on Banking Supervision, see Task Force on Islamic Finance, *Islamic Finance and Global Financial,* appendix I and II. It is claimed that while these Western standards are borrowed, specificities of Islamic financial firms, their risks and *Shari'ah* compliance are also taken into account. One wonders here if *Shari'ah* compliance is given priority over the conventional standards.
12. Task Force on Islamic Finance, *Islamic Finance and Global Financial,* p. 43.

15. Venture capital

I am of the opinion that venture capital is going to be the rising star of Islamic finance. This is because venture capital (VC) is a *Shari'ah* based instrument and though risky, embodies huge profit potential. In this chapter, we will discuss the remarkable Islamicity of this Silicon Valley instrument and its incorporation into the Islamic capitalism of the future.

As it is well known, venture capital is a highly dynamic financial system that has successfully introduced the most advanced technology, provided tens of thousands of new jobs and created massive export potential, first for the American economy, and now increasingly, for Europe[1] and India.[2]

The American venture capital industry has invested a total of US$7 343 238 700 in 1995. This amount shot up to more than US$100 billion in 2000 and was then reduced to US$18 billion in 2009 due to the latest crisis. Numbers of deals were 1863 in 1995, which increased to 7979 in 2000 and reached 2916 in 2009.[3] In Malaysia, by contrast, the total committed funds under management as at 31 December 2007 was RM3.3 billion.[4] But this may increase rapidly because over the next five years American VC funds plan to increase their commitments in emerging markets. Asia is expected to receive 70 per cent of VC investments in these markets. Malaysian ICM believes that Islamic venture capital will be the distinguishing factor that differentiates Malaysia from other emerging markets.[5]

Let us now describe the classical venture capital industry as it emerged in the mid twentieth-century USA and then discuss its Islamicity. A few hard facts should substantiate this argument: after the Second World War a French officer, General Doriot, who was teaching at Harvard, established in 1946 the *American Research and Development Co*. This was the very first venture capital company. It invested US$70 000 in 1957 for 77 per cent of the common stock of a new company, the DEC, created by four MIT students. By 1968, when the DEC went public, this investment was worth US$355 million. So, from US$70 000 to US$355 million in 11 years – this is a return of 500 times on the investment and an annualized rate of return of 101 per cent.

In 1975, Arthur Rock, a famous venture capitalist, invested US$1.5 million in a start-up company, called Apple Computer. In 1978, only three years later, that investment was valued at US$100 million.

Fed Ex constitutes another dramatic story. When financing the Fed Ex, venture capitalists lost US$1 million per month for 29 consecutive months.

But when the Fed Ex went public, the US$25 million that the venture capitalists had invested was worth US$1.2 billion.

The famous VC Company Kleiner & Perkins invested US$7 million during the period 1973–80. Four years later this investment was worth US$218 million.

So, this is what venture capital is all about: a high risk–high gain investment. It is also defined as large probability of a small loss combined with small probability of a fantastic gain. Indeed, a survey that covered 383 American portfolio companies (i.e., entrepreneurs financed by venture capital) revealed that between 1969 and 1985 just 6.8 per cent of these firms yielded returns of ten times or more on the invested capital. More than 60 per cent of all these investments either lost money or failed to exceed savings account rates of return.[6]

Venture capital gives birth to new companies with all the macroeconomic implications. A survey based on 235 venture-capital-backed companies revealed that in the early years of the industry, these companies, on average, were only 1.9 years old; but they had created, from 1985 to 1989, 36 000 new jobs. Their total exports reached US$786 million; they spent about the same amount on research and development and they paid US$170 million in corporate taxes.

In the 1990s, the job creation capability of the venture capital industry increased greatly. In 2005, companies that were once backed by venture capitalists accounted for 17 per cent of America's GNP. In the year 1995, 1887 venture deals were signed and US$7 313 402 700 were invested. In 2010, these figures had reached 3447 and 23 262 929 500 respectively.[7]

Moreover, venture capital companies fill a great vacuum in the world of finance. This vacuum is known as the MacMillan gap and refers to the conventional banking system's failure to finance entrepreneurs. Small family enterprises can obtain finance from the family or friends. Large firms can obtain finance from the conventional banking sector. But entrepreneurs, whose financial needs are too big for family and who, at the same time, cannot meet conventional banks' stringent lending criteria, simply cannot obtain capital.

Indeed, to finance an entrepreneur, conventional banks first demand hefty collateral. Second, in the USA, unless a company has sales of about US$15 million, assets of US$10 million and a good profit history, it cannot get loans from the banking system. Yet, less than 2 per cent of the more than five million companies in the USA have more than US$10 million in revenues. So the young entrepreneurial companies starve for funds. In short, the conventional banking system is entrepreneur unfriendly. Venture capital enters into this void and finances young entrepreneurs without collateral and other conditions imposed by the conventional banking system. We can even argue that the conventional system would have normally killed entrepreneurship in the West. If despite these impediments entrepreneurship still flourishes, particularly in the USA, this is in large part thanks to venture capital.

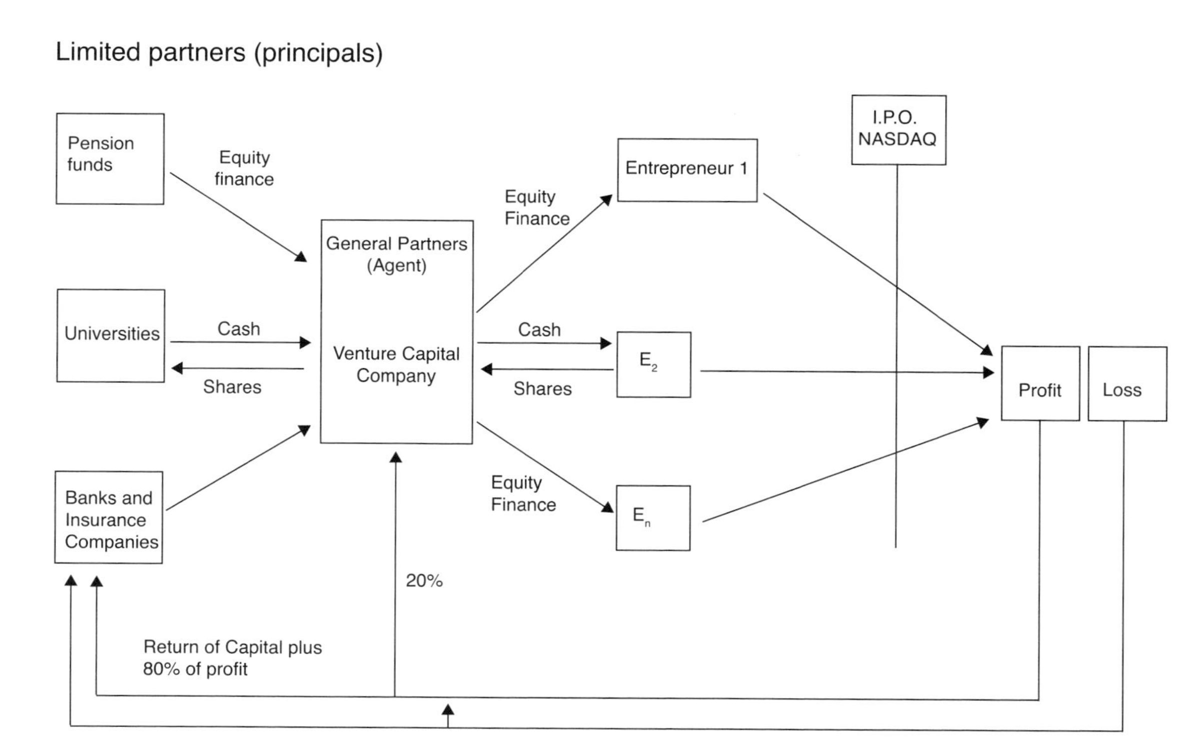

Figure 15.1 Classical venture capital (USA)

How does venture capital do this? To answer this question we need to study the structure of the classical American venture capital sector, which is depicted in Figure 15.1.

A US venture capital company functions as a partnership, that is, a partnership of limited and general partners.

It is the limited partners who provide capital in the form of equity finance, that is, buying the shares of the venture capital company. There are primarily five groups of limited partners: pension funds, university endowments, banks, insurance companies and rich individuals. They invest a small part of their investment portfolio in venture capital companies and expect an annual return of 25–35 per cent. Venture capitalists try to fulfil these goals by choosing the right entrepreneur, in the right industry, that is, a growth industry. These limited partners are passive partners not involved in day-to-day management. The venture capital company acts as their agent. Equity finance is the usual method of finance applied. This means that the limited partners provide finance to a venture capital company by purchasing its shares.

Those who manage the venture capital company are known as general partners. These general partners are active partners and act as agents for the limited partners. Limited partners supply the funds and are promised 75–80 per cent of the realized gains in return. The venture capital company gets 20–25 per cent of the profits. After the funds are thus collected, the venture capital company must invest. This brings us to the asset side.

On the asset side also equity finance prevails. Indeed, a classical US venture capital company provides primarily equity finance to young entrepreneurs. This is done as follows: an entrepreneur, usually a young engineer with a very promising, feasible and potentially lucrative project, applies to the VC company. First, a ruthless process of selection, due diligence, is applied. Highland Capital Partners receives about 10 000 business plans a year and conducts about 1000 meetings. This is followed by 400 company visits. The company ends up making 10–20 investments a year.

If his application is accepted, the entrepreneur is asked to form an incorporated joint-stock company. This is a company established by an unknown entrepreneur. Normally, no-one would be interested in the shares of this company. Only the VC company would be interested in these shares and therefore the share prices would be very low. It is these cheap shares that the VC company buys. The VC company pays the cash to the entrepreneur that he needs and, in return, obtains his shares.

How much of the shares are transferred to the venture capital company is decided as a result of bargaining between the venture capital company and the entrepreneur. Generally, the riskier the enterprise, the greater is the number of shares given to the venture capitalist. This is equity finance and a partnership is born.

The essence of venture capital is to enable the entrepreneur to succeed. When this is achieved, this success is reflected in share values. The venture capital company earns its profits by selling these shares. In a nutshell, the venture capitalist buys the entrepreneur's shares cheaply, nurtures him for a short period of time, then sees to it that he succeeds and the shares he holds gain in value. The venture capitalist then sells these shares with huge gains, often with the help of an investment banker.

Selling the shares occurs at the so-called over-the-counter markets. The best known over-the-counter market is *NASDAQ*.[8] The process of selling the shares of an unknown company for the first time is known as initial public offering (IPO).

Alternatively, the venture capitalist would be equally happy if the entrepreneurial company he has financed is bought by a giant conglomerate. This is known as merger and acquisition (M&A). Whether IPO or M&A, the goal of the venture capitalist is to exit from the partnership with the entrepreneur by selling the shares he holds with great profit. This is because, normally, the venture capitalist is not in the business of managing a company forever but he is rather in the business of picking an otherwise unknown winner, making him succeed and then sell the shares he possesses, and then exit. Thus a venture capital company is like a fertile mother who gives birth to many successful infants. The profits obtained in this process are then shared between the venture capitalist and the limited partners at 20/80 or 25/75 ratio respectively.

But how can we claim that a system so closely identified with Californian Silicon Valley is actually Islamic? This is best explained by focusing on the *modus operandi* of a hypothetical Islamic venture capital.

It is my contention that the classical multiple *mudaraba* (liability and asset sides) constitutes the basic underlying structure of the Islamic venture capital.

ISLAMIC VENTURE CAPITAL

The Liability Side

Basically four participants (limited partners) are envisaged for an Islamic venture capital company:

1. *Tabung Haji*;
2. private investors or corporations;
3. pension funds;
4. Islamic banks;
5. waqfs, particularly university endowments.

The first four are obvious enough, but waqfs and university endowments are of special interest. The rise of Google from a Stanford University PhD research project to a multibillion dollar giant provides an excellent example of how waqfs may be involved in venture capital. While Larry Page and Sergey Brin, the founders of Google, were students at Stanford, the university endowment was one of the earliest providers of capital to the infant company. When Google went public, Stanford University gained US$200 million in stocks.[9] Based upon this example we conclude that waqfs and particularly university endowments are best suited to become major venture capitalists in the Islamic world as well. This is simply because university foundations have the great advantage of becoming aware, before everybody else, of the potential of research being conducted in their own laboratories.

These five groups provide equity capital to the Islamic venture capital company by purchasing its shares. Such equity financing would be tantamount to a *mudaraba* arrangement. This is because the bulk of the pecuniary loss of the venture capital company would be shouldered by the financiers (limited partners). It is also possible to extend the private investors category so as to include the general public. It is indeed possible for the general public to participate in venture capital activities by purchasing *muqarada/mudaraba* bonds.

This creates the difficult problem of the investing public losing their capital. This problem has been solved in Jordan by issuing these *muqarada* bonds.[10] These bonds can be issued by venture capital companies and allow the public to invest in a project in exactly the amount that they wish to. They are also provided with third party, in this case the state, guarantee. The guarantee provided by the state opens the way for the participation of the masses to Islamic venture capital. Thus, members of the public may now buy *mudaraba/muqarada* bonds to be redeemed at a certain time in the future.[11] Their initial investment would be guaranteed by the state and if at the time of redemption a profit has been generated, the participant would obtain his/her share pro rata. The bond holder does not suffer any loss of his capital due to the state guarantee.[12] Third party (government) guarantee is also practised in Malaysia.[13]

At this point, we need to elaborate on the question of third party guarantee. The AAOIFI approved of third party guarantee with its *Shari'ah* standards no. 17 on the condition that the issuer of the certificates does not accept any liability to compensate the owner of the certificates nor that he guarantees a percentage of profit. It is, however, permitted for an independent third party to provide a guarantee free of charge. But this guarantee must not be linked in any manner to the *mudaraba* or the *muqarada* contract.[14] Despite the AAOIFI approval, the subject of guarantees is still not free of controversy.[15] This is because the question of the fairness of state-financed third party guarantee arises. Why, indeed, should tax-payers finance losses of investors? It will be argued here that the average tax-payer benefits substantially from *mudaraba/*

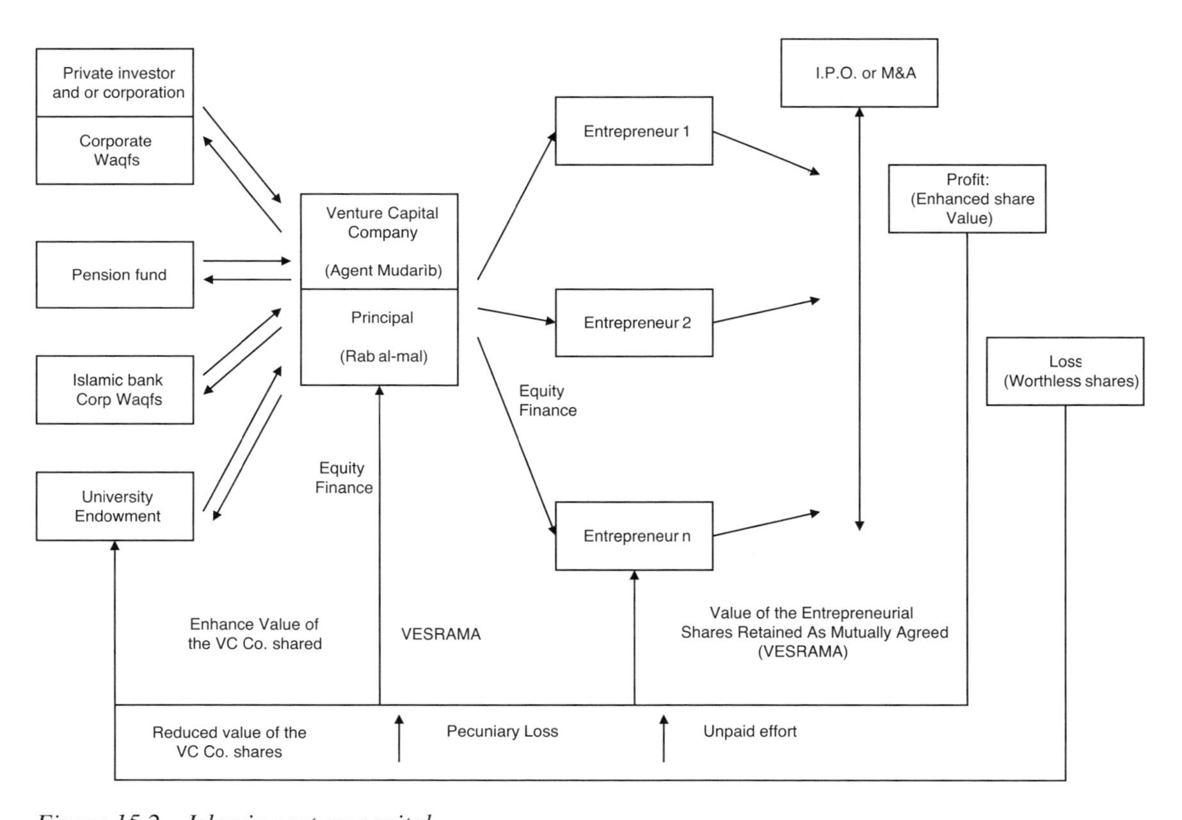

Figure 15.2 Islamic venture capital

musharaka activities. These benefits accrue from the high technology to be developed by the *mudaraba/musharaka* financed entrepreneurs, the employment generated by the entrepreneurial companies and the taxes to be paid by these companies themselves as well as by their shareholders and employees. It is my contention that these benefits would be well above the losses that may accrue to tax-payers as a result of providing third party guarantee. Moreover, subject to the conditions described above by AAOIFI, third party guarantee does not violate the *Shari'ah*.

The Asset Side

The asset side also exhibits characteristics of a classical multiple *mudaraba* partnership. This is because the entire capital is provided by the principal (VC company) and the Islamic rule of profit and loss sharing is applied. The Islamic rule is applied because profit is shared according to mutual agreement (partners, i.e., venture capital company and each of the entrepreneurs, decide mutually how many shares the VC company should obtain in return for finance) and it is the actual number of shares held between the partners which determine how the profit will be shared.

Loss is not shared: it accrues entirely to the VC company in the form of worthless shares. This is again in accordance with the Islamic rule that 'loss follows capital'. Since the entire capital was provided, when the VC company bought the entrepreneur's shares, if the entrepreneur ends up with a loss, entire pecuniary loss accrues to the VC company. However, the venture capital company protects itself by forming a portfolio of entrepreneurs financed. Consequently, the loss that an entrepreneur makes would be compensated by the gain of the other. The entrepreneur's loss, on the other hand, is in the form of unpaid effort. This is, once again, identical to the classical Islamic *mudaraba*.

In reality, venture capital partnerships only rarely lose money. Indeed, American experience has shown that these companies enjoy between 11 and 27 per cent compound annual rates of return over the long run.[16] But in exceptional circumstances, like the present crisis, losses can be inevitable. The Draper, Fisher, Jurvetson Fund, for instance, which raised US$640 million in 2000, has yielded a –2 per cent return as of 30 September 2009.[17] But on the upside, venture capital partners agree to return all of the investors' capital before sharing the upside.

Even when we accept that most of the entrepreneurs will at best return only the original investment and at worst be total losses, it has been observed that only 10–20 per cent of the entrepreneurs funded need to be real winners to achieve the targeted return rate of 25 per cent to 30 per cent.[18] Consequently, a depletion of the limited partners' capital is extremely unlikely.

Let us now sum up the argument about the Islamicity of venture capital. The system is not *Shari'ah* compliant but *Shari'ah* based. This is for the following reasons:

1. Venture capital is identical to *mudaraba*. *Mudaraba* was part of the Prophet's *sunnah*.
2. Unlike a loan or a credit transaction, there is neither interest nor collateral in a venture capital transaction. Finance is simply provided in return for shares. This is equity finance.
3. Since the entire system is based upon equity finance, there are no loans and where there is no loan, there is definitively no *riba*. If a third party guarantee is provided in order to encourage the public, only the principal is guaranteed by the state.
4. Venture capital is a profit-and-loss-sharing system. Profit-and-loss sharing takes place in accordance with Islamic rules. Profit in a venture capital company is shared according to mutual agreement. This mutual agreement is expressed in the amount of shares the venture capital company obtains from the entrepreneur. Loss goes entirely to the venture capitalist financier. This is without any doubt *mudaraba*.
5. A venture capital company is established just like a classical Islamic *shirkat*, that is, as a partnership for limited duration, usually ten years.
6. Risks are truly shared and the venture capitalist does not demand collateral from the entrepreneur.

Since Islamic law does not impose any restriction on the number of agents financed by the principal, an Islamic venture capital company can finance a multitude of entrepreneurs. Not only is this desirable for enhancing entrepreneurship, it is also desirable for risk diversification purposes. But each one of these entrepreneurs must be financed through equity financing, that is, swapping cash for shares.

As a result, the principal, that is, the VC company, ends up having collected the shares of several entrepreneurial companies. Herein lies the great profit potential of VC companies. Every VC company hopes that the shares it has collected cheaply from the entrepreneurs will gain in value as the entrepreneur succeeds.

The Islamic venture capital company would generate profits from the difference in the share prices, that is, by selling the cheaply acquired shares expensively, hopefully with a huge margin. For this, two conditions must be fulfilled:

1. The entrepreneur selected must succeed. This increases the value of his shares.
2. The venture capital company must be able to sell the now valuable entrepreneurial shares in its possession to the public.

In short, the VC company makes profit when it sells its shares at the over-the-counter market. These profits are shared with the entrepreneur as previously mutually agreed, that is, both partners can sell their shares and would enjoy profits according to the number of shares retained. I call this VESRAMA: Value of the Entrepreneurial Shares Retained as Mutually Agreed. Thus both partners, the VC company and the entrepreneur, enjoy VESRAMA. Or put differently, profits are in the form of VESRAMA.

As for the original principals, that is, the limited partners, they also enjoy the enhanced value of shares. But these shares are not VESRAMA. Limited partners enjoy the enhanced value of the VC company's shares itself. The values of these shares are enhanced in proportion to the VESRAMA in the portfolio of the venture capital company.

If the entrepreneur fails, loss would be encountered. This loss would be in the form of worthless shares. Both the VC company and the entrepreneur would end up possessing worthless shares. In this case, as with the classical *mudaraba*, the agent/entrepreneur would end up incurring no pecuniary loss. His loss would be in the form of unpaid effort. This is because the entrepreneur had not invested any capital of his own to start with. The entire pecuniary loss would accrue to the VC company. Failure would reduce the value of the VC company as well, which, in turn, would be reflected on the limited partners (principals).

The entrepreneur's failure would result in all parties (entrepreneur himself, the venture capital company, the principals) holding worthless shares. This is precisely why the whole set-up is Islamic, because profits as well as losses are shared among all the parties concerned. Losses may take different forms but each partner loses. The only exception is the members of the general public holding *muqarada* bonds guaranteed by the state. In case of loss, these bond holders do not obtain any profit share.

Venture capital companies form a portfolio of entrepreneurs on the asset side, which diversifies the entrepreneurial risks substantially. In the long run, this seems to have worked: indeed, as already mentioned, US VC companies enjoy between 11 and 27 per cent annual rate of returns over the long run.

Finally, I would like to respond to the argument that *mudaraba/musharaka* is not equity.[19] First of all, what is equity? Equity is defined as 'shares in a corporation that pays the holder some of its profits. It is the value of what the stockholders own and have risked in the business, which is known as stockholders' equity.'[20]

The argument that 'equity is divisible but *mudaraba/musharaka* is not, therefore they are not the same' is not acceptable, because *Shari'ah* does not prohibit shares. This is confirmed by the fact that Muslims have established partnerships for centuries with shares. There are hundreds of examples of such partnerships.[21]

Moreover, beginning from 1775 onwards the bulk of the Ottoman state finance was based upon shares known as *esham*. There is also a 1905 *fatwa* permitting Muslims even to establish waqfs with shares.[22]

So, if Muslims were able to establish business partnerships with shares, finance their state with shares, establish waqfs with shares and do all this from the sixteenth to the twentieth centuries, why can't they do so now? Thus, we conclude, since shares have been permitted and used for centuries, this constitutes established custom, *'urf*, and there is no reason why a modern *musharaka/mudaraba* should not be set up with equity, shares.

Moreover, it has also been argued that equity is liquid but *musharaka/mudaraba* is not. The *Mecelle* clearly states that in case one of the partners dies, a *musharaka* (*inan* partnership) with more than two partners continues and is not dissolved. But the share of the deceased partner can be converted to cash and be paid to his descendents.[23] Thus, there is no legal impediment to the liquidity of a *musharaka*. It is certainly permitted to convert a *musharaka* share to cash, providing the partners agree to do so and clearly state this in the initial contract.

It has been argued further that equity exists in perpetuity but *musharaka* has a time limit. This is also an oversimplification and applies only to *musharaka*s with two partners. But *inan/musharaka* partnerships with more than two partners can perpetuate. Besides, Shafi'i and Maliki schools refuse to restrict *mudaraba* to a fixed time.[24]

Another reason why equity finance perpetuates is due to the judicial personality of a corporation. But it has been argued that judicial personality is not recognized in Islam. This is not correct: *Shari'ah* does not prohibit judicial personality either and has recognized it for centuries in waqfs and *bayt al-mal*. Therefore 'it is totally untrue that the Islamic legal system does not recognize the concept of the juristic person'.[25]

Finally, it has been argued that 'profit sharing in equity is not necessarily equal but under *musharaka* it has to be equal'. This is also simply untrue! The Hanefi school insists that profits in all partnership forms must be divided according to mutual agreement. If the partners decide to divide the profit unequally, they certainly can. All other *madhabs* rule that profit division must be made according to the capital contribution. So if partners contribute to the venture with unequal amounts of capital, they would divide profits also unequally. The only exception to these rules is the *mufawada* partnership. This is the only partnership where everything, including the profit, must be shared equally.

As made clear above, venture capital cannot exist without joint-stock companies. This is because the entrepreneur is asked to form a joint-stock company and the venture capitalist purchases the shares of this company. The entrepreneur then uses this money to bring his invention to the market. Thus, joint-stock companies form a *conditio sine qua non* for venture capital. Consequently, it is inevitable that while discussing the Islamicity of venture capital we should also be discussing the Islamicity of joint-stock companies as well.

The modern joint-stock company constitutes a synthesis of the classical *mudarabah* and the *sharikat al-inan*. All the shareholders are unequal partners, each having contributed to the partnership with varying amounts of capital. These shareholders are considered as the *rab al-mal*. However, shareholders who also act as directors are like *mudarìbs* by virtue of their responsibility for the management of the company. They are in fact agents through whom the company acts. Such directors are therefore considered as both *rab al-mal* and *mudarìbs*.[26]

Contemporary jurists have approved the joint-stock company based on analogy (*qiyas*) and public interest (*masalih mursalah*) on the condition that capitals as well as objectives of such companies do not contradict the Islamic law. Obviously, it is required that such a company should not be involved in transactions involving the prohibited goods and activities. It is also required that the company in question should not borrow money on interest nor keep its surplus in an interest-bearing account. This boils down to the requirement that all banking activities should be limited to Islamic banks or windows. To ensure this, a process called *stock-screening* is required. In addition, equality, pertaining to equal rights in the event of bankruptcy, is encouraged.

In an effort to increase the number of *Shari'ah* compliant joint-stock companies traded in the stock exchange, the *Securities Commission of Malaysia* has introduced the concept of partial compliance. Thus, companies are now classified as 5 per cent, 10 per cent, 25 per cent, etc., *Shari'ah* compliant. It is envisaged that such classification will not only provide transparency to the prospective investors but also encourage joint-stock companies to be fully *Shari'ah* compliant.

It has been recommended that stock exchanges should be reformed such that share prices reflect real values and not speculative motives.[27] But as long as information asymmetries exist, outside investors have no choice but to make the best estimate. Investing in stocks is not an exact science and this cannot be any different in an Islamic stock market.

Thus we conclude that *mudaraba/musharaka* financing is identical to equity finance as well as to venture capital.[28] We reach this conclusion not only because of the structural similarities between these, but because other aspects of venture capital, such as joint-stock companies and stock exchanges, also do not violate any Islamic law.

INTRODUCING VENTURE CAPITAL TO ISLAMIC COUNTRIES

Having concluded that venture capital is identical to the traditional Islamic modes of finance, we may now discuss the actual introduction of venture capital to Islamic countries. This is a timely discussion in view of the fact that the classic US venture capital industry is in the midst of a great transformation. Latest research has revealed that about 50 per cent of the US venture capital firms intend to shift their investments to Asia. It is imperative for the future development of Islamic capitalism that Muslim countries and entrepreneurs should fully participate in this process.[29]

Probably the very first attempt to introduce venture capital to an Islamic country, Turkey, was made by the present author who co-authored a book on this specific topic together with Tansu Çiller. Although Çiller, shortly after the publication of this book, became the Prime Minister, a viable venture capital sector could not be established in Turkey.[30]

An in-depth account of the failure cannot be expounded here and must form the subject of a special research. Suffice it to say that when, despite the warnings of the present author, the *Turkish Capital Market Board* in 1993 insisted that the initial capital of a venture capital company should not be less than TL100 billion (US$9.1 million) and the registered capital TL300 billion (US$27.3 million), it effectively prevented the emergence of a venture capital sector in Turkey – a capital-scarce country, where the prevailing rate of interest (treasury bill auctions) ranged from 63 per cent to 93 per cent.[31] To the extent that these high interest rates reflect the opportunity cost of capital, insisting on such demanding amounts of initial and registered capital was a huge mistake. This mistake was also shared by the Prime Minister Çiller, who though well aware of the importance of venture capital, did not interfere. When the present author tried to contact and warn her, she was not available.

We will now focus on Malaysia, which has identified the establishment of a viable Islamic venture capital sector as a national goal and considers venture capital as another asset class in the country's broad range of Islamic products.

To achieve this goal, Malaysian state allocated RM1.6 billion (US$500 million) for venture capital under the Ninth Malaysia Plan (2006–10). This constitutes a hefty two-fold increase from the previous plan.[32] In 2009, the overall size of the Malaysian venture capital industry stood at RM4.5 to RM5 billion. Malaysian pension funds' contribution to this remains quite limited and constitutes merely 5 per cent.[33]

The state also established the *Malaysian Venture Capital Development Council* in January 2005. The *raison d'être* of this council is to see to it that all the prevailing rules and regulations in the Malaysian finance industry are venture capital friendly. The MVCDC is expected to facilitate the development of the venture capital industry by coordinating government initiatives. The government has also introduced various tax incentives in addition to liberalizing equity ownership for venture capital corporations. For instance, fund managers applying Islamic profit-and-loss-sharing instruments are granted 100 per cent tax exemption until 2016. Shareholders of these funds are also granted the same exemption. SPVs as well as foreign currency *sukuk* profits have also been granted tax exemption. In order to encourage managers to learn about Islamic finance, those who take courses at INCEIF can claim up to RM5000 tax returns annually.[34]

Furthermore, the government has established its own venture capital companies such as *Malaysia Venture Capital Management* (MAVCAP), *Malaysian Technology Development Corporation* (MTDC) and *Kumpulan Modal Perdana* (KMP).

Of these companies, MAVCAP received about RM1 billion from the government. Regarding the management, the government has taken the correct decision and has delegated the management responsibility to professionals.

At this point, it would be appropriate to make an objective assessment of these efforts and make policy recommendations. Let us start with the establishment of the venture capital company itself and focus on the liability side, that is, flow of funds to VC companies. In this process some fundamental principles must be borne in mind.

To start with, the state must facilitate, not hinder, the establishment of venture capital companies. Imposing very high paid-in capital requirements impedes the establishment of such companies. This is the mistake that the *Turkish Capital Market Board* made in the early 1990s. In a country where the opportunity cost of capital was very high, imposing such requirements killed the sector right at the beginning. A venture capital company should not be confused with a bank. These companies do not collect deposits and therefore do not create risks for the public. If they make mistakes they only hurt their own shareholders. Therefore insisting on very large paid-in capital requirements does not make sense. No such requirement should be imposed at all and venture capitalists should be allowed to establish such companies with whatever capital they can muster. Granted, being undercapitalized is a serious risk, but this risk belongs to the venture capitalists and the government should not interfere in it.

It must be remembered that venture capital is strictly a private sector activity. Finding the right entrepreneur to finance and nurture and then bringing him up to the initial public offering (IPO) state or having it acquired by a powerful outsider, merger and acquisition (M&A), takes a very special partnership between the venture capitalist and the entrepreneur. This is not a process that a bureaucratic government office can handle. This observation has been confirmed by the German case of the so-called *Wagnisfinanzierungsgesellschaft*, which was established by the German government in order to establish a viable venture sector in Germany. The attempt failed miserably.

A better method of channelling government funds would be fund matching. In other words, the government may declare that if a venture capital company is established with private capital, it will match up to 49 per cent of this privately committed capital as equity finance. Less than 50 per cent government equity finance ensures that the venture capital company will be run as a private enterprise. This suggestion serves two purposes: it reduces the risk of undercapitalization and commits public funds only after private investors have already committed theirs.

Still another form of government support is taking place in Europe. Probably drawing upon the German experience, Europeans have learned that venture capital is strictly a private sector activity. They have therefore started providing government finance indirectly through 'fund of funds'. The European Investment Bank and the European Union jointly own the European Investment Fund, 'fund of funds' placing money with other funds rather than directly in start-ups, which by the end of 2009 had invested €4.1 billion. Much of this investment, however, is wasted as it goes to big banks and insurers, which operate most funds and charge hefty fees: on average, 38 per cent of the initial investment over eight years, as reported by the French Finance Ministry.[35] Obviously, it would have been far more effective had the French government channelled these funds directly to venture capital companies through fund matching as proposed above.

Tax breaks are also emerging as an important government support to the venture capital industry. In France, for instance, citizens can cut their wealth tax by up to 75 per cent if they invest an equivalent amount in venture capital funds or directly in start ups. This policy has been obviously effective: France raised nearly €2 billion in 2009.[36]

Interstate competition has long been recognized as a great advantage of Europe.[37] Thus, it is argued, European countries discover which nation within the continent has the best practice and then start imitating it. For this purpose the EU has now established an Innovation Commissioner, which is to produce a plan to make life easier for the European start-ups. It is to be seen with what kind of advice the commissioner is going to come up with and whether the models that will be developed will have any relevance for the Islamic world.

Pension funds constitute one of the most important contributors of equity capital to venture capital companies. In the USA their participation in the industry was made possible by the 1974 *ERISA* Act,[38] which allowed pension funds to invest a maximum of 2.5 per cent of their portfolio in venture capital companies. When four years later two more very important acts were introduced, the American VC industry really took off. These were the *Bayh-Dole Act* of 1980 and the reduction of the *Capital Gains Tax* to a maximum of 28 per cent. Thus, establishment of a viable VC industry necessitates pension fund participation, as well as low or, preferably zero, *Capital Gains Tax* and university participation. The last condition was provided by the *Bayh-Dole Act* and will be explained in detail below.

In the Islamic world, participation of the public with equity capital in the formation of a venture capital company has been made possible by the so-called *muqarada* bonds mentioned above. These bonds provided with third party guarantee should play an important role in introducing venture capital companies to the Islamic world.

If we now look at the asset side, that is, investing the funds collected by the venture capitalist, the most important condition to remember is that the ultimate aim of the venture capitalist is to sell the shares he holds of the entrepreneurial company and exit from the partnership. For profitable exits, a number of conditions must be fulfilled.

First, as mentioned above, the *Capital Gains Tax*, which taxes the profits gained in selling shares in the stock exchange, should be low or preferably zero. The current tax policies in both Malaysia and Turkey, therefore, are correct.

Second, as already mentioned, shares of entrepreneurial companies are sold off at *NASDAQ*. This is a special stock exchange, where shares of young entrepreneurial companies can be traded. Unlike traditional stock exchanges, it is easier for an entrepreneurial firm to be listed in *NASDAQ*. The Malaysian version of *NASDAQ* is *MESDAQ* (*Malaysian Exchange of Securities Dealing & Automated Quotation*), which was launched on 6 October 1997 as a separate market mostly for technology-based companies listing. But the important question here is, just how easy is it for a Malaysian entrepreneur to be listed in *MESDAQ*? A detailed institutional comparison of the entry and exit procedures between the two stock exchanges, *MESDAQ* and *NASDAQ*, needs to be made.

But well before an entrepreneur is registered with the stock exchange, the entrepreneurial firm first must be created. The breeding ground of entrepreneurs is the universities. Venture capitalists need to establish close links with, particularly, the engineering, biology and medicine faculties of universities. Universities should also have flexible structures, allowing their faculties to be involved in VC-related research. As already mentioned above, university endowments (waqfs) can also play an important role and techno-parks adjacent to university campuses can play host to companies established by entrepreneurial professors and their research students.

The government can do its part by transferring patents to researchers. Reference is made here to the *Bayh-Dole Act* of 1980, which gave new life to the American industry on the brink of collapse due to the Japanese competition. This act unlocked all the inventions and discoveries that had been made in laboratories throughout the USA and paid for with tax-payers' money. It is generally accepted that, more than anything, this single act helped to reverse the USA's precipitous decline to industrial irrelevance in the last two decades of the twentieth century. Before the act, companies did not have access to government-owned patents, which had been financed with tax revenue and created in the universities. Indeed, of the 28 000 patents that the US government owned in 1980, fewer than 5 per cent had been licenced to industry. This meant that although tax-payers were paying the bill for 60 per cent of all academic research, they were getting hardly anything in return. The act hit two birds with one stone: on the one hand, it transferred ownership of an invention from the government agency that had financed it to the academic institution where the actual research was carried out; and on the other, it ensured that the researchers themselves got a piece of the action. Overnight, universities across the USA became hotbeds of innovations as entrepreneurial professors took their inventions and their graduate students, who carried out the actual research as their PhD work, just across the campus to the techno-parks. In these techno-parks the professors were allowed to start their own companies jointly with their students without having to abandon their academic careers.

The result of all this was impressive: since 1980, American universities have witnessed a ten-fold increase in the patents they generate, spun off more than 3200 firms to carry further basic research done in their labs, created 260 000 jobs in the process and now contribute US$40 billion annually to the economy. Remarkably, this huge success has invited criticism. Some have argued that it is immoral for the government to privatize the crown jewels of academic research.

In view of the fact that a dollar's worth of academic invention requires about US$10 000 of private investment to bring it to market, such criticism should, obviously, not be heeded. Thus, far from getting a free lunch, companies that licence ideas from universities end up paying over 99 per cent of an innovation's final cost.[39] It goes without saying that it is the venture capital companies that finance this 99 per cent.

It is not difficult to transform all this into a possible Islamic context, which would be completely *Shari'ah* based. Assume the government of an Islamic country suddenly has money to spare and decides to invest it for research and development.[40] The question is how to do this most effectively. My basic argument is that it should be done as follows.

First, the government gives this money in the form of grants to waqfs of various universities. Waqfs are preferred to the usual bureaucratic university organizations in view of their more flexible, dynamic and transparent nature.

Second, each university waqf then distributes this research grant it is assigned among the various research teams within the university. Each research team is made up by a leading professor and graduate students writing their theses. As the research progresses, each team gradually establishes a company in the form of a classical Islamic partnership. The company then moves to the techno-park adjacent to the campus, thus allowing the researchers to continue their academic work and pursue the research without interruption. The *sine qua non* condition for this is that the university must have a flexible attendance system. A university that treats its academic staff as bureaucrats and insists on nine-to-five attendance automatically disqualifies itself from this system. Such universities should never be treated as research universities and tax-payers' research money should not be wasted on them. This implies further that universities should be put into two categories: research universities and teaching universities. The former would best be distinguished from the latter by their flexible attendance requirements. It goes without saying that research grants should only go to research universities.

A partnership established by the researchers can be envisaged as a *mudaraba*, with the university waqf being the first *rab al-mal* providing the initial capital, and researchers being the *mudarìbs*. The partners agree to distribute profits the Hanefite way, that is, by mutual agreement. The Hanefite distribution according to mutual agreement is necessary in this case as it assigns a profit share to the researchers, who do not contribute capital. This is not possible in other schools, which insist on profit distribution according to the ratio of the capital contributed.

If the research is successful and a patent is obtained, the next step is to transform the invention into a marketable product. This necessitates further and much larger injection of capital. Islamic law permits obtaining capital from different *rab al-mals*. The second *rab al-mal* would be a venture capital company. If the *mudarìbs* succeed in persuading the venture capitalist, they have to give up more shares of their company in return for the additional capital. The rest of the *modus operandi* has already been discussed in detail: the venture capitalist provides a whole spectrum of help to the researchers. If the success is achieved, either an initial public offering (IPO) or a merger and acquisition (M&A) is organized and the venture capitalist exists by selling the shares it possesses either to the public or to the company that has acquired the research team's company.

The total profit is then shared among the three groups: the university waqf, the research team and the venture capitalist. Each group enjoys the profit in proportion to the shares it actually possesses. The relevance of the American *Bayh-Dole Act* of 1980 should be obvious here. The whole scheme would fail if the state short-sightedly demands a lion's share in the profits. It should be well understood that tax-payers are the ultimate winners in what has been described above. This is because every research team that has succeeded means new firms, additional employment, taxes to be paid by the entrepreneurial firms, exports and further taxes. It is therefore essential that a law is passed which gives the patent right directly to the university waqf/research team/entrepreneurial company and not to some bureaucratic government department.

The Guidelines and Best Practices on Islamic Venture Capital, issued by the *Malaysian Securities Commission* in May 2008, has given great importance to the employment of *Shari'ah* Advisors and *Shari'ah* Compliance Officers in Islamic VC companies. Such officers may be of some use in attracting foreign, particularly Arab, capital to the fledgling Malaysian VC industry. But since, unlike Islamic banking, venture capital is by definition *Shari'ah* based, these officers will not have much to do. This is because VC collects its funds through equity finance and focuses on high technology investments – a hardly *Shari'ah* incompliant activity. In any case, it would be a good idea to limit the compliance controls of these officers to the pre-IPO or M&A levels. Because if *Shari'ah* compliance conditions are extended by these officers to companies willing to acquire the entrepreneurial companies, a self-defeating situation may emerge and instead of facilitating the exit of the venture capitalist it would, in fact, be impeded. Ultimately, it would be far more preferable if these *Shari'ah* officers are withdrawn altogether. Because, since Islamic credentials of venture capital industries are beyond any doubt, there is no use for these officials.

Finally, all the measures I have pointed out pertain to the tip of the iceberg. We must realize that venture capital constitutes a culture, and the most difficult part of the whole process is to transfer this culture across borders. A culture which places great value on entrepreneurship is needed. In the USA, for instance, a failed start-up is considered a badge of honour. In continental Europe, by contrast, it often spells professional death. How Islam approaches the risks of business needs to be specially investigated. But in this context it will suffice to say that Islam assigns an honest merchant struggling to earn and enlarge his assets legitimately the highest social status. Indeed, it is believed that such a merchant/businessman/entrepreneur will be exalted and shall join the ranks of the prophets and the martyrs.[41] This means that concerning the social importance attached to entrepreneurship, Islam holds a position closer to the USA than to Europe.

Much of this venture culture is shaped by the prevailing government policies. In Germany, for instance, any equity stake is immediately taxed. It is necessary to make share options more attractive than salaries. If this is not done, then potential entrepreneurs would prefer to work for salaries instead of establishing their own companies.

Newly established companies need large markets. The existing fragmented state of the Islamic markets constitutes a great impediment to venture capital. In this context the recent abolishment of import taxes by the Turkish government on Syrian industrial products is certainly a step in the right direction. Syria, in return, has promised to abolish its taxes on Turkish industrial goods within three to twelve years. The first such agreement was signed on 1 January 2007, covering only certain products. The list of goods exempted from customs taxes is being mutually expanded. Another such agreement was also signed between Turkey and Jordan on 1 December 2009.[42] Similar agreements are needed among all Islamic countries if a viable venture capital sector is to be established in the Islamic world.

A change in government policies with respect to immigration can also play an important role in the development of a viable venture capital industry. After all, it should never be forgotten that any successful venture capital industry has two essential components, the venture capitalist and the entrepreneur. The greater the pool of entrepreneurs that a venture capitalist can draw upon, the more probable is the success. Even the US venture capital sector, although functioning in a vast country with a huge indigenous entrepreneurial pool, has rapidly become dependent on, particularly, Indian and Chinese entrepreneurs. The sector has benefited enormously by attracting these entrepreneurs who had come to study in American universities. Without immigration laws, which made it possible for these foreign students to stay on in the country, this would have been impossible. It is now well known that after 9/11, these laws have become far more restrictive, which may well be an important reason for the stagnation observed in the US venture capital industry. The lesson to be drawn for an aspiring Muslim country to become a venture capital hub is to design its immigration policy accordingly. To put it succinctly, talented entrepreneurs with feasible and potentially lucrative projects invited by the local venture capitalists should be given easy entry visas and eventually even permanent residence permits.

We have already seen in detail how universities play a hugely important role in the development of venture capital. This they do both by educating/inspiring/training, in general, producing the entrepreneur, and by providing them with the seed finance they desperately need through their often sizable endowments. These endowments have, of course, the enviable position of being the first at scene when a major technological breakthrough occurs at the laboratories. As we have already seen above, the Islamic equivalent of the Western endowment is the waqf. A thorough waqf reform therefore becomes important not only for everything else that the waqf represents but also for an Islamic venture capital industry. This is another area where Europe lags behind the USA. Indeed, Europe's pool of capital from the university endowments is about 8 per cent of the USA's.[43] If we remember the hugely important role that waqfs have played in Islamic history and culture, we may argue that *potentially*, and subject to a thorough reform of this institution, the Islamic world, once again, stands between the USA and Europe. Put differently, if properly reformed, Islamic waqfs, and through them waqf financed and organized universities in the Islamic world, can advance by leaps and bounds and progress much farther than the European system. The early signs of such a progress are already visible in the Turkish waqf universities. These universities, however, have not yet become active players in the venture capital sector.

Latest reports indicate that venture capital activities are emerging in the Gulf as well. It seems high-net-worth pious Muslims in the region, disenchanted with the way mainstream Islamic finance has been heading, have started to take matters into their own hands and started to invest in equity. We are informed that such individuals finance venture capital companies in the region. These VC companies identify the entrepreneurs to be financed, conduct due diligence and then often acquire their companies. Since it is estimated that the region has approximately US$1.5 trillion in excess liquidity, it should not be surprising that some of this cash should be directed to risky but totally *halal* investments. Indeed, the *Gulf Venture Capital Association* recently reported that in the Gulf alone US$7 billion was raised in 2007, up from US$4.3 billion in 2005.[44] There is definitive evidence that at least US$4 billion of these funds are Islamic. This means that the entrepreneur is ethically screened and *Shari'ah* based financing is used for the acquisition and funding. Moreover, even the risk adverse Islamic banks have belatedly started to join the bandwagon and have established their own private equity funds.

These latest developments appear to have dumbfounded some financial analysts ignorant about Islamic finance. These individuals are astounded because what they observe in the Gulf is diametrically opposed to worldwide trends. They report with alarm a substantial divergence in global versus Islamic asset management. This has apparently occurred with Islamic private equity in the GCC comprising about 50 per cent of the total Islamic mutual funds. It is reported further that this is a vastly different ratio than the ratio of private equity as a percentage of mutual funds worldwide, which is not more than 15 per cent. Experts report further that there are already trillions of dollars of assets under management in the Gulf. But they find it surprising that these continuously growing funds are flowing not towards mutual funds – not even Islamic mutual funds – but that they are flowing towards private equity funds, that is, venture capital or *mudaraba*/*musharaka* investments.[45]

At this stage, although our knowledge is very rudimentary and we urgently need specialized research on the fundamentals of this new phenomenon, I prefer to interpret these developments, at the risk of making a premature statement, as the response of high-net-worth pious Muslims who are disenchanted about the way mainstream Islamic finance has moved from *Shari'ah* based instruments towards quasi-Islamic instruments mimicking conventional finance. It seems that these individuals have taken matters into their own hands and shall soon give new directions to Islamic finance.

All of this means that there is a great demand for *Shari'ah* based financial instruments. In what follows, I would like to propose a new synthesis combining some of the most potent *Shari'ah* based Islamic financial instruments.

WAQF OF STOCKS, ISLAMIC VENTURE CAPITAL AND MICROFINANCE: A PROPOSAL

In what follows, I will present a new model, which will combine some of the most important, yet, so far, relatively little known, institutions of Islamic finance – waqf of stocks, Islamic venture capital and microfinance. It is envisaged that combining these powerful institutions in its structure, this simple model may play an important role in the eradication of poverty, enhancement of entrepreneurship and building up of human capital in Islamic countries.

The *modus operandi* of this model can be explained as follows. A Government agent establishes the First Global Waqf of Stocks. It is envisaged that the funds for this enterprise will be provided by investors throughout the world. Hence the term: First Global Waqf of Stocks. The government agent can do so, because it is considered to have judicial personality. Thus the government agent is the *de facto* founder of this global waqf of stocks. Highly respected international institutions, such as the Islamic Development Bank (IDB) or the Organization of Islamic Countries (OIC), or central banks of Islamic countries, can also initiate such a waqf. In Malaysia, both the *Bank Negara* and the *Tabung Haji* have the potential.

Since, according to the *Shari'ah*, the founder of a waqf can appoint himself or herself as the trustee, the government agent can also be the trustee of this waqf. Normally, of course, a waqf should be established by a private person with his personal capital. But there are examples of waqfs established by government agencies in the twentieth century.[46]

During the establishment it will be declared that this waqf will be active, according to the *hadith*: '*sawab ba'd al wafat*'. This is the well-known *hadith*:

> Abu Hurairah reported Allah's messenger as saying: When a person dies, all his acts come to an end, but three; recurring charity, or knowledge by which people benefit or a pious offspring, who prays for him.[47]

This means that the global waqf will focus on three basic activities: on-going charity (*sadaqa jariyah*), education and family waqfs. On-going charity can be interpreted as poverty alleviation. Poverty alleviation, on the other hand, can be addressed by focusing on the extremely poor through providing Islamic microfinance. The methodology of microfinancing is already fully developed by the 2006 Nobel Laureate Professor Muhammad Yunus and need not be repeated here. It should only be mentioned that as the founder of the Grameen Bank, Professor Yunus was not considered worthy of a Nobel Prize in economics and was given the Nobel Peace Prize in a roundabout way on the grounds that poverty threatens peace. If an institution that has rescued some seven millions of Bangladeshi peasants living in 73 000 villages from poverty is deemed not fit for a Nobel Prize in economics, this only serves to illustrate to what extent the discipline has distanced itself from what should be its main goal: eradication of poverty. The discipline, apparently, has more important things to do!

The Grameen Bank and microcredit finance attack poverty by focusing on the poorest of the poor. But poverty can also be alleviated by supporting the entrepreneurs. Indeed, creating entrepreneurs by providing equity financing to venture capital companies creates brand new companies and leads to capital accumulation. Venture capital companies help poverty alleviation by increasing employment, increased exports, creating the most advanced technology and additional tax revenue. Finally, family waqfs ensure the future of a family for generations to come and also alleviate poverty at a personal microlevel.

In Figure 15.3, boxes D1–D*n* represent *n* number of donators. Once the First Global Waqf of Stocks is founded, members of the public will be invited to participate. These individuals, the donors D1 to D*n*, will contribute to the waqf by purchasing its shares according to their respective means. Their motive will be purely religious, *fisebilullah*. The donors can determine in which activity their funds should be spent. Thus, they may choose any of the four basic activities depicted in the figure. Since from the *Shari'ah* perspective, contributing to a waqf is like establishing one and will be rewarded in the hereafter as such, it is to be expected that large numbers of contributors would participate. Their participation will also be facilitated by the fact that not only persons of high net worth but also even individuals with modest means can purchase such shares.

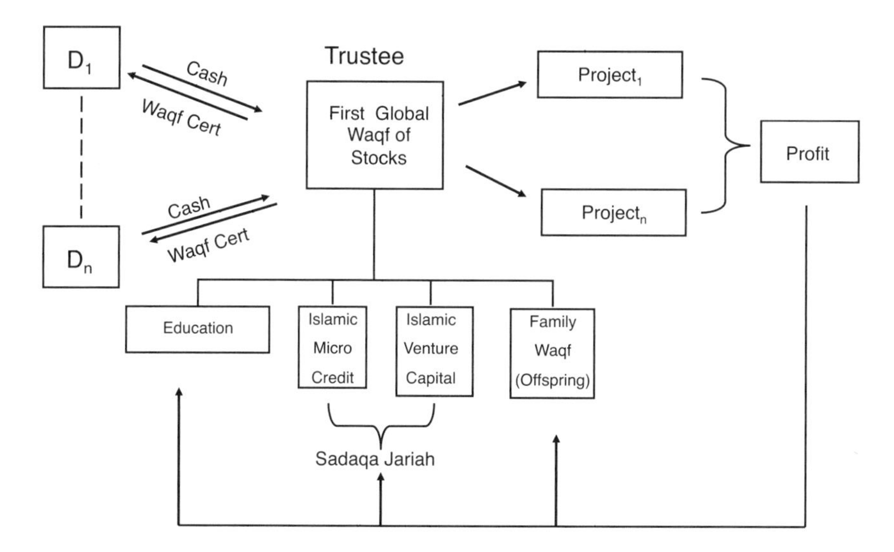

Figure 15.3 The First Global Waqf of Stocks

The Government agent/waqf will invest the accumulated cash contributions in various projects. These investments occur in the form of equity financing and would be tantamount to *mudaraba* or *musharaka*, both 100 per cent *Shari'ah* based.[48] It is important that such investments constitute a portfolio so as to diversify risks. We have indeed observed in the previous chapter that losses incurred in some projects are amply compensated by profits generated by the others.

The profits generated will be spent for education, Islamic microfinance, venture capital and family waqfs. The exact distribution of these profits between the four activities will reflect the desires and original donation of the donors. Put differently, although all the donations will be pooled and invested in various projects and the net profits will also be pooled, the exact distribution of the pooled profits among the four beneficiary activities will be done in proportion to the original donations reflecting the preferences of the donors.

What has been described above is *Shari'ah* based, not compliant. The reader will observe here that we have not identified a Western instrument and tried to Islamize it by reverse engineering – the prevalent method of the *Shari'ah* compliant approach. Instead, we have started out with a well-known *hadith* and the institutionalization of this *hadith* has led to the structure described.[49]

Moreover, as already discussed above in this chapter, there is absolutely no doubt about the Islamicity of venture capital. This is because equity finance is practically identical to the classical Islamic partnerships of *mudaraba* and *musharaka*. As for the Islamic microfinance we can envisage a modified microfinance system functioning along the lines of Professor Yunus's Al-Grameen Bank. The modification pertains to the loans. Instead of charging borrowers' rates of interest, the Islamic microfinance company resorts to interest-free *qard hasan* loans. The borrowers may be charged an administrative fee merely to cover administrative and operational expenses.[50] But the Islamic microfinance institution can operate as a non-profit since it is a component of a broader non-profit, the First Global Waqf of Stocks.

The First Global Waqf of Stocks would essentially function like a multiple *mudaraba*, with the government agent acting as the trustee (*mutawalli*)/principal (*rab al-mal*) with the difference that the profits generated would not be shared but would be channelled directly to the four activities which the donors have chosen: education, Islamic microfinance, venture capital and family waqfs. Since the First Global Waqf of Stocks would not operate with *istiglal* but with equity finance with the profits accruing to the beneficiaries, it would be 100 per cent *Shari'ah* based. The donors would sacrifice their rights to the equity/*mudaraba* profits when they purchase their waqf certificates, thus in fact declaring that the four activities are the recipients of the profits.

In modern financial institutions participants usually insist on liquidity. That is, they want to be able to withdraw their investments when needed. Since the structure we have been discussing is essentially a waqf, this boils down to the question whether a donation made to a waqf can be revoked and the donors demand their payment back.

According to Imam Hanefi, in case of emergency, the founder of a waqf can revoke his waqf. But according to Imam Shafi'i, the waqf, once established, is irrevocable. Thus there is no consensus among the scholars and the state can take a decision for the good of the society (*maslaha*). Such a decision must be obeyed by the Muslims according to the Qur'an.[51] Therefore, the government agent, representing the state, can allow the revocability of the waqf certificate and return the capital endowed, if so desired by the donor. Alternatively, instead of revoking his endowment, a donor can sell his shares. Indeed, waqf shares can be negotiable and be sold to third parties. For instance, the donor D_1 can sell his waqf share to D_2 and simply inform the government agent. In such a case, all the government agent has to do is to re-channel the profit shares accruing to the beneficiaries designated by D_1 to those designated by D_2.

Another difficulty may stem from the riskiness of venture capital investments. Indeed, waqf funds cannot be subjected to risky VC investments. At this point the third party guarantee provided by the state can come into the picture. Since we have discussed this possibility above, no further details will be provided here.

I have designed this model as a government initiated enterprise on the grounds that a respected government would be better able to attract global funds. But there are highly respected private sector conglomerations in the Islamic world. It should be possible for, say, an Islamic bank to organize the above scheme as a for-profit enterprise as well. In such a case, the trustee can be a bank and simply obtain a part of the profits generated for its services with the rest going to the four designated areas.

NOTES

1. In 2005, some US$970 million were channelled to the start-ups in Europe. This is more than twice the levels of 2002. In France there are 233 000 new businesses. In the USA this number is 671 000. American venture capitalists most recently poured US$727 million into alternative energy start-ups. See Tagliabue, 'Start-ups Become Old Hat', and Richtel, 'Silicon Valley Investors'.
2. Indian Venture Capital Association (IVCA) shows that overall funds committed are around US$1.3 billion.
3. Buckman, 'Venture to Nowhere', p. 26.
4. Shaikh, 'Private Equity?', US$1 is equal to RM3.42.
5. *Malaysian ICM,* April 2008, vol. 3, no. 2. pp. 14–15.
6. Bygrave and Timmons, *Venture Capital*, pp. 1–2, 9.
7. *The Economist*, 14–20 March 2009: Special Report, p. 9. Pricewaterhouse Coopers/NVCA, MoneyTree Report, Data: Thomson Reuters, retrieved 24th April 2011.
8. North American Securities Dealers' Automated Quotation.
9. *The Economist*, op. cit., p. 10.

10. *Muqarada* comes from the word *qirad,* which is the synonym of *mudaraba.*
11. Redemption at a specific time in the future is considered to be strictly between the bond holder and the state. Neither the entrepreneur nor the venture capitalist can promise redemption – if they do, the exercise would no longer be venture capital.
12. Sanusi, '*Muqarada* Islamic Bonds', pp. 49–52.
13. Kamil, 'Introduction to Sukuk', p. 27.
14. Al-Amine, '*Sukuk* Market'. See also *AAOIFI Shari'ah Standards* no. 5 on Guarantees.
15. For details, see ibid.
16. Bygrave and Timmons, p. 151.
17. Buckman, 'Venture to Nowhere', *Forbes Asia,* 12 January 2009, p. 26.
18. Zider, 'How Venture Capital Works', p. 136.
19. Platinum Partner/CIMB Islamic, 'Islamic Capital Market: Business Approach and Structuring Methodology' in RAM Rating Services Berhad, *Malaysian Sukuk Market Handbook* (Kuala Lumpur: RAM, 2008), no page number given.
20. *Encarta Encyclopaedia.*
21. Çizakça, *Comparative Evolution*, chs. 4, 5.
22. Çizakça, *Philanthropic Foundations*, pp. 34–8.
23. Çizakça and Kenanoğlu, 'Ottoman Merchants'. Halebi, *Mülteka'l Ebhur*, 1884; Bilmen, *Hukuku İslamiyye*, p. 86; İbn Abidin, *Redd al-Muhtar*, pp. 332–57; *Al-Mavsuat al-Fıkhiyye*, p.89; Gözübenli, '*Inan*', pp. 260–61; Siddiqi, *Partnership and Profit-Sharing*, p. 93.
24. Usmani, 'The Concept of *Musharaka*', pp. 203–20.
25. Sanusi, 'The Concept'.
26. Sanusi, *Critical Issues,* p. 186.
27. Sanusi, ibid., p. 188.
28. The identity of these forms of finance has been confirmed by Ahmad al-Naggar, in a conference in Istanbul in 1989. On details of this conference see; Çizakça, *Risk Sermayesi*, pp. 6–12.
29. Zakaria, 'Is America Losing Its Mojo?', 2009, p. N37.
30. Çiller and Çizakça, *Türk Finans Kesiminde Sorunlar*, 1989.
31. In 1993, US$1 was equal to TL10,986. On the prevailing rates of interest, see Celasun, 'Currency Crisis', p. 29. For further details on the capital requirements imposed by the Capital Market Board, see *Resmi Gazete*, 6 July 1993, no. 21629, p. 11.
32. Mahmood, 'Malaysia Leads Robust Islamic Venture'.
33. Salleh, 'The State of the Industry'.
34. Chang, 'Incentives from the Malaysian Government'.
35. *The Economist,* 12 June 2010, p. 81.
36. *The Economist,* 12 June 2010, p. 81.
37. Jones, *Miracle.*
38. *Employee Retirement Income Security Ac*t.
39. *The Economist,* 14 December 2002, p. 3.
40. This is expected in Turkey, where it has been estimated that a peace deal over the divided island of Cyprus will enable the Turkish state to save some €14 billion annually.
41. Zaim, 'Ekonomik Hayatta', p. 105.
42. Internet. http://www.dtm.gov.tr/dtmweb/index.cfm?action=detay&yayinID=1583&icerikID=1703&dil=TR. Also see http://www.muhasebenet.net/makale_eyupyuceli_turkiye%20ile%20suriye%20arasindaki%20ticarette%20inc %20noktalar.html.
43. *The Economist*, 12 June 2010, p. 81.
44. Shaikh, 'Private Equity'.
45. Sandwick, 'Divergence of Views', vol. 6, Issue 2, no. 17, p. 21. But these investments appear to differ from classical high technology oriented American venture capital, probably because of the lack of ambitious universities as well as the university–industry linkages described above. Standard & Poor's has reported that real estate investment constitutes some 20 per cent of the total loans of the IFIs rated by them. See *Islamic Finance News*, 13 March 2009, p. 20.

46. Consider for instance the *Diyanet Vakfi* in Turkey and the *Bunyad-i Mustaz'afan* in Iran. For further details about these, see Çizakça, *Philanthropic Foundations,* pp. 95, 101, 102, 158–9.
47. Muslim, *Sahih Muslim*, *hadith* 14.
48. A government agent being involved in equity finance is not a novelty anymore. As we have seen in the previous chapter, the Malaysian *Tabung Haji* has obviously been involved in such financing for some time now.
49. On details of how this *hadith* has led to the institution of waqf, see Çizakça, *Philanthropic Foundations*, p. 6.
50. This is permitted. See Ul Haq, *Economic Doctrines of Islam*, 1996.
51. An-Nisa'a, 59.

16. Democracy and the modern Islamic capitalism

MAQASID AL-SHARI'AH AND ITS BRIEF HISTORY

Neither Islamic capitalism nor its institutions described throughout this book can operate in a vacuum. Indeed, even the best financial model cannot function unless it is operating in a country governed by a trustworthy state which respects the rule of law. Moreover, governments need guidance to enable them to decide what policies to pursue and what to avoid. All of the above are provided by the *maqasid al-Shari'ah*, which if reinterpreted, can provide the essence of a trustworthy state within which Islamic capitalism and its financial institutions can flourish and the governments be properly guided.

I will first provide a brief history of the development of *maqasid al-Shari'ah*, to be followed by an attempt to reinterpret it. I am of the opinion that *maqasid al-Shari'ah*, so reinterpreted, will provide the necessary framework. For too long, it has been assumed in the Islamic world that financial institutions can operate in a vacuum regardless of the political environment. This is simply not true and it is appropriate to complete this book by describing the broader framework within which Islamic capitalism and its financial institutions can best function.

Maqasid al-Shari'ah is largely concerned with the philosophy of Islamic law rather than its actual formulations. Consequently, it is often omitted in classical *fiqh* books. But not any more; recently important works have emerged which consider the *maqasid* as a fundamental methodology of *fiqh*.[1] Auda goes even further and considers the *maqasid* as one of today's most important intellectual means and methodology for Islamic reform.[2] Moreover, this method is not borrowed from the West but emerged from within Islamic thought.

The term *maqasid al-Shari'ah* appears for the first time in the writings of Abu Abd-Allah al-Tirmidhi al-Hakim during the fourth/eleventh century. But the most important developments in the formulations of *maqasid al-Shari'ah* were made by al-Ghazali (d. 1111) and then al-Shatibi (d. 1388).[3] It was al-Ghazali who pointed out that the *Shari'ah* pursued five basic objectives: life, intellect, faith, lineage and property and that these were to be protected as absolute priorities.[4] Sayf al-Din al-Amidi (d. 1233) pointed out for the first time that the *maqasid al-Shari'ah* actually provides criteria to ascertain preference among conflicting policies – a crucial information for the day-to-day functioning of the institutions described in this book.

The list of the five essential values was evidently deduced from the Qur'an and the *Sunnah*. It was observed that each *hudud* punishment prescribed in these sources was actually designed to protect a certain very important social value. The value that each of these penalties sought to defend was identified as an essential *maqsud*, purpose.

Al-Shatibi, who, together with al-Ghazali, is considered to be one of the chief exponents of *maqasid al-Shari'ah*, has argued that induction is one of the most important methods for identifying the purposes of the *Shari'ah*. Indeed, there is no specific declaration in the Qur'an or the *Sunnah* that the five values constitute the very purposes of the *Shari'ah*. But this conclusion is reached by induction, *istiqra*, and is generally accepted by the scholars.[5]

Ibn Taymiyya was probably the first ever scholar to depart from the fixed five purposes and add such things as the fulfillment of contracts, respect for the rights of one's neighbours, etc. This is tantamount to transforming the *maqasid al-Shari'ah* to a completely open-ended list of values. Contemporary scholars including Yusuf al-Qaradawi and Ahmad al-Rasuni have added human dignity and freedoms to the list.[6]

The most obvious and important principle that must be remembered while adding a component (purpose) to the *maqasid* is that the new component is not valid unless it leads to the fulfillment of some good, *maslaha*, or the avoidance of some mischief, *mafsada*.[7] I would like to rephrase this general statement and make it more specific by arguing that a new component is not valid unless it contributes to at least one of the existing components without harming any of the others. We will have more to say on this method below.

REINTERPRETING *MAQASID AL-SHARI'AH*

In presenting this reinterpretation I am encouraged, first of all, by the *fiqh* rule *istishab*, which prefers a positive approach to a new problem and considers prohibition as exceptional.[8] I am also encouraged by the modern critiques advanced by contemporary theorists, who proposed that justice, freedom, women's rights and human dignity should also be added.[9] In what follows, I will support each reinterpretation not only with contemporary research but also with evidence from the original sources of Islam. This was the method used by al-Ghazali, who did not accept a new proposal based only upon its apparent current need unless it was also supported by the classical sources.

As we have seen above, each of the five criteria of *maqasid al-Shari'ah* were deduced from the *hudud* punishments prescribed in the Qur'an and the *Sunnah*. Traditionally, it is considered as the duty of the Muslim individual to protect his religion (*hifz al-din*), his mind (*hifz al-aql*), his property (*hifz al-mal*), his own life or the lives of others (*hifz al-nafs*) and the next generations (*hifz al-nasl*).[10] But I was intrigued by this and wondered if the duty to protect each criterion must, indeed, be considered exclusively as the duty of an individual Muslim or that of the Islamic state. When I put this question to Alparslan Acikgenc, a professor of Islamic philosophy, we discovered to our amazement that if we view each traditional criterion to be protected not as the duty of the individual Muslim but as the duty of the Islamic state, a totally different picture emerged.[11]

Consider, for instance, *hifz al-din*, the duty to protect the religion. Traditionally, this has been interpreted as the duty of the Muslim individual and more specifically it is understood as his obligation to participate in the *jihad*. But if, in addition to this traditional interpretation, we interpret this as the duty of the Islamic state to protect religion, we quickly reach to an enormously important concept, the freedom of worship. Freedom of worship is the essence of any civilized society, without which there would be complete chaos and bloodshed. This freedom is clearly pronounced in the Qur'an. Consider the following verses:

> To you be your religion and to me mine.[12]

And,

> If it had been thy Lord's will they would all have believed, all who are on earth! Will though then compel mankind against their will to believe?[13]

And,

> Let there be no compulsion in religion.[14]

The Qur'an also orders Jews and Christians to live by their faith:

> So let the people of the Gospel judge by that which Allah has revealed therein, for he who judges not by that which Allah has revealed is a sinner.[15]

From these verses it is clear that an Islamic state must protect religious freedom and pluralism even to the extent of permitting multiple legal systems.[16] Thus, our reinterpretation of *hifz al-din* as the freedom of worship is strongly supported by the Qur'an as well as Islamic history.[17] There is, indeed, substantial historical evidence that Islamic empires admirably fulfilled this duty and protected their minorities for centuries. Indeed, it is well known that minorities flourished in and contributed greatly to the Islamic states throughout history.[18] The Ottoman state failed to fulfil this duty only when it was taken over by a modernist military dictatorship of the Young Turks, shortly before its final demise at the end of the First World War, with disastrous consequences for Christian Armenians. Both the Young-Turk policies as well as the latest round of violence against the Christians of Bagdad are, therefore, in flat contradiction of the *maqasid al-Shari'ah*.

Of the five components, *hifz al-aql* has been traditionally interpreted as the duty of a Muslim to protect his mind and has been deduced from the alcohol and drugs prohibition. This author prefers to interpret *hifz al-aql* as the duty of the state to protect freedom of thought including the freedom of press.[19] Indeed, we can argue, what good is *aql* (mind) if it is not allowed to express its absolutely most important product, the thought?[20]

Freedom, in general, is given such importance in the Qur'an that it is considered as one of the three goals of the prophethood of Muhammad.[21] The importance of the specific form of freedom, the freedom of thought, is supported by the *sunnah* of the Prophet and Omar bin al-Khattab, the second Caliph. Indeed, it is well known that, when the Prophet made a statement, the companions used to ask him if this was a revelation or his own personal opinion. If the latter, a discussion would follow. In fact, the decision to dig trenches around Mecca was the result of just such a discussion. There is also a *hadith* which proclaims that the best form of holy struggle, *jihad*, is to tell a word of truth to a tyrannical ruler.[22]

It has also been reported by Ibn-i Abbas that when Omar bin al-Khattab had found out that Damascus was hit by plague, he consulted several groups in his army before taking the decision not to go into the city.[23] The implication is clear: if the companions could freely argue with the Prophet himself or with a powerful Caliph like Omar bin al-Khattab, freedom of thought existed and was practiced in the very origins of Islam.

'Commanding good and forbidding evil' is a cardinal principle of the Qur'an which lies at the root of many Islamic laws and institutions.[24] Known as *hisbah*, this principle constitutes the ethical core of governmental power. The *hisbah* lays down the foundation of freedom of speech in Islam, because only thanks to this freedom can the ruler be informed about what good or evil prevails in the society. Thus, since without this freedom it would be inconceivable to command good or to forbid evil, freedom of speech becomes a *conditio sine qua non* of *hisbah*.[25] The *hisbah* entitles every Muslim to speak for a good cause and criticize a bad one. This has been recently recognized and acknowledged by the *Universal Islamic Declaration of Human Rights*. This document refers to *hisbah* as the right and duty of every person to speak for and defend the rights of others.[26]

Hifz al-mal has been traditionally interpreted as the right of a Muslim to protect his property. This can be interpreted alternatively as the duty of the state to protect the property rights of individual citizens as well as institutions. This is an absolutely important condition for economic development. Indeed, without effective property rights none of the financial institutions described throughout this book can function. If this right is not sufficiently protected, Muslims would hide their capital under the mattress, a condition not only strictly prohibited by the Qur'an[27] but one which would also render all of the Islamic financial instruments discussed in this book non-functional. All of this is supported by Douglas North, a Nobel laureate in economics, who showed that secure property rights support economic growth and without it an economic system, and ultimately the state associated with that system, will stagnate.[28] It has also been shown that economies of nations that protect property rights grow more rapidly than those that do not and the nature of a political regime influences economic growth indirectly through its commitment to property rights.[29]

Hifz al-nefs has been traditionally interpreted as the duty of a Muslim to protect his/her health and has been probably deduced from the prohibition to commit suicide. An alternative interpretation much more in line with economic development would be the duty of the state to protect human rights. These rights pertain to the rights of citizens vis-à-vis the state. Persecution of innocent citizens by a powerful ruler is considered to be a great sin by the Qur'an and such tyrants are warned with hell fire.[30] This concept is also an inseparable component of the Rule of Law, which subjects everybody, even the ruler, to the law. Indeed, protection of the unarmed citizens from the overwhelming power of the modern state constitutes the essence of contemporary human rights.

What is needed here is the formation of a state that is strong enough to protect the country from external aggression but at the same time capable of controlling itself so as to respect the basic rights of its unarmed citizens. The concept of Rule of Law enables the individual citizen to sue the omnipotent state in case the state has violated the law. The idea to recognize the protection of human rights as a *maqasid* component has been gaining acceptance recently. The process started in 1981 when an Islamic Universal Declaration of Human Rights was initiated by Muslim scholars associated with the UNESCO.[31]

Hifz al-nesl has been traditionally interpreted as the duty of the Muslims to protect future generations. This has been deduced from the harsh *hudud* punishments inflicted upon the adulterous. But *hifz al-nesl*, if interpreted within the framework of the recent literature on intergenerational Pareto efficiency, grants the whole argument an intergenerational dimension.[32] Indeed, *hifz al-nasl* interpreted from the perspective of Pareto optimum provides a powerful tool with policy implications.

Inspired by the well-known Pareto optimum, the argument can be restated as follows: when considering a policy application, we progress towards the *Al-Ghazali–Al-Shatibi Optimum* if the policy in question improves any one of the components of the *maqasid al-Shari'ah* without inflicting any harm on any of the others.[33] The optimum is reached when it is no longer possible to improve one of the five components without harming any one of the remaining in the current *or some other future generation*. Thus the *hifz al-nesl* criterion renders the *Al-Ghazali–Al-Shatibi Optimum* relevant over time and space because it accounts for all periods.

To sum up, by reinterpreting *maqasid al-Shari'ah* we reach the conclusion that in an ideal future Islamic society not only the basic freedoms observed in every modern advanced society such as freedom of thought and press, freedom of worship, freedom from confiscation of property and human rights exist, it is also the most profound duty of any Islamic state to provide these freedoms. This is because the duty to provide these freedoms constitute the very purposes of the *Shari'ah*. Thus, there is absolutely no reason, according to Islam, why any of these freedoms should not be provided and be carefully safeguarded by an Islamic state.

ADDING ANOTHER COMPONENT: DEMOCRACY

Although the above-mentioned freedoms may, indeed, constitute the very purposes of the *Shari'ah*, they should be viewed as necessary but insufficient conditions for Islamic financial institutions to function. For these institutions to flourish, democracy and a host of institutions embodied in it are also needed. We have already mentioned that Ibn Taymiyya had added other components to the original five, such as fulfilment of contracts, respect for the rights of one's neighbour, etc. Thus, it has become possible to add additional components to *maqasid al-Shari'ah*.[34] I will argue here that democracy and its supporting institutions should be considered as additional components of *maqasid al-Shari'ah*. I am making this proposal, which hopefully will receive a positive reaction from the global Islamic scholarly community. In doing this, I will continue the approach I have used throughout this chapter and focus not only on the current needs of the society, *maslaha*, but also on the basic principles of Islam.

The question of democracy's importance and its proposed inclusion in *maqasid al-Shariat* needs to be examined from the perspectives of several social sciences. Let us start with that of the political scientists. To do so, first of all, an accurate definition of democracy is needed. Ahlmark has suggested that a country is considered to be democratic:

1. if the leaders of the executive and legislative branches of the government are elected in competitive and honest elections;
2. if at least two independent political parties compete in these elections;
3. if at least half of the adult population votes in the elections;

4. if the political party in power has been changed at least once through free elections.[35]

I do not consider these conditions to be sufficient and add the following, which I derive from the experiences of Turkey and Malaysia.

1. If the political parties are able to function freely: they are not shut down or threatened with being shut down and their leaders are freely allowed to compete for power.
2. If the following preconditions of democracy are fulfilled:
   (a) the rule of law must be supreme, entailing equality of all citizens before the law and the obligation of the *state* to obey the law;
   (b) while the judiciary must be independent of the executive and legislative branches, it should also be objective and should not be bound by an ideology;
   (c) the legislative should be superior to the executive;
   (d) the military must be under the authority of the democratically elected civilian government.

Do Islamic countries meet these conditions? Turkey meets Ahlmark's conditions, but not all of my conditions. In only four Arab countries (Palestine, Yemen, Algeria and Sudan) are presidents elected from among competing candidates with presidential term limits.[36] But if we apply a rigorous test, combining Ahlmark's and my own criteria, no Islamic country, including Turkey, can pass. At this point, one may say, 'So what? Why does it matter?' To answer that question, it is necessary to understand fully why democracy is so important and what the Islamic world is missing for the lack of it.[37]

We may begin with the relationship between democracy and waging war as revealed by European history. The democratic countries considered here are those that satisfy the conditions described above in the period after the battle of Waterloo (1815). We will now focus strictly on the link between democracy and war. It has been observed that a total of 70 wars were waged between 1816 and 1991, a period of about 175 years from the end of the Napoleonic wars roughly to the present. These wars were fought between 353 'pairs' of hostile countries. Among those 'pairs' of countries at war, while a non-democracy fought another non-democracy in 198 cases, and a democracy fought a non-democracy in 155 cases, *a democracy never fought against another democracy*.[38] From this it may be concluded that democratic countries do not fight wars against each other.

The economic and financial implications as well as the relevance of this observation for this book should be obvious. Wars are terribly destructive, much more so in our days with the ever more potent weapons. Therefore, in a world dominated by democracies, destructive wars and massive armies with their hugely expensive armaments can be avoided. The funds thus saved can be channelled to human and economic development projects instead. This is one of the reasons why there is a strong link between democracies and economic development.[39]

But to reach to this happy state of affairs and avoid wars, the number of democratic countries should increase and democracy should become the predominant system of world politics. While this idea is correct, recent events have shown that how this is achieved assumes great importance. Indeed, Iraq taught the world an important lesson that democracies should expand democratically! Or that democracy should first be desired by the population, and that it cannot be imposed by a foreign power, much less a hostile one. This is precisely why the latest democratic explosion in North Africa, Yemen and Syria are so important: they demonstrate the committment of Muslims to democracy.

During the period 1900–87, 170 million civilians were killed for political reasons not on battlefields but often by their own governments. Totalitarian and authoritarian countries killed 166 millions, while democratic countries killed, mainly by aerial bombardments, about two millions. Thus 98 per cent of the victims were civilians killed by their own dictators. If we add the American bombardments of civilians in Vietnam and Iraq,[40] the figure would probably be reduced slightly to about 95 per cent. So we reach the conclusion: governments kill civilians. But most of these killers are dictatorships and the number of people killed by democratic governments is far less. Moreover, the latter do not, usually, kill their own people.

Thus, about 95 per cent of the civilians so killed were murdered by the dictators. Here are the details of some of the twentieth-century massacres, where non-democratic states killed their own citizens:

1. The Soviet Union, under Stalin, killed about 62 millions,
2. Communist China, under Mao, killed about 35 millions,
3. Nazi Germany, under Hitler, killed 21 millions,
4. The Pol Pot regime in Cambodia killed two millions (out of a population of only seven millions),
5. In Rwanda within three months one million civilians out of seven millions were killed,
6. And most recently the Serbs in Bosnia killed 200 000, raped 40 000 and displaced two million Muslims.

The total number of those massacred by the Communist regimes adds up to about 110 million. This is about two-thirds of the 170 million killed during the period 1900–87.

Why was it that the communist regimes were particularly so murderous? There are two reasons:

1. the state controlled all the economic and political power,
2. all the civil society institutions which could inform, criticize and protest were silenced.

Thus the more overwhelmingly the power of the modern state is concentrated in the hands of a certain group, and the more political freedoms are curtailed, the greater is the potential for crimes. This shows clearly the importance of the democratic principles of separation of powers and checks and balances.

The murder of 170 million peoples is like a modern plague.[41] There are three medicines against this plague:

1. the separation of the executive, legislative and judicial powers,[42]
2. establishment of the Rule of Law, and
3. expanding the basic freedoms.

I have already demonstrated above that the basic freedoms of the expression of thought, worship, property and human rights are included in the reinterpretation of *maqasid al-Shari'ah*. Thus, if this interpretation is correct, Islam not only endorses the importance of these freedoms but it also assigns them a profound place by considering them as the very purposes of the *Shari'ah*.

It used to be argued that democracy is a luxury only the rich could afford, and that the poor countries needed to focus all their resources to avoid famines. Amartya Sen, a Nobel laureate in economics, proved these arguments wrong.[43] He showed that the great Bengal famine of 1943 with 3 million people dead, occurred when India was under the British rule. But after India became an independent democracy, there has not been a single famine in India. So, Sen has concluded that independent democratic countries with a free press do not experience famines.

Moreover, not only the rich Western democracies, but also the newly independent poor democracies such as India, Botswana and Zimbabwe, successfully avoid famines. Famines occur either in colonies ruled by foreign powers, such as the nineteenth-century Ireland and British India, or in countries governed by the Communists, or by dictators. Indeed, the most recent serious famines occurred in Sudan and in North Korea, both dictatorships.[44]

Thus, to sum up, the political scientists and the economists have observed that:

1. ever since Napoleon, there has never been a war between two democracies;
2. democratic states do not kill their own civilians – they kill enemy civilians during warfare with non-democracies. But the numbers are

significantly less than the crimes committed by dictatorships against their own citizens;
3. famines never occur in independent democratic regimes with a free press.

These are the most obvious reasons why democracies are associated with sustained economic development. But there are equally important, yet less obvious reasons as well.

I now turn to a sociological perspective. A well-known Polish sociologist Piotr Sztompka has shown that democracies institutionalize distrust.[45] They do this first by assuming that all governments are corrupt and then by establishing institutions which act as quasi-insurance agencies and minimize our risks of trusting others, particularly those who govern us. Such risk minimization takes place through the separation of powers which control, check and balance each other. I am referring here to the executive, legislative and judiciary powers of the state.

As a result, power invested on democratic governments is diluted between different institutions. Because the prevalent risks in the society are thus effectively minimized, people in democracies trust their governments more, and this reduces transaction costs and enhances growth.

The essential question that we must ask ourselves now is Islam's position towards democracy. A mere neutral position does not suffice here because we are interested whether we may indeed include democracy within the *maqasid al-Shari'ah*. This inclusion can only be made if, in addition to the current social needs, *maslaha*, explained above, a powerful endorsement of democracy can be found among the basic teachings of Islam. This, it will be remembered, was the method Imam al-Ghazali had used.

ISLAM AND DEMOCRACY

Let us now view Islam's position vis-à-vis democracy. To start with, while the Qur'an does not provide Muslims with any injunction about how to choose or appoint a ruler, it ordains them to consult.[46] Moreover, there is an indirect and subtle message among the *sunnah* of the Prophet. It is well known that when asked to appoint his successor, Prophet Mohammad refused to do so. This is a subtle message given on his death bed that Muslims should elect their own leaders. His refusal to appoint his successor can therefore be interpreted as an endorsement of an important democratic principle.

The *sunnah* of the righteous Caliphs give mixed messages.[47] Both Abu Bakr and Ali can be considered to have been elected. These were, naturally, limited elections participated by the inhabitants of the city of Medina alone. But these elections were neither dominated by just a few aristocratic individuals, nor were they determined by the masses. They were as close to general elections as possible under the prevalent conditions of the time.

All four *Sunnite* schools agree on two methods for the determination of the ruler: elections and appointment. Elections were accompanied by *bi'at*, which means mutual agreement. Through *bi'at* inhabitants declare that they shall obey the ruler as long as he remains within the framework of the laws, and the ruler pledges that he will rule subject to the existing laws. This mutual agreement, which also implies the existence of the rule of law, used to take place by the electors solemnly placing their right hands, one by one, on the right hand of the ruler.[48]

The second method for the determination of the ruler was appointment by the previous ruler. Indeed, Abu Bakr appointed Omar to replace him. But this appointment took place after consultation. The details are as follows: Abu Bakr was aware that the Prophet had refused to appoint his successor lest his choice might have been confused with a divine inspiration. Since his own decision would obviously not be considered as such, he felt free to appoint his successor. But before doing so, he did ask the opinions of those who had come to visit him during his sickness. When he asked if they would offer their *bi'at* to Omar, they declared that they would.[49] Thus Omar was appointed after consultation.

But when Omar was asked to appoint his follower he was reluctant to do so. This is because Abu Bakr had appointed him after consultation, but the Prophet had refused to appoint any one, obviously opting for elections. So, when the community leaders insisted that he should appoint his follower, Omar declared six candidates, one of whom was to be elected as the next Caliph, thus combining the *sunnah*s of the Prophet with that of Abu Bakr.[50] It is noteworthy that Omar followed Abu Bakr's example and did not include his own son among the six candidates. In fact, none of the virtuous Caliphs attempted to establish a dynasty.

After Omar's death, of the six candidates four withdrew and only Othman and Ali remained. Of these two candidates, Othman was elected by the public. When Othman died, Ali was elected by the majority.[51]

An early example of a concrete structure of the Islamic political system can be found in the *hutbah* of Abu Bakr, which he read when he came to power. The structure had five items:

1. unlike kings, the Caliph has limited power;
2. people should trust him as long as he does not transgress the *Shari'ah*;
3. people would be justified to remove the Caliph in case he transgresses the *Shari'ah*;
4. the Caliph should rule with consultation;
5. the public has the right to control the Caliph as well as the other administrators.[52]

Elections were applied in determining provincial officers as well. When the question came up of appointing revenue officers of Kufah, Basrah and Syria, Omar ordered that the people of these provinces should select from their midst a person whom they considered to be the most honest and capable.[53]

It is well known that, despite these early democratic examples, the governance of the Islamic world was taken over by the Umayyad dynasty. Imperial dynasties continued until well into the twentieth century and were gradually replaced by military dictatorships. Thus, dictatorships and absolutist monarchies, which prevail in most of the Islamic countries today, contravene the very spirit of Islam. This is because true governance, *hakimiyah*, belongs to *Allah*, and what belongs to *Allah* should not be usurped by a man.

Powerful evidence for the very clear preference of Islam for democracy can be deduced from the interest prohibition. For it is clear that the primary motive of interest prohibition is to lead Muslims to an economic system characterized by a spirit of sharing. Risks, profits and losses must be shared in a true spirit of partnership. Indeed, partnership and contract/covenant are considered to be at the very heart of Islam.[54]

Thus, if partnership, profit and loss sharing and contract are at the very heart of Islam and the whole economic system is supposed to be based upon these, then it is only to be expected that these concepts be reflected in the Islamic political system as well. There is therefore no doubt that the Islamic political system must also be characterized by partnership, sharing and brotherhood. Obviously, what is to be shared here is political power. As a principle, such a system cannot be hierarchical and the leader's tenure must be temporary. This is because it would not be normal for one of the brothers to continuously rule and the others to be continuously ruled. A political system by which the rulers are regularly and continuously rotated through elections would therefore be in harmony with the spirit of Islam.[55] In short, if we deduce from the interest prohibition that profits, losses and risks must be shared in Islamic finance, by analogy, *qiyas*, we deduce further that power too must be shared in an Islamic political system. Democracy is, therefore, perfectly harmonious with Islam because it is the institutionalization of the idea of power sharing. Put differently, the Islamic concept of power sharing deduced from the interest prohibition is implemented and institutionalized through democracy.

If, notwithstanding the favourable beginnings and inclinations to democracy, dictatorships have come to dominate the Islamic world, this is not because of an inherent preference for dictatorship within the classical teachings of Islam but because of Sasanid and Byzantine influences. Indeed, it is well known that the Umayyads were particularly influenced by the Byzantine, and the Abbasids by the Sasanid traditions and institutions. Indeed, when Muaviye moved the capital to Damascus, for instance, he made Servilianus, the former Byzantine governor of Damascus, his chief consultant.[56]

In short, Muslims need to relinquish these un-Islamic imperial influences and return to their own democratic origins. This is not really difficult, because some elements of democracy and its related institutions can be traced back to the initial years of Islam. Indeed, both the *sunnah* of the Prophet as well as that of the righteous Caliphs and Islamic political philosophy support democracy.

But democracy and republicanism should not be confused. Going to the opposite extreme and creating a French-style republic is not necessary for establishing a democracy. A combination of monarchy with democracy is also perfectly possible as demonstrated by the European democratic monarchies. A monarchy that provides a symbol of unity for the nation and which voluntarily and gradually relinquishes power to the democratically elected legislative and executive branches as well as to an independent judiciary would also be perfectly acceptable and legitimate. Put differently, democracy can exist without a republic, but a republic without democracy quickly evolves into a dictatorship.

Consider the following verse in the Qur'an:

> Those who respond to the call of their Lord, and establish the prayer, and who consult each other and spend of what we have granted them of sustenance...[57]

In this verse four types of people are mentioned: 'those who respond to the call of their Lord and establish the prayer' refers to the pious prayers; 'spend of what we have granted them of sustenance' refers to the payers of *zakat*. The important point here is that consultation is mentioned together with prayer and *zakat*. The implication is crystal clear: the Qur'an assigns a role to consultation commensurate with prayer and *zakat,* the two pillars of Islam.[58]

The next Qur'anic verse is even more direct and *ordain*s Muslims to consult.

> ...and consult them in affairs of moment, then, when though hast taken a decision, put thy trust in God.[59]

This verse ordered the Prophet, and by extension every Muslim ruler, to consult his companions, or by extension, the public.

Based upon these verses, modern thinkers have begun to argue about the appropriateness of democracy for the Islamic world. Kamali has argued that if *Allah* commanded his Prophet to consult, despite the fact that he was the recipient of the divine revelation, how much more would ordinary rulers, who have no access to direct revelation, be ordained to consult the public! Muhammad 'Abduh has also held that in this verse consultation is not just a recommendation but an obligatory *command* addressed to the ruler.[60] Sadek Sulaiman concluded that democracy and *shura* are synonymous in conception and principle and are thus one and the same. This is supported by Mohammad Khalaf-Allah, who interpreted the *Shura* as the authority of majority vote.[61]

There is also strong evidence that this Qur'anic command was carefully observed by the virtuous Caliphs. It is well known that Omar the second Caliph had regularly consulted people after the prayers at the mosque. This can be considered as an early attempt to institutionalize consultation. Omar practised this after every Friday prayer. When a major problem surfaced and he needed a more thorough consultation, as the one that emerged about dividing the conquered lands of Sawad, he asked additionally the opinions of the leaders of the society. Omar explained his practices succinctly as follows:

> There is no *Khilafet* without consultation.[62]

Consultation without the freedom of speech, however, is meaningless. Thus the order to consult should also be understood as an order to the ruler to safeguard this freedom. In fact, as Mahmud Shaltut and al-Sibai reiterate, the Qur'anic principle of consultation takes the freedom of speech for granted.[63] Consultation can either be invited (*Shurah*) or takes place regularly in democratic elections. Indeed, *hisbah* and *nasihah* (advice) are realized best through elections, where millions give advice to the government. Governments are alerted most effectively when their votes fall in elections, which therefore constitute the most effective *nasihah*.

In view of all this I propose that democracy should be considered as the sixth purpose, *maqsud*, of the *Shari'ah*. There are five reasons behind this proposal. First, Muslim rulers have been ordained to consult. Second, in modern times consultation means elections and a parliamentary system, in one word, democracy. Third, as various social sciences have revealed, Muslims need democracy. Fourth, democracy cannot be separated from and would support all the other five components of *maqasid al-Shari'ah*.[64] Fifth, if so, and as Al-Shatibi has concluded, whatever is complimentary to the *maqasid* and in service thereof is also a part of the *maqasid*.[65]

CONCLUSION

This book started with a comment by Professor Reich, former US Secretary of Labour, wondering whether there is a third type of capitalism, an alternative to the two existing ones, and has provided a definitive confirmation that another form of capitalism, actually older than both, exists. This is Islamic capitalism. Yet, whether this Islamic capitalism can provide an alternative to the existing two depends on to what extent Muslims can avoid being influenced by the powerful temptations of Western capitalism and utilize their imaginative and creative powers to develop new powerful tools inspired by their own religion and history.

Islamic capitalism, indeed, constitutes one of the earliest and most successful forms of capitalism experienced by humanity. This capitalism and at its core, Islamic finance, have made a remarkable return in modern times after the Second World War, when the Islamic world emerged independent from the grip of Western imperialism.

There is, however, a limit to how much Islamic financial capitalism can flourish without an appropriate political system. There is no doubt that parliamentary democracy is the appropriate system within which modern Islamic capitalism and finance shall flourish. All the dictators in the Islamic world who refuse to consult the public are actually violating a most fundamental principle of Islam enshrined in the Qur'an – power sharing. This principle is institutionalized and implemented through democracy. Therefore the dictators cannot last long and eventually shall be replaced by democracies in the Islamic world. Whether these democracies will emerge in the form of monarchies or republics is of secondary importance and will depend on the ability of the monarchs to voluntarily relinquish power to the elected parliaments. Islamic capitalism, democracy and freedoms are all compatible with the basic teachings of Islam and shall prevail in the Islamic world in the long run.

Equally important, civilizational survival is at stake. Western imperialism, which destroyed three Islamic empires and then colonized the bulk of the Islamic world, was financed and led by Western capitalism. Huge Islamic territories like the Indian subcontinent and Indonesia were colonized by Western joint-stock companies. As the famous saying goes, defensive weapon must match the offensive one. If so, the survival of the Islamic civilization would only be possible if Muslims were able to develop their own capitalism. This means that the struggle for survival, *Jehad*, should take another form. It must be in the form of creating an Islamic capitalism which can compete with that of the West and stand tall on its own.[66] In this book, I have tried to explain how this can be brought about.

NOTES

1. Auda, *Maqasid as Philosophy*, p. xxv.
2. Auda, *Maqasid as Philosophy*, p. 8.
3. Kamali, *Principles of Islamic Jurisprudence*, p. 400. See also Al-Raysuni, *Imam Al-Shatibi's Theory*, p. 139.
4. In Arabic: *hifz al-nafs, hifz al-aql, hifz al-din, hifz al-nasl, hifz al-mal*.
5. Kamali, *Principles*, p. 404.
6. Kamali, *Principles*, p. 402.
7. Auda, *Maqasid as Philosophy*, p. 2.
8. Orman, 'Cagdas Arap Dunyasinda Demokrasiye', pp. 233–4. For further details of the concept of *istishab*, see Auda, *Maqasid as Philosophy*, p. 132.
9. Auda, *Maqasid as Philosophy*, p. 5.

10. Some scholars are of the opinion that there might be an order of priority among the components with faith and life having the highest priority to be followed by the next generations, the mind and property. I disagree with this suggested priority and consider each component as equally important. This is because each component can support and may become indispensable for the other. See on this Kamali, *An Introduction to Shari'ah*, p. 127, as well as Sen, *Development as Freedom*.
11. An earlier version of this reinterpretation has been published: Çizakça, 'Democracy', pp. 101–18.
12. 109: 6.
13. 10: 99.
14. 2: 256.
15. 5: 47–50.
16. Also see Muqtedar, 'The Islamic State', internet. This appears to conflict with the death penalty given to the apostates from Islam. This, however, is not a Qur'anic injunction but a solitary *hadith* reportedly stated under very special circumstances. For further details, see Kamali, *Introduction*, pp. 215–16.
17. Modern scholars such as Ibn Ashur and Jasser Auda are also of the opinion that *hifz al-din* can be reinterpreted as the 'freedom of faiths'. See Auda, *Maqasid as Philosophy*, p. 24.
18. For exhaustive evidence from the Ottoman archives, see Kenanoğlu, *Osmanlı Millet Sistemi*, 2004.
19. I adhere here to the definition of freedom as 'a choice for the better', *ikhtiyar*, as discussed by Al-Attas in his *Prolegomena,* p. 33. This differs significantly from the Western concept of the freedom of press, which does not take into consideration such finesse. Had it been able to do so, the Danish caricature scandal would not have occurred, harming Denmark, insulting the whole Muslim world and seriously harming East–West relations. The decision as to what constitutes 'a choice for the better' should be taken not by an authority with its own agenda but by the individual concerned.
20. In 2003 the Middle East was declared to be the region with the least freedom of press. See UNDP, *Arab Human Development Report*, 2004: 4.
21. 'and removes from them the burdens and the shackles which were on them before.' (7: 157).
22. Kamali, *Freedom of Expression in Islam*, p. 11.
23. I am grateful for these points to Sabri Orman. See also Nevevi, *Riyazü's-Salihin*, c. III, s. 299.
24. 31: 17. Even the *jehad* was an offshoot of this command. See on this, Al-Raysuni, *Al-Shatibi's Theory*, p. 139.
25. Kamali, *Expression*, p. 28.
26. Ibid., p. 29.
27. 9: 35.
28. North, *Economic History*, pp. 11–13.
29. Leblang, 'Property Rights', pp. 5–26.
30. 85: 10.
31. The Islamic declaration includes the entire list of the basic rights mentioned in the *Universal Declaration of Human Rights*, such as right to life, freedom, equality, justice, fair trial, protection against torture, asylum, freedom of belief and speech, etc. The Islamic declaration has triggered an intense debate. For details, see Auda, *Maqasid as Philosophy*, p. 23.
32. Todd Sandler, 'Intergenerational Public Goods, Strategies, Efficiency and Institutions', p. 28.
33. This approach is only possible if each of the components are considered to be of equal importance. The Nobel laureate Amartya Sen's view that freedoms support each other and therefore cannot be prioritized has already been explained above. But there is also at least a partial Islamic counterpart of this view. Al-Sarakhsi, a prominent classical Hanefite jurist, has given equal importance to *hifz al-mal* (property rights) and *hifz al-nafs* (protection of life itself). Babacar Mbengue, *Islamic Finance*, forthcoming.
34. For an extensive treatment of modern expansion of the maqasid, see Auda, *Maqasid as Philosophy*, pp. 5–8.
35. Ahlmark, 'Conclusions from the Twentieth Century', p. 186.

36. UNDP, *Arab Human Development Report* (New York: United Nations, 2004), p. 5.
37. There are, however, reasons for optimism. The post-2001 election results in Pakistan (2001), Turkey, Bahrain (2002), Morocco, Jordan (2003) and Indonesia (2004) manifested the increased presence of pro-democratization Islamic parties and the most recent developments in Tunisia, Egypt, Libya, Yemen and Syria are simply mind-boggling! For further details on this, see Kamali, *An Introduction*, p. 204.
38. Ahlmark, 'Conclusions', p. 185–7.
39. Sen, *Development as Freedom*, pp. 146–89; Hayek, *The Road to Serfdom*; Friedman, *Capitalism and Freedom*. According to the IMF, of the ten richest countries in terms of GDP in 2009, nine are democracies. See IMF, World Economic Output, Oct. 2010. According to other databases, all ten are democracies. See www.aneki.com. Retrieved on 19 November 2010.
40. American invasion of Vietnam is estimated to have caused 700 000 Vietnamese casualties as admitted by Dean Rusk (internet) while that of Iraq is estimated to have caused about 100 000 Iraqi deaths (UNDP, *Arab Human Development Report*, 2004: 4). Ahmedinejad has argued that this figure reached 700,000 in 2007. (*Newsweek*, Special Edition/Issues, December 2007: 24).
41. Indeed, in 1348 about half of the population of Europe was killed by the Black Death. Remarkably, 170 millions was 56 per cent of the population of the Euro area in 2005.
42. Legislative power should be above the executive and the judicial power should be independent of the two.
43. Sen, *Development*, p. 180.
44. Ahlmark, 'Conclusions', p. 194.
45. Sztompka, 'Trust, Distrust'.
46. This will be discussed in detail below.
47. Ameer, *The Spirit of Islam*, pp. 127–33.
48. Aydın, *Türk Hukuk Tarihi*, p. 109.
49. Erkal, *İslam'ın Erken Döneminde*, p. 80.
50. Aydın, *Türk Hukuk Tarihi*, pp. 110–11 and Erkal, *İslam'ın Erken Döneminde,* p. 81.
51. Erkal, *İslam'ın Erken Döneminde*, p. 82.
52. Ibid., p. 79.
53. Shibli, *Al-Farooq*, p. 214.
54. Man is considered to be bound in a covenant, *ahd*, with God. Al-Attas, *Prolegomena*, pp. 144–5.
55. Orman, 'Cagdas Arap', pp. 236–7.
56. Bulac, 'Seriat ve Orf', p. 10.
57. 42: 38.
58. Kamali, *Expression,* p. 41.
59. 3: 159.
60. Kamali, *Expression*, p. 41.
61. Auda, *Maqasid as Philosophy*, p. 174.
62. Shibli, *Al-Farooq*, p. 213.
63. Kamali, *Expression*, p. 42.
64. That democracy is in basic harmony with the *maqasid* is also the conclusion of Kamali. See his *An Introduction to Shari'ah*, p. 218.
65. Kamali, *An Introduction*, p. 124.
66. This is what Tan Sri Dato' Muhammad Ali Hashim, the CEO of the Malaysian Johor Corporation, has called 'business jihad'.

Glossary

Adl	Justice.
Ahadith (pl. of *hadith*)	Statements of the Prophet.
Ahd	Promise.
Ahdname	A statement of promise.
Ahilik, Ahis	A medieval Turkish/Islamic order closely associated with craft guilds.
Akçe	Ottoman silver-based coin.
Al-aqilah	Ancient Arab custom considered to be the essence of modern Islamic insurance.
Al-diyah or *diyah*	Compensation for harm inflicted or a return paid for a favour.
Al-mafalis	Bankrupt.
Aman	Security granted by a Muslim conqueror to the conquered peoples.
Amanah	Entrustment.
Anatolia	Turkey in Asia.
Aqad izin	The authorization granted by depositors to *Tabung Haji* to invest their deposits.
Awqaf al-nuqud	Cash waqfs.
Bai' Bithaman Ajil	A controversial financial instrument utilized by some Islamic banks.
Bai' inah	Sale on credit for payment at a future time.[1]
Bancatakaful	Insurance (*takaful*) marketing through Islamic banks.
Bay' al-dayn	A controversial pre-Islamic sale contract involving an exchange of credit for credit.[2]
Bayt al-mal	Public treasury.
Ber vech-i malikâne	In the manner of *malikâne*.
Berat	A document of permission, a document attached to *esham* shares.
Bi'at	Mutual agreement between a ruler and subjects.
Bona fide	Genuine, real.
Bumiputra	Endogenous Muslims of Malaysia.
Caveat	Warning.
Caveat emptor	The principle that the risk of a purchase belongs to the buyer alone.

Ceteris paribus	Assuming that other conditions are held constant.
Conditio sine qua non	An indispensable condition.
Consol	Fully transferable and negotiable English annuities.
Consolato del Mare	European mercantile law borrowed from the world of Islam.
Corpus	Capital of a waqf, main body of.
Dar al-Islam	The world of Islam.
Darrura	Compulsory, necessity, a dire need.
Defterdar	Ottoman Minister of Finance.
Denarius	Ancient Roman coin, eventually borrowed by Muslims.
Dhimma	Islamic concept similar to judicial personality.
Dominium eminens	Originally the Roman element of land ownership claimed by the state.
Erfelijke rente	The traditional Flemish perpetual hereditary rent.
Esham	(plural of *sehm* meaning share) Ottoman institution of *riba* free domestic borrowing.
Fatwa	Verdict of a Muslim judge.
Fellahin	Egyptian peasants.
Fi sanduq wahid	Capital pooling in a single box.
Fi sebilallah	Charitable fund.
Fiqh	Collection of Islamic juridical opinions regarding the application of the *Shari'ah*.
Fructus	The element of land ownership claimed by the peasant actually cultivating it.
Fütüvvetname	Rules of conduct for the Anatolian *ahi* orders.
Ganimah	Booty.
Gelire Endeksli Senet	Modern Turkish bonds indexed to the revenues to be generated by certain state economic enterprises or projects.
Gharar	Deception, a certain type of uncertainty or risk.
Gruş	Ottoman coin.
Habs	To keep, to preserve.
Hadith (pl. *ahadith*)	The statements of the Prophet.
Hakimiyah	Governance.
Halal	Permitted.
Hamish jiddiyah	Security deposit.
Haram	Prohibited.
Hawala	Transfer of revenue.
Hiba	Gift.
Hifz al-aql	Protection of the mind.
Hifz al-din	Protection of religion.
Hifz al-mal	Protection of property.

Hifz al-nasl	Protection of the future generations.
Hifz al-nefs	Protection of life.
Hijrah	The migration of the Prophet and his followers from Mecca to Medinah.
Hisbah	The Qur'anic principle of 'Commanding good and forbidding evil'.
Homo-economicus	The Western rational man/person.
Homo-Islamicus	Islamic man/person.
Hudud	Punishments prescribed in the Qur'an and the *Sunnah*.
Hujjat al-Islam	A learned judge.
Hums al-ganaim	One fifth of the booty.
Hutbah	Public sermon after the Friday or *Bayram* prayers.
Ibdal	Exchanging the original capital of a waqf with cash, selling the waqf property.
Ijara tawilah	Long-term rent.
Ijaratayn	Double rent.
Ijtihad	Independent reasoning by an Islamic scholar of law.
Iltizam	Ottoman tax farming.
Imdad-ı seferiye	Extra taxes imposed during wartime.
Imtiyazat	Privileges/protection granted to foreign/non-Muslim merchants.
Inan	A classical Islamic partnership, where both partners contribute to the capital.
Inter vivos	Gift among the living.
Iqta'	Assignment of land as private property or military fief.
Iqta' al-qabala	A land grant for the payment of a fixed amount of tax.
Istibdal	Exchanging the original waqf property with another.
Istiglal	A sale/lease/buy-back contract used by Ottoman cash waqfs.
Iştirak	Participation.
Istishab	Existence of a thing established by evidence. Thus a practice once proved to be widespread may be presumed to be both ancient and continuing.
Istisna	A contract to purchase now, for a definite price, something that may be manufactured later according to agreed specifications, an exception.
Jagird	Tax farmer in India.
Jehad	Struggle, struggle for survival.
Jizya	Poll tax.
Jugum	The Roman unit of land that could be cultivated by a pair of oxen in a day.

Juros	Spanish *rentes*.
Juros de heredad	Hereditary *rente*s, shares.
Kadi	Islamic judge.
Kafala	See kefalet.
Kalimah	A statement every Muslim must make to the effect that 'there is no God but *Allah* and that Prophet Muhammad is His messenger'. A non-Muslim converts to Islam by making this statement.
Karz	Loan.
Karz hasene (qard hasan)	A beautiful loan (without charging interest).
Kazeruniyya	A Sufi order.
Kefalet	Surety, guarantee.
Kefil	A person who stands as surety, a guarantor.
Kharaj al-mukasamah	An agricultural tax imposed according to the productivity of land.
Kharaj al-muvazzafa	A fixed amount of tax imposed on the size as well as the location of the land.
Kharaj	Land tax.
Khoms	One fifth.
Kulliyah	A complex of buildings and functions, a complete system. Usually used for a college campus and is believed to be the original word for college.
Kurum	Establishment, institution.
Lijfrent	The Flemish life-rent.
Madhab	An Islamic school of thought, a sect.
Maisir	Gambling.
Malikâne	Ottoman tax-farming system, important primarily during most of the eighteenth century.
Maqasid al-Shari'ah	Objectives and purposes of the *Shari`ah*.
Mare liberum	A free ocean to trade, the Indian Ocean.
Masalih mursalah (Maslaha)	Public interest.
Mazlama	Injustice, usurpation.
Medieval	The long period in European history from the fall of the Western Roman empire during the fifth century to roughly the fall of the Eastern Roman empire during the middle of the fifteenth century. Thus a period of roughly one thousand years. When the term is used for the Islamic world, it covers the period from the seventh century to the fifteenth.
Monte Vecchio	'Mountain of debt'.

Muaccele (mu'ajjal)	Lump sum payment made by the *malikâneci* in a public auction in order to obtain a *malikâne*.
Mudaraba	Classical Islamic capital–labour partnership.
Mudarìb	Agent in a *mudaraba*.
Mufawada	Classical business partnership where both partners are considered equal.
Muhtesib	Official in charge of markets.
Mültezim	Ottoman tax farmer.
Muqata'a	Tax source to be farmed out.
Murabaha	Cost plus profit sale contract.
Musharaka	Modern term for *inan* partnership.
Mutawalli	Trustee of a waqf.
Mutawwif	Specially trained *imams* who help Malaysian pilgrims during the pilgrimage.
Muzara'a	Share cropping, agricultural partnership.
Namaz	Daily prayer.
Narh	Maximum price allowed, price fixing.
Nasihah	Advice.
Nisab	A minimum amount of wealth beyond which a Muslim becomes liable to pay *zakat*.
Pir	An elderly person, a religious figure, someone believed to be the original founder of a craft guild.
Qabala	Egyptian tax farms.
Qirad	Synonym of *mudaraba*.
Qirat	A measure of landholding or jewellery, a ship-share.
Qiyas	By way of analogy.
Rab al-mal	A business partner who provides the whole or bulk of the capital.
Raison d'être	The reason why something exists.
Raqaba	*See Dominium eminens*.
Reaya	Ottoman civilians, ordinary folk, non-military, non-official, tax payer not tax recipient.
Rente	European financial instrument that pays fixed annuities.
Riba	Interest, usury.
Rikaz	Buried treasury.
Rizq	Livelihood.
Sa'	A measure of weight.
Sadaqa jariya	Ongoing charity.
Sadaqa	Alms.
Salam	A sale contract.
Sawad	A region comprising parts of Syria and Iraq.

Sehm (pl. *Esham*)	A share.
Şeyhülislam	The highest religious official in the Ottoman hierarchy.
Shari'ah	The revelation that Prophet Muhammad received and made practising it the mission of his life.[3]
Shirkat	Company.
Sparkassen	A German bank of savings.
SPV	Special purpose vehicle.
Suftaja	Letter of exchange used for transferring capital across time and space.
Sukuk (pl. *sakk*)	Certificates of equal value that represent the ownership of an underlying asset.
Sunnah	The deeds and actions of the Prophet.
Ta'amul	Custom.
Ta'bid	Condition of perpetuity of a waqf.
Taawun	Principle of helping one another.
Tabarru	Donation.
Tadawul	Exchange, circulation of money in the economy.
Takaful	Islamic insurance.
Takalif-i örfiye	Customary taxes.
Tamam	Complete.
Tasarruf	See *Usus*.
Tawarruq	Modern application of the historical *wujuh* or the so-called *Sharikat al-Mafalis*. A sale contract.
Tawhid	Unity.
Tawliah	A form of sale.
Tekalif-i örfiyye	Ottoman taxes imposed by the state.
Tesis	Establishment.
Thaman hall	Immediate payment.
Thaman muájjal	Deferred payment.
Thawab	Good deeds.
Thawab ba'd al Wafah	Reward after death.
Timar	Ottoman military fief.
Umrah	Visiting Mecca at a time not during the pilgrimage.
'Urf	Custom.
'Urf khass	Special recognized practice.
Ushr	Agricultural tax, usually one-tenth.
Usus	The element of Roman land ownership claimed by the landlord, a commander or a tax farmer.
Vakıf	Waqf.
Vakıflar Bankası	The Turkish Bank of Waqfs.
Völkerwanderung	Peoples' wandering, a major event of primary importance in European history.

Wa'd	Promise to purchase.
Wadia	A gift; in Islamic banking the term refers to deposits that do not earn any return.
Wagnisfinanzierungsgesellschaft	A German institution established to introduce venture capital to Germany.
Wakala	Representation.
Wakil	A person who is authorized to represent.
Waqf	Charitable/philanthropic foundation.
Waqf *ahli* or *khas*	Family waqf.
Waqf *khayri*	Charitable waqf.
Wujuh	See *tawarruq*.
Yasa	Law.
Zakat	The most basic Islamic tax.
Zimmis	Non-Muslims whose lives and properties were protected.

NOTES

1. Abdullah 'Alwi Haji Hassan, *Sales and Contracts in Early Islamic Commercial Law* (Islamabad: Islamic Research Institute, International Islamic University, 1994), p. 62.
2. Ibid., p. 65.
3. Auda, *Maqasid al-Shari'ah as Philosophy*, p. xxiii.

Bibliography

Abd Hamid, Abu Bakar and K. T. Joseph. 'Ungku A. Aziz – A Man For All Seasons', in Hashim Yaacob et al. (eds), *The Renaissance Man* (Kuala Lumpur: University of Malaya Press, 2010).

Abdel Mohsin, Magda Ismail. *Cash Waqf, A New Financial Product* (Kuala Lumpur: Pearson, 2008).

Abdullah, Mohamed Ridza. 'Regulatory Issues: Innovations and Application in *Sukuk*', in Securities Commission Malaysia, *Sukuk* (Kuala Lumpur: SCM, 2009).

Abidin, A. Anwar Zainal. 'The Fiscal Policy of Umar Ibn 'Abd al-Aziz', in Taher (ed.), *Islamic Culture*, 8: 120–24.

Ackerman-Lieberman, Phillip Isaac. 'A partnership culture: Jewish economic and social life seen through the legal documents of the Cairo Geniza', Princeton University PhD Thesis, 2007.

Ahlmark, P. 'Conclusions from the Twentieth Century: How War, Mass Murder and Famine Are Related to Democracy and Dictatorship', *Wissenschaftskollegjahrbuch*, 1998–9.

Ahmad, Nor Hayati, Abmalek F. Abubakar and Mohamad Yazid Isa. 'Practices and Issues of Risk Management in Financing and Investment of Islamic Financial Institutions in Malaysia', paper presented at INCEIF, Kuala Lumpur, on 20 February 2009.

Ahmed, Ausaf. 'The Evolution of Islamic Banking', in Muazzam Ali (ed.), *Encyclopaedia of Islamic Banking and Insurance* (London: Institute of Islamic Banking and Insurance, 2006).

Ahmed, Salahuddin. *Islamic Banking, Finance and Insurance* (Kuala Lumpur: Noordeen, 2006).

Akcam, T. *A Shameful Act: The Armenian Genocide and the Question of Turkish Responsibility* (New York: Metropolitan Books, 2006).

Akgündüz, Ahmet. *Islam Hukukunda ve Osmanlı Tatbikatında Vakıf Müessesesi* (Ankara: TTK, 1988).

Akkoyunlu, Pınar. 'Osmanlı Maliyesindeki Esham Sisteminin Günümüzdeki Uzantısı, Gelir Ortaklığı Senetleri', *Sosyal Bilimler Dergisi* I (2) 1994.

Akram Khan, Muhammad. *Economic Teachings of Prophet Muhammad* (Islamabad: Institute of Policy Studies, 1989).

Al-Amine, Muhammad al-Bashir Muhammad. '*Sukuk* Market: Innovations and Challenges', paper submitted at the International Conference on Islamic Capital Markets, 2008.

Al-Amine, Muhammad al-Bashir Muhammad. *Risk Management in Islamic Finance* (Leiden: Brill, 2008).

Al-Attas, Syed Muhammad Naquib. *Prolegomena to the Metaphysics of Islam* (Kuala Lumpur: ISTAC, 1995).

Alhabshi, Syed Othman and Shaikh Hamzah Shaikh Abdul Razak. 'Takaful: Concept, History, Development and Future Challenges of Its Industry', forthcoming.

Al, Hüseyin. *Ondokuzuncu Yüzyılda Ülke Riski, Finans Politik, İngiliz Tahvil Sahipleri ve Babıali* (İstanbul: Istanbul Üniversitesi Doktora Tezi, 2005).

Ali, Muazzam (ed.). *Encyclopaedia of Islamic Banking and Insurance* (London: Institute of Islamic Banking and Insurance, 2006).
Ali, Rahail. 'Legal Certainty for *Sukuk*', in Securities Commission Malaysia, *Sukuk,* (Kuala Lumpur: SCM, 2009).
Al-Jarhi, Mabid Ali and Muhammad Anas Zarqa. 'Redistributive Justice in a Developed Economy: An Islamic Perspective', *Proceedings of the Sixth International Conference on Islamic Economics, banking and Finance, 21–24 November 2005, Jakarta*, vol. I (2006).
Al-Qur'an. Translated by A. Yusuf Ali (Cairo: Dar al-Kitab al-Masri, 1934).
Al-Qusi, Abd al Mun'im Mahmud. 'Riba, Islamic Law and Interest', Temple University PhD Dissertation, 1981–82.
Al-Raysuni, Ahmad. *Imam Al-Shatibi's Theory of the Higher Objectives and Intents of Islamic Law* (Herndon, VA.: International Institute of Islamic Thought, 2006).
Al-Tirmidhi, Sunan. *Kitab al-Ilm al-Kutub al-Sittah wa Shuruhuha* (Istanbul: Çağrı, 1992).
Al-Zuhayli, Wahbah. *Financial Transactions in Islamic Jurisprudence*, vols. I and II, translated by Mahmoud A. El-Gamal (Damascus: Dar al-Fikr, 2003).
Ameer A. S. *The Spirit of Islam* (Lahore: Sang-e-Meel, n.d.).
Amin, Muhammad. 'The UK Tax Law for *Sukuk*', *Islamic Finance News,* 4 July 2008.
Anderson, Kate. 'Waqf and Jersey Foundation: Common Grounds', www.newhorizon-islamicbanking.com/index.cfm?section=features&id=10871&act, 13 February 2010.
Ariff, Mohamed. *The Malaysian Economy: Pacific Connections* (Oxford: Oxford University Press, 1991).
Aslantepe, Cengiz. *Nostalgia for Ottoman Bonds and Shares* (Istanbul: Alfa Securities, n.d.).
Auda, Jasser. *Maqasid al-Shari'ah as Philosophy of Islamic Law* (Washington D.C.: International Institute of Islamic Thought, 2008).
Aydın, Davut et al. *Kâr Amacı Gütmeyen Sektör Olarak Vakıflar* (Eskişehir: EESAM, 1999).
Aydın, Mehmet Akif. *Türk Hukuk Tarihi* (Istanbul: Beta, 2009), seventh edn.
Aziz, Zeti Akhtar. 'Enhancing the Resiliences and Stability of Islamic Financial System', Regulators forum *Global Islamic Finance Forum* 2010, Kuala Lumpur, 26 October 2010.
Aziz, Zeti Akhtar. *Islamic Banking and Finance Progress and Prospects, Collected Speeches: 2000–2006* (Kuala Lumpur: Bank Negara Malaysia, 2006).
Aziz, Zeti Akhtar. 'Developing Islamic Banks and Capital Market' in Z. A. Aziz, *Islamic Banking and Finance Progress and Prospects, Collected Speeches: 2000–2006* (Kuala Lumpur: Central Bank of Malaysia, 2006).
Aziz, Zeti Akhtar. Key-note Address at the Seminar on Labuan IOFC, 2–3 May 2006.
Baigent, Michael and Richard Leigh. *The Inquisition* (London: Penguin Books, 2000).
Bakanlar, Kurulu . *Kamu Ortaklığı Fonu Yönetmeliği, Resmi Gazete,* no. 13/09/1984–18514, madde 6.
Ballar, Suat. *Yeni Vakıflar Kanunu* (Istanbul: Beta, 2000).
Baloğlu, Adnan Bülent. 'Law of Sales in the Works of Marwazi, Quduri, and Sarakhsi', University of Manchester PhD Thesis, 1991.
Bank Negara Malaysia. Annual Report 2007 (Kuala Lumpur, Bank Negara Malaysia, 2008).
Bank Negara Malaysia. Financial Sector Stability (Kuala Lumpur: Bank Negara Malaysia, 2001).
Bardakoglu, A. et al. (eds), *Islam ve Demokrasi* (Istanbul: Ensar, 2000).

Barkan, Ömer L. 'Bazı Büyük Şehirlerde Eşya ve Yiyecek Fiyatlarının Tesbit ve Teftişi Hususlarını Tanzim Eden Kanunlar', *Tarih Vesikaları*, 1/5, 1942.

Barkan, Ömer Lütfi and E. H. Ayverdi. *Istanbul Vakıfları Tahrir Defteri (953/1546)*, (Istanbul: Istanbul Fetih Cemiyeti, 1970).

Barkan, Ömer Lütfi. *Edirne Askeri Kassamına Ait Tereke Defterleri, 1545–1659, Belgeler*, c. III, s. 5–6 (Ankara: TTK, 1968).

Barkan, Ömer Lütfi. 'H. 933-934 Tarihli Bütçe Cetveli ve Ekleri', *İstanbul Üniversitesi İktisat Fakültesi Mecmuası*, c. 15, no. 1–4, 1953–54.

Bayındır, Servet. 'Menkul Kıymetleştirme Uygulamaları ve Fıkıhtaki Yeri', *İstanbul Üniversitesi İlahiyat Fakültesi Dergisi*, XVI, 2007: 249–73.

Behrens-Abouseif, Doris. *Egypt's Adjustment to Ottoman Rule, Institutions, Waqf and Architecture in Cairo* (Leiden: E.J. Brill, 1994).

Berman, H.J. *Law and Revolution, the Formation of Western Legal Tradition* (Cambridge, MA: Harvard University Press, 1983).

Bi, Farmida. 'Islamic Capital Markets Respond to the Financial Crisis', *Islamic Finance News*, 4 September 2009.

Billah, Mohd Ma'sum. *Applied Takaful and Modern Insurance* (Kuala Lumpur: Sweet and Maxwell Asia, 2007, 3rd edn.).

Billah, Mohd Masum. *Applied Islamic Law of Trade and Finance* (Kuala Lumpur: Thomson, 2007), third edn.

Billah, Mohd Masum. 'A Model of Life Insurance in the Contemporary Islamic Economy', *Arab Law Quarterly*, vol. XII, no. 3, 1997.

Bilmen, Ömer Nasuhi. *Hukuku İslamiyye ve Istılahatı Fıkhıyye Kamusu*, vol. 7 (Istanbul: Bilmen Yayinevi, 1970).

Blockmans, Wim. *Emperor Charles V, 1500–1558* (London: Arnold, 2002).

Boone, M. et al. (eds), *Urban Public Debts* (Turnhout: Brepols, 2003), passim.

Braudel, Fernand P. and F. S. Spooner. 'Currencies, Precious Metals and Money Markets', in E. E. Rich and C. H. Wilson (eds), *The Cambridge Economic History of Europe*, vol. IV (Cambridge: CUP, 1967), pp. 474–9.

Braudel, Fernand. *Maddi Cambridge University Press, Ekonomi ve Kapitalizm, XV–XVII Yüzyıllar*, 3. cilt, (Istanbul: Gece, 1993).

Braudel, Fernand. *Civilization and Capitalism 15th–18th Centuries, vol. I, The Structures of Everyday Life, The Limits of the Impossible* (New York: Harper and Row, 1981).

Buckman, Rebecca. 'Venture to Nowhere', *Forbes Asia*, 12 January 2009.

Büker, S., D. Aydın, N. Saglam. *Son Değişikliklere Göre Vakıflar Kuruluşu Yönetimi ve Muhasebesi* (Eskişehir: Birlik, 1998).

Bulaç, Ali. 'Seriat ve Orf, Toplum ve Devlet', *Bilgi ve Dusunce*, vol. 1, No. 2, 2002.

Business Jihad (Kuala Lumpur: Corporate Bureau, Malaysian Islamic Chamber of Commerce).

Büyükçelebi, İsmail. *İslam Hukukunda İnan Şirketi ve Nevileri* (Erzurum: Atatürk Üniversitesi Doktora Tezi, 1981).

Bygrave, W.D. and J.A. Timmons. *Venture Capital at the Crossroads* (Boston: Harvard Business School, 1992).

Canan, Ibrahim. *Hadis Külliyatı Kütüb-i Sitte Tercüme ve Şerhi* (Compilation of *Ahadith*, the six books) 18 vols (Ankara: Akçag, 1995).

Casale, Giancarlo. 'The Ottoman Administration of the Spice Trade in the 16th Century Red Sea and Persian Gulf', *Journal of the Economic and Social History of the Orient*, 2006.

Cavaciocchi, S. (ed.). *XXXIX Settimana di Studi: La Fiscalita nell'economia europea secc. XIII–XVIII* (Florence: University of Florence Press, 2008).
Celasun, Oya. 'The 1994 Currency Crisis in Turkey', Macro-economic and Growth Group, Development and Research Department, The World Bank, internet: www.econturk.org/Turkisheconomy/kriz.pdf.
Cezar, Yavuz. *Osmanlı Maliyesinde Bunalım ve Değişim Dönemi* (Istanbul: Alan Yayıncılık, 1986).
Chang, Jennifer. 'Incentives from the Malaysian Government', paper presented at the Second Islamic Venture Capital and Private Equity Conference, 2009, convened at the Kuala Lumpur Convention Center, 20–21 May 2009.
Chapra, Umar. *The Future of Economics, An Islamic Perspective* (Leicester: The Islamic Foundation, 2000).
Chapra, Muhammad Umer. 'Monetary Management in an Islamic Economy', *Islamic Economic Studies,* 1996, vol. 4, No. 1.
Chapra, M. Umer. *Islam and the Economic Challenge* (Leicester: The Islamic Foundation, 1992).
Çiller, Tansu and Murat Çizakça. *Türk Finans Kesiminde Sorunlar ve Reform Önerileri* (Istanbul: ISO, 1989).
Çizakça, Murat and Muhammad Muhaizam bin Musa, 'Tabung Haji and Its Performance', ISRA, forthcoming.
Çizakça, Murat. '*Gharar* and Risk Aversion in the History of Islamic Public Finance – Evidence from the Ottoman Archives, 1500–1774', (ed. Mohammad Ariff) (Cheltenham, UK and Northampton, MA, USA: Edward Elgar, forthcoming).
Çizakça, Murat. 'Waqf', in Brahimi, Kahf, Siddiqi (eds), *Encyclopaedia of Islamic Economics*, (London: BPR, 2009).
Çizakça, Murat. 'The Economy', in S. Faroqhi and K. Fleet (eds), *Cambridge History of Turkey* (Cambridge: Cambridge University Press, forthcoming), vol. II.
Çizakça, Murat. '*Gharar* in Public Finance and the Origins of *Sukuk* – 1500–1800', submitted at the Symposium on Sukuk Financial Instruments, jointly sponsored by the Graduate School of Business, University Putra Malaysia and the Dubai International Financial Centre, convened on 3 May 2010 in Dubai at the DIFC conference centre.
Çizakça, Murat. 'Was *Shari'ah* Indeed the Culprit?', MPRA Paper no. 22865, posted 23 May 2010. http://mpra.ub.uni-muenchen.de/22865.
Çizakça, Murat. 'Thc British Legislation in Malaya and Its Impact Upon the Malaysian Waqf System', paper submitted at the Second Harvard Conference: 'Law of Waqf, Modern State Control and Nationalization', 16–18 May 2008, Harvard Law School.
Çizakça, Murat and Macit Kenanoğlu. 'Ottoman Merchants and the Juriprudential Shift Hypothesis', in S. Faroqhi and G. Veinstein (eds) *Merchants in the Ottoman Empire* (Leuven: Peeters, Collection *Turcica*), vol. XV, 2008: 195–215.
Çizakça, Murat. 'Democracy, Economic Development and *Maqasid al-Shari'ah*', *Review of Islamic Economics,* vol. 11, No. 1, 2007.
Çizakça, Murat. 'Cross-cultural Borrowing and Comparative Evolution of Institutions between Islamic World and the West', in S. Cavaciocchi (ed.), *Relazioni Economiche tra Europa e Mondo Islamico, Secc. XIII–XVIII* (Prato: Istituto di Storia Economica, F. Datini, Serie II, 38, 2006), also available at www.mcizakca.com
Çizakça, Murat. 'Islam und Christentum: Symbiose Zweier Zwilizationen', paper presented on 13 November 2006, Munich, Germany at the Ludwig Maximillians Universitaet on the occasion of the inauguration of the Third Allianz Professorship.
Çizakça, Murat. *Demokrasi Arayışında Türkiye: Laik-Dindar/Demokrat Uzlaşmasına Bir Katkı* (Ankara: Yeni Türkiye, 2002).

Çizakça, Murat. *A History of Philanthropic Foundations, The Islamic World From the Seventh Century to the Present* (Istanbul: Bogazici University Press, 2000).
Çizakça, Murat. 'Awqaf in History and Its Implications for Modern Islamic Economies', *Islamic Economic Studies,* vol. 6, no. 1, 1998.
Çizakça, Murat. *A Comparative Evolution of Business Partnerships, Islamic World and Europe with Specific Reference to the Ottoman Archives* (Leiden: E. J. Brill, 1996).
Çizakça, Murat. 'Cash Waqfs of Bursa, 1555–1823', *Journal of the Economic and Social History of the Orient,* vol. 338, part 3, 1995.
Çizakça, Murat.'Tax-farming and Financial Decentralization in the Ottoman Economy', *The Journal of European Economic History*, vol. 22, No. 2, fall 1993, pp. 219–50.
Çizakça, Murat. *Risk Sermayesi, Özel Finans Kurumları ve Para Vakıfları* (Istanbul: ISAV, 1993).
Çizakça, Murat. *Türk Finans Kesiminde Sorunlar ve Reform Önerileri* (Istanbul: ISO, 1989).
Çizakça, Murat. 'Price History and the Bursa Silk Industry: A Study in Ottoman Industrial Decline', *Journal of Economic History,* 1980, No. 3, pp. 533–51.
Crecelius, Daniel. 'Introduction', *Journal of the Economic and Social History of the Orient,* vol. 38, 1995, no. 3.
Davudoglu, Ahmed. *Mevkufat Mülteka Tercümesi* (Istanbul: Sağlam Kitabevi, 1980).
Dawud: Book 10, *Kitab al-Manasik wa'l-Hajj,* hadith 1730.
DeLorenzo, Yusuf Talal. 'The Total Returns Swap and the *Shari'ah* Conversion Technology', http://www.dinarstandard.com/finance/DeLorenzo012308.htm. Retrieved on 10 November 2010.
Demir, Abdullah. 'Ebussuud Efendi'nin Osmanlı Hukukundaki Yeri' (Istanbul: Marmara University PhD Thesis, 2004.)
Demirci, Mustafa. 'İkta', *İslam Ansiklopedisi, Türkiye Diyanet Vakfı Islam Ansiklopedisi* (Istanbul: ISAM, 2007).
Dincecco, Mark. 'Fiscal Centralization, Limited Government and Public Revenues in Europe, 1650–1913', *Journal of Economic History,* vol. 69, no. 1, 2009.
Döndüren, Hamdi. *Günümüzde Vakıf Meseleleri* (Istanbul: Erkam, 1998).
Döndüren, Hamdi. *Ticaret ve İktisat İlmihali* (Istanbul: Altınoluk/Erkam, 1993).
Döndüren, Hamdi. *Islam Hukuku'na Göre Alım-Satımda Kar Hadleri* (Balıkesir: İnce, 1984).
Dusuki, Asyraf Wajdi Dato'. *Islamic Finance: An Old Skeleton in a Modern Dress* (Kuala Lumpur: ISRA/INCEIF, 2008).
El-Gamal, Mahmoud A. *Islamic Finance, Law, Economics and Practice* (Cambridge: Cambridge University Press, 2007, reprint).
Ensminger, Jean. 'Transaction Costs and Islam: Explaining Conversion in Africa', *Journal of Institutional and Theoretical Economics,* vol. 153, 1997.
Epicentre, the MIFC eNewsletter, 26 October 2009.
Erkal, Mehmet. *İslam'ın Erken Döneminde İslam'ın Erken Döneminde Uygulamaları* (Istanbul: ISAM, 2009).
Esen, Adem and Kemalettin Çonkar. *Orta Anadolu Girişimcilerinin Sosyo-Ekonomik Özellikleri, İşletmecilik Anlayışları ve Beklentileri Araştırması* (Konya: Konya Ticaret Odası, 1999).
Essid, Yassine. *A Critique of Islamic Economic Thought* (Leiden: Brill, 1995).
Evensky, Jerry. *Adam Smith's Moral Philosophy: A Historical and Contemporary Perspective on Markets, Law, Ethics and Culture* (Cambridge: Cambridge University Press, 2005).

Farook, Sayd. '*Salam* Based Capital Market Instruments', Securities Commission Malaysia, *Sukuk* (Kuala Lumpur: SCM, 2009), pp. 161–85.
Faroqhi, Suraiya. *Artisans of Empire, Crafts and Craftspeople Under the Ottomans* (London: I. B. Tauris, 2009).
Faroqhi, Suraiya. *Coping with the State* (Istanbul: ISIS, 1995).
Faroqhi, Suraiya. 'A Great Foundation in Difficulties' in id. *Making a Living in Ottoman Lands* (Istanbul: ISIS, XVIII, 1995), pp. 281–84.
Faroqhi, Suraiya. *Herrscher über Mekka, die Geschichte der Pilgerfahrt* (München: Artemis Verlag, 1990).
Faure, David. 'Charity Halls and the History of Charity in China', paper submitted at the conference: Historical Studies of Charity Institutions Across Culture, sponsored by the Chinese University of Hong Kong, 6–7 November 2008.
Faure, David. *China and Capitalism, A History of Business Enterprise in Modern China* (Hong Kong: Hong Kong University Press, 2006).
Friedman, M. *Capitalism and Freedom* (Chicago: University of Chicago Press, 1982).
Fritschy, Wantje. 'Indirect Taxes and Public Debt in the World of Islam Before 1800', in S. Cavaciocchi (ed.), *XXXIX Settimana di Studi: La Fiscalita nell'economia europea secc. XIII-XVIII* (Florence: University of Florence Press, 2008).
Froozye, Nikan. '*Tawarruq*: *Shari'ah* Risk or Banking Conundrum?', www.opalesque.com/OIFI12/Featured_Structure_Tawarruq_Shariah_Risk_or_...
Furat, Ahmet Hamdi. *Hanefi Mezhebi'nin İlk Oluşum Dönemi, Kufe Ekolü* (Istanbul: Yayın Yayıncılık, 2009).
Gaudiosi, Monica. 'The Influence of the Islamic Law of Waqf on the Development of the Trust in England: The Case of Merton College', *University of Pennsylvania Law Review,* vol. 136, no. 4, 1988.
Genç, Mehmet. 'Osmanli Dunyasinda Dilencilik', in Suvat Parin (ed.), *Bir Kent Sorunu: Dilencilik Sempozyumu Tebligler Kitabi* (Istanbul: B.B. Zabita Daire Bsk., 2008).
Genç, Mehmet. 'Malikâne', *İslam Ansiklopedisi* (*Türkiye Diyanet Vakfı Islam Ansiklopedisi* (Istanbul: ISAM, 2007).
Genç, Mehmet. 'Osmanlılar: Ticari ve İktisadi Yapı', *Türkiye Diyanet Vakfı Islam Ansiklopedisi* (Istanbul: ISAM, 2007).
Genç, Mehmet and Erol Özvar (eds). *Osmanlı Maliyesi, Kurumlar ve Bütçeler,* c. 1 (İstanbul: Osmanlı Bankası Arşiv ve Araştırma Merkezi, 2006).
Genç, Mehmet. 'Osmanlı İmparatorluğu'nda Devlet ve Ekonomi', in Mehmet Genç, M. *Osmanlı İmparatorluğu'nda Devlet ve Ekonomi* (Istanbul: Ötüken, 2000).
Genç, M. 'Esham'. *İslam Ansiklopedisi* (Ankara: Türkiye Diyanet Vakfı, 1995).
Genç, Mehmet. 'Osmanlı Maliyesinde *Malikâne* Sistemi', in O. Okyar (ed.), *Türkiye İktisat Tarihi Semineri* (Ankara: Hacettepe University Press, 1975).
Gerber, Haim. 'The Muslim Law of Partnerships in Ottoman Court Records', *Studia Islamica*, 1981, vol. 53.
Geremek, Borislaw. *Poverty, A History* (Oxford: Blackwell, 1994).
Gilbar, Gad. 'Muslim Tujjar of the Middle East and Their Commercial Networks in the Long Nineteenth Century', paper submitted at the XIV International Economic History Congress, Helsinki, 21–25 August 2006, Session 121.
Global Investment House. '*Sukuk* Market – Down But Not Out (Final Part)', *Islamic Finance News,* 6 March 2009.
Goitein, S.D. 'The Rise of the Middle-Eastern Bourgeoise in Early Islamic Times' in S. D. Goitein, *Studies in Islamic History and Institutions* (Leiden: Brill, 1968).
Gomez, Terence and K. S. Jomo. *Malaysia's Political Economy* (Cambridge: Cambridge University Press, 1999).

Gözübenli, Beşir. 'Inan', *Türkiye Diyanet Vakfı Islam Ansiklopedisi* (Istanbul: ISAM, 2007).
Gulaid, M. A. and M. A. Abdullah (eds). *Readings in Public Finance in Islam* (Jeddah: IRTI/IDB, 1995).
Gülen, Fethullah. *Enginliğiyle Bizim Dünyamız: İktisadi Mülahazalar* (Istanbul: Nil, 2009).
Güler, Mustafa. *Osmanlı Devleti'nde Haremeyn Vakıfları* (Istanbul: TATAV, 2002)
Halebi, Ibrahim. *Mülteka'l Ebhur* (Istanbul: 1884)
Hamidullah, Muhammad. *The First Written Constitution in the World* (Lahore: Sh Muhammad Ashraf, 1981).
Haneef, Muhammad Aslam and Emad Rafiq Barakat. 'Must Money be Limited to Only Gold and Silver?', *Journal of King Abdulaziz University: Islamic Economics,* 2006, vol. 19, no. 1, pp. 21–34.
Haneef, Rafe. 'Islamic Treasury Money Market Instruments for Liquidity Management', *Islamic Finance Bulletin,* October–December 2008.
Haneef, Rafe. 'The Sukuk Market, the Challenges Ahead', Paper presented at INCEIF, June 2008.
Hanna, Nelly. *Making Big Money in 1600* (Cairo/Syracuse: The American University in Cairo Press/Syracuse University Press, 1998).
Hansmann, Henry et al. 'Law and the Rise of the Firm', *Harvard Law Review*, 119, 2006: 1337–43.
Harris, Ron. 'Institutional Dynamics: The Commenda and the Corporation', http://www.usc.edu/schools/college/crcc/private/ierc/conference_registration/papers/Harris_final.pdf.
Hartwell, R. M. and Stanley L. Engerman. 'Capitalism', in J. Mokyr (ed.), *The Oxford Encyclopaedia of Economic History*, vol. I (Oxford: Oxford University Press, 2003).
Hasan, Zubair. 'Islamic Finance: What Does It Change, What It Does Not?', paper submitted at the Workshop on Islamic Finance, Université de Strasbourg, Institut d'Etudes Politiques, 17 March 2010.
Hasan, Zubair. 'Commodity *Murabaha* : Does It Violate Islamic Norms?', *MPRA,* no. 11736, 2008.
Hasan, Zubair. 'Ensuring Exchange Rate Stability: Is Return to Gold (Dinar) Possible?', MPRA Paper No. 8134, posted 8 April 2008.
Hasan, Zubair. 'Islamic Banking at the Cross-Roads: Theory vs. Practice', *MPRA*, paper no. 2821, 2007.
Hasan, Zubair. '*Mudaraba* As a Mode of Finance in Islamic Banking: Theory, Practice and Problems', *MPRA*, no. 2951, 2007.
Hasan, Zubair. 'Theory of Profit: The Islamic Viewpoint', *Journal of Research in Islamic Economics,* vol. I, no. 1, 1983: 3–14.
Hashim, Muhammad Ali. *Waqf An-Nur* Corporation Berhad Annual Report, 2008.
Hassan, Kabir M. and Mervyn K. Lewis. *Handbook of Islamic Banking* (Cheltenham, UK and Northampton, MA, USA: Edward Elgar, 2007).
Hassan, Taufiq., S. Mohamad and M. K. I. Bader. 'Efficiency of Conventional vs. Islamic Banks: Evidence from the Middle East', *International Journal of Islamic and Middle Eastern Finance and Management,* vol. II, no. 1, 2009, p. 60.
Hayek, F. A. *The Road to Serfdom* (Chicago: University of Chicago Press, 1994).
Heck, Gene W. *Charlemagne, Muhammad and the Arab Roots of Capitalism* (Berlin: De Gruyter, Studien zur Geschichte und Kultur des islamischen Orients, Beihefte zur Zeitschrift 'der Islam', Band 18, 2006).
Hesse, Heiko, Andreas A. Jobst and Juan Solé. 'Trends and Challenges in Islamic Finance', *World Economics,* vol. 9, no. 2, April–June 2008.

Himmelfarb, Gertrude. *The Roads to Modernity, The British, French and American Enlightenments* (New York: A. A. Knopf, 2005)
Hodgson, Marshall G. S. *The Venture of Islam* (Chicago: University of Chicago Press, 1974).
Hoexter, Miriam. *Endowments, Rulers and Community, Waqf al-Haramayn in Ottoman Algiers* (Leiden: Brill, 1998)
Hoexter, Miriam. 'Adaptation to Changing Circumstances: Perpetual Leases and Exchange Transactions in Waqf Property in Ottoman Algiers', *Islamic Law and Society*, vol. 4, no. 3: 319–33.
Hoffmann, Gerhard. 'Interdependencies Between the Military and the Economy in the Near East and Egypt', in J. Heitzman and W. Schenkluhn (eds), *The World in the Year 1000* (Lanham, MD: University Press of America, 2004).
Hooker, Barry. 'Fatawa in Malaysia 1960–85, Third Coulson Memorial Lecture', *Arab Law Quarterly,* vol. VIII, no. 2, 1993.
Hookway, James. 'Malaysians Go for Gold as Alternative Currency', *The Wall Street Journal,* September 7, 2010, p. 10.
Hudson, Leila Olga. 'Cultural Capital: Wealth and Values in Late Ottoman Damascus', The University of Michigan PhD Thesis, 1999.
Hussain, A. *The Islamic Law of Succession* (Riyadh: Darussalam, 2005).
Ibn Abidin. *Al-Mavsuat al-Fıkhiyye* (Kuwait: 1992), vol. 26, 89.
Ibn Abidin. *Redd al-Muhtar* (Istanbul: Kahraman, 1984), 8 volumes.
Ibn Ashur. *Treatise on Maqasid al-Shari'ah* (London: International Institute of Islamic Thought, 2006).
Ibn Khaldun. *The Mukaddimah, An Introduction to History* (Princeton: Princeton University Press, 1967), translated by F. Rosenthal.
Ibrahim, Monsor H. 'Monetary Dynamics and Gold Dinar', *Journal of King Abdulaziz University*, vol. 19, no. 2, 2006, pp. 3–20.
IFIS (Islamic Finance Information Service), *IFIS Global Sukuk Market, Sukuk H2-2010 Report*, 2010.
IMF. *World Economic Output Database*, October 2010.
Inalcık, Halil. *Turkey and Europe in History* (Istanbul: Eren, 2006).
Inalcık, Halil and Donald Quataert. *An Economic and Social History of the Ottoman Empire* (Cambridge: Cambridge University Press, 1994).
İnalcık, H. 'Cizye'. *İslam Ansiklopedisi* (Istanbul: ISAM, 1993).
Inalcık, H. 'Imtiyazat', *Encyclopaedia of Islam* (Leiden: E. J. Brill, 2nd edn.).
Iqbal, Munawar and P. Molyneux. *Banking and Financial Systems in the Arab World* (London: Palgrave Macmillan, 2005).
Iqbal, Munawar and P. Molyneux. *Thirty Years of Islamic Banking* (London: Palgrave Macmillan, 2005).
Iqbal, Zafar and M. K. Lewis. *An Islamic Perspective on Governance* (Cheltenham, UK and Northampton, MA, USA: Edward Elgar, 2009).
IRTI. *Tabung Haji as an Islamic Financial Institution* (Jeddah: IRTI/IDB Prize Winners Lecture Series, no. 4, 1995).
Islam Mahbubul. *Freedom of Religion in Shari'ah* (Kuala Lumpur: Noordeen, 2002).
Islamic Finance in Practice, www.gmbpublishing.com.
Islamic Finance News, www.islamicfinancenews.com.
Islamic Financial Services Board. *Exposure Draft, Guiding Principles on Governance for Islamic Insurance* (Takaful) *Operations,* (Kuala Lumpur: IFSB, December 2008).

Jacobs, Jennifer. 'Laughing All the Way to the Bank'. *Islamic Finance Asia,* 27 August 2009.
Jasin, Kadir. 'The NEP Was Not a Failure', *Malaysian Business,* 16–31 July 2009.
Jastram, Roy. *The Golden Constant* (Cheltenham, UK and Northampton, MA, USA: Edward Elgar, 2009).
Johor Corporation. *Johor Corporation's Intrapreneur Development Programme* (Johor Bahru: Internal Paper dated 26 January 2009).
Jones, Eric. *The European Miracle, Environments, Economies and Geo-politics in the History of Europe and Asia* (Cambridge: Cambridge University Press, 2003).
Kahf, Monzer. 'The Use of Assets, *Ijara* Bonds, for Bridging the Budget Gap', in IDB/IRTI (ed.), *Islamic Financial Instruments for Public Sector Mobilization* (Jeddah: IDB/IRTI, 1997).
Kahf, Monzer. 'The Use of Assets, *Ijara* Bonds, for Bridging the Budget Gap', *Islamic Economic Studies,* vol. 4, no. 2, 1997.
Kahf, Monzer. 'Taxation Policy in an Islamic Economy', *Readings in Public Finance in Islam* (Jeddah: IDB/IRTI, 1995).
Kala, Ahmet. 'Türk Sanayiinin Öncü Müteşebbisi Ahi Evren', *Çerçeve,* 2005, XIII/35.
Kallek, Cengiz. *Hz. Peygamber (S.A.S.) Döneminde Devlet ve Piyasa* (Istanbul: Bilim ve Sanat Vakfı, 1992).
Kamali, Mohammad Hashim. *An Introduction to Shari'ah* (Kuala Lumpur: Ilmiah, 2006).
Kamali, Mohammad Hashim. *Equity and Fairness in Islam* (Kuala Lumpur: Ilmiah, 2006).
Kamali, Mohammad Hashim. *Islamic Commercial Law* (Kuala Lumpur: Ilmiah, 2002).
Kamali, Mohammad Hashim. *Principles of Islamic Jurisprudence* (Kuala Lumpur: Ilmiah, 3rd edn, 2000).
Kamali, Mohammad Hashim. *Freedom of Expression in Islam* (Kuala Lumpur: Ilmiah, 1998).
Kamali, Mohammad Hashim. *Istihsan (Juristic Preference) and Its Application to Contemporary Issues* (Jeddah: IRTI, 1995).
Kamil, Wan Abdul Rahim. 'Introduction to *Sukuk*', in Ram Ratings, *Malaysian Sukuk Market Handbook* (Kuala Lumpur: Tijanimas, 2008).
Karaman, Hayreddin. 'Gelire Endeksli Senetler', *Yeni Şafak*, 15 February 2009.
Karaman, Hayrettin ve Ali Şafak. *Islam Hukuna Göre Alış Verişte Vade Farkı ve Kâr Haddi* (Istanbul: ISAV, 1987).
Karaman, Hayreddin. 'Islam Hukukunda Alış Verişte Kâr Haddi Araştırmasına Tenkidi Görüş', in Karaman, Hayrettin ve Ali Şafak, *Islam Hukuna Göre Alış Verişte Vade Farkı ve Kâr Haddi* (Istanbul: ISAV, 1987).
Karaman, Hayreddin. '*Zekat*', *İslam Ansiklopedisi* (Istanbul: Kültür ve Turizm Bakanlığı, 1986).
Kardavi, Yusuf al. *İslam Hukuku'nda Zekat* (Istanbul: Kayıhan, 1984).
Kaul, Inge, Isabelle Grunberg and Marc A. Stern (eds). *Global Public Goods* (Oxford: Oxford University Press, 1999).
Kawach, Nadim. 'GCC *Sukuk* Issues Plunge 57 Percent in 2008', *Emirate Business,* 24/7, 12 February 2009.
Kaya, Süleyman. 'Osmanlı Toplumunda Şahıslar İçin Kredi Kaynağı Olarak İcareteyn Uygulaması', paper submitted at the Second Congress of Ottoman Economic History, Elazığ, 24–25 June 2010.
Kenanoğlu, Macit. *Osmanlı Millet Sistemi* (Istanbul: Klasik, 2004).
Keay, John. *The Honorable Company, A History of the English East India Company* (London: HarperCollins, 1993).

Khan, Ahmad Zafar. *Islamic Banking and Its Operations* (London: IIBI, 2000).
Khan, Muhammad Akram. *Economic Teachings of Prophet Muhammad* (Islamabad: Institute of Policy Studies, 1989).
Khan, Salman H. 'Why *Tawarruq* Needs To Go', *Islamic Finance News*, 4 September 2009.
Khnifer, Mohammed. 'Maslaha and the Permissibility of Organized Tawarruq', https://mail.inceif.org/exchange.
Kindleberger, Charles P. *A Financial History of Western Europe* (London: Allen & Unwin, 1984).
Kıraç, Can. *Anılarımla Patronum Vehbi Koç* (Istanbul: Milliyet Yayınları, 1995).
Kuran, Timur. *Islam and Mammon, the Economic Predicament of Islamism* (Princeton: PUP, 2004).
Kuran, Timur. 'Why the Middle East is Economically Underdeveloped: Historical Mechanisms of Institutional Stagnation', *Journal of Economic Perspectives*, vol. 18, No. 3, 2004: 78–9.
Kuwait Finance House. *Islamic Finance Research,* 16 February 2009.
Labib, Subhi Y. 'Capitalism in Medieval Islam', *Journal of Economic History*, vol. 29, No. 1, 1969.
Laldin, Mohamad Akram. '*Shari'ah* Compliant vs *Shari'ah* Based Product', *ISRA Bulletin,* vol. 2, April 2009.
Laldin, Mohamad Akram. 'Islamic Financial System', *Humanomics,* vol. 24, no. 3, 2008.
Laldin, Mohamad Akram. *Fundamentals and Practices in Islamic Finance* (Kuala Lumpur: ISRA/INCEIF, 2008).
Lambton, Ann. *Landlord and Peasant in Persia* (London: I. B. Tauris, 1991).
Lane and Commentators, 'Meanings of Capitalism', *The Journal of Economic History,* vol. XXIX, No. 1, 1969.
Leblang, David A. 'Property Rights, Democracy and Economic Growth', *Political Research Quarterly,* 1996.
Lewis, Mervyn K. 'An Islamic Economic Perspective on the Global Financial Crisis', in Steve Kates (ed.), *Mainstream Economic Theory and Its Failings: Alternative Perspectives on the Global Financial Crisis* (Cheltenham, UK and Northampton, MA, USA: Edward Elgar, 2010).
Lewis, Mervyn K. 'An Islamic Economic Perspective on the Global Financial Crisis', Lecture given on 16 April 2009 at the *Securities Exchange Commission* in Kuala Lumpur.
Macdonald, James. *A Free Nation Deep in Debt, The Financial Roots of Democracy* (Princeton: University of Princeton Press, 2006).
Mahmood, Nik Ramlah Nik. 'Malaysia Leads Robust Islamic Venture Capital Industry', Keynote address delivered at the Islamic Venture Capital and Private Equity Conference, on 7 May 2008.
Mahmood, Nik Ramlah. *Insurance Law in Malaysia* (Butterworths: Utopia Press, 1992).
Majed, Salleh. 'Removing the Clutches Slowly', *Malaysian Business,* 16–31 July 2009.
Majer, Hans Georg (ed.). *Das osmanische Registerbuch der Beschwerden (Şikayet Defteri) vom Jahre 1675* (Wien: 1984).
Malik, Book 31 (Business Transactions), *hadith* 31.12.21, www.imaanstar.com.
Mallat, Chibli Wajdi. 'The Renaissance of Islamic Law: Constitution, Economics and Banking in the Thought of Muhammad Baqer as-Sadr' (London: SOAS PhD Thesis, 1989).
Mandaville, Jon E. 'Usurious Piety: The Cash Waqf Controversy in the Ottoman Empire', *International Journal of Middle East Studies*, vol. 10, no. 3, 1979.
Mannan, M. A. 'Cash Waqf Certificate – An Innovation in Islamic Financial Instrument: Global Opportunities for Developing Social Capital Market in the 21st Century

Voluntary Sector Banking', paper submitted at the Third Harvard University Forum on Islamic Finance, October 1999.

Mannan, Mohammad Abdul. *Islamic Socioeconomic Institutions and Mobilization of Resources with Special Reference to Hajj Management of Malaysia* (Jeddah: IRTI/IDB, Research Paper No. 40, 1996).

Martinez, Manuel Sanchez . 'Dette publique, autorites princieres et villes dans les pays de la Couronne d'Aragon', in M. Boone et al. (eds), *Urban Public Debts* (Turnhout: Brepols, 2003).

Mbengue, Babacar. *Islamic Finance: Back to the Spiritual Roots of Capitalism?*, forthcoming.

McCormick, Michael. *Origins of the European Economy, Communications and Commerce* (Cambridge: Cambridge University Press, 2001).

Meera, Ahamed Kameel Mydin. *The Islamic Gold Dinar* (Kuala Lumpur: Pelanduk, 2002).

Menard, C. and M. M. Shirley (eds). *Handbook of New Institutional Economics* (Dordrecht: Springer, 2005), p. 26.

Milgrom, P. and J. Roberts. *Economics, Organization and Management* (London: Prentice-Hall, 1992).

Mirakhor, Abbas and Idris Samawi Hamid. *Islam and Development, the Institutional Framework,* forthcoming.

Mirakhor, Abbas and Iqbal Zaidi. 'Profit and Loss Sharing Contracts in Islamic Finance' in M. Kabir Hassan and Mervyn K. Lewis (eds), *Handbook of Islamic Banking* (Cheltenham, UK and Northampton, MA, USA: Edward Elgar, 2007).

Mirakhor, Abbas and Zamir Iqbal. *An Introduction to Islamic Finance, Theory and Practice* (Singapore: John Wiley and Sons, 2007).

Mohamad, Yusoff and Al-Qassar. 'Ground Rules', in Securities Commission Malaysia, *Sukuk*.

Mokhdar, Shabnam. 'The Relationship Between Leakage in Commodity *murabaha* and *Sukuk* Pricing', *ISRA Bulletin,* Vol. 1, Dec. 2008, ISSN 1985-7497.

Morimoto, Kosei. *The Fiscal Administration of Egypt in the Early Islamic Period* (Kyoto: Dohosha, 1981).

Mukhtar, Shabnam and Arfa'eza A. Aziz. 'Is AAOIFI Irrelevant?', *Islamic Finance News,* 4 April 2008.

Munro, John. 'The Usury Doctrine and Urban Public Finances in Late Medieval Flanders', paper submitted at the XXXIX Settimana di Studi, *Fiscal Systems in the European Economy,* Prato, 22–25 April 2007.

Munro, John. 'The Medieval Origins of the Financial Revolution: Usury, *Rentes* and Negotiability', *The International History Review,* vol. XXV, No. 3, 2003.

Muqtedar Khan. 'The Islamic State and Religious Minorities', *Islam for Today.*

Muslim, Book 10 (Book of Transactions), *hadith* 3861.

Muslim, Imam. *Sahih Muslim; Al-Kutub al-Sittah wa Shuruhuha* (Istanbul: Çağrı, 1992).

T.C. Başbakanlık Hazine Müsteşarlığı. *Basın Duyurusu, Sayı 2009/63, 17* Nisan, 2009.

T.C. Başbakanlık Hazine Müsteşarlığı. *Gelire Endeksli Senetler Tanıtım Klavuzu.*

Nadim Khan, Paul McViety et al. 'Scholarly Debate Drives Reform', *International Financial Law Review*, August 2008.

Nair, Sridharan and Adelyn Chen, 'The Evolving Malaysian *Takaful* Industry', *Islamic Finance News,* 11 April 2008.

Nevevi, Muhyiddin-i. *Riyazü's-Salihin* (Ankara: Diyanet İşleri Bşk., 1993).

Nienhaus, Volker. *Islam und Moderne Wirtschaft* (Wien: Styria, 1982).
North, Douglas. 'Institutions and the Performance of Economies Over Time' in Menard and Shirley, *New Institutional Economics*, 2005.
North, Douglass C. *Institutions, Institutional Change and Economic Performance* (Cambridge: Cambridge University Press, 1990).
North, Douglass and Barry Weingast. 'The Evolution of Institutions Governing Public Choice in 17th Century England', *Journal of Economic History*, 1989.
North, Douglas C. *Structure and Change in Economic History* (New York: W. W. Norton & Co., 1981).
Orman, Sabri. *Gazali'nin Iktisat Felsefesi* (Istanbul: Insan Yayinlari, 2002).
Orman, Sabri. *Iktisat, Tarih ve Toplum* (Istanbul: Küre Yayınları, 2001).
Orman, Sabri. 'Cagdas Arap Dunyasinda Demokrasiye Gecisin Onundeki Engeller', in Bardakoglu et al, *Islam ve Demokrasi I* (Istanbul: Ensar, 2000).
Ortayli, Ilber. *Kirk Anbar Sohbetleri* (Istanbul: Aşina, 2006).
Öniş, Ziya. *State and the Market: the Political Economy of Turkey in Comparative Perspective* (Istanbul: Bogazici University Press, 1998).
Özdemir, Şennur. *MÜSİAD, Anadolu Sermayesinin Dönüşümü ve Türk Modernleşmesinin Derinleşmesi* (Istanbul: Vadi, 2006).
Özdevecioglu, Mahmut. *Kayseri Tüccar Profili Araştırması* (Kayseri: KTO, 1997).
Özvar, Erol. 'Fiscal Crisis of the Ottoman Empire in the Seventeenth Century', paper presented at the the XIth International Congress of the Economic and Social History of Turkey, Ankara, 17–20 June 2008.
Özvar, Erol. 'Osmanlı Devleti'nin Bütçe Harcamaları', in M. Genç and E. Özvar (eds.), *Osmanlı Maliyesi Kurumlar ve Bütçeler* (Istanbul: Osmanli Bankası, 2006), 2 volumes.
Pamuk, Şevket. 'Batı Avrupa İle Karşılaştırmalı Çerçevede Osmanlı Devleti'nde Kişi Başına Gelir', paper submitted at the Economic History Congress, Marmara University, Istanbul, 7–8 September 2007.
Pamuk, Şevket. *A Monetary History of the Ottoman Empire* (Cambridge: Cambridge University Press, 2000).
Pamuk, Şevket. *İstanbul ve Diğer Kentlerde 500 Yıllık Fiyatlar ve Ücretler, 1469–1998* (*500 Years of Prices and Wages in Istanbul and Other Cities*) (Ankara: DİE, 2000).
Pamuk, Şevket. *Osmanlı İmparatorluğu'nda Paranın Tarihi* (İstanbul: Tarih Vakfı, 1999).
Panzac, Daniel. 'Le Contrat d'Affrément maritime en Mediterranée', *Journal of the Economic and Social History of the Orient,* vol. 45, No. 3, pp. 351–8.
Parker, Mushtak. '*Shari'ah* Advisories Must be Regulated', *Islamic Banker,* May/June, no. 8, 2009.
Parker, Mushtak. '*Sukuk* and the Efficacy of *Shari'ah* Governance', *Islamic Banker,* 18, March–April 2008.
Parliamentary Debates, Dewan Ra'ayat, vol. IV, Fourth Session, Part I, April 1962–December 1962.
Pense, Alan. 'The Decline and Fall of the Roman Denarius', *Materials Characterization,* vol. 29, no. 2, 1992.
Permodalan Nasional Berhad, *Annual Report*, 1978.
Permodalan Nasional Berhad, *Annual Report*, 2005.
Permodalan Nasional Berhad, *The Fabric of a Nation* (Kuala Lumpur: PNB, n.d.).
Peter Baum, Hans. 'Annuities in Late Medieval Hanse Towns', *Business History Review*, Spring 1985.

Pistor, K., D. Berkowitz, J.-F. Richard. 'Economic Development, Legality, and the Transplant Effect', *European Economic Review* 47, 2003.
Pistor, K. *The Standardization of Law and Its Effect on Developing Economies*, G-24 Discussion Paper No. 4, June 2000.
Postan, M. M., E. E. Rich and E. Miller (eds). *The Cambridge Economic History of Europe* (Cambridge: At the University Press, 1965).
Powers, David S. 'The Islamic Inheritance System: A Socio-Historical Approach', *Arab Law Quarterly,* vol. 8, No. 1, 1993: 14–15.
Prather, Doug. 'The Ducat', *World Internet Numismatic Society Newsletter,* 2004.
Prodromidis, Prodromos. 'Economic Environment, Policies and Inflation in the Roman Empire up to Diocletian's Price Edict', *Journal of European Economic History*, 2009, no. 3, pp. 567–609.
Rahman, Khalid. 'Towards Islamic Banking: A Case Study of Pilgrims Management and Fund Board, Malaysia', www.eldis.org/fulltext/rahman.pdf (2004).
Ram Ratings. 'Malaysian *Sukuk* Taxation', *Islamic Finance News*, 10 April 2009.
Ram Ratings. *Malaysian Sukuk Market Handbook* (Kuala Lumpur: Tijanimas Communications, 2008).
Richtel, Matt. 'Silicon Valley Investors Lobby for Clean Fuel', *International Herald Tribune*, 30 January 2007.
Riza, Reşid and Hayreddin Karaman. *Gerçek Islam'da Birlik* (Istanbul: Iz, 2003).
Rodinson, Maxime. *Islam and Capitalism* (New York: Penguin Books, 1974).
Rosly, Saiful Azhar; Ahcene Lahsasna and Muhammad Arzim Naim. 'Shari'ah Risk and Clawback Effect of *Al-Bai-Bithaman Ajil* in Default', *Journal of Islamic Accounting and Business (Emerald),* under review.
Rosly, Saiful Azhar. *Critical Issues on Islamic Banking and Financial Markets* (Kuala Lumpur: Dinamas, 2008, third print).
Ruhanie, N. and S. Mahavera. 'Permodalan Nasional Launches *Amanah Saham Gemilang*', *New Straits Times,* 18 March 2003.
Saeed, A. *Islamic Banking and Interest, A Study of the Prohibition of Riba and Its Contemporary Interpretation* (Leiden: Brill, 1996).
Sahillioğlu, Halil. 'Bursa Kadı Sicillerinde İç ve Dış Ödemeler Aracı Olarak 'Kitabül Kadı! ve 'Süfteceler''', O. Okyar (ed.), *Türkiye İktisat Tarihi Semineri* (Ankara: Hacettepe Üniversitesi Yayınları, 1975).
Salamon, Lester M. and Stefan Toepler. *The International Guide to Non-Profit Law* (New York: John Wiley and Sons, 1997).
Salehabadi, Ali. *Essays on Islamic Finance* (Teheran: Imam Sadigh (A.S) University Press, 2008).
Salleh, Husni. 'The State of the Industry Address: Market Practice Regionally', paper presented at the Second Islamic Venture Capital and Private Equity Conference, 2009, convened at the Kuala Lumpur Convention Center, 20–21 May 2009.
Sandler, Todd. 'Intergenerational Public Goods, Strategies, Efficiency and Institutions' in Inge Kaul, Isabelle Grunberg, Marc A. Stern (eds), *Global Public Goods* (Oxford: Oxford University Press, 1999).
Sandwick, John. 'Divergence of Views, Divergence of Allocations', *Islamic Banking and Finance,* vol. 6, Issue 2, No. 17.
Sanusi, Mahmood Mohamed. *Critical Issues on Islamic Banking, Finance and Takaful* (Kuala Lumpur, INCEIF, 2010).
Sanusi, Mahmood Mohamed. 'The Concept of Legal Entity and Limited Liability in Islamic Legal System', *Malayan Law Journal* (*Lexis Nexis*), vol. 3, 2009.

Sanusi, Mahmood M. '*Muqarada* Islamic Bonds as an Alternative to *Bay' al-'Inah* and *Bay' al-Dayn* Bonds: A Critical Analysis', *International Journal of Islamic Financial Services,* 1999, No. 2.
Satoğlu, Emine Beyza. 'Anatolian Tigers: Local Adaptability to Global Competitiveness in Kayseri', Bogazici University/Atatürk Institute for Modern Turkish History MA Thesis, 2008.
Sayın, Abdurrahman Vefik. *Tekâlif Kavaidi (Osmanlı Vergi Sistemi),* (Ankara: Maliye Bakanlığı, yayın no: 1999/352, 1999).
Saylan, Ş. Cankut. *Kira Sertifikası Sistemi Üzerine Kısa Bir İnceleme* (Istanbul: Unpublished Report for Türkiye Katılım Bankaları Birliği, 2009).
Sayous, Andre. *Le Commerce des Européens à Tunis depuis le XII Siècle jusqu'à la fin de XVIé* (Paris: Lacademie des Sciences Coloniales, 1929).
Schlicht, Ekkehart. *On Custom in the Economy* (Oxford: Clarendon Press, 1997).
Schoon, Natalie. 'Application of Islamic Products in Treasury', *Islamic Finance News*, 19 December 2008.
Securities Commission Malaysia, *Sukuk* (Kuala Lumpur: Sweet and Maxwell Asia, ICM Series, 2009).
Sen, Amartya. *Development As Freedom* (Oxford: Oxford University Press, 1999).
Şekerci, Osman. *Islam Şirketler Hukuku* (Istanbul: Marifet Yayınları, 1981).
Şencan, Hüner. *İş Hayatında İslam İnsanı, Homo-Islamicus* (Istanbul: MÜSİAD, 1994).
Sezgin, Fuad. *Einführung in die Geschichte der Arabisch-Islamischen Wissenschaften* (Frankfurt am main: Johann Wolfgang Goethe Universitaet, 2003), vol. I.
Shaikh, Omar. 'Private Equity – Modern Day Musharaka?', *Islamic Finance News* Volume 4, Issue 45. Currently 2 January 2010.
Shari'ah Advisory Council of Bank Negara Malaysia. *Shari'ah Parameter Reference 1: Murabaha* (Kuala Lumpur: BNM, 2009).
Shatzmiller, Maya. *Her Day in Court: Women's Property Rights in Fifteenth Century Granada* (Cambridge, MA: Harvard University Press, 2007).
Shibli, Nu'mani. *Al-Farooq, the Life of Omar the Great* (New Delhi: Idara Isha'at-e-Diniyat, 1996).
Siddiqi, Mohammed Nejatullah. 'Islamic Banking and Finance in Theory and Practice: A Survey of State of the Art', *Islamic Economic Studies*, Vol. 13, No. 2, 2006.
Siddiqi, Muhammad Nejatullah. *Partnership and Profit-Sharing in Islamic Law* (Leicester: The Islamic Foundation, 1985).
Siklos, Pierre. 'Barter and Barter Economies', *Oxford Encyclopaedia of Economic History* (Oxford: Oxford University Press, 2003), vol. I, pp. 242–44.
Sin, Kam Fan. *The Legal Nature of the Unit Trust* (Oxford: Clarendon, 1997).
Spufford, P. 'Coinage and Currency', in Postan, Rich and Miller, *The Cambridge Economic History of Europe* (Cambridge: Cambridge University Press, 1965), Vol. III.
Standard & Poor's. *Outlook 2008*.
Standard & Poor's. 'Chief Drivers Behind Islamic Finance's Global Expansion', *Commentary Report*, April 2007.
Standard & Poor's. '*Sukuk* Market Picks up Pace Despite Gloomy Conditions', www.Islamicfinancenews.com, 19 September 2008.
Standard & Poor's. *Islamic Finance News,* 13 March 2009.
Standard and Poor's. '*Sukuk* Market Continues to Grow Despite Gloomy Global Market Conditions'. *Ratings Direct*, 9 September 2008.
Standard & Poor's. '*Sukuk* Market Grows Despite Roadblocks (part 1)', *Islamic Finance News*, 11 September 2009.

Steensgaard, Niels. 'The Companies as a Specific Institution in the History of European Expansion' in E. Blusse and F. Gaastra (eds), *Companies and Trade* (Leiden: Leiden University Press, 1981).
Suhrawardy, A. al-Ma'mun. 'The Waqf of Movables', *Journal of the Royal Society of Bengal*, June 1911, vol. VII, no. 6, new series.
Sunan Al-Tirmidhi. *Kitab al-'ılm, al-Kutub al Sittah wa Shuruhuha* (Istanbul: Çagri, 1992).
Sztompka, Piotr. 'Trust, Distrust and Two Paradoxes of Democracy', *European Journal of Social Theory,* vol. 1, No. 1, 1998.
Taeschner, Franz. 'Das Zunftwesen in der Türkei', *Leipziger Vierteljahrschrift für Südosteuropa* 5, 1941: 172–88.
Tagliabue, John. 'Start-ups Become Old Hat for Europeans', *International Herald Tribune*, 2006.
Taher, Mohamed (ed.). *Encyclopaedic Survey of Islamic Culture* (New Delhi: Anmol Publications, 1998).
Task Force on Islamic Finance and Global Financial Stability. *Islamic Finance and Global Financial Stability* (Kuala Lumpur/Jeddah: IFSB/IDB/IRTI, 2010).
The Malaysian Reserve, 14 September 2009.
Togoslu, Erkan. 'Hizmet: From Futuwwa Tradition to the Emergence of Movement in Public Space', Submitted at the Gülen Conference held in Washington DC, on 20 November 2008.
TÜSEV. *Elektronik Bülten*, No. 18, January 2009.
Udovitch, Abraham. 'Bankers Without Banks', in *The Dawn of Modern Banking* (New Haven: Yale University Press, 1979).
Udovitch, Abraham. *Partnership and Profit in Medieval Islam* (Princeton: Princeton University Press, 1970).
Udovitch, Abraham. 'At the Origins of the Western Commenda: Islam, Israel, Byzantium', *Princeton Near East papers no. 9* (Princeton: Princeton University Press, 1969).
Ul Haq, Irfan. *Economic Doctrines of Islam* (Herndon, VA: International Institute of Islamic Thought, 1996).
United Nations Development Programme. *Arab Human Development Report* (New York: United Nations, 2002).
Usmani, Mufti Muhammad Taqi. 'Sukuk and Their Contemporary Applications', http://www.muftitaqiusmani.com/ArticlePublication.aspx, 5 October 2008.
Usmani, Muhammad Taqi. 'The Concept of *Musharaka* and Its Application as an Islamic Method of Financing', *Arab Law Quarterly,* XIV, No. 3, 1999.
Utku, Nihal Şahin. *Kızıldeniz'de Denizcilik, Ticaret ve Yerleşim, VII-XI. Yüzyıllar* (Istanbul: Marmara Üniversitesi Sosyal Bilimler Enstitüsü, Doktora Tezi, 2005).
Vakfi, Diyanet. *Faaliyet Raporu* (Ankara: Türkiye Diyanet Vakfi, 1997).
Vallario, Angela M. 'Death by a Thousand Cuts: The Rule Against Perpetuities', *Journal of Legislation,* vol. 25, no. 141, 1999.
Van Der Wee, Herman. *A History of European Banking* (Antwerp: Mercator, 1994).
Van Dillen, J. G. *Van Rijkdom en Regenten, Handboek tot de Economische en Sociale Geschiedenis van Nederland Tijdens de Republiek* ('s-Gravenhage: Martinus Nijhoff, 1970).
Van Leur, J. C. *Eenige Beschouwingen Betreffende den Ouden Aziatischen Handel* (Middelburg: 1934).
Venardos, Angelo M. *Islamic Banking and Finance in South-East Asia* (Singapore: Scientific Press, 2005).

Vollmer, Uwe and Ralf Bebenroth. 'Policy Reactions to the Financial Crisis in Japan: Lessons from the 1990's', Discussion Paper Series RIEB, Kobe University, DP2010-16, May 7, 2010. Also see http://www.reuters.com/article/idUSN3017278720100730 retrieved on 15 October 2010.
Wallerstein, Immanuel. *Historical Capitalism with Capitalist Civilization* (London: Verso, 1996, 8th edn).
Wansbrough, J. 'Imtiyazat', *Encyclopaedia of Islam* (Leiden: Brill, 2nd edn).
Waqaf An-Nur Corporation Berhad. *Annual Report, 2008.*
Weber, Max. *The Protestant Ethic and the 'Spirit' of Capitalism* (New York: Penguin Twentieth Century Classics, 2002).
Weitzman, Martin. *The Share Economy, Conquering Stagflation* (London: Harvard University Press, 1984).
Weitzman, Martin. 'Some Macro-economic Implications of Alternative Compensation Systems', *The Economic Journal,* vol. 93, December 1983.
Wilson, Rodney. 'Innovation in the Structuring of Islamic *Sukuk* Securities', *Humanomics*, vol. 24, No. 3, 2008.
Wilson, Rodney. 'Islamic Financial Instruments', *Arab Law Quarterly,* VI, 2, 1991.
Wink, Andre. *Al-Hind, The Making of the Indo-Islamic World*, vol. I (Leiden: Brill, 1991).
Yaacob, Hashim et al. (eds). *The Renaissance Man* (Kuala Lumpur: University of Malaya Press, 2010).
Yavuz, M. Hakan. *Islamic Political Identity in Turkey* (Oxford: Oxford University Press, 2005).
Yener, Serhat. *Dernekler-Vakıflar Kanunu ve İlgili Mevzuat* (Ankara: Seçkin, 1995).
Zahraa, Mahdi. 'Legal Personality in Islamic Law', *Arab Law Quarterly*, vol. X, No. 3, 1995: 202–6.
Zaim, Sabahaddin. 'Ekonomik Hayatta Müslüman İnsanın Tutum ve Davranışları', paper submitted at the First World Congress of Islamic Economics convened Mecca on 5–11 April 1976, in Hüner Şencan (ed.), *İş Hayatında İslam İnsanı, Homo-Islamicus* (Istanbul: MÜSİAD, 1994).
Zakaria, Farid. 'Is America Losing Its Mojo?', Newsweek, 23 November 2009.
Zakaria, Rosli. 'Dr. M Launches Another PNB Unit Trust Scheme for Education', *New Straits Times,* 21 April 2001.
Zamir and Mirakhor. See, Mirakhor.
Zider, Bob. 'How Venture Capital Works', *Harvard Business Review*, November–December 1998.

Index